The Cognitive Sciences

The Cognitive Sciences:
An Interdisciplinary Approach

Carolyn P. Sobel
New College of Hofstra University

Mayfield Publishing Company
Mountain View, California
London ■ Toronto

Library of Congress Cataloging-in-Publication Data

Sobel, Carolyn P.,
    The cognitive sciences : an interdisciplinary approach / Carolyn P. Sobel.
       p. cm.
    Includes bibliographical references and index.
    ISBN 0-7674-0213-8
    1. Cognitive science. I. Title.

  BF311.S637 2001
  153—dc21   00-036168
                                                CIP

Manufactured in the United States of America
10   9   8   7   6   5   4   3   2   1

Mayfield Publishing Company
1280 Villa Street
Mountain View, California 94041

Sponsoring editor, Franklin C. Graham; production editor, Deneen M.Sedlack; manuscript editor, Margaret Moore; design manager, Jeanne Schreiber; text designer, Linda Robertson; cover designer, Lisa Buckley; art editor, Rennie Evans; illustrator, Dartmouth Publishing, Inc.; photo researcher, Laura Katis; manufacturing manager, Randy Hurst. The text was set in 10/12.5 Garamond Light by Thompson Type and printed on acid-free 50# Finch Opaque by R. R. Donnelley & Sons Company.

Cover art: Judy Dunworth, *And Sometimes Y,* 53" × 39".

Acknowledgments and copyrights continue at the back of the book on pages 319–320, which constitute an extension of the copyright page.

This book is dedicated to the memory of my parents,
Martin Panzer and Pauline K. Panzer,
who taught me the excitement of asking questions,
to my sons, Daniel and Jonathan Sobel,
who gave me the pleasure of watching intelligence unfold,
and to Fred, for more than I can say.

Contents

PART TWO
Neuroscience: Our Incredible Brain

3   Exploring the Brain   76

Preface

Many people are intrigued by cars. To some, they represent status; to others, power. Some people respond to the design of cars and can recite the features of every style produced by every manufacturer in any given year. Others, like me, view a car as a means of transportation only—one that should perform well and with minimal care and preferably be equipped with certain comforts, such as air conditioning and power steering. Beyond that, they do not give cars a thought.

There are times, though, when aspects of a car do claim the attention of even such nonenthusiasts. For instance, once, when stopped at a red light, I found myself behind a Honda CIVIC (a fairly frequent occurrence, given the number of Honda CIVICS on the road). Staring at the back of the car, I noticed that the word *CIVIC* is a palindrome—a word or sentence that, like *eve* or *mom* or *Madam I'm Adam,* reads the same forward and backward. Now, CIVIC is strictly a spelling, or symbolic, palindrome, not a visual one, because the final *C* faces the same direction as the initial *C*. Of course it does—it's a *C,* after all, and that's what a *C* looks like. But if you mentally rotate the final *C,* you will see that CIVIC is now a *visual* palindrome: a pattern that *looks* the same forward and backward. But it is no longer a symbolic palindrome, because a backward *C* is not really a *C;* it's just a meaningless mark, and the pattern no longer spells the word.

But as I was saying, I was waiting at a red light. When it changed, my palindrome pulled away. I followed suit, and, because the road was a familiar one, I put the car on automatic pilot, as it were, and continued to think. I wondered whether the company had been aware of the palindromic nature of the name and had chosen the name deliberately for that reason, and whether anyone else on the road was struck by it or even noticed it was a palindrome.

Remembering this now, I'm sure that if anyone had asked I would have been unable to report the color of the car or the number of passengers in it or anything but that it had in fact been a palindromic Honda CIVIC. I was, instead, following my own train of thought, which led to a new question: How does it happen that people notice such different aspects of a situation? And is that why, when remembering, their recollections are so different? What is it that causes them to notice different things in the first place? Does it have to do, perhaps, with what was in their minds just before the experience in question? I knew that the effect of one experience could somehow "prime" people's mental associations, call forth an idea or a name suggested by that experience even though it was not itself uppermost in their minds at the moment.

My own mind was "wandering"—suddenly I was home and without a sense of having traversed the route at all, having failed to notice anything about where I was or where I was going until I got there—an experience surely familiar to you. I had been conscious only of my thoughts, yet something had enabled me to find my way home without mishap. At some level, parts of my mind had been ticking away, doing what needed to be done, without my having consciously directed them. And now I was busy thinking about my thinking and marveling that I was, even then, thinking about how I was thinking about my thinking. . . .

Contained in the little episode just recounted are a number of the mental phenomena addressed by the field of cognitive science: memory, associative thinking, abstract thinking, mental imagery, language, consciousness. But what exactly *is* cognitive science? The field is not as familiar to most people as are the subjects traditionally offered in educational institutions. We all have some notion, for example, of the concerns of history, physics, and literature. But the focus of cognitive science is the human mind itself, and thus it necessarily cuts across many disciplines. These disciplines include some that have been around for a long time and some that have come onto the scene relatively recently. Issues traditionally addressed by philosophers about the nature of meaning and the nature of knowing are examined today through the various lenses provided by cognitive psychology, neuroscience, linguistics, artificial intelligence, and, of course, philosophy itself, which is alive and well. As long as researchers in each of these fields peer only through the lenses of their own fields, relevant material from the others is not available to them. Valuable insights may thus be lost—insights that can increase our understanding of the burning questions for humanity, motivated by a powerful wish to understand ourselves: What exactly is the intelligence with which we seem uniquely endowed? Are we correctly characterized as animals that think? Machines that feel? What is the thing we experience as consciousness—and is our species alone in it as each individual is alone in it? At its most simply stated but most fundamental, the pivotal question for humanity is Who are we?

There is a greater likelihood of our being able to answer this question, and all the questions that go with it, if the different perspectives of the fields concerned with them are accessible to, and invited to inform, the others. Integrating into a more coherent whole the knowledge gained by each field will contribute to a clearer understanding of the entity that has long mystified our species: our own human mind. New ways of thinking, some arising from technologies newly developed, permit us now to reconsider this old enigma.

This integration is what the field of cognitive science is seeking. The present volume will introduce the perspectives and contributions to this endeavor of each of the primary participating disciplines, in the following order: cognitive psychology, neuroscience, linguistics, artificial intelligence, and philosophy. The book is organized into five units, each one devoted to one of these disciplines. A unit consists of two chapters, the first providing historical background to the field as a framework for its more recent work. The second chapter in each unit describes and discusses the more recent work and the current approaches of the field.

To the Instructor

In a work of this nature there is no one predetermined "best" organization of material. The subject matter of each participating discipline overlaps and inter-twines with that of the others so that, no matter where one chooses to begin, one is bound to trip over an approach, a theme, an issue that has also arisen—and will surely arise again—elsewhere. Choose a chronological approach, and one finds oneself ever and again referring to the same issues. Organize the material around these issues, and one finds oneself shuttling back and forth between historical periods. Follow the approaches of the different disciplines, and one finds so many interconnections that in discussing the relevant aspects of any of the disciplines one is forever referring to work carried out in the others. I have opted to treat the disciplines individually, each in its own unit, while generally following a chrono-logical ordering of developments within the units.

Presenting the material in this fashion leads to the continual recurrence of certain key issues in the quest to understand the human mind. Fundamental to these issues is the degree to which cognitive functions are localized in specific regions of the brain, functions such as thought, knowledge representation, mem-ory, language, and consciousness. These are explored from the vantage points of the various disciplines.

Similarly fundamental are the methods by which science proceeds in its explo-ration of the brain and its functions. Those methods employed before the devel-opment of recent technological advances seem primitive by today's standards. But these earlier explorations raised questions with which we are still grappling. Un-derstanding the nature of the questions and of the quest is aided by acquaintance with the contexts in which they have been undertaken.

In line with this point, I have chosen to present material on the way human intelligence has been regarded in the past and the methods that have been devised in an attempt to measure it. Although it is not precisely on the cutting edge of cognitive science today, the issue is nevertheless being actively addressed by well-known researchers. Even more important, it is a subject familiar and of interest to students: They often feel the effects of IQ labeling and what IQ tests purport to indicate about them. In this regard, I see it as a lead-in for those new to cognitive science, a bridge between a familiar realm of personal interest and the current search for understanding of the human brain.

With regard to the order of the units in the book, it is one that seems logical to me. However, the units lend themselves to rearrangement according to the instruc-tor's preference. Furthermore, each faculty member who adopts this book is expert in his or her discipline(s) and has more or less firm expectations regarding how that discipline is best treated in the realm of cognitive science. My field is linguistics, and in teaching students its contributions to cognitive science I import concepts and illustrations that range well beyond what appears here in Chapters 5 and 6. I assume that those who adopt this book will similarly complement the material pertinent to their specialties. The subject matter is vast; one volume cannot hope to be comprehensive in scope or in detail. It was necessary—if the volume was ever to be completed—to be selective, to choose important representative issues. Users will have their own preferences with regard to the subject matter they consider it important to include. Where they find my selections wanting, they should certainly supplement with the materials they have accumulated as experts in their fields.

I have provided in the Instructor's Manual teaching resources for each of the areas covered in this book, as well as examples of syllabi and exams, additional thought questions for discussion and for written assignments, recommended readings, and suggestions for lecture content. I would appreciate being informed of any significant oversights in the text or in the recommended readings, and of any suggestions for inclusion in the Instructor's Manual, which is available online at http://www.mayfieldpub.com/sobel, or by request on CD-ROM or disk.

Acknowledgments

I could not have completed this volume in a timely manner—or at all—without the assistance and encouragement provided me from many quarters. I am grateful to my students over the years, who have been my stimuli and my testing ground. Some have been of direct help; I therefore particularly thank my research assistants Ed Bringas, Amy Gallaher, Ginger Morawski, and Alan Rorie.

I am also indebted to colleagues who have answered my innumerable questions and provided practical assistance, among them Evelyn Altenberg, Alessandro Adragna, Jessica Anderson, Valerie Barr, Ron Bloom, Cynthia Breazeal, Heidi Contreras, Brian Cox, Silvia Federici, Ignacio Götz, Heather Johnson, David Knee, John Kreniske, Charles Levinthal, Natalie Naylor, Eric Partridge, Gail Satler, Diane Swick, Roy Udolf, Elizabeth Unruh, Stavros Valenti, Stefan Waner, and the wonderful Hofstra University Axinn Library staff members who have gone out of their way to facilitate my research: Domenica Barbuto, Marge Burke, Elena Cevallos, Lydia Di Domenico, Howard Graves, Maureen Haugh, Martha Kreisel, Jim Mellone, Marie Miller, Anne Mott, Lorraine Palmer, Rachel Plimack, Sandra Reynolds, Charles Secter, Laura Thompsen, Beatrice Thompson, Janet Wagner, and Deb Willett.

I would be remiss if I omitted those at the Hofstra Computer Center whose expertise and patience have kept me functioning in tandem with my computer: Barry Germond, David Klein, Shari Ross, Adam Scinto, Julie Sullivan—and those anonymous voices at the Help Desk who either talked me through problems immediately or really did return my calls, as promised.

I wish also to acknowledge the assistance provided by individuals who do not fit neatly into the above categories: Jennifer, Allison, and Jim Drieves, for help with assorted tasks—and for providing food for thought; my son Jonathan Sobel, for research assistance at the very outset; and my sister and colleague Lenore Szuchman, for ideas, insights, and moral support.

I am indebted to Frank Graham, sponsoring editor at Mayfield Publishing Company, for his valuable guidance throughout the project; and to Rennie Evans, Marty Granahan, and Deneen Sedlack of Mayfield for their help in the preparation of the manuscript (and for patiently answering my many questions). I am grateful also to Margaret Moore for her painstaking editing, and to the reviewers whose careful reading and constructive suggestions have produced a considerably improved product—with special appreciation to Joel Alexander. Errors in and omissions from the text are mine alone, perhaps due to my failing to heed some of their counsel.

Thanks are due also to New College staff and students: Bonnie Hedstrom, for her help with matters ranging from Band-Aids to bookshelves, Emily Greenfield, Renae Hart, Pierre Ligonde, and Jennifer Springer; to David Christman who, as Dean of New College, has provided all manner of support; and to Hofstra University, source of funds and facilities without which the project would not have been possible.

Finally, I wish to recognize the invaluable contributions to this project of my husband and colleague, Alfred Cohn. Fred has lent his extensive knowledge, his editorial expertise, his time and energy, his library, and his emotional support and comfort through the long and sometimes trying period of preparation. I hope I do as well by him.

Introduction

A number of years ago, while waiting for some friends in the lobby of the American Museum of Natural History, I observed a young mother pushing a twin stroller. A boy of less than two years walked beside the stroller, holding on obediently. A second toddler, identical in looks and clothing, ran ahead. Their mother called to him: "Jimmy! Jimmy!" The child ignored her. She could not abandon the stroller with its attached toddler, so she called again, louder: "Jimmy! Come back here!" The boy continued his progress toward the exit, this time indicating defiance by a gesture of his shoulder. Before scooping up the other child and taking off after her disobedient son, the mother tried a different tack: "Bobby," she called, "Come back." Immediately the child turned and ran toward her. As he did so she caught my eye and exclaimed, "That's the last time I dress them alike!"

This little episode stayed in my mind. I marveled at its implications. Here was a very small person indeed, but one who clearly had not only a mind of his own, but just as clearly a strong sense of his own identity. He already knew very firmly that he was not his brother. Moreover, he did not appreciate being taken for his brother, and if anyone erred in this way he would refuse to respond. He understood the meaning of his mother's verbal commands, and he himself had at his disposal at least the gestures that would convey his displeasure and his refusal. All in all, I thought at the time—and still think—it was a remarkable performance, indicating remarkable abilities. The nature of these and other abilities of which even the very young human being is capable is something students of the human mind have sought for a long time to explain. How is it, for example, that anyone, let alone such a young person, understands so much: the language that is used to communicate with him; the concept of who he is; the subtle and changing requirements of his society? How is it that people think—even what does it *mean* that people think? Is language crucial to thought? What *is* thought? Are there in human brains representations of what is out there in the world? If so, of what sort are they? Are some of them pictures? If so, how do they get there? What are they made of? If we look inside a human brain, we don't see pictures of concepts. Nor do we see words. Pictures we seem to see in our "mind's eye" and words we can "hear" long after voices have ceased—how are these related to or created by the structures we do in fact see? With the technologies now available to us, what inferences can we make about the activities of the brain, and what can we learn by having computers attempt to do what we humans do?

The questions are myriad. Answers and explanations are being sought by researchers in all the fields that have traditionally (some for centuries or millennia) posed some of the questions, as well as by those in new fields arising from new technologies. Cognitive psychologists have been concerned with questions about intelligence, learning, memory, problem solving, and many other aspects of human cognition. Neuroscientists are learning more every day about the structures and functions of the human brain and how they relate to the behaviors we observe in people, such as using language, solving problems, and remembering. Linguists offer hypotheses concerning the human capacity for language and what it indicates about the nature of the human brain. Since the middle of the 20th century, computer scientists have been developing the field of artificial intelligence. They have been attempting to model human capacities, to design machines that do at least part of what humans do in a variety of areas, from motor activities to problem solving and learning language. And of course philosophers have long addressed such issues as the nature of knowing, and the mind-body and mind-brain distinctions.

The proliferation of ideas, of experiments, of knowledge is so great that no one person can possibly become familiar with or absorb all of it. Yet if all of these disparate fields remain separate, important insights may be missed and relevant connections will not be made. The approach that is being taken by the relatively new field of cognitive science is an attempt to capture the connections, to coordinate insights gained in the several areas as their practitioners work and learn so that, for example, questions posed by cognitive psychologists about how the brain goes about solving problems may be refined or redefined by attempts on the part of researchers in artificial intelligence to solve the problems by computer. Questions about which areas of the brain control or affect language may find answers in neuroscientists' experiments using their new scanning techniques. Observations such as the one with which I began this introduction, of the subtle workings of a small child's mind, as well as contemplation of the complexity of the infrastructure that underlies such workings, seem to me to lead inevitably to a desire to know more about the organ in each of us that contains such a universe. What could be more interesting and exciting to study than the object that makes us human—and, furthermore, incites us to ask questions about its very self?

This book is designed to introduce the reader to this fascinating field, to the questions with which its participants grapple, and to some of the avenues they follow in their endeavor to answer these questions.

CHAPTER 1

Early Approaches to the Study of Human Cognition

In the preface, I indicated that cars as such are of little interest to me. But I do like to drive—though I haven't much sense of direction. So whenever I have to drive somewhere unfamiliar, I make sure to get very clear directions. People are always wanting to draw me a map, and I'm sometimes embarrassed to have to admit that I have a rather hard time with maps. I can eventually figure out where the route is and which direction I am going on the map, but I often have to turn the map around so that it faces the same way *I* am facing. I do much better with verbal instructions, repeating segments of them to myself as I drive. As long as the words remain in my ears, so to speak, I follow my route and get to where I am going.

The return trip, however, is another story. At each turn I must consciously—and verbally—convert a "turn right" instruction into a "turn left" one, because to me coming back looks so different from going. I don't seem to have a "feel" for the spaces I have traversed or the turns I have taken.

It is encouraging, however, to think about what I *can* do well. I seem to be one of those "verbal-symbolic" individuals, rather than a "visual-spatial" one. I learn other languages rather easily, for example. Although I may be missing a "feel" for the road, I have a good "feel" for words. I hear the different sounds and imitate them pretty well, and I remember lots of them and how to make sentences in the new language with less difficulty than some of my friends report having.

I also have some musical ability. When I sing while driving, I generally hit the right notes, which I seem to hear in my "mind's ear," even without music to help me. (I think, by the way, that this is the same "mind's ear" that helps me retain directions as I repeat them aloud. Only in this case, the "sounds" are not generated externally; rather, they are somehow produced, or remembered, inside me. But more of that later.) So when I'm feeling rather stupid, losing my way or being flustered by a map, I can tell myself, "Never mind, you have other abilities."

We have all observed that within a given individual certain abilities are rather well-developed, whereas others, though not entirely absent, are relatively *un*developed. We have all known individuals who do enviably well in school but who are awkward on the playing field, or those who are not at all attuned to the subtleties of a social situation and will often say "just the wrong thing" in interacting with someone. And we wonder how it can be that someone so "smart" can be so graceless—athletically or socially or in some other way.

At school we are made uncomfortably aware of the importance of certain kinds of abilities, and through various tests we are often classified as intelligent or not so intelligent. We ourselves make such judgments about people in an intuitive way, and in doing so we rely on certain assumptions about what being smart *is*—what, in fact, constitutes human intelligence. But what are these assumptions, and how can we decide whether they are correct?

I have presented the issue of intelligence from an intraspecies perspective. But as well as considering what distinguishes Michelangelo from Machiavelli, Michael Jordan from Michael Jackson, Freud from Franklin Roosevelt, Jane Austen from Martha Graham, one member of your family from another, we may also consider the question of what distinguishes all the individuals I have named, together with all the other members of our species, from members of any other species. Another way of framing the question, then, is: How do our singular human brains contribute to the formation of the varied individuals we are, and how do the cognitive functions and capabilities we share because of our uniquely human brain distinguish us from other species? What we learn about these capabilities and functions encompasses both perspectives.

Considered at different times and for different purposes by many different people, the nature of our human brains and their uniquely human capabilities lie at the heart of cognitive science. Certain key areas of inquiry and investigation have emerged over the years in our attempt to understand this phenomenon. Among the most important of these areas, which are still very much the foci of research, are sensation, **perception** (interpretation or understanding of sensory experiences), problem solving, learning, memory, and in addition, the location of these capacities. We take for granted the sensations and perceptions that underlie our various cognitive abilities, but it has taken much work over many years to reach our current level of understanding of these functions. We have long known that we humans are "problem solvers," but our mechanisms of problem solving are not transparent to us. We are "master learners," but there is much we have yet to learn about *how* we learn. Certainly, memory is involved in problem solving and learning, as it is in virtually everything we do. But how does memory work? And pertinent to every aspect of our investigation is the large question of *where* in the brain all these varied activities take place.

The purpose of this chapter is to provide a framework within which to place the various approaches of contemporary cognitive scientists to the functions that together constitute human intelligence. We will therefore review the notions of, and the types of work engaged in by, some of those who have addressed this issue over the past 200 years or so.

Accounting for Differences

Localization of Function: Early Approaches

People have always noticed individual differences of the sort I have mentioned even among members of homogeneous groups: the most salient ones, such as height and hair color; the somewhat subtler ones, such as nose size and eye color; the less concrete ones, such as behavior and temperament. And because part of the human "stock in trade" is curiosity—a strong desire to *know*—there has always been interest in finding an explanation for these differences. Research into the factors that account for *physical* characteristics has been carried out since the Moravian monk and botanist Gregor Mendel (1822–1884) gave us the first real insights into genetics. Although much is still unexplained, our knowledge of the subject has expanded and continues to expand greatly as modern technology and techniques are continually developed and refined. With respect to those human characteristics that are harder to describe or account for, such as even-temperedness, moodiness, optimism, persistence, insightfulness, artistic gifts, gracefulness, coordination, and academic ability, the picture is not so clear. Nor is it easy to explain why different members of the same family (who may physically resemble each other a good deal) differ so greatly in these and other ways.

An early attempt to account for certain kinds of differences among people was that of the German anatomist Franz Joseph Gall (1758–1828). Gall's interest was sparked by his own experiences in studying. Difficulty with memorization placed him at a disadvantage with respect to his schoolmates, both early on and subsequently in medical school. He observed that there were students who, without understanding the material, were nevertheless able to memorize it easily. Sometimes he even found himself deprived of the rank among them that his written work had earned him. At the time, Gall made an observation that today, given the more sophisticated state of knowledge, would not lead to the conclusion he reached: He noticed what he took to be a connection between the ability of those students to memorize with ease and their "large and protruding eyes" (not, presumably, one of his own features), and he concluded that this bodily structure was related to the ability to memorize that they possessed and he lacked. This notion led him to search for other such relationships.

From his work in **anatomy** (the structure of the body) and **physiology** (life processes and functions), Gall became interested in the functioning of the brain. His conclusion that structure and function were related led him, with his student J. G. Spurzheim (1776–1832), to seek to explain the functioning of the human brain by relating what he thought was its structure to people's behavior. Gall's early conclusion was mistaken: The ability to memorize is in no way related to the size or shape of one's eyes! The idea that there is a relationship between brain structure and function, however, is still recognized as valid and has proven productive. It led ultimately to the hypothesis that various functions are localized in particular physical structures, a hypothesis that was long at the center of debate among researchers. As you will see in Part 2, although modern interpretations differ from Gall's, the notion has achieved new importance in more recent times with the development of methods of direct observation.

Gall's conclusions concerning the functions of the brain are founded on three basic principles:

> (1) The brain is the sole organ of the mind. (2) The basic character and intellectual traits of man are innately determined. (3) Since there are differences in character and intellectual traits among individuals as well as differences in various intellectual capacities within a single individual, there must exist differentially developed areas in the brain, responsible for these differences! Where there is variation in *function*, there must be variation in the controlling *structures*. (Krech, 1963, p. 33)

(The sources of much of the material in this section have not been published in English and are therefore not readily available in the United States. I have cited both Krech and Tuddenham, in Postman, 1962, so that readers can easily find translations and references to the material covered here.)

The first principle, that the brain is the sole organ of the mind, is indeed generally accepted today. The second, which holds that the nature of character and intellect is innate, is still a controversial issue as evidenced by the stir caused by the 1994 publication of Herrnstein and Murray's *The Bell Curve*. But despite occasional manifestations of the debate over whether traits are inherited or are acquired through exposure to the environment (the **nature-nurture question**), most scientists today recognize the essential contributions of each and so are less inclined than they once were to ascribe the origin of a particular trait so rigidly to one cause or the other. Because both are necessary for virtually any behavior more complex than a reflex, most researchers do not consider it productive to try to tease out the relative contributions of nature and nurture.

The third principle proposed by Gall, that the structures differ according to their function, has significant implications. If it is true, then (innately determined) behavioral traits, such as being musically gifted or good at *spatial relations* (and therefore at finding one's way both to a destination and home again!), will be governed primarily by different areas of the brain. (**Spatial relations** refers to one's ability to perceive the relationship of objects to each other and to oneself in space.) Further, these areas should develop differently, depending on the individual's inherent potential. What we have learned since Gall's time is that **neurons** (the nerve cells of which the brain is composed) do in fact respond to repeated experiences by adding links (**synapses**) to other neurons. Thus the total area involved in a particular function develops to a greater extent than it would without the repeated experiences. A concert pianist, for example, spends years, beginning in childhood, listening to and practicing music. The areas of the pianist's brain involved in these behaviors will develop in response to these activities over and above what heredity alone would have produced. Without a piano, Mozart would never have become Mozart.

A further condition Gall assumed is that, as they develop, these areas will cause a corresponding development in the shape of the skull to accommodate them. According to his theory, then, it should be possible to infer these traits by examining the shape of the skull. If both notions were true—that the structures will be located in different areas and that, as they develop in different individuals, they will cause the shape of the skull to vary accordingly—Gall's suggestion would be quite reasonable. Anthropological study today sometimes does make use of the imprint of the brain when it is found preserved on the *inside* of fossil crania. From these fossil remains, inferences are drawn about the relative state of development of areas of the brain of hominid species. (The term "hominid" refers to the various species of humans, including the extinct *Homo erectus* and *Homo habilis* and the current *Homo sapiens*.) From measurements of the imprints, inferences are made about the abilities of the species in question.

However, Gall was not entirely on the right track. Because he found that those faculties of mind that were accepted by philosophers of his day were too general or vague, he listed a large number of faculties that were far more specific, such as having mechanical or musical ability, or being cautious or affectionate. Some of these faculties would today be considered talents; some would be regarded as

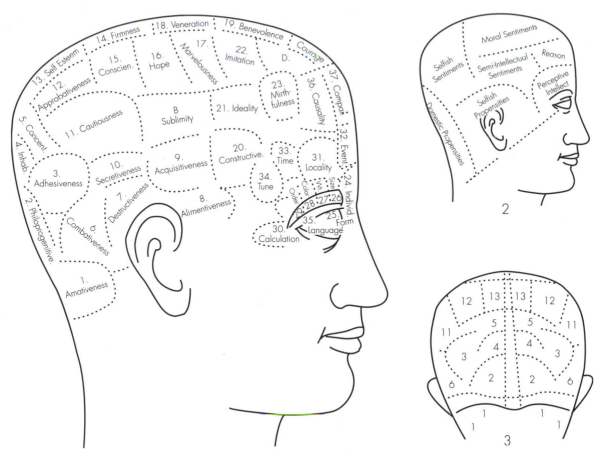

FIGURE 1.1 The Faculties That Phrenologists Claimed to Have Located in Different Regions of the Brain

personality traits. Gall's system, which came to be known as **phrenology** (from the Greek *phren*, "heart" or "mind," and *logos*, "science"), was based on this list (Figure 1.1). Interestingly, for a time, a lucrative profession exploited the presumed possibility of predicting people's abilities or personality traits by measuring the "bumps on their skulls." This application of phrenology won widespread attention and acceptance, but the more the public accepted it, the more it lost the credibility it initially had among scientists. We now know that portions of Gall's theory were quite incorrect: There is no "area of affection," for example, that can be isolated from surrounding brain areas, much less attributed to a particular development of the skull. Such structural characteristics of the skull as are in fact related to behavior are not those assumed by phrenologists. They involve, rather, anatomical asymmetries associated with the localization of function involved in, for example, language (see the next section).

Although we now recognize the flaws in Gall's theory, we can also appreciate the element of that theory that anticipated current research interests. **Localization** of function is today accepted as an important aspect of the brain's structure, although the functions that contemporary researchers study in different areas of the brain are not for the most part those Gall suggested. We will return to this area of research in Part 2.

Following Gall's work, a hundred years or so of research into the subject of localization of function of the brain produced a variety of approaches and conclusions. These began with an attempt by the experimental neurologist Pierre Flourens (1794–1867) to demolish Gall's theory. Through experiments on the brains of living pigeons, chickens, and rats, Flourens reached the conclusion that "all the intellectual faculties reside exclusively in [the brain], but they all reside there coextensively, and without any one being separable from the others" (Krech, 1963, p. 41). But Gall had been interested in important human mental faculties such as imagination and language—and on these, experiments on rats and fowl could shed no light.

Somewhat later, the French surgeon Paul Broca (1824–1880) worked with patients whose language function was compromised through injury or stroke. Broca naturally accepted the prevailing notion that the larger the brain the more intelligent the individual. It follows from this notion that by measuring cranial capacity, or the size of the skull, one can rate the degree of intelligence of the individual. As with phrenology's incorrect assumption (that from the structure of a person's skull one can infer abilities or traits), so **craniometry**'s assumption (that from the size of the skull one can assess intelligence) also led its proponents astray. (See Stephen Jay Gould's *The Mismeasure of Man,* 1981, in which Gould summarizes the history of this area of research and identifies a number of its shortcomings.)

These considerations apart, Broca's work on the language function of the brain provided evidence for the theory of localization of function. As we will see in Chapter 6, Broca had been working with patients suffering from **aphasia** (language loss). In one famous case, so much speech ability had been lost that all the patient could articulate was the single syllable "tan." After the patient's death, Broca examined his brain and found a **lesion** (an area of damage) in the left **frontal lobe**, the portion just under the forehead. In another patient who had exhibited very limited speech, Broca also found, again on autopsy, damage to that area of the brain. In 1861 he presented this evidence of localization of function to members of the Anthropological Society in Paris, and thus it became known to the scientific world and to the world at large as Broca' area (Krech, 1963).

Localization of Function: More Recent Approaches

A little earlier I indicated some of the major areas that have emerged in our quest to understand our own intelligence. Sensation, perception, memory, and problem solving were all examined in the research on localization of function later in the 19th century and in the 20th. Some of this research involved the sensory functions of the brain. Clinical observation and experimental research (notably by Hughlings-Jackson, Fritsch and Hitzig, and Ferrier, discussed in Chapter 3) led to the recognition that sensory and motor functions, at least, can be localized in specific regions of the brain. Once this was demonstrated and accepted, the way was opened to the study of mental processes within this framework. A prominent researcher was the psychologist Karl S. Lashley (1890–1959), who studied the effects of experimentally induced brain lesions on other major areas of **cognition** that recur in our quest for understanding, notably learning and problem solving. Naturally, Lashley did not induce brain lesions in humans; instead, he studied the learning and problem-solving behavior of white rats raised specifically for these experimental purposes. This research convinced Lashley that the more complex a behavior the less it can be linked to a particular region of the brain. He contended that his experiments "lend support to the theory which conceives intelligence as a general capacity" (Lashley, 1929, p. 173), a position consistent with his conclusion, like that of Flourens in the previous century, that specific **cortical functions** (activities of the outer layer of the brain's gray matter) cannot reasonably be assigned to specific areas.

In fact, his review of research on dogs, monkeys, and human beings led Lashley (1929) to conclude that "aside from [the] function of spacial [sic] orientation, there is little evidence of a finer cortical differentiation in man than in the rat" (p. 156). Although pertinent evidence may have been lacking, largely because the techniques for this research had not yet been developed, it has since become clear that the human brain is indeed more differentiated than Lashley thought. Extrapolating to humans from information gleaned from other species is risky, constituting what H. A. Murray, the distinguished American personality theorist, euphoniously called "the audacious assumption of species equivalence" (A. Cohn, personal communication, 1998). It is, to be sure, quite a leap from the learning and problem-solving behavior of the white rat to the nature of *human* intelligence.

How we approach human intelligence depends crucially on whether brain function is conceived as unitary—a "general capacity"—or as comprising identifiably different aspects. The contributions of Lashley, significant as they were, did not settle the question. A new era was ushered in by **neurosurgeons**, physicians whose field of expertise is the brain itself (rather than the behavior for which it is responsible). The discovery that patients could provide information about the functioning of their brains, even as this organ was exposed for surgery, led to additional evidence regarding localization of function. Although even Lashley's results pointed to localization of sensory and motor skills, other functions, such as speech skills, were now being shown to reside in quite specific areas.

Very important in this regard was the work of the Canadian neurosurgeon Wilder Penfield (1891–1976). Working with human patients who required surgery for various medical conditions, Penfield performed operations in which the brain of an awake individual was exposed, under local anesthesia of the scalp. Surprising as it may seem, patients can remain conscious for certain types of brain surgery because the brain itself has no **sense receptors** and thus the patient feels no pain. Penfield found that stimulating certain areas of the **cortex** (the brain's outer layer) with a weak electric current evoked specific motor effects, whereas stimulation of other areas caused patients to report sensory events. For example, there may be the clenching of a fist, or a tingling in the tongue, when a specific spot on the brain is stimulated. But what was even more exciting to cognitive scientists was the discovery that hallucinations and memories (or experiences reconstructed as memories) can also be elicited in this way, or that access to words can be blocked for the duration of the stimulation (Penfield, 1958, 1959; Penfield & Roberts, 1959). (**Hallucinations** are perceptions of, for example, sounds or sights that aren't really there.) These are among the functions that Lashley could not study in rats, and the findings led researchers in new directions in their pursuit of knowledge about the motor, sensory, and especially the *intellectual* (**perceptual** memory) functions of the human brain.

During the past 20 years or so, there have been breathtaking technological developments by means of which, without performing surgery or otherwise disturbing them, we can now actually see structures deep within the brain of a conscious person. We can observe which areas of the living brain are activated as the individual attempts to solve problems or responds to events in the environment. These amazing developments will be elaborated in Part 2 when we examine the contributions of neuroscience to cognitive science.

The Emergence of Modern Psychology

Meanwhile, as this kind of work was providing new information about human intelligence, other paths were being followed in Germany by scientists whose training in medicine and physiology led them to an interest in this direction and to the founding of the modern discipline of psychology. An important 19th-century example is Hermann Helmholtz (1821–1894), who contributed to science in fields ranging from physics and geometry to perception, one of the cornerstones of psychology. An experiment for which Helmholtz is particularly famous was in the area of perception. It had earlier been thought that signals sent from the sensory organs traveled to the brain at least at the speed of light. Given that the distance the signals were traveling—the length of a nerve—was so short, this assumed speed was too fast to measure. However, with the invention of an instrument capable of recording short durations and rapid changes (the **chronograph**), this measurement could be attempted. Helmholtz did attempt it, first on frogs and then on humans, proving that the conduction time was not, as had been thought, as rapid as the speed of light. Measuring the reaction time to stimuli at two different points on a body, such as the shoulder and the wrist, he learned that it takes longer to react to a stimulus applied to the receptor that is farther from the brain. Neither of these results seems surprising to us, but to an establishment convinced that nerve impulses are transmitted to the brain instantaneously, it was astounding.

In his consideration of perception, Helmholtz also worked with illusions, especially visual illusions, concluding that these are the result of unconscious processes and characterizing visual perceptions as based on unconscious inferences. He explained that an astronomer computing "the positions of the stars in space, their distances, etc., from the perspective images he has had of them at various times" bases his conclusions on his conscious knowledge of the laws of optics. Ordinary people, in the act of seeing, do not base their conclusions about what they

see on any such laws. Nevertheless, Helmholtz argues, they are, in the course of ordinary perception, coming to conclusions— *"unconscious conclusions"* (Helmholtz,
1910, p. 4, in Hochberg, 1962, p. 293). Early in its development, then, the field of
psychology recognized a role for unconscious processes, which are part and parcel
of what occurs at the conscious level. An explicit concern with issues of consciousness was largely submerged in American psychology at least, from about 1912 until
the mid-1950s. It became a hot topic at the end of the 20th century and continues
to be so as we enter the 21st.

Another towering figure in the scientific world in the late 19th and early 20th
centuries was Wilhelm Wundt (1832–1920). A somewhat younger contemporary
of Helmholtz, he too had wide-ranging intellect and expertise encompassing medicine, physiology, anthropology, and psychology. One of the psychological methods he employed in his experiments was **introspection,** or "looking inside" of
one's own experience, attending to and becoming conscious of one's own mental
states. It is a practice we all engage in sometimes, and as you will see later in the
discussion of philosophy, it is a technique that has long been employed by those
who think about thinking. Over the years we have developed more objective—
more scientific—methods of research so that when we have recourse to it today
introspection functions as a starting point for ideas rather than as an experimental tool.

Wundt established the very first psychology research laboratory. His Institute
of Experimental Psychology drew students from many countries. Along with his
many publications in various areas within psychology, the institute contributed to,
and may even be said to have largely shaped, the newly developing field of experimental psychology.

Like Helmholtz, Wundt also arrived at the idea that "unconscious inferences
can determine perception" (Murray, 1999, p. 897). He dealt as well with attention,
which is another aspect of consciousness. "Paying attention" means that certain
features of what one is generally conscious of at a given time are perceived most
clearly; they are "in focus," so to speak, while the rest fades into the background.
What attention is and how it functions are actively being studied in cognitive
science today.

Still another of Wundt's ideas relating to areas of exploration within cognitive
science today is that a "mental representation" exists for a speaker before he or
she forms a sentence and that variations in the use of grammar allow the speaker
to emphasize one or another aspect of this mental representation (Murray, 1999).
This foray into the psychology of language indicates Wundt's interest in the language function. **Generative transformational grammar,** which revolutionized the
field of linguistics beginning in the mid-1950s, was prefigured by Wundt, who
"viewed language as generative: utterances are the product of the creative synthesis of one or more mental contents, following specific grammatical rules" (Wertheimer, 1987, pp. 64–65). Many of Wundt's ideas thus anticipated those with which
scientists in the 20th century have been concerned, among them the relation of
thought and language and the issue of mental representation. We will examine
these ideas further in subsequent chapters.

Memory is another component of cognition that has received much attention in recent times. In this area, too, groundwork was laid in Germany in the late 19th and early 20th centuries. In this case, the researcher was Hermann Ebbinghaus (1850–1909). Ebbinghaus devised ingenious experimental methods for studying memory and, using only himself as a subject, provided much information about remembering and forgetting that subsequent research has confirmed. According to Roediger (1999), "Ebbinghaus solved the three problems faced by all cognitive/ experimental psychologists in their work: to convert unobservable mental processes into observable behavior; to measure the behavior reliably; and to show how the behavior is systematically affected by relevant factors and conditions" (p. 252). One of the experimental techniques Ebbinghaus devised required learning lists of nonsense syllables (syllables that have no meaning in the language and hence bring with them no connotations or easy means of connection to anything in a subject's experience—*mur* or *nim,* for instance). Wertheimer (1987) describes Ebbinghaus's methods in this way:

> His primary techniques were complete mastery and savings. That is, he counted how many trials it took to memorize a list of syllables so that he could recall it at least once without an error; alternatively, for the savings method, he memorized some material at a particular time, then had no further contact with it for awhile, and finally determined how much easier it was to relearn later on—the difference in the number of trials required to relearn, relative to the number required for original learning, or the saving, could then constitute a measure of the amount retained. (p. 77)

Although Ebbinghaus was the only subject in these experiments, they were logically and carefully constructed and later replication by others—on many subjects—produced the same results. This held true as well for the results of variations of the experiments, with which Ebbinghaus obtained new information about, for example, the relation between the number of repetitions and forgetting, about the rate of forgetting over time, and about the strength of forward and backward associations. His work was important in setting the stage for later study of various aspects of cognition.

In addition to his important work on memory and association (and what I have mentioned here constitutes for Ebbinghaus, as for Helmholtz and Wundt, only a hint of their seminal contributions to science), Ebbinghaus concerned himself with the testing of children's intelligence. He was "the first to publish a paper on the intelligence testing of school children, using a completion test which is still included in some current test batteries" (Wertheimer, 1987, p. 76). Thus, Ebbinghaus anticipated a large and important movement in the field of psychology—**psychometrics**, the theory and measurement of psychological variables—years before it came into its own.

Another early giant in psychology, one who also made crucial contributions to the field—and in particular to cognitive psychology, as it is now known—was the American psychologist William James (1842–1910). While much work of great significance to psychology was under way in Germany, James was establishing a groundwork for it in the United States. Like Helmholtz and Wundt, James began his studies and his work in medicine and physiology. From there he moved into psychology and finally philosophy. James was a man of many interests, and the topics in psychology with which he concerned himself were varied. He is well known for his two-volume work titled *The Principles of Psychology,* published in 1890, in which he discusses subjects ranging from localization of function to the **stream of consciousness** (the process of one thought leading to another), from sensation and perception to attention and memory, and from emotions to the will. For example, here is how James (1890) distinguishes between sensation and perception:

> Any quality of a thing which affects our sense-organs does also more than that: it arouses processes in the hemispheres which are due to the organization of that organ by past experiences, and the result of which in consciousness are commonly described as ideas which the sensation suggests. The first of these ideas is that of the *thing* to which the sensible quality belongs. *The consciousness of particular material things present to sense* is nowadays called *perception.* (vol. II, p. 76)

James goes on to explain that one may be more or less conscious of such things, but one cannot distinguish between the "more" and the "less" with regard to consciousness, because "the moment we get beyond the first crude sensation all our consciousness is a matter of suggestion, and the various suggestions shade gradually into each other, being one and all products of the same psychological machinery of association" (p. 76). In this passage, he identifies several of the concerns of contemporary cognitive psychology and cognitive science: sensation, perception, consciousness, and association.

Elsewhere, James (1890) takes up problem solving, another of today's foci:

> In the theoretic as well as in the practical life there are interests . . . taking the form of definite images of some achievement, be it action or acquisition, which we desire to effect. The train of ideas arising under the influence of such an interest constitutes usually the thought of the *means* by which the end shall be attained. If the end by its simple presence does not instantaneously suggest the means, the search for the latter becomes an intellectual *problem.* The solution of problems is the most characteristic and peculiar sort of voluntary thinking. (vol. I, p. 584)

One often hears the comment that today's knowledge explosion requires individuals to restrict the scope of their areas of expertise; there is so much to know about a given subject in order to be an expert in it that each person, in effect, is constrained to know "more and more about less and less." It is interesting to note how many scholars and scientists of eras preceding our own were versed in a broad range of fields. It was not as unusual then as it is now for a scholar's or scientist's work to encompass, as was the case with those I have been discussing, both physical and psychological aspects of the human experience. Knowledge thus gleaned from many areas by one mind can also be synthesized and integrated by that mind. In more recent times it is truly not possible for a single individual to keep abreast of all the developments in his or her field as well as of those in several other fields. Cognitive science today is in the process of synthesizing and integrating what is continually being learned by researchers in its constituent fields about the workings of the human mind/brain. It is therefore particularly interesting for cognitive scientists today to observe that the foundation for many of the threads they are now pursuing was laid by *individuals* such as Helmholtz, Wundt, Ebbinghaus, and James, who consolidated and extended the knowledge of their day.

Measuring Differences

Earlier in the chapter I referred to the interest we have always had in the differences we observe among human beings, particularly with regard to the abilities that, taken together, constitute intelligence. And in discussing some of the precursors to the field of cognitive psychology today, I mentioned Ebbinghaus's paper on the intelligence testing of school children, which anticipated an entire movement in the field of psychology. Beginning in the mid-19th century, while the research carried out by anatomists, physiologists, and neurosurgeons was addressing the *location* of events in the brain, researchers known as **psychometricians** were addressing the nature of human intelligence. Their focus was on *measuring* the diverse intellectual abilities of humans. Once again attention was focused on the sensory and perceptual functions of the brain.

Sensory Discrimination

The first to address the issue of measurement of individual differences was Sir Francis Galton (1822–1911), a versatile (and controversial) pioneer in many fields. Galton observed the diversity of mental abilities among people and set about devising ways to measure these abilities objectively. In 1883 the first edition of his *Inquiries into Human Faculty and Its Development* gave an account of his measurement of variation in human mental capacity. The dominant British philosophical stance of the period, **empiricism**, holds that we derive all knowledge from our senses and our reflection on the sensations they yield. Consistent with this stance, Galton (1883/1928) concluded that "the more perceptive the senses are of difference, the larger is the field upon which our judgment and intelligence can act" (p. 19). That is, the better we are at noticing sensory differences, the more information we accumulate about our environment, and hence the better we are able to perform intellectual tasks. He therefore constructed tests to measure **sensory discrimination**, which he hoped would lead to an objective index of human mental capacity.

One of the tests Galton devised was intended to measure "the delicacy with which weights may be discriminated by handling them" and was carried out by means of an apparatus consisting of "a number of common gun cartridge cases filled with alternate layers of shot, wool, and wadding, and then closed in the usual way. They are all identical in appearance, and may be said to differ only in their specific gravities." These were weighed precisely, numbered, and given, three at a time, to subjects whose eyes were closed. The subjects were instructed to arrange the gun cartridge cases in their proper order "by the sense of their weight alone." The scale interval that the subject could just detect was then recorded "as being the true measure of the coarseness (or the inverse measure of the delicacy) of the sensitivity" of the subject (Galton, 1928, p. 24).

Another test devised by Galton was performed in order to ascertain the upper limits of audible sound in different people. To accomplish this, Galton made a small whistle from a brass tube whose internal diameter was less than one tenth of an inch. Into the lower end of this tube he fitted a plug, which could be pulled out or pushed in to vary the length of the bore of the whistle. Low notes were produced from a long bore, high notes from a short one. The bore was graduated so that precise readings of what was audible to the subjects could be taken and recorded (Galton, 1928).

Galton's early attempts to measure sensory differences in order to infer differences in intelligence were carried out by means of devices simple in design, but the reasoning behind them was sophisticated. In 1890 an American psychologist, James McKeen Cattell (1860–1944), devised still more elaborate and refined tests of the sort Galton had initiated. Cattell referred to these as "mental tests." The field of psychology was coming into its own, and Cattell (1890) argued that "psychology cannot attain the certainty and exactness of the physical sciences unless it rests on a foundation of experiment and measurement" (p. 373). He therefore proposed that a series of tests be designed, including measurement of "Least noticeable difference in Weight; Reaction-time for Sound; Time for naming Colours; and Number of Letters remembered on once Hearing" (p. 373). (**Least noticeable difference** refers to the smallest amount of change in sensory perception that a person is able to notice.) Although some such tests (for example, remembering a series of numbers after one hearing) do tap certain mental abilities directly, the primary emphasis of most of them is on sensory discrimination. Sensory awareness in and of itself is a relatively less complex process than are those processes, such as categorizing and remembering, that are involved in intellectual tasks. Despite Galton's reasoning that the one can be inferred from the other, it is a large step from sensory discrimination to intellectual ability.

Psychometrics

The leading psychologist in France at the turn of the century, Alfred Binet (1857–1911), had begun his research within the tradition of craniometry established earlier by his countryman Paul Broca. But painstaking studies ultimately convinced Binet that the degree of intelligence of any given individual could not be determined by measuring the capacity of his or her skull. His later approach to the problem was influenced by the type of measurement of sensory discrimination carried out by Galton and Cattell. However, he was convinced that measuring sensory discrimination would not lead, any more than craniometry did, to insights into general mental capacity.

Therefore, along with his student Victor Henri, Binet proposed tests that would assess the most important differences in "*higher* mental faculties" among individuals as well as the relationship of these faculties to each other within a given individual. In addition to motor skill, he proposed to study memory, imagination, comprehension, and perceptual skill in spatial relations. Binet recognized that tests used to make comparisons among individuals must be sensitive to the backgrounds of these individuals (Binet & Henri, 1895). Comparisons made without regard to people's (varied) experiences can lead to incorrect conclusions. A test item designed to assess ability in comprehension may use words that refer to objects or **concepts** unfamiliar to an individual. For example, if one has grown up in a culture not yet touched by computer games, not much could be learned about one's understanding of a question if the question required knowledge of, say, "Tetris," "Myst," or "Super Mario Brothers." It would be absurd to conclude that a person who had no experience with computers was somehow less "intelligent" if he or she did not know what these are. Binet was very well aware of this fact.

The First "Intelligence Tests"

Binet and a fellow researcher, Théophile Simon, produced in 1905 what is regarded as the first successful test of general intelligence (Tuddenham, 1963). The purpose of the test was practical and humane: to ensure that education could be directed appropriately to children of different levels of ability. Binet and Simon's scale marked the beginning of what is known as **IQ** (intelligence quotient) testing, although that term was not applied until 1912 when Stern, in Germany, took Binet's concept of mental age and divided it by chronological age. Multiplying this quotient by 100 yields "IQ," a number since used to classify children, rightly or wrongly, as to their levels of intelligence. By the end of the 20th century, it had become evident that this way of conceiving intelligence is so problematic as to be, in the minds of many, worse than useless.

More recent work in this area has demonstrated that there are statistical difficulties inherent in using the IQ ratio, and because these difficulties have not always been appreciated, there has been a good deal of misunderstanding and misinterpretation with respect to the IQ score and its use. Much has been written on this subject, but because the focus of this book is on intelligence and not primarily on tests to assess or measure it, I will not devote much space to that aspect.

One risk involved in intelligence testing is that instead of simply identifying children who need help so that help can be provided (as Binet intended) test scores may become the sole basis for assigning them to one or another track (for example, the college-bound track) in school. Implicit in this use of intelligence tests is the assumption, prevalent in Gall's time, that intelligence is inborn and fixed for life.

A second risk is that disallowing creative interpretations of test questions serves both to emphasize conformity with expectation (as dictated by cultural factors) and to downgrade originality of thought as a factor in intelligence (Gould, 1981). When this attitude is carried over into the schools, and students' freedom to be creative and original is limited, they unquestionably feel the effects. No doubt many readers remember school experiences in which departures from expected responses, or from rigid rules, were penalized. Certainly this is not entirely attributable to the nature of intelligence tests, but the assumption underlying these influential tests, that originality and creativity are not major aspects of intelligence, must have left its mark. This is borne out, for example, by my son's experience some years ago, when Danny, a child with humor and originality (and who liked to bend rules), was in second grade. One day, instead of writing his name at the top of the page in the usual manner, he wrote "Perfesser Sobel." The teacher humorlessly not only corrected the spelling (a not surprising pedantic response) but indicated as well, in an unpleasantly stiff manner, that Danny was to limit himself in the future to simply writing his name. It is easy to see, and to feel, the damping effect such a response can have on a child.

Third, most standard tests of "intelligence" came to weigh their verbal and abstract aspects disproportionately heavily. More recent attempts at testing and defining intelligence have incorporated a more diverse set of components, as we shall see. It seems clear, then, and is, in fact, inevitable, that investigators' own notions of what intelligence consists of influence the nature of the tests they construct. David Wechsler (1896–1981), for example, included in his tests "performance" subtests. Known as the Wechsler Adult Intelligence Scale (WAIS) and the Wechsler Intelligence Scale for Children (WISC), these are currently in wide use. Wechsler's approach is based "not on the theory that there are different kinds of intelligence, but on the hypothesis that either through habit, training or endowment, some individuals are able to deal better with objects than with words" (Wechsler, 1958, p. 159). Therefore he incorporated components that addressed this ability, such as the "object assembly test," in which, like a jigsaw puzzle, an object is cut up asymmetrically and given to the person being tested, with instructions to reassemble it.

Wechsler's (1958) definition of intelligence as "the aggregate or global capacity of the individual to act purposefully, to think rationally and to deal effectively with his environment" (p. 7) anticipates more recent work.

The earlier British psychologist Charles Spearman (1863–1945), having a grasp of mathematics unusual among psychologists and also involved in the measurement of intelligence, carried out careful experiments and made skillful use of correlational techniques. These showed him that there was a high degree of relationship among diverse mental tests. From these observations, he concluded that all tasks of an intellectual nature make use not only of those abilities that are specific to any given test but also of a single capacity that relates to all of them. This he referred to as *general intelligence,* a factor that has come to be known as *g.*

Spearman's proposal touched off fierce debate over whether *g* is a real property of the brain. Gould (1981) is among those who believe that *g* has no real existence but is simply a mathematical artifact. He points out that a mathematical device, such as Spearman's use of correlations, should not lead one to infer the *reality* of an entity (such as *g*), much less to compound the error by assuming a physical substrate for it.

The concept of *g* remains with us. In its most recent incarnation, Arthur Jensen (1999) conceives of it as "a biological property of the brain, highly correlated with measures of information-processing efficiency, such as working memory capacity . . . and perceptual speed" (Abstract). If *g* does indeed play a role in cognitive functioning, we should expect, or hope, that its biological (neural) basis would someday also be revealed. This eventuality would place the notion of *g* squarely within the realm of current research in localization of function.

Recent Approaches to the Study of Intelligence

We have touched on some of the most influential early approaches to the study of cognition and some of those proposed in the more recent past. Much of this description has had to do with attempts to characterize and assess intelligence, but the whole story has not yet been told.

We turn now to some quite different contemporary approaches to the study of human intelligence, those of Robert Sternberg, of Yale University, and Howard Gardner, of Harvard University. Because Binet's original purpose was to identify those students who were unable to do the work generally required in school, his original tests, and those based on them, necessarily focused on abilities that are tapped, and rewarded, in school. Sternberg finds that other aspects of intelligence— insight and originality, for example—are not adequately addressed in such tests. **Insight** is what we sometimes call "getting it," grasping the nature of an idea or solving a problem intuitively.

Sternberg's Approach

Sternberg (1982) regards intelligence as "goal-directed adaptive behavior" (p. 3), comprising "those abilities that order and make the most of our daily environment, not just environments artificially created in psychologists' tests or laboratories" (Sternberg, 1988, p. 6). Or, stated somewhat more formally, "Intelligence in everyday life is defined as the *purposive adaptation to, selection of, and shaping of real-world environments relevant to one's life and abilities*" (p. 65).

In his 1985 book *Beyond IQ,* Sternberg elaborates his "triarchic theory of intelligence," the first element of which has to do with this everyday-life aspect. As he explains it, in our day-to-day lives intelligence generally leads us to try to adapt to our environment. A person unhappily married, for example, may try very hard to adapt, to "manage" in the marriage. But he or she may not succeed in adapting, may not be able to "manage." At this point, the everyday-life sort of intelligence might lead one to try a better means of coping, such as leaving the marriage and trying a different environment. Some, however, would find it impossible to leave: if, for example, there are small children or if there is not enough money to support two households. In such instances, a possible third strategy dictated by this aspect of intelligence might be to try to make the environment more comfortable by making changes in the marriage.

The second component of Sternberg's triarchic theory of intelligence encompasses two skills: "the ability to deal with novel kinds of task and situational demands and the ability to automatize the processing of information" (Sternberg, 1985, p. 68). These skills are also involved in everyday life. We base our assessment of someone's intelligence to a large degree on how well he or she manages in novel situations.

With experience, aspects of a task do become familiar and we do them without conscious attention. Much of the activity we engage in is highly complex—for example, driving a car. When we first confront this task, all the procedures it requires are new, and we must keep them all in mind simultaneously. At this stage, we may drive rather haltingly, often exasperating other drivers. (We prefer, for example, not to find ourselves behind a "driver ed" car, with its rooftop sign.) At some point in the learning process, however, it is no longer necessary to juggle all the required procedures by shifting awareness from one to another as fast as we can. Rather, a good deal of the process becomes automatic, allowing us to perform smoothly and with much less conscious effort. Indeed, Sternberg (1988) describes this phenomenon as the "automatizing" of aspects of a task (p. 62), and he maintains that in this way part of the mind is freed to do other work. We all engage in this sort of behavior a good deal of the time, accomplishing what needs doing with only "part of our minds" as it were—much as I did when I drove home thinking about the Honda Civic. I used a similar metaphor when I described what I had done as putting the car on "automatic pilot," allowing me to think about palindromes, **mental imagery** (images present only to the "mind's eye"), and all of those other notions suggested to me on that occasion.

According to Sternberg, intelligent people do spend time in planning a problem's solution, but they have also trained themselves to deal with familiar aspects of a task by rote so that more of the mind is available to attend to what is new. Here, Sternberg holds out the possibility of increasing the skills that comprise one's intelligence—the possibility of *learning* to be more intelligent.

The third aspect of Sternberg's triarchic theory of intelligence concerns the components involved in thinking, or the performance of tasks. The mental processes involved are of three kinds: **metacomponents**, the executive processes used to plan, monitor, and evaluate problem solving; *performance processes,* which implement the commands of the metacomponents; and *knowledge-acquisition components,* those involved in gaining new knowledge. These three types of process are interdependent and interactive (Sternberg, 1988). If one sets out to write a term paper, to use Sternberg's example, one employs the metacomponents of thinking to "decide on a topic, plan the paper, monitor the writing, and . . . evaluate how well the finished product succeeds in accomplishing its goals. Knowledge-acquisition components are used for research. Performance components are used for the actual writing" (Sternberg, 1988, p. 59). All three kinds of components are clearly necessary and interdependent. Figure 1.2 summarizes Sternberg's analysis.

If, as Jensen has argued, information processing efficiency is related to *g,* it follows that Sternberg's formulation is consistent with the idea of a general factor underlying diverse manifestations of intelligent behavior. Thus, it too may someday be linked to sites or networks in the brain.

Sternberg points out that one aspect of intelligence that has received short shrift in considerations of the nature of intelligence—and hence in many formulations of intelligence testing—is *insight.* The well-known nine dots problem is an

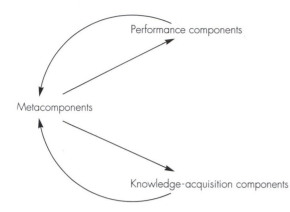

FIGURE 1.2 The Relationship Among Metacomponents, Performance Components, and Knowledge-Acquisition Components

example of the sort of insight problem he discusses. Figure 1.3 presents the problem; its solution is given at the end of the chapter. (The reader is advised to try the problem *before* reading the solution.)

The task here is to connect all nine dots with straight lines, without lifting the pencil off the page and without using more than four distinct line segments or retracing a line. Most people, confronted with this challenge, find it difficult, if not impossible. The reason, Sternberg maintains, is that most of us approach this task with the assumption that the lines must be drawn within the boundaries formed by the dots. A person endowed with *insight,* however, is able to find solutions to tasks that require thinking *outside* of the constraints or somehow to ignore those constraints that are generally—though perhaps for no obvious reason—assumed (Sternberg, 1988).

Yet another facet of intelligence described in *Beyond IQ* is "practical intelligence"—the sort that rests on "tacit knowledge," the kind of knowledge one is not taught in school. The stereotypical college professor, for example, is perceived as lacking just this type of intelligence (what we generally refer to as "common sense") and so is often presented as somewhat ridiculous outside the classroom. In real life, we all know people who seem oblivious to the obvious requirements of a given situation and who suffer socially or professionally because of this trait. Indeed, Sternberg maintains that success in life may depend more on this type of knowledge than on explicit information. He considers that this sort of tacit knowledge can in some degree be made explicit, and thus taught, again leading to an increase in intelligence.

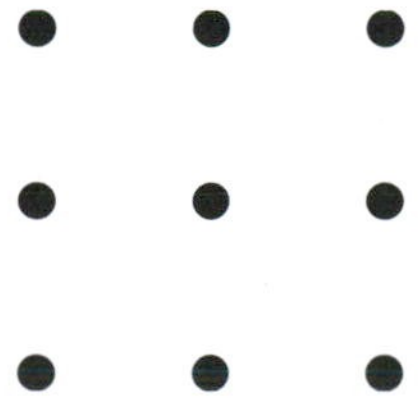

FIGURE 1.3 The Nine Dots Problem: The Pattern

The notion that intelligence consists of sets of skills and types of knowledge that can be taught is a somewhat different view from that often put forward. It is frequently held, implicitly or explicitly, that one is born with a certain capacity, which can be encouraged by the environment but which cannot, strictly speaking, be *taught*.

Gardner's Approach

Howard Gardner's research provides another perspective on intelligence, one that is more explicitly linked to issues of localization of function. Like Sternberg, Gardner addresses the issue of the specific aspects of intelligence that are identifiable, based on various types of evidence, examples of which we will see. In his description of human intelligence, Gardner must of course take into account the same phenomena Sternberg does. In fact, anyone who considers the issue must consider such realities as the different sorts and degrees of ability that characterize different people. But in his book *Frames of Mind: The Theory of Multiple Intelligences* (1983), Gardner analyzes these phenomena somewhat differently and proposes a different sort of organization. Like Sternberg, Gardner sees intelligence as having various aspects. His focus is on the diversity of human abilities or talents, which he calls "frames of mind." Each is viewed as an "intelligence" in its own right, distinct from the others, although, like Sternberg, he stresses that among normal individuals, in normal, ordinary living, all the intelligences are interdependent and function in harmony. Gardner's approach fits with the types of explanation being offered by cognitive science particularly because the components he suggests, his "candidate intelligences," may be studied by means of neuroscience's new technologies for viewing the activity of different areas of the brain as these components are called into play. Gardner's approach, in effect, describes many of the phenomena cognitive science must account for.

To explain and support his hypothesis, rather than stressing intelligence as it functions in everyday life and is exercised by *everyone,* Gardner focuses on *unusual* development—or unusual *lack* of development—of given abilities as a path to understanding the nature of intelligence. (Having a problem with maps and sense of direction in general certainly seems consistent with this view, although I like to think I am not *that* unusual in this regard!) Gardner reviews evidence from a broad and varied set of perspectives, whose objects have not generally been perceived as related to one another. These include people considered to be "gifted" in one or another area; those who suffer from brain damage that interferes with some aspect of intelligent functioning, such as language; child prodigies; normal children; normal adults; people from diverse cultures; and ***idiots savants***— those rare individuals who, though they may in other respects be unable to function on a level with people of normal intelligence, nevertheless are endowed with far more than is usual of a *particular* ability, such as the ability to play a complex piece of music on the piano after hearing it only once (Gardner, 1983).

The first of Gardner's set of "intelligences"—proposed as a first approximation to the range of human talents—is linguistic intelligence. This aspect of intelligence, a distinguishing characteristic of human beings, stands out most clearly, as Gardner (1983) points out, in poets. Poets manipulate language more effectively than the majority of us by virtue of their "sensitivity to the meaning of words . . . to the order among words . . . to the sounds, rhythms, inflections, and meters of words . . . and . . . to the different functions of language—its potential to excite, convince, stimulate, convey information, or simply to please" (p. 77). Gardner cites as evidence for this as a distinct component of human intelligence those cases in which people lose their linguistic capacity (through damage to the brain due to disease or trauma) while many of their other cognitive functions remain unimpaired.

The second intelligence Gardner identifies is musical intelligence. Here again he focuses on those who possess an ability to an unusual degree, in this case, composers. This choice is based on the fact that composers present "instances of unambiguous musical accomplishment in adulthood," representing what he calls the "end-state of musical intelligence" (Gardner, 1983, p. 100). This "end-state" is reached by a relatively small number of people, even if we include among them composers of works (such as popular songs) that are less complex than those of, say, Mozart or Beethoven. As in the case of language, most of us have "musicality" to some degree. Music is constructed of elements such as patterns of rhythm and melody, and all of us have internalized at least some of these elements. But those who achieve at the level of the unusual few recognized as "geniuses"—or even the somewhat lesser lights in the realm of musical composition—are unquestionably endowed with a highly developed and specialized capacity not possessed by the rest of us. (A challenge to the neuroscientist is the identification of neural correlates of such unusual capabilities, assuming that there *are* such correlates.) This capacity, given the right conditions (a musical family, for instance), often manifests itself unexpectedly early, as in the case of Mozart, who was a prodigy. The young Mozart's first published works, two *Sonates pour le clavecin* (piano sonatas), appeared in 1764, when he was only 8 years old (Banks & Turner, 1991).

Both music and language are constructed of small elements combined by sets of rules into complex patterns. But Gardner (1983) cites evidence that, for example, "the mechanisms by which pitch is apprehended and stored are different from the mechanisms that process other sounds, particularly those of language" (p. 117). Furthermore, studies of individuals who have suffered brain damage indicate that in cases of language loss (aphasia) musical ability may remain unimpaired and that when the loss is of musical ability language may remain unimpaired (Gardner, 1983).

Logical-mathematical intelligence is Gardner's third "frame of mind." As with musical talent, logical-mathematical ability emerges early in the gifted individual. This ability, however, is more difficult to examine because so much specialized training is required not only for the mathematician or scientist to *produce* interesting results but also for others to be apprised of and to *understand* them. An appreciation of both the math wizard's results and the intellectual achievement they represent is beyond most people.

Next in Gardner's set of intelligences is spatial intelligence, which involves being able to recognize that different visual experiences of an entity are, in fact, experiences of the same entity, though the perspective may have changed. For instance, the path one has traversed in one direction is the same path when one is going the other way, though every object along it is now seen from the opposite direction. Another capacity involved in this aspect of intelligence allows us first to see in our mind's eye an object, say a brick, and then to imagine what it looks like from a different angle. (We return to this capacity for mental imagery in the next chapter.) These abilities allow us, for example, to orient ourselves in space and to recognize objects when they appear in a different context or orientation from the one in which we first encountered them. Without these capacities, we'd feel "lost in space" and constantly confronted with objects we could not recognize, though we'd seen them countless times before in many different places and situations.

Research in neuroscience supports Gardner's treatment of spatial intelligence as distinct from other types of intelligence. Clinical studies indicate that lesions in certain areas of the brain (notably the right parietal region, at the top of the brain, toward the back), caused by stroke or other trauma, result in difficulties, among which is difficulty in spatial representaion and orientation (Gardner, 1983).

Bodily-kinesthetic intelligence is Gardner's next candidate intelligence. Is there anyone among us who has not noticed—or, worse, *been*—the unfortunate student always chosen last for a team in gym? Even being considerably superior to most of one's peers in linguistic or logical-mathematical intelligence in no way compensates for the humiliation of always being, and knowing one will always be, the last chosen when physical prowess and grace count heavily. What such a student would not give for bodily intelligence, "control of . . . bodily motions and capacity to handle objects skilfully" (Gardner, 1983, p. 206).

Someone who can make an audience believe that he or she is actually talking on the telephone when there is no telephone present and no words are being spoken, eating when there is no food, or engaged in any sort of activity that is not in fact taking place—such a person exhibits a high degree of this sort of intelligence. Similarly, dancers who are able to express emotion by means of their bodily movements alone, and in the process afford the audience aesthetic pleasure by the grace and shape of these movements, demonstrate bodily-kinesthetic intelligence. And the actor whose movements, use of voice, and sense of timing, for example, make an audience believe he or she is someone else entirely, or transport the audience into another time and another place, also displays a high degree of bodily-kinesthetic intelligence.

Finally, Gardner cites two personal intelligences. One, the *intra*personal, involves *"access to one's own feeling life*—one's range of affects or emotions: the capacity instantly to effect discriminations among these feelings and, eventually, to label them, to enmesh them in symbolic codes, to draw upon them as a means of understanding and guiding one's behavior." The other, the *inter*personal, involves *"the ability to notice and make distinctions among other individuals* and, in particular, among their moods, temperaments, motivations, and intentions" (Gardner, 1983, p. 239).

Gardner's inclusion of the personal intelligences in his scheme, like Sternberg's inclusion of a practical intelligence, makes explicit the important point that these are at least as crucial to one's successful functioning in the world as are more generally accepted indications of intelligence. With respect to the intrapersonal, at one end of the continuum are those individuals who are not aware of their own feelings, their own emotions. Many will recognize "Bob," for example. A physician, Bob is considered very intelligent by his colleagues. He is also attractive and personable, and he had no difficulty in finding girlfriends and eventually a wife. But Bob does not recognize that much of his behavior, like everyone else's, results from his emotions. Neither can he comprehend his wife's emotional responses. He insists on "rationality" in himself and others, without acknowledging (indeed, without *noticing*) that occasionally his own responses are not rational. Those who interact with people like Bob may find this aspect of their personalities frustrating or exasperating. One might wish to help but be unable to, because these individuals can't recognize or pinpoint what their own feelings are—let alone what is causing them—and may reject or take offense at any efforts to "help."

At the other end of the continuum are those who have such a solid understanding of themselves that they become sources of stability whom others lean on. There is often a member of a group of school friends, for example, who is the "listener" to whom others go with their troubles and who provides both a strong shoulder and sensible advice. Or think of the author Marcel Proust, who was enormously sensitive and alert to every shade and nuance of his own feelings. Endowed in addition with a superior linguistic intelligence, Proust contributed to society an influential work of literature, *À la recherche du temps perdu* (published in English as *Remembrance of Things Past*), in which he captured these feelings for others to recognize and appreciate.

With respect to the interpersonal intelligence, one extreme is the individual who can't seem to put himself in another's shoes, who sees that people have some kind of intuition about each other's responses but somehow doesn't grasp what it consists of or how to do it. As we will see in Chapter 9, a condition known as Asperger's syndrome, more descriptively known as "mindblindness," may be responsible for this deficiency in some individuals. As with all the intelligences, if the personal intelligences, which normally act in concert with the others, are, as Gardner proposes, discrete entities, their neural correlates may someday be found. The study of Asperger's syndrome will no doubt play a role in locating them.

More recently, Gardner has added one more intelligence to his list (and still another may be forthcoming): the naturalist intelligence. I leave it to the reader to consider whether it falls into the same category of separable but interdependent intelligences as those he originally proposed.

> The core of the naturalist intelligence is the human ability to recognize plants, animals, and other parts of the natural environment, like clouds or rocks. All of us can do this; some kids (experts on dinosaurs) and many adults (hunters, botanists, anatomists) excel at this pursuit. While the ability doubtless evolved to deal with natural kinds of elements, I believe that it has been hijacked to deal with the world of man-made objects. We are good at distinguishing among cars, sneakers, and jewelry, for example, because our ancestors needed to be able to recognize carnivorous animals, poisonous snakes, and flavorful mushrooms. (Gardner, 1998, p. 2)

Gardner (1983) perceives these human intelligences as extremely important aspects of human ability, that have "tended to be ignored or minimized by nearly all students of cognition" (p. 241). One type of evidence he cites for considering them distinct from other abilities is neurological. The identification of consistencies between types of neurological damage and behavioral or cognitive deficits is a foundation stone in Gardner's theoretical structure.

As with the other intelligences, brain damage can affect intrapersonal and interpersonal knowledge. Very striking in this regard is the famous case of Phineas Gage, who, in 1848, at the age of 25, suffered a terrible wound. Gage was a railway construction foreman, very competent at his job—a job requiring both technical and social skills. Due to an accidental explosion, he was struck by an iron rod traveling at great speed. The rod passed through his left cheek, pierced his skull, and exited through the top of his head, damaging his brain en route. (Figure 1.4).

Surprisingly, Gage made a quick physical recovery from this bizarre accident, but his personality underwent a radical change. Whereas before the accident he had exhibited normal social behavior, afterward he was unable to get along with people and could not make advantageous decisions about his own future. He was no longer able to work as a construction foreman; indeed, he was unable to hold a regular job at all. In a way, he had become a different person. Neurologist Antonio Damasio cites the case of Phineas Gage as an early hint that, in addition to the specific area of the human brain that supports language, there is a specific area involved in rationality that when impaired, leads to inappropriate life choices and unacceptable social behavior. Damasio's recent work with patients suffering similar brain damage (although as a result of stroke rather than of bizarre and dramatic accidents) bears out what Gage's case suggests: that when a certain area of the frontal lobes is damaged one may apparently recover health and reasoning ability yet be unable to put this ability to work as before, becoming, in the eyes of friends and family, "somebody else" in terms of character and personality (Damasio, 1994).

Although the perspectives on intelligence of both Sternberg and Gardner are useful in a variety of ways, they are not intended as *explanations* of intelligence. The first step in arriving at an explanation (i.e., an understanding) of a phenomenon is accurately *describing* it and, in so doing, making very clear what it is that requires explanation. When I offer as an explanation of how the light works in my study the statement "I just flick the switch and the light goes on or off," I have provided a description of what I do to make it work. Someone who wished truly to understand what is going on in the process would be frustrated by my answer and would follow it with the question "Yes, but how does it *work?*" There are different levels of explanation, depending on the field of study. Each field seeks explanations at a certain level for the phenomena with which it is concerned. For instance, in attempting to explain human behavior, the psychologist's account may rest on observations of behavior or reports of a person's upbringing and other past experiences, as well as factors likely to be influenced by genes, for example, temperament. The chemist will look for explanations at the level of the chemical structure and interaction of the substances that are produced by the brain and

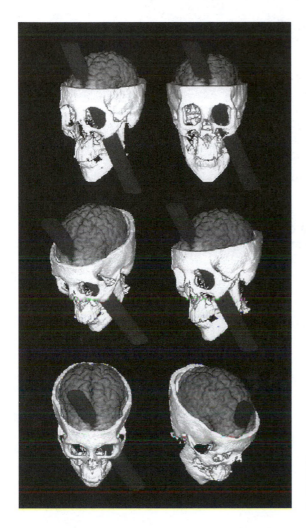

FIGURE 1.4 Contemporary
Drawing of the Rod and the
Path It Took Through the Skull
of Phineas Gage

influence or affect behavior. The physicist's explanation will be given in terms of the ultimate particles out of which these substances—and the brain itself—are made. Cognitive science seeks answers to questions about how the human mind actually works. What must be in there, in terms of actual physical entities, to allow us to function as we do? How is the mind actually organized? Is there a center where, for example, Sternberg's metacomponents operate or where our experience of the external world is passed along from perception (visual, auditory, etc.) to organization into what we recognize as "making sense"? Is there a specific location where Gardner's personal intelligences reside or where their various components are coordinated? If there is a portion of our mind devoted to one kind of ability, say, language or mathematics, just how does it connect with other such portions devoted to other kinds of abilities? We shall return to such questions in the following chapters.

The End of the Beginning

The quest to understand intelligence lies at the heart of cognitive science. Each discipline participating in this endeavor contributes its own data, its own methods, its own perspective. We began our journey by reviewing cognitive psychology's early efforts to explore human intelligence, starting with Gall's early work in accounting for differences among people. En route we have noted the experimental approach of Lashley; the contributions of neurosurgeons such as Penfield; the attempts on the part of Galton to measure intelligence, and those as well of the psychometricians Binet and Wechsler, whose IQ tests (and their derivatives) are in wide use today; and we have briefly examined the approaches of Sternberg and Gardner, who regard human intelligence as a set of capacities that can be studied independently but that function interdependently in the normal individual. Fortified with this background, we are ready to proceed on our journey into cognitive science. Chapter 2 provides an introduction to areas currently under research in the field of cognitive psychology.

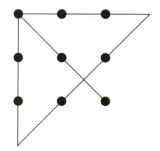

The Nine Dots Problem: A Solution

Questions to Think About

1. Many people operate under the assumption that all of us think in the same way. This chapter suggests a very different point of view. What is *your* view of the matter? Is everyone pretty much alike? Are we all pretty much like you?

2. What do you think are the likely reasons for the disappearance of phrenology as a serious scientific enterprise? If you had been a contemporary of Gall's, would you have believed what Gall said?

3. Penfield's epileptic patients were awake during their brain surgery so that their experiences could be reported as he probed different points of their brains. What might be some of the advantages to the surgeon (and, of course, to the patient) of this technique?

4. Ebbinghaus is one of those early psychologists who used themselves as the subjects of their research. How better to study learning, he reasoned, than to

observe oneself learning? His findings have held up well over the years. Why does observing oneself learning in order to study learning make sense or fail to make sense, especially if we have many different intelligences and levels of intelligence?

5. Galton believed our ability to discern very low intensity stimuli should be closely related to our ability to solve problems, indeed, to function intelligently in all areas. Do you agree with this view? Might you wish to modify it in the light of other material in this chapter? Explain.

6. IQ has been a very controversial issue in the past 30 years or so. Have you known anyone whose intelligence was greatly underestimated (or overestimated) by a standard test? What kind of intelligence? Do you think tests like the SAT measure intelligence? If not, do they measure *anything*? What?

7. What does Sternberg's approach add to your understanding of your own intellectual functioning?

8. Are there intelligences identified by Gardner that you recognize in yourself or in your friends but had not previously dignified with the label "intelligence"? Do you think they merit that name? Why or why not?

9. Are there types of intelligence that you have recognized that you don't see discussed in this chapter?

The Approach of Cognitive Science

Sitting near me the other day was my friend Amy. We were companionably working at our computers, and Amy's fingers and keyboard were going a mile a minute. I was for the moment just thinking—thinking, in fact, about thinking, which is essentially the subject of this chapter. Then I noticed that Amy's fingers had become still, and I turned to look at her. "I just asked my computer to 'find' something for me in this document," she explained. But, for reasons unknown, the little icon that indicates that the command is being processed remained on the screen—and remained, and remained, and remained. After a while Amy said, "It's thinking," then a bit later, "It's still thinking." And still later, "It's never thought for *this* long!" Finally, Amy concluded that the computer was stuck and had to be restarted.

Some time later, I asked Amy if the computer ever did find the place on the document she had been looking for. "No," she replied, "I was afraid to ask it again." "Well," I said, "you can probably find it on yesterday's printout over there on the table."

"Good thinking," she replied.

When Amy described her computer's activity as "thinking," we had both smiled a little, as though we humans, secure in what we know, understood that the computer wasn't *really* thinking; only *we* can do that. In searching its memory for information, it was indeed doing something that we do when we think. But when *I* sometimes get stuck trying to retrieve something from my memory, I am not obliged to "restart" the entire mechanism; I simply go on to a new thought. Although we knew the information Amy was looking for was in its memory (because she had put it there), after Amy had given up, restarted, and gone on with her work it would not retrieve it on its own. Computers don't do anything without instructions.

Suppose *we* couldn't retrieve a bit of information we wanted, and instead of giving up and hoping for the "spontaneous" phenomenon to occur, we pursued our thought. Suppose what we sought was a word. If one avenue, say, searching through words of similar meaning, did not produce it for us, we might try another, perhaps thinking of words beginning with the same letter or words having the same number of syllables (What street *is* that—Boardman? Burnside? Oh, yes, Milburn!)—providing that we recalled information of this sort. Or suppose we followed the path of associations of ideas this word triggered, associations available to us though the word itself was not. Or perhaps the word, though missing, was yet able to conjure up for us a visual image, a picture in our mind's eye of, say, a person with whom the word (or the concept the word expressed) was associated.

Before this era of scientific experimentation, one of the chief means of learning about what goes on in the mind was introspection. I pointed out in the preceding chapter that this is an activity in which anyone can engage—and most of us do. We notice, for example, that it *is* possible to pursue a missing word in a variety of ways, as described a moment ago. And if this activity fails to produce the word, we notice that it may spring to mind when we are thinking of something else altogether, appearing suddenly, as if unbidden, and causing us to exclaim, "Obfuscation! That's the word—I *knew* it began with an *o*!" At the same time we may even notice that we are noticing all of this; in thinking about it, we are using our minds to introspect about how we are introspecting . . . In imagining how it happens that a word we were looking for unexpectedly appears when we are no longer attending to the problem, we may hypothesize, for example, a searcher of some sort continuing its operation unattended—and unintended—down pathways and byways until it hits the right entry. When that happens, it has what we may call a "Bingo!" reaction. And perhaps in its wake comes our attempt to explain what we meant by "unattended" operation: how we can perform such a complex function without intending to.

Cognitive psychologists seek explanations for all the functions introspection suggests that our minds carry out. Some of this research has been stimulated by attempts to design machines that can carry out these functions. We name the computer functions after our own: Amy's computer was retrieving from its "memory." And then we turn around and use computer terminology to describe our own mental activity: "information processing." After all, in order to do this successfully, we must first know what it *is* that we are doing when we are, for instance, remembering the word "obfuscation," solving problems (such as how to get the information the computer got stuck on), or envisioning in our mind's eye Aunt Sally's fat old gray cat. And so cognitive psychologists now try to explain these functions, as opposed to describing them or measuring them, as earlier psychologists did. They have offered accounts of what sort of "machinery" must be in there—what the "cognitive architecture" that supports the functions might be.

Our focus in this chapter, then, is on the types of cognitive processes our brains engage in and on the mechanisms that have been proposed to account for them. Cognitive psychologists are engaged in two tasks: developing a theoretical framework to explain the workings of the brain and devising experiments whose results serve to illuminate that framework.

Concepts and Categories

Why is it that the notion that Amy's computer was "thinking" made us smile? Perhaps we have an implicit awareness that our own brand of thinking involves much complex, if silent, "whirring and humming" that is not performed by the computer. If we know anything at all about this machine, we know that however well it may perform certain types of tasks, even outperforming us in some of them, it has not (yet?) achieved the ability to orchestrate the great variety of tasks our brains execute effortlessly—simultaneously. Let us look now at some of the cognitive processes we need to consider, starting with a very fundamental one: the crucial process that allows us to organize our experience of the world so that we can function in it.

Think for a moment about what organizing our experience of the world entails. You have notions or ideas of what things are: This is a washing machine, that is a tree, and there in the sky (also something you recognize) is an airplane. Another way of referring to these notions or ideas is as *concepts*. As you go about living your life, you constantly compare the items you encounter with a selection of your concepts to see whether any of them fits. If so, you consider that item, perhaps a washing machine, to be "one of those."

We speak of notions, ideas, and concepts rather casually, expecting our words to be understood. And so they are, for all practical purposes. But if our purpose is scientific—for example, if we wish to study the workings of the human mind—we must be precise in our use of such terms. Harvard psychologist W. K. Estes offers a definition of "concept" that begins with the one given in the *American Heritage Dictionary:* "a general idea or understanding, especially one derived from specific instances," and continues with the stipulation ". . . and taking the form of a knowledge structure that enables or mediates categorizations." Says Estes (1994), "The mark of having mastered a concept is the ability to categorize objects or events of a domain in ways that could not be accomplished in the absence of the concept" (p. 241). In other words, without having mastered and stored a given concept, we would not be able to assign instances of it to a *category*; our own idiosyncratic world would be that much less organized.

Estes then makes precise the everyday understanding of **categorization** by introducing the notion of "coherence," a property defined by Murphy and Medin (1985). A category may be defined in any way one wishes, but some categories seem to make sense, whereas others do not. He uses as an example the classifying of trees encountered in a walk through the woods as "odd trees" and "even trees," pointing out that such a classification provides no information about the classes other than their position relative to each other (Estes, 1994). That information serves no practical purpose. If, however, we were to classify them on the basis of the shapes of their leaves and the types of bark that covered them, we could assign this one to the category *pine* and that one to the category *oak*. These categories are characterized by coherence; that is, there is sense in such a category—we can make use of the information the category suggests. We have no such use for "odd" or "even" in this situation. Given the right concept, we would be able to predict that the seeds of some of these trees will be acorns and those of others pleasantly scented pine cones. Prediction is a very important aspect of dealing with the world; I may wish to plant oak trees, and if I know where to find acorns, my task will be facilitated. Or, if I wish to take a walk, and I know that there are acorns underfoot, I will take care not to step on them. If, while on my walk, I recognize that a tempting berry belongs to a particular category, I will know whether or not it is safe to eat it.

Forming concepts via categorization, and recognizing members of a category by virtue of the concepts we have formed, are major—indeed, crucial—achievements. Consider for a moment the experience of a newborn baby. From the limited, enclosed, and comfortable environment it experiences before birth, it is suddenly thrust into a world in which sights, sounds, smells, touches, and tastes abound. It experiences all of these by means of senses that are alert—but unaccustomed—to the "booming, buzzing confusion" of the new environment, as William James put it. What is the baby to make of all this confusion? Shapes move in and out of its field of vision; it is picked up, jiggled, stroked, put down; sounds of all types, all pitches, all intensities assail its ears; objects with different tastes are thrust into its mouth; and odors waft through the air around it. How is it possible for the new little one to make sense of all this?

We undoubtedly take for granted the obvious differences between the appearance of a face and that of an umbrella, the blast of a car horn and the soothing sound of a lullaby, the sourness of a pickle and the luscious taste of a peach. But the question of how we have managed to make all these distinctions in the first place is a difficult one to answer. Reason tells us that we need a mechanism that experiences all the different stimuli presented by the environment and sorts them, placing some together with others along a particular dimension or according to a particular characteristic, to arrive at coherent concepts. Faces, for instance, first perceived by infants as shapes appearing in the air above, must be sorted along with—what? More or less oval items? Curved entities with a regular assortment of objects protruding from them? Colored objects occurring in conjunction with certain specific noises? The question is not simply "What other objects does this resemble and in what ways?" but also "What are the salient features or attributes of this object that I should take note of as I decide what other objects it resembles and in what ways?" That is, what are the attributes that *matter*? In the earlier example of trees on a path, it does not really matter that every other one is "odd" and the ones separating them are "even." Does it matter that a given object in the infant's environment, later to be identified as a face, has two items on the top, one in the middle, and one across the bottom? Is it relevant to its "faceness" that this one is relatively pink, that one is lighter in color and has little brown dots on it, and the one over there is uniformly rather brown? Does it matter that this stuff in my mouth makes my lips pucker, but that other stuff slides right down? Is that distinction more relevant than, say, the fact that the puckery stuff (a pickle) is long, green, and crunchy, and that the smooth and slidey stuff (a peach) comes in an orangey-pink, round, fuzzy package?

It is clear why we must have a mechanism for concept and category formation: first, simply because we do form concepts and categories; and second, because it is crucial to our survival to be able to divide the objects around us into those that are safe and those that are not, those that are desirable and those we should avoid, those that are necessary and those we can do without. Reason gets us this far, but what reason cannot tell us is *how* it is done: how babies make sense of the world around them by dividing it up into "some of these, some of those, and some of that other kind of thing"—in other words, how they categorize the elements in their environment to arrive at concepts, which in turn allow the classification of newly encountered elements.

In our discussion of language (Part 3), we will see that the infant begins very early to distinguish among sounds so that speech is perceived not only as something distinct from other types of environmental noise but as distinct even from other *human* noise, say, humming. Experiments have indicated an even more sophisticated ability on the part of the infant, that of distinguishing one *speech* sound from another. Such experiments support the notion that the ability to categorize is innate in humans. This is not a surprising notion; it is intuitively reasonable that an ability so fundamental to survival is, like the impulse to suck, inborn, as indeed it appears to be in other species. The newborn kitten, for instance, instinctively seeks its mother's nourishment; to do this it, too, must be able to distinguish "source of milk" from "table leg." There is experimental evidence that other species categorize. For example, in the realm of color, honeybees, pigeons, and monkeys have been shown to divide the spectrum into categories. (See in this regard, e.g., von Frisch, 1971, on the European honeybee; Wright, 1972, and Wright & Cumming, 1971, on the pigeon; and Sandell, Gross, & Bornstein, 1979, on macaques.)

Distinguishing among speech sounds depends on both hearing and noticing. Categories based on sensory input are basic types of categories for humans (as for other species). We have already noted that it is our senses that bring us information from "outside." We must and do categorize this information in order to make sense of and live successfully in the world.

But humans do not stop with perceptual categorization; we categorize abstractly as well. We refer to "feelings," for example, sorting them into physical sensations and emotions. We sort the physical ones into, for example, hot/cold, sweet/sour, loud/quiet; and we categorize emotions as fear, anger, joy, and so on. We categorize other kinds of abstractions: intelligence/stupidity, democracy/dictatorship, melodic/atonal. Categorization is a function so fundamental that we cannot think without engaging in it. Indeed, we can, with assurance and good reason, consider categorization (along with memory, of which more shortly) the base on which human cognition rests.

According to Emory University psychologist Lawrence Barsalou (1992), "Categorization provides the gateway between perception and cognition" (p. 15). And as psychologist Edward E. Smith (1995) of the University of Michigan puts it, categorization is "perhaps our primary means for coding experience," allowing us to infer "invisible properties from visible ones" (pp. 5–6). That is, when we categorize an object as a grape—based on its size, shape, and the fact that it is on a vine—we infer that some of its properties that we *can't* see are that it is edible, it will be juicy, and, if we don't pluck it, its juice may find its way into a wine bottle.

Not surprisingly, cognitive psychologists have paid a good deal of attention to the subject of concepts and categories over the course of the last 30 years or so, approaching the phenomenon in various ways, in part because it may be that we employ different means for different kinds of categories. Because information from the environment comes to us by means of our senses, the properties of environmental stimuli are intimately involved in the way we categorize those stimuli. We possess sensory mechanisms specific to the different senses, for example, the retina of the eye for visual stimuli and the taste buds on the tongue for gustatory stimuli. Speech, which reaches us primarily through our ears, is one such stimulus that has been extensively analyzed in this regard. We have devised sophisticated techniques for describing speech sounds in terms of their physical properties (acoustic phonetics) and in terms of the way in which we produce them (articulatory phonetics). In infancy, we observe these sounds and sort them, for example, according to how loud or soft they are; we sort them too according to whether, among other characteristics, they are produced with closed or open lips and with or without the voice—and also according to combinations of these qualities. Researchers have determined that the ability to recognize certain sounds as speech sounds—and even as different *types* of speech sounds—probably indicates an innate predisposition to respond to sound by categorizing it. But we have not determined *how* infants, or we, do it.

Sorts of Sorting

Once, in response to my request to look through old family photos, my father took down from a closet shelf several manila envelopes of varying sizes. As we sat down and began to go through their contents, I was struck by what seemed an odd assortment within each envelope. Pictures of me in early childhood rubbed elbows, so to speak, with photos of my aunt on a fishing boat, holding up a large fish—taken years before my birth—and shots of dinner party guests I did not recognize, gathered around a restaurant table. Another envelope yielded snapshots of my children at a birthday party, faces adorned with ice cream and cake, in company with pictures of my sister's college graduation and a set of views taken on someone's trip out west in some unspecified year.

My own collection of photos, although stored somewhat helter-skelter in drawers and shoe boxes, nevertheless was in an intelligible order that made sense to me: One shoe box contained pictures of my children at various ages, another those of my sister and her family, another of the cats that had been my pets over the years. There was an envelope devoted to pictures of my friends' children, one containing photos of high school friends long scattered, and so on.

"*How* have you organized these?" I demanded of my father, looking in some consternation at the envelopes on the table. "Why," said my father, in a tone of great reasonableness, "by size, of course."

Sorting items is often what we do to keep order in our lives. When it comes to tackling the sorting of items such as family photos, we consciously choose arrangements, perhaps sorting chronologically or by family groups—making use of categories that have meaning for us, categories that "make sense." It made no sense to *me* to sort them by size, at least not until my father explained that his choice was based on the sizes of the envelopes. . . . Not a factor that would influence me, this was at least comprehensible. (Need I add that my father was endowed with a playful sense of humor?)

Now suppose you were given the task of sorting objects, say marbles, in order to store them in an organized fashion. What criteria might you use for assigning some to one jar and some to another? That is, what characteristics of the various marbles serve to distinguish them from one another? Not shape, surely: They are all spherical. Not texture: They are all smooth. Size? Perhaps: Some may be larger than others. Color? Surely: Some are blue, some red, some clear, some streaky, or "marbled." But they share enough features for you to recognize them all as marbles. You would be unlikely to confuse them with lollipops, though their colors might be similar and some lollipops are roughly spherical. Lollipops, even those shaped like a large marble, have a stick by which to hold them; marbles do not.

Now suppose there were many different types of objects on the table, and you were asked to sort them. If some were marbles, some lollipops, some colored plastic spoons, and some colored plastic forks, you'd probably put all the marbles together, based on the characteristics they shared, and likewise the lollipops. Would you separate the forks from the spoons? You might, based on the differences in shape. But you might not, figuring that they were all very different from marbles and lollipops but similar to each other in function. Marbles are not for eating. Lollipops are for eating. Spoons and forks are for eating *with*. Thus you would probably end up with three or four sets of items, depending on how you regarded the spoons and forks. If at this point a family of gerbils were added to the assortment, you might decide that they form a separate set, leaving you with four or five sets; or, noticing that they are the only living things on the table, you might redefine your sets: gerbils in one set and everything else in the other.

What you would be doing is organizing the items on the table in terms of shared characteristics. Some of these characteristics seem more important than others as a basis for sorting, providing coherent categories: Most people would separate the marbles from everything else rather than placing the red marbles with the red lollipops, spoons, and forks and the green marbles with the green lollipops, spoons, and forks. Why? On what basis do we make such decisions? In other words, what accounts for the sets, or categories, that we perceive and make use of in such tasks? If we could answer this question, we might be a step further along in understanding how our minds set up and then recognize categories. As we consider this issue, we must also bear in mind that categorization depends crucially on memory: Without the ability to remember what we have experienced in the past, we would have nothing to relate new experiences to, hence no categories. (The topic of memory is considered later in the chapter.)

Plato and others have suggested that we might be born with categories already in place. Could this be the case? There certainly seems to be an innate aspect to certain categories in various species of animals. If a new kitten didn't distinguish at birth "mother" from "table leg," for example, it would not survive. But it is the environment that shows us marbles, lollipops, spoons, forks, and families of gerbils. It is difficult to believe, as Plato did, that we come into the world with categories already specified for everything we might someday come across. Most of the categories we ultimately use are based on our experience. Categorization is such a fundamental aspect of human cognition that, if we hope to understand how our minds work, we need to learn what factors in our experience contribute to forming our categories and what part of our cognitive equipment is involved in doing so. Various approaches have been taken in studying categorization. Three major ones are described in what follows.

The "Exemplar" Approach to Categorization   As we develop through childhood and beyond, we are presented with bits and pieces of the world around us, from which we must construct the categories that will allow us to function in that world. Some of those bits and pieces are, for instance, individual experiences of dogs. One could assume that people construct the category *dog* out of these. Say your Uncle Joe's dog is about waist high and brown all over, with pointy ears and a long tail. The dog next door, much smaller, is white with black spots and has long, droopy ears. Your best friend's dog is intermediate in size, gray, with longish fur hiding its ears and forming a fringe that falls in its eyes. According to this model, all of these experiences, or **exemplars**, get lumped together into a category *dog*. Should you encounter a new example that resembles one in this collection, you will assign it to this category. If what you encounter looks like Uncle Joe's dog, it goes in; if it is small and black with a white stripe down its back, and it douses you with an evil-smelling fluid when you approach, it probably does not resemble any instance of dog you have come across; hence you will not assign it to that category.

Many if not most of these categories, such as *dog*, are fairly stable across a particular culture and remain so through many generations. It is interesting to observe, however, the changes that sometimes occur even in the categories we might expect to remain stable. In eliciting from students the features of the category *brother*, I found, to no one's surprise, that they judged "male" to be an essential one. I assumed that another was "having the same parents." My students disagreed, basing their categories on a conception of family structure quite different from mine. I realized that I was operating from the cultural perspective of the period during which I grew up, in which family relationships were based on intact nuclear families (irrespective of whether any of the children were adopted). My students were accustomed to a world of stepparents, stepgrandparents, and perhaps whole contingents of stepsiblings who were referred to as and considered brothers and sisters, at least when emotional closeness was felt.

A difficulty with the exemplar approach to categorization is that the entities that are eventually assigned to a particular category are frequently very different from each other. One might, on first impression, judge a chihuahua to be less like a great Dane than like a cat. What makes us consider these two breeds of dog, along with wire-haired terriers, beagles, collies, and whippets, members of the same category—one which excludes cats and rabbits? And what causes us to assign to the category a *new* instance, as different from the other members (and from each other) as a collie and a Mexican hairless? It does seem that there must be more to the process of categorization than the accumulation of already encountered individuals. In going beyond the instances encountered to organize a meaningful category, we seem to abstract from all of them some characteristic or set of characteristics, that then constitutes the basis of a category.

In arriving at coherent categories, people we regard as "creative" may make unusual judgments about which features are involved. They may find salient features that most of us would not notice. What they abstract from the elements of their environment may be quite different from what the majority of us would single out, faced with the same elements. This would account for that sense we have, on experiencing the work of creative people, of "seeing things in a new light"—having been shown by their work a novel way of constructing concepts.

The "Feature" Approach to Categorization   A second approach to categorization is to specify those characteristics of a category that are both necessary and sufficient for membership in that category; if an entity possesses them, it qualifies. Because it requires only a few clear-cut identifying features to characterize it, the category *bachelor* is often cited, its features being adult, human, male, and unmarried. All of these **features** must be included or the category is not adequately specified. (Test this claim yourself by subtracting first one and then another of these features.) Furthermore, no characteristic other than these four is necessary to define the category; these are sufficient. (Again, test *this* claim: Add a feature, say, happy. Is this one necessary?)

Identifying the necessary and sufficient features for any category one might choose is not always as easy as it is for *bachelor,* however. What, for instance, uniquely specifies *dog*—that is, characterizes *dog* so that every dog, but nothing else, possesses those features? In all the instances of *dog* I described previously, I cited only differences: differences in size, color, shape of ears. But surely all of these exemplars share important characteristics. Try for a moment to think what they are. People generally come up with a set that includes "animate, canine, domesticated, furry, four legs, tail, and barks." Which of these features is absolutely necessary in order to characterize *dog*? Animate is important; it distinguishes *dog* both from *rock* and from *statue of a dog* (though perhaps not from *tree*). *Canine* is not really a feature; it is a category of its own, comprising dogs, wolves, and others. Thus, domesticated is an important feature, serving to distinguish *dog* from non-dog members of this larger category. Having four legs and a tail is certainly part of being a dog. It is perhaps necessary to the category, but not sufficient to distinguish *dog* from *cat, horse,* or, for that matter, *skunk.* That it *barks,* however, serves to make that distinction. So, excluding *canine,* we have perhaps identified the features necessary and sufficient to specify the category *dog.*

Often at this point I meet with protest from my students; they point to instances of dogs that accidents have left with only three legs. They mention the Siberian husky, which does not bark, and a breed of dog that has no fur. After discussion—sometimes heated—it is usually agreed that these instances constitute exceptions to a norm. Membership in the category *dog* still requires certain features; their absence in individual instances does not invalidate the category.

The "Prototype" Approach to Categorization   A third model of categorization rests on the notion of a *norm*; this is the model based on **prototypes**. A prototype is a version of an entity that one might think of as the "average" of the type, that is, a representation formed of average values for the features characterizing the entity. You might think of a prototype as the typical dog or the typical house or the typical summer day. Upon encountering a new entity, according to this model, one presumably compares it with the prototypes represented in one's mind and assigns it to the category whose prototype it most resembles. To be assigned to a category, an entity need not be similar to the prototype in any specific characteristic or characteristics, as it must in the feature-based model. If it has two legs, two wings, and a shape something like the one illustrated in Figure 2.1, then it is readily

FIGURE 2.1 The Savannah Sparrow, Which Fits Our Expectation of What a Typical Bird Looks Like

FIGURE 2.2 The Emu, Which Is Far From Our Expectation of a Typical Bird

assignable to the category *bird*. If, however, it has two legs, two wings, but is shaped like the one illustrated in Figure 2.2, we may find it more difficult to place it in the bird category. But because there is no requirement in such a model that a given instance of the category have any specific features, the problem my students find with the feature approach is not encountered.

Categorizing by the prototype method is categorizing "heuristically." That is, instead of doing a complete search, which would entail considering every entity in our collection that has features in common with the new one until we find a precise match (which is the way a computer would do it), we look only for similarity to prototypes. This kind of approximate search is the sort of activity human beings do well. It may not be one hundred percent accurate, but it is fast, and for most purposes and most of the time, it works perfectly well. We return to this topic in Part 4, on artificial intelligence.

Experimental Evidence for Categories

We have touched on three major models of the processes by which humans acquire perceptual and conceptual categories. No single one of these provides an adequate account; it is probable that we make use of a combination of strategies that includes at least these three. Our discussion so far has been theoretical, but a large number of experiments exists that provide relevant data. Because real-life experience varies so much from one individual to another, it is not possible for a researcher to know either what information someone may have about categories of entities encountered in ordinary living or how this information is organized. Therefore, experimenters typically construct artificial situations in the laboratory. They decide what information the subjects will be exposed to so that they don't have to be concerned with experiential differences among subjects or with other factors that might confuse the issue. There is always a question as to the validity of generalizations made from laboratory results to real life, but according to Barsalou (1992), who has carried out much research in this area, the phenomena relating to artificial categories produced in laboratory experiments occur in **natural categories** (those arising from real-life experience) as well.

Important research was carried out fairly early in the game in the perceptual domain of color. A hypothesis had been advanced by the American linguist Edward Sapir (1884–1939) and Benjamin Lee Whorf (1897–1941), who had been his student. Known as the **linguistic relativity hypothesis**, or the **Sapir-Whorf hypothesis**, it held that the distinctions within a particular domain expressed in a given language will not be the same as those in any other language. An example often cited in support of this hypothesis comes from the realm of color. It had generally been thought that the way the color spectrum was segmented—as evidenced by the names assigned to colors in different languages—varied arbitrarily from language to language. The Sapir-Whorf hypothesis is discussed more fully in Chapter 5.

In 1969 the results of experiments designed to test this hypothesis were published. The primary data were drawn from 20 different languages, representing various language stocks. Speakers of these languages first provided the basic color terms in their languages. Then the researchers presented them with 320 color chips ranging over what we perceive as the spectrum from violet to red, differing in brightness (or dullness) and in saturation (i.e., purity of color; Berlin & Kay, 1991). The subjects first decided what the different color categories were and then selected which chip best represented each of them (the "prototypical" instance of the color). They were also instructed to identify the chips that marked the boundaries, that is, the last chip in each case that could still be considered to belong to the category before another category began.

Among the researchers' interesting findings were that (1) human beings perceive 11 basic color categories, for which languages have 11 or fewer basic color terms, and that (2) if there are fewer than 11 basic color categories encoded in a language there are strict limitations on which they may be. There are terms for white and black in all languages; if a language has only three color terms, the third one is for red; the fourth term in languages with four terms is for green or yellow, but not both; for languages with five terms, both green and yellow are included; in languages with six terms the sixth is for blue; in seven-term languages the seventh is for brown; and languages with eight or more color terms include purple, pink, orange, gray, or some combination of these. These striking results were taken by many as disconfirmation of the Sapir-Whorf, or linguistic relativity, hypothesis.

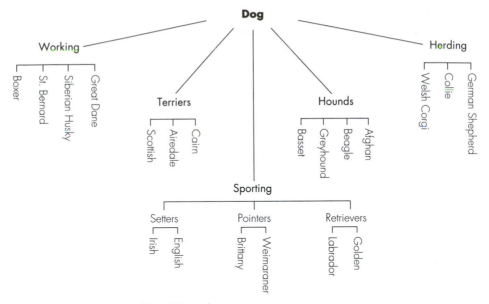

FIGURE 2.3 Illustration of Dog Hierarchy

There has since been much debate on the subject, and in the process a good deal of research has been stimulated. Subsequent major surveys of color terms have been conducted that seem to support the notion that certain perceptual categories are universally present in human beings.

Researchers in the area of categorization study other sorts of categories as well, both those that occur naturally, such as *fruit* or *dog,* and those consisting of artifacts, such as *car* and *chair.* Each category occupies a place within a hierarchy; for example, *dog,* as we saw earlier, falls under the larger heading, *canine,* which includes, along with domestic dogs, wild dogs, foxes, and wolves. As well as falling *within* a category, each member of the category subsumes members. For the category *dog,* members include a great variety of types: dachshunds, poodles, spaniels, terriers, and "mutts," for example. Within each of these types there may be yet another level: French poodles, toy poodles, cocker spaniels, English springer spaniels, wire-haired terriers, fox terriers, shepherd-collie mixes, and so forth. Figure 2.3 shows a dog hierarchy and Figure 2.4 a fruit hierarchy.

The category at the top (e.g., *canine, dog,* or *terrier,* depending on how far up the line you wish to draw your distinctions), from which the others branch out, is called a ***superordinate*** **semantic category**, and those below it constitute ***subordinate*** **semantic categories**. Within each category will be found "family resemblances," deriving from the characteristics that the members have in common. In an important set of experiments, Rosch and Mervis (1975) studied the role of family resemblance in categorization. They sought to identify the principles that dictate formation of category prototypes and gradients of category membership. They viewed natural semantic categories as

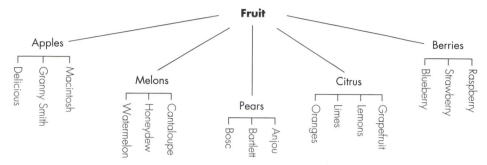

FIGURE 2.4 Illustration of Fruit Hierarchy

networks of overlapping attributes; the basic hypothesis was that members of a category come to be viewed as prototypical of the category as a whole in proportion to the extent to which they bear a family resemblance to (have attributes which overlap those of) other members of the category. Conversely, items viewed as most prototypical of one category will be those with least family resemblance to or membership in other categories. (Rosch & Mervis, 1975, p. 575)

Rosch and Mervis asked their experimental subjects to list the attributes of 20 items in each of six common superordinate categories of concrete noun. Some of these represented manufactured, and some natural, items: furniture, vehicles, fruit, weapons, vegetables, and clothing. Based on these attributes, a "family resemblance score" was computed for each item within a category. The higher the score, the closer to the typical, or the prototype, the category member was judged to be. For example, within the category *vehicles,* the attributes of car, airplane, and sled might include those listed in Table 2.1. The overlaps are clear; the "vehicle prototype score" for each car, airplane, and sled would be the total number of instances in which one of its attributes was also given as an attribute of another.

TABLE 2.1 Some Attributes of the Category *Vehicles:* Car, Airplane, and Sled

Car	*Airplane*	*Sled*
holding passengers	holding passengers	holding passengers
having four wheels	having wings	having runners
for getting from one place to another	for getting from one place to another	for getting from one place to another
made by people	made by people	made by people
used outdoors	used outdoors	used outdoors
made of metal	made of metal	made of wood
having an engine	having an engine	pushed, pulled, or moved by the force of gravity
riding on land	flying in the sky	gliding on snow

In another of their studies, Rosch and Mervis (1975) demonstrated a relation-ship between family resemblance and judgments of prototypicality. Subjects were given instances of category names and asked to rate, on a 7-point scale, the degree to which each accorded with their notion of the meaning of the category name. The result was that the instances of category names judged more prototypical were those with the greatest number of shared attributes, or, in other words, those that showed the most family resemblance.

Of course the conclusions reached in the research we have just looked at have not been the last word on the subject of categorization. Much work continues to be done in this area. For example, in a more recent set of experiments, Ahn and Medin (1992) investigated category construction based on free sorting, as opposed to the family resemblance principle. They pointed out that much of the earlier research on categorization had addressed the questions of how and why people create family resemblance categories. But when people confront the world, as opposed to the laboratory, they face two sorts of categories: the ones already constructed (the color categories employed by their culture, for example, or family systems, or pets as opposed to wild animals) and the ones they must construct for themselves both early in their development and later on. There had been few experiments that required the subjects actually to *construct* the categories rather than to choose among predefined categories. Ahn and Medin's (1992) results sug-gested that people do not in fact use the family resemblance principle to sort examples.

You can see even from this brief discussion something of the way research works: A model is proposed (in this case to explain the process of categorization) and experiments are designed to test it; then researchers find greater complication in the phenomenon, leading them to design studies to address the complication. With regard to the understanding of categorization, there are a wide range of issues under investigation. Consider, for example, categorizing engaged in by infants. There have been studies on, among many others, the perceptually based catego-ries of young infants (Eimas, Quinn, & Cowan, 1994), the contribution of parents' "labeling" to the development of infants' vocabulary (Dubois, Graham, & Sippola, 1995), and the perceptual cues that allow infants to differentiate among animal species (Quinn & Eimas, 1996). This very small sample will give the reader an idea of the variety of ways in which research into categorization by infants—only one of many definable populations—is being approached.

Category Loss

We have been focusing on the ways in which we acquire categories, the types of categories we acquire, and experimental evidence regarding our hypotheses about categorization. There is, however, another interesting source of information about our categorization function: category *loss*. Suppose we came across a person who had previously had no difficulty in recognizing and describing animate or inani-mate objects, but who, after an injury to a particular part of the brain, could no longer do so. We would consider the unfortunate deficit evidence that such a

TABLE 2.2 Performance on Definition Task of Two Patients with Impaired
Knowledge of Living Things

Name: Definition	Name: Definition
JBR Parrot: don't know	Tent: temporary outhouse, living home
Daffodil: plant	Briefcase: small case used by students to carry papers
Snail: an insect animal	Compass: tools for telling direction you are going
Eel: not well	Torch: hand-held light
Ostrich: unusual	Dustbin: bin for putting rubbish in
SBY Duck: an animal	Wheelbarrow: object used by people to take material about
Wasp: bird that flies	Towel: material used to dry people
Crocus: rubbish material	Pram: used to carry people, with wheels and a thing to sit on
Holly: what you drink	Submarine: ship that goes underneath the sea
Spider: a person looking for things, he was a spider for his nation or country	

category had indeed been conceptualized by that person—that is, that it *had* been
"in there." In fact, there are reports of cases of such category-specific recognition
deficits, which are known as **agnosias**. Individuals with a particular type of agnosia
may well be able to *perceive* the objects within the category they have lost, but
they are no longer able to identify them. One type of agnosia, known as **prosopagnosia**, is the loss of ability to categorize or recognize faces (see, e.g., Farah's 1990
book *Visual Agnosia*). This deficit can lead to the bizarre situation in which afflicted people cannot recognize the faces of family members, friends, or even their
own reflection in a mirror!

Other types of agnosia involve such stimuli as artifacts or animals. Sheridan
and Humphreys (1993) reported the results of their experiments with a young
woman who, following an encephalitis infection, had more trouble identifying and
demonstrating knowledge about animals and foods than about inanimate objects.
Smith (1995) cites two interesting patients who were told the names of common
objects and were then tested on whether they could define these objects. They
had no problem defining the artifacts but could not manage to define the animals.
Table 2.2 illustrates these patients' definitions.

There are still many unanswered questions about agnosias. For example, are
visual and verbal agnosias—involving categorization by means of sight or by
means of words—aspects of the same deficit, or do they represent two different
deficits? Even so, the existence of such selective deficits in patients who have
suffered damage to various areas of the brain constitutes yet another kind of evidence regarding the human capacity to categorize.

Mental Representation

Accepting that as a matter of course humans acquire concepts and engage in the process of categorization we also accept that our concepts and categories are stored somehow in our brains. It remains for us to understand and explain *how*.

The Representation of Concepts

At the beginning of our discussion of concepts and categories we saw that the two are intimately connected. We construct categories from instances, and these categories result in concepts—the representations we have of the totality of a category. These representations then allow us to judge, based on (at least) those considerations we have just examined, whether an item is most appropriately assigned to one category or to another. From Uncle Joe's dog, the boy next door's dog, our best friend's dog, and all the other instances of dog we have encountered, we have arrived at our concept of *dog*. But where *is* it? To be sure, this and all of our other concepts are somehow "in our brains," but a very important question cognitive scientists would like to be able to answer is "*How* are such concepts represented in our brains?"

On introspection, we note that concepts are often related. For example, as you are walking down the street you happen to see a woman wearing a colorful scarf. You may be reminded of your Aunt Frances, who wore scarves like that. Your train of thought may take you from there to the summer you spent staying with your Aunt Frances in Manhattan, and from there to the summer job you had that year, and the time you had lunch in a local cafeteria where they served the best macaroni and cheese you ever had. "That would be good for dinner tonight," you think. So a woman with a colorful scarf you saw in passing has led you to thoughts of tonight's dinner! Whether or not you have an Aunt Frances, and whether or not you like macaroni and cheese, you are certainly familiar with this process, because it is one in which we all engage constantly. One thing is sure to remind us of another and that of yet another; sometimes when we are conversing with a friend we keep following up on the new associations, forgetting about—and never completing—our original discussion.

The observation of this phenomenon of associated concepts is far from new. As we introspect on the subject, so did thinkers far back in history. Aristotle described it in 350 B.C. thus: From a starting point, people "pass swiftly in thought from one point to another, e.g. from milk to white, from white to mist, and thence to moist, from which one remembers Autumn (the 'season of mists')." And he continues, "From the same starting point a movement can be made in several directions. . . . [The mind] tends to move to the more customary. . . . Custom now assumes the role of Nature. Hence the rapidity with which we recollect what we frequently think about" (McKeon, 1941, p. 614).

As the phenomenon of associated concepts is not a new one, so reflecting on it and describing it are not occupations introduced in our time. Yet there *is* something different now: In the intervening period, **empirical** methods of inquiry, based on experiment and observation, have developed and, with them, new fields, such as cognitive psychology and artificial intelligence. The interplay among the perspectives of these fields allows us now profitably to address such questions as "How does it all work, this process of association of concepts?" The first step after the observations, as always, is the hypothesis. A fruitful one with which cognitive psychologists have been working is that concepts are represented in our brains as a *network:* One concept leads to another because aspects, or features, of that concept are linked to features of other concepts. Thus a brightly colored scarf, through its visual properties, its function, its fabric, may be linked to another such scarf in an individual's set of representations, and this other scarf will be linked to a quite different sort of concept: a person, perhaps Aunt Frances. Thoughts of Aunt Frances may trigger links to any number of other concepts: other aunts, uncles, Uncle Joe's dog, fur, allergic reaction . . .

The concepts and their representations that this illustration suggests are mixed. I referred to color, which is visual, and to function, or use, which is not directly perceivable but must be inferred; it's more of an abstraction. If, as this suggests, there are different sorts of concepts, we may need to hypothesize different means of representation for them, with various means for those that can be directly perceived through the senses, and a means for those that are abstract and thus must be inferred. If someone asks us, for instance, to describe *dog,* it is likely that we will "see" one in our mind's eye—perhaps the last one we encountered, perhaps the one we encounter most often, perhaps the one we like best, or perhaps some other one entirely. The notion of a mind's eye is familiar to all of us; we all "see" things that are not present, "envisioning" the *Mona Lisa* or tonight's dessert—a rich, brown fudge cake. We will return to this process later in the chapter and to research of the past few decades that has revealed a great deal about it.

The Representation of Propositions

First, though, we turn to the topic of the representation of thoughts that are not strictly visual. When we think of something—anything—it is likely to be couched in what has been termed a **proposition**. That is, it is a thought that is in some sense complete: not just an object, say, a piece of that fudge cake, but *That is fudge cake,* or *Fudge requires chocolate,* or the somewhat more complex *That piece of fudge cake looks good.* Perhaps that thought sparks another: *I want a piece of that fudge cake,* and from there still other thoughts take off: *The fudge cake I had last week at the diner wasn't very good; The waitress at the diner was slow; Diners are not my favorite restaurants; Restaurants these days are pretty expensive; I need more income; I'll ask the boss for a raise; I don't like the boss; I think I'll quit my job.* From a wish for a piece of fudge cake, I have now arrived at the decision to quit my job!

In fact, *proposition* is defined more formally. In one formulation, "A proposition is a unit of meaning that can take a **truth value**" (McKoon & Ratcliff, 1980, p. 369). That is, it is a unit of meaning that can be either true or false; questions and commands, for instance ("Are you ready?" "Get lost!"), are not propositions because the notions of true and false cannot be applied to them. *That is a fudge* *cake* or *Fudge requires chocolate* is a unit of meaning about which it makes sense to speak of truth value: Either it is true or it is not true. In this last case, the concepts are fudge, chocolate, and the relation between them. The concepts standing in a relation to each other are sometimes called the **arguments** of the relation. This terminology may seem at first glance to be unnecessarily formal, but here, as in any field of study, defining terms in a clear and precise manner makes it possible to develop testable hypotheses. We will need these terms in what follows.

Notice that these propositions have been expressed in *language*. There is an intimate relationship between propositions and language: Language is our means of encoding both the concepts from which propositions are constructed and the propositions themselves. That wedge of cake is not a concept until we have categorized it, which involves first recognizing it as "one of those"—a process that involves both sorting and *naming,* or encoding its meaning in language. Wanting a piece of that fudge cake is not in itself a proposition; *I want a piece of that fudge cake* is—or more precisely, it is the expression in English of a proposition.

But lest we assume that propositional *thought* occurs via the medium of language (as our use of English examples might suggest), a word of caution is in order. The point will be made by the following experience of mine. Some years ago, as I was waiting in line at the Empire State Building for the elevator to the top, a woman approached the line and asked me, "Is this the line to go up to the top?" I answered immediately, "Yes, it is"—not realizing until she had thanked me and walked back toward the end of the line that her question *and my response* had been in French! I had reacted to the meaning of what had been said to me, selecting without a moment's hesitation the appropriate language in which to encode my response.

Furthermore, the fact that it is possible to translate a sentence (which embodies a proposition or propositions) from one language to another demonstrates that there is not a single way of rendering a given proposition. Despite the intimate connection between thought and language, it is clear that propositions need not be represented in a *particular* language; rather, we may regard them as being represented in some language-*like* fashion, not to be confused with any *specific* human language. In other words, it makes sense to regard our stored (and largely unconscious) **propositional representations** as entities not yet converted into ordinary language but translatable into such language when we need them, whether to talk about them or, perhaps, even to think about them.

Experimental Evidence for Propositional Representation

I cited the little episode of my unnoticed comprehension of and response in French as a small piece of evidence for the storage of propositions in some kind of prelinguistic form. This type of evidence is generally referred to as "anecdotal." We all have stories that we use to illustrate or support points we are making, but such anecdotal evidence is not necessarily convincing. How often have you heard one person's "evidence" refuted by someone else's equally convincing anecdote supporting precisely the opposite position? Sometimes it takes considerable ingenuity to design an experiment that will provide truly convincing evidence for a hypothesis.

Such was Sachs's (1967) experiment, which presented subjects with taped narrative passages. After listening to each passage, the subjects heard an additional sentence. They were then asked to report first whether this sentence was identical to one that had occurred in the preceding passage, called the base sentence, or whether it had been changed in one of a few specific ways. The base sentence occurred in the passage in one of three conditions: immediately before the end of the passage, with no intervening syllables, 40 syllables before the end of the passage, or 80 syllables before the end of the passage. Second, they were asked to report how sure they were of their judgments.

Sentences that were not identical to the base sentence could differ in one of three ways: first by being made passive, second by being made more formal in tone—both of these retaining the meaning of the sentence—and third by being semantically altered so that although the form remained (syntactically) similar to the original the meaning was changed. The base taken from one of the passages, and the three sentences derived from it, were

> Base: He sent a letter about it to Galileo, the great Italian scientist.
> Passive: A letter about it was sent to Galileo, the great Italian scientist.
> Formal: He sent Galileo, the great Italian scientist, a letter about it.
> Semantic: Galileo, the great Italian scientist, sent him a letter about it.
> (Sachs, 1967, p. 439)

What Sachs found was that the more material that intervened between the end of the passage and a test sentence the less well subjects remembered the exact form of the sentence. But no matter how much material had intervened, the subjects remembered very well the *meaning* of the sentence. According to Sachs (1967), "That original sentence which is perceived is rapidly forgotten, and the memory then is for the information contained in the sentence" (p. 442). This finding supports the hypothesis that propositions are comprised of meaningful concept/relation combinations not yet clothed in language, because it is not necessarily the precise language in which they are expressed that is later remembered but rather the meaning, or the proposition, itself.

Propositional Networks

If thought rests on the mental representation of propositions, and if, as has been recognized by both classical thinkers and contemporary researchers, thought is associative, moving rapidly from one idea to another, it is likely that the associations are due to the shared elements in the associated thoughts. In the precise terms introduced earlier, a proposition that surfaces at a conscious level may be drawn out of memory by the repetition of arguments. That is, if two propositions share an argument, say, *fudge,* then these two propositions may be close to each other in one's mental representation. *Fudge requires chocolate* and *Fudge is brown* share the argument *fudge* (though not the other arguments nor the relations involved in the two propositions).

Of course thinking—and the concepts it depends on—requires our having stored word meanings and the links between them. When we speak of "storage," we mean that the concepts we have acquired have somehow remained in that portion of our memory that keeps material around for a long time. This is known as long-term memory, as distinct from the type of memory that stores information for brief periods, to be accessible to us for immediate use. Without memory there is no propositional, or semantic, representation, for having concepts "in there" depends crucially on our ability to store them over long periods. Memory is another of the very important areas studied in the past from various perspectives, and it is now the focus of interesting and productive research in cognitive science, as will become clear later in the chapter.

An important hypothesis about how the associative process works is that meanings and links are stored in a propositional, or semantic, network. Under this hypothesis, concepts in a semantic network are represented by *nodes,* and the properties that relate them to other concept nodes and the associations between them are represented by lines, or *links.* Associated with the links are values that indicate how essential they are to the meanings of the various concepts with which they are associated (Collins & Loftus, 1975; see Figure 2.5 for a schematic representation of a fragment of concept relatedness).

To explain the associations we make so rapidly between and among the nodes, a **theory of spreading activation** has been proposed. Interestingly, this theory originated in the process of creating a computer program that would simulate human memory search (Quillian, 1968) and has been extended to help explain human memory retrieval (Collins & Loftus, 1975). This theory involves several assumptions. First, when a concept is being processed (e.g., when you are thinking of Uncle Joe), its **node** is activated to a certain level; think of it as a kind of "charge." This charge, or activation, spreads out in every direction in the network, lessening at weaker links and strengthening at stronger ones. Second, activation released from a concept node continues as long as the node is in use, for example, by hearing it, reading it, or thinking about it. Humans are designed to process material one element at a time (think of the linear aspect of language, for example; we hear and process speech one sound, one word, at a time). Thus activation can *start* at only one node at a time, but as it reaches other nodes, they continue the spread of the activation outside the "thinker's" conscious awareness. Many of these associated nodes become activated and continue their simultaneous activation in parallel fashion. Even as we are trying our hardest to remember the name of Uncle Joe's dog by whatever associative means we can come up with (e.g., "two syllables, begins with *t,* means 'very small'"), other associations will also become activated relating to Uncle Joe, to dogs in general, to anything, in short, that is related in any way to our target.

Now imagine this process, as so far described, in action. Imagine asking someone, for example, "What is your Uncle Joe's dog's name?" Not only is the node associated with the concept *uncle* activated, but its activation will spread in all directions, stimulating each node in its path. As this node is activated, each of these other nodes will do the same. Simultaneously, every node associated with the

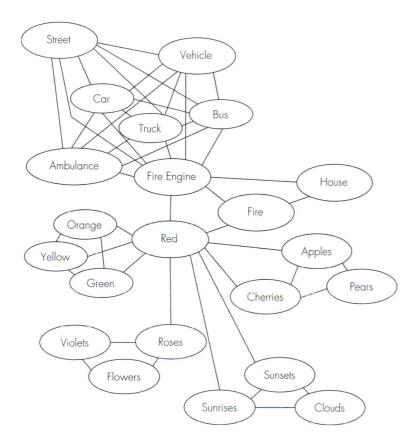

FIGURE 2.5 A Schematic Representation of Concept Relatedness in a Stereotypical Fragment of Human Memory (where a shorter line represents greater relatedness)

name "Joe" will be activated, and the same process set in motion. A similar process will occur, at the same time, at every node associated with the concepts *dog* and *name*. There must be limits on the operation of this process; otherwise, in no time at all, the spread of activation will set up in the brain of this poor individual a commotion, a tumult of activity so overwhelming as to make normal functioning difficult or impossible. And we have not even considered the effects of other aspects of the environment, which are impinging simultaneously on the individual's awareness, causing similar lines of activation to be set in motion!

Two further assumptions enable constraints on the activation so that it will not produce such a disastrous effect. The first is that activation decreases over time, or when other activity intervenes, dissipating gradually unless something (repetition of a word, perhaps) occurs to strengthen it. The second is that the greater the number of concepts being stimulated by this process of spreading activation, the less activation is available for each one.

A final assumption of this hypothesis concerns what happens when activation at a particular node derives from more than one source. This assumption is that activation from all the different sources is *cumulative*. It adds up, and when it reaches a certain amount, called a **threshold**, we become aware of it. If we are in the process of trying to retrieve a piece of information, and the node representing it becomes sufficiently activated, we will have access to the information. Put another way, that is when the thought "pops into" our consciousness. This process may thus explain our suddenly finding a word we have ceased consciously to look for.

Some nodes will be in a relatively greater state of activation than others at any given time; those whose level of activation is strong enough will reach the level of consciousness. They will be the ones involved in the person's thoughts at that moment. In the case of the question "What is the name of Uncle Joe's dog?", as one seeks the name of the dog, the relative strength of the nodes associated with the name will be great, whereas those involved in propositions having to do with irrelevant uncles and dogs will weaken—and ultimately the name itself, "Tiny," will be retrieved. (When the constraints are relaxed, say, in the situation of psychoanalysis, where one is supposed to free-associate, some of the "irrelevant" paths may be pursued, allowing thoughts usually kept in check to surface and the feelings they arouse to be recognized.)

The theory of spreading activation is supported by neuroscientific evidence. The richly networked neural structures of the human brain seem well suited to function as the theory proposes, as we will see in the next chapter, when we turn our attention to the field of neuroscience. And as noted, the original impetus for the notion of **parallel processing** of information and the theory of spreading activation came from the field of artificial intelligence, in which researchers seek to design intelligent computers that can perform complex tasks requiring such interconnected networks working in parallel. In Chapter 8 we will examine recent work in this area.

Experimental Evidence for Propositional Networks

In an interesting set of experiments, McKoon and Ratcliff (1980) obtained evidence for the structure of **propositional**, or **semantic**, **networks**, using a prediction suggested by the theory of spreading activation. In the first of these experiments, they organized a text by presenting its component propositions in an order such that an argument of one was shared by the next, as in the following set of sentences of a paragraph. (This somewhat simplified example is only a small part of a set of experiments. The interested reader will find the complete account in McKoon and Ratcliff, 1980.)

1. The youth stole a car.
2. The car sideswiped a pole.
3. The pole smashed a hydrant.
4. The hydrant sprang a leak.
5. The leak sprayed water.
6. The water flooded the flowers.

The purpose of this arrangement was to allow the measurement of distance between propositions. The first proposition is connected to the second by virtue of the argument *car,* and the second is connected to the third through the shared argument *pole*. In this manner, the relative distances between the propositions can be defined; *car,* for instance, is closer to *pole* than to *hydrant,* and *hydrant* is closer to *leak* than to *car.* If mental representation of a paragraph of text follows such a structure, then, the researchers hypothesized, associations among the propositions nearer to one another (in terms of the shared arguments) would be made more rapidly than associations to those farther away. Triggering one concept would "prime" others down the line. Much as one primes a pump to prepare it to work at a high level of efficiency, one might consider the less highly activated nodes in a network to be "primed"—more ready to participate in the particular thought process than those not activated at all.

Priming is based on the activation of nodes and links associated with a particular concept or proposition. When a portion of a semantic network has been activated, the activation is hypothesized to spread from it in all directions to concepts and propositions that share its arguments, and from them to those that share *their* arguments. Thus somewhere down the line a proposition relatively unrelated to the initial one will be activated. The process of priming makes use of the earlier activation; access to a concept down the line will be faster if an associated concept has already been activated; and the closer the relation between the two, the faster the access of one by the other.

In this experiment, McKoon and Ratcliff tested subjects on words that appeared in paragraphs they had been given to read, asking the subjects whether or not the words had occurred in the paragraphs. They reasoned that a "yes" response (indicating awareness that the word *had* appeared in the paragraph) would be produced faster if a closely connected word were presented first than if one occurring farther away had been presented first. That would mean that if, for example, the test word *water* was presented just before *flowers,* the subjects would respond "yes," faster than if the word *pole* had been presented just before *flowers*. And indeed, this was what happened. The subjects did respond more quickly to words when presented first with the more closely connected words. Thus the hypothesized propositional network structure and the theory of spreading activation provide mutual support.

The Notion of Scripts

So far our discussion of knowledge representation has concerned conceptual and propositional knowledge. But we of course realize that the store of knowledge any one of us possesses is considerably more vast than what has been discussed up to now. We know, for instance, a great deal about how to behave in different circumstances: put the dollar bill into a vending machine face side up; wear clean clothes to a job interview. We know how various people are likely to react in all kinds of situations, what is involved in preparing a meal, how to distinguish between a good banana and a bad one and between truth and falsehood. All of us have as well a unique store of knowledge specific to our own upbringing, education, occupation, and experience. The picture presented up to now, as complex as it has been, has in fact been too simple. To understand the representation of knowledge requires considering many additional factors.

Cognitive scientists have found it useful, for example, to draw a distinction between the following two types of knowledge: **declarative**, or **factual**, **knowledge**, which is the kind of knowledge embodied in concepts and propositions, and **procedural knowledge**, the kind required for tasks that are performed so often that they become automatic. The procedures involved in driving a car, for instance, become so ingrained after one has had a certain amount of practice that one no longer has to think about them individually. They are tapped and activated as a unit.

It has been suggested that this kind of activation of knowledge-as-a-whole applies as well to declarative knowledge. In their 1977 book *Scripts, Plans, Goals, and Understanding,* Schank and Abelson consider the question of how people organize all the knowledge they must have in order to understand and function in the world. They recognize "two classes of knowledge that people bring to bear during the understanding process: general knowledge and specific knowledge. General knowledge enables a person to understand and interpret another person's actions simply because the other person is a human being with certain standard needs who lives in a world which has certain standard methods of getting those needs fulfilled." Specific knowledge, on the other hand, is used to "interpret and participate in events we have been through many times. Specific detailed knowledge about a situation allows us to do less processing and wondering about frequently experienced events" (Schank & Abelson, 1977, p. 37). Seen in this light, the use of declarative knowledge is analogous to that of procedural knowledge: The specifics of a situation, given sufficient familiarity (like practice in a procedure such as driving), become activated as a whole, allowing us to function in a given situation without having to expend time and energy plowing through all of its pieces separately. As Schank and Abelson (1977) put it,

> We need not ask why somebody wants to see our ticket when we enter a theater, or why one should be quiet. . . . Knowledge of specific situations such as theaters allows us to interpret the remarks that people make about theaters. Consider how difficult it would be to interpret "Second aisle on your right" without the detailed knowledge about theaters that the patron and the usher both have. (p. 37)

You have certainly stored the concepts *second, aisle, on,* and *right,* and the proposition that a particular aisle is the second one on the right, but without your knowledge of the whole situation, you'd have no idea why the usher happened to mention it. (Might the aisle be already filled to capacity? Is there bubblegum on its floor? Should you look for a seat there, or are you not supposed to enter it?)

Schank and Abelson refer to these sequences of stored knowledge as **scripts**. Just as actors work from scripts to guide their behavior while on stage or on camera, so each of us is continually following scripts as we move from one activity or task to another. The difference is that actors' scripts are written out for them by screenwriters or playwrights, whereas ours have been written into our nervous systems over the course of our lives.

The notion of scripts ties in nicely with the network theory of propositional representation we have been considering and with the theory of spreading activation. Much as concepts participate in the propositional, or semantic, networks stored in memory, so these networks themselves may participate in larger sets of stored knowledge. According to the theory of spreading activation, the concept *doctor*, or any of many, many possible concepts (e.g., *nurse, waiting room, examining room, injection*), may activate the set of propositions related to this situation. This set constitutes an entire complex script representing the knowledge one has about the familiar sequence of events involved in visiting the doctor. The script then becomes activated as a whole when any of the concept nodes related to "doctor visit" is activated, allowing one to know what to expect and what to do: sign in, take a seat in the waiting room, perhaps leaf through a magazine while waiting to be called. When one is finally summoned to the examining room, one will not be surprised to be told to "open your mouth and say 'ah,'" or to be asked certain routine questions, to be given a paper gown and told to disrobe, and so forth, until it is time to offer one's arm and grit one's teeth, as the immunization needle finds it mark. (As with propositional representation, there is experimental evidence for scripts; the interested reader is referred, for example, to important early work reported by Bower, Black, & Turner, 1979, and to more recent work, for example, by Custers, Boshuizen, & Schmidt, 1996, and Lojek-Osiejuk, 1996.)

Mental Imagery

Up to now we have been considering the representation of the kind of knowledge we think of as language-like: concepts, propositions, semantic networks, scripts. But it is abundantly clear that not all of our knowledge is stored in this fashion. As I mentioned earlier, the notion of a mind's eye is a familiar one; all we need do to be convinced that we conjure "mental images," or visual representations, is to think of what happens if we are told "not to think of a pink elephant." Not only do we immediately think of one, but more than likely we do so not by recalling the set of features that constitutes the concept, but by "seeing" or "imaging" one— and in this case the image present to our mind's eye is not even of an entity we have ever seen with our real eyes. Elephants don't come in pink. Just as we can *conceptualize* a nonexistent state, say, Utopia, so we can *visualize* a nonexistent entity such as a pink elephant, or a flying toaster, or a little green person with three eyes, four ears, and a dorsal fin. (It is interesting that all of these examples make use of elements of "real" entities. Can we think of anything new at all that is not a novel arrangement of the building blocks that are found in our perceptual environment?)

A number of questions can be asked about the nature of these mental images. One that comes to mind right away is "*Why* do we see them?" and another is "*How* do we do it?" Stephen Kosslyn (1995), a major researcher in the area of mental imagery, points out the resemblance of imagery to visual perception and the similarity of their purposes: "We use vision primarily . . . to identify objects, parts, and characteristics (such as color and texture); and to track moving objects, to navigate, and to reach appropriately. Similarly, one purpose of imagery is to identify properties of imaged objects, which allows us to retrieve information from memory" (p. 268). For example, if you were asked how long a pink elephant's trunk is compared to its body, you would "scan" your mental image in order to make the comparison. And if you were then asked how you had done that, you would probably describe the process in the same terms you would use had you been at the zoo, looking at a real elephant. You might say something like this: "I looked at the elephant in my mind and saw how long its trunk was."

Like vision, imagery is also used to track, navigate, and reach. Consider the judgments involved when you cross a city street: It is part of the task of mental imagery to "see," given its current speed, where that nifty silver BMW Z3 roadster, now a block away, will be at the moment you wish to step off the curb. It is also a function of imagery to allow you to reach far enough, but not too far, in grasping the drink your host offers you as you arrive for dinner. Reach not quite far enough and your host drops the drink; reach just a little too far and you grab his tie!

A more difficult question is the "how" of seeing mental images. It seems most unlikely that there is a little screen inside your brain, on which are projected or generated your mental images. But research in the area of mental imagery in the past couple of decades has produced a good deal of information that yields some answers and promises yet more. An important part of the explanation has to do with the relation between our visual processes and our imaging processes.

Of course there is no way to observe mental images directly. The information about imagery that was available before the 1970s came primarily from introspection and people's reports about their own images. But interesting experiments have been performed since then that have produced objective evidence concerning the structure of mental imagery—experiments involving what might be thought of as "the quantification of introspection" (Kosslyn, 1980, p. 4).

Experimental Evidence for Mental Imagery

In a 1971 paper, Shepard and Metzler reported an experiment that indicated very strongly that people perform much the same operations on mental images as when looking at *actual* objects. For example, imagine the face of a clock with its second hand moving around the dial, passing each number in turn. One does have the impression, from imaging in this way, that images can be rotated. The researchers reasoned that if this impression is valid, the process should take longer if images pass through intermediate positions as they are rotated than if the images just jump from here to there. In designing their experiment, they took advantage of the fact that people can often tell when two-dimensional pictures represent the same object, even when the object's orientation in space differs from one picture to another (as, for example, a rightside-up clock and an upside-down clock). In this experiment, the subjects were presented with pairs of perspective line drawings (i.e., line drawings that represented three-dimensional objects). As you see in Figure 2.6, these drawings look like arrangements of blocks in space. The pairs are of two

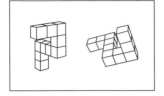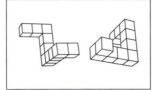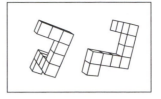

FIGURE 2.6 **Examples of Pairs of Perspective Line Drawings.** Either both drawings in a pair represent the same object in two different orientations in space, or they represent two different objects.

types: Either both drawings in a pair represent the same object in two different orientations in space, or they represent two different objects. Shepard and Metzler were careful to avoid cues that would allow the subjects to recognize the drawings as anything familiar (that's why they chose objects that are relatively meaningless) or as having anything in particular, apart from their orientation in space, to distinguish them from each other.

Shepard and Metzler wanted to learn whether the amount of difference in the angle of rotation would in fact affect the length of time it took subjects to decide whether or not the two objects represented were the same. They designed two types of three-dimensional drawings of objects. In the simpler type the two objects were rotated in the same plane, and in the more complex type the rotation involved depth. The subjects reported that in order to compare the two objects within each pair they had to imagine one rotated so that it was in the same position as the other, and that because the objects seemed to be in three-dimensional space they could imagine this rotation around whichever axis would allow them to make the comparison.

The results of the experiment were striking. As you see from Figure 2.7, whether subjects were faced with plane or depth images, the time required for deciding that two images in different rotation are the same increased *linearly* with the difference in the angle. The greater the difference in the angle of rotation, the longer it took subjects to make the judgment that the two depicted objects were identical—about 1 second longer for every 60 degrees. That it should take longer was not surprising; that the relationship between difference in angle of rotation and judgment time should be linear *was* striking.

Shepard and Metzler (1971) point out that these results are consistent with the subjects' own reports of what they were doing during the experiment and conclude that "if we can describe this process as some sort of 'mental rotation in three-dimensional space,' then the slope of the obtained functions indicates that the average rate at which these particular objects can be thus 'rotated' is roughly 60° per second" (p. 703). It seems reasonable to interpret their findings as evidence for **mental rotation** (turning imagined objects in the mind's eye as if one were looking at real objects turning) and thus for the psychological reality of mental imagery.

Since Shepard and Metzler's important experiment, there has been a good deal of further work that supports the interpretation of their results that what goes on

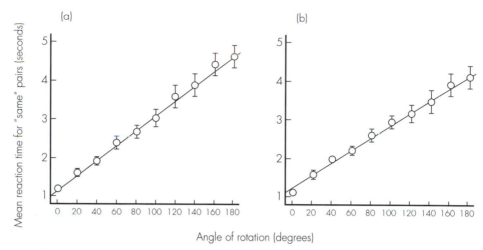

FIGURE 2.7 **Mean Reaction Times to Two Perspective Line Drawings Portraying Objects of the Same Three-Dimensional Shape**. (a) Picture-plane pairs. (b) Depth pairs.

in the brain as one sees with one's mind's eye corresponds directly to what goes on when one sees with one's actual eyes. Think of what happens when you stop along the road to look at a scenic vista. You let your eyes rove over the view, rightward from the snow-covered top of one mountain on your left to another peak, across a valley, and past yet another mountaintop. It takes a certain amount of time to view the whole scene as your eyes move from left to right. Now imagine you have closed your eyes and are scanning the same view, left to right, as you remember it. How long will it take to do so, and will that length of time correspond in any way to the time it took for you to scan the scene in front of you with your eyes open? Based on the results of the experiment on mental rotation, you would probably expect that there *would* be a systematic correspondence between the actual scanning of the scene and your "imaging" of it. And that is in fact what researchers found when they carried out experiments in image scanning. In a 1978 set of experiments, Kosslyn, Ball, and Reiser asked subjects to scan visual images of letters of the alphabet, looking for a particular "target" letter, which they were to classify as either upper- or lowercase. To reach the target, they had to scan past a certain number of intervening letters and spaces. As the researchers predicted, the scanning times increased with increases in the distance the subjects had to scan in order to reach the target. The time also increased as the number of intervening letters (which of course had to be "inspected") increased.

In a second experiment, subjects learned and then visualized a fictional map (Figure 2.8). They focused on a location on their imaged map and then decided whether an object named by the experimenter was on it. If it was, they were to scan to it and push a button when they arrived at it. After measuring all the times the subjects needed to scan between all possible pairs of locations, the experi-

FIGURE 2.8 Fictional Map Used in Experiment 2 to Test Subjects' Ability to Visualize Objects and Their Locations

menters found that, as with mental rotation, the time increased linearly with the distance to be scanned. They interpret this finding as suggesting that distances are embodied in *mental* images in the same way as in one's *actual* visual perception of pictures.

Our knowledge about mental imagery has increased since the years of those early experiments, as Kosslyn makes clear in his 1994 book *Image and Brain*. For example, it is now widely accepted that imagery and visual perception share the same underlying mechanisms (Kosslyn, 1994). The scanning technology that neuroscience has in recent years provided illuminates the activity in the brain that underlies both visual perception and mental imagery. Thus aspects of knowledge gained via both physiological and psychological research are brought together by neuroscientific developments, illustrating once more the overlap among disciplines within cognitive science and the resulting contribution to our understanding of cognitive phenomena.

Problem Solving

Every day, throughout the day, we are required to solve problems. Some of them are trivial and easily solved, for example, finding one's mislaid car keys in order to drive to work. There are clear-cut ways to solve that one: First we look in all the places we habitually put the keys: pockets, purse, briefcase, hall table. If they are not there, we look to see if we have dropped them in the car or just outside it. Aha! There they are!

Some problems are not so easily dealt with. Suppose the keys are in none of those places. Perhaps we have a spare set. If so, our immediate problem is solved. If not, we must try another tack—getting a lift from a friend. But if the friend has already left . . . When all avenues are exhausted and we still have not solved the problem, we must approach it from another angle. Maybe we can accomplish our tasks at our home computer, or maybe we will decide it's not worth the effort, call in sick—and go back to bed.

Other problems may be crucial to our well-being, such as how to equip ourselves for a particular occupation and, having done so, how to get a job. Some problems, such as math problems or finding a topic for a research paper, are set for us as part of a school curriculum. Some are presented as "brain teasers," such as the nine-dot problem we saw in Chapter 1, and some arise in games—how to win at chess, for example. Some are even more complex than these, for example, how to design a computer to *beat* us at chess.

One aspect of human cognition is unquestionably problem solving. Whenever we have to figure out how to get from point A to point B, in a geographical or in a more abstract sense, we are attempting to solve a problem. We use the term "problem" freely, knowing pretty well what we all mean by it, though recognizing, of course, that one person's "problem" may be another's "challenge" or no problem at all to a third. But in order to study this aspect of our cognitive functioning, once again it is necessary to define our terms carefully. If we want to understand what "problem solving" is, we must be explicit in our definition of "problem" and also in our description of what it takes to solve one. That is, we must have a clear idea of the cognitive processes we engage in when we approach a problem with the intention of solving it.

Research in Problem Solving

The Problem   Exactly what, then, is a problem? In their 1972 book *Human Problem Solving,* Newell and Simon define "problem" as the situation people face when they want something but don't know right away what to do to get it. What an individual wants may be tangible (the car keys) or abstract (a mathematical proof). The way to go about obtaining it may involve physical actions such as reaching or writing, perceptual activities such as looking or listening, or mental activities such as remembering where the object, tangible (keys) or not (a proof), may be found (Newell & Simon, 1972).

Within this definition, one may classify different types of problems. Greeno (1978) suggests three, the first being the *comprehension* sort. In problems of this kind, one must come to understand the structure of a domain, or field, in order to know how it works and to be able to predict behavior within it. For example, one may be presented with some elements of a structure, such as the various members of a committee at a meeting at which one is substituting for a regular member; the substitute must figure out the relationships among those present in order to behave in an appropriate and constructive manner.

Greeno's second category of problem is that of *transformation* problems, in which one faces an initial situation and a goal, and there are possible sets of operations that will produce changes in the situation. The task here is to find such a set so that the initial situation is transformed into the goal.

The third type of problem identified by Greeno involves *arrangement*. Here the problem solver confronts some elements of the problem and must arrange them so that they satisfy a particular criterion. When playing Scrabble, for instance, you have seven letters in front of you, and you must arrange them—or some of them—into a real word, using elements (letters) already on the board. There may in fact be more than one word possible using your letters, and one of them may produce a higher score for you than another. Greeno (1978) characterizes the main skills here as "skill in composition, a process of constructive search, where the problem solver is required to find the solution in a search space but must also know how to generate the possibilities that constitute the search space" (p. 241).

This is not, of course, an exhaustive list of problem types, and many problems involve *at least* all three of these categories. It does serve, however, to give you an idea of what researchers consider and the kind of precision characterizing their approach when examining the nature of problems within the context of the issue of problem solving.

The Problem Solver   The problem solver and the problem are of course intimately connected. Nevertheless, when conducting research it is always necessary to choose a specific focus. Newell and Simon (1972) focus primarily on the problem solver. They begin their analysis of problem solving by asking two questions that are easily stated but not so easily answered. The first is "How can a problem be solved?" and the second is "What makes a problem difficult?" "The answers to these questions constitute a theory of problem solving, one that should be applicable to man, beast, and machine alike, insofar as they can be represented as information processing systems" (Newell & Simon, 1972, p. 87). Taking the second question first, we note that there are different ways of measuring the difficulty of a problem, such as how long it takes to arrive at a solution and whether or not it is finally solved. But whichever measures one chooses, the difficulty of a problem depends on the interaction of the problem solver and the task environment, such as our example of locating those missing car keys.

With regard to the question of how a problem can be solved, Newell and Simon (1972) undertake to "introduce a suitable abstract information processing system to describe how man processes task-oriented symbolic information" (p. 5). Influenced by the development of the field of artificial intelligence, their theory assumes that a human being operates as an information processing system. Such systems can be very precisely—if mechanistically—rendered. Their components include, for instance, a set of instances of symbols connected by a set of relations, and a memory that stores these for processing. Given an environmental situation (e.g., the need to telephone someone in order to obtain some information), a task environment is laid out in which the problem is situated. This is translated into an internal representation from which, given a store of general knowledge, a method of approaching the problem can be selected. "A method is a process that bears some rational relation to attaining a problem solution, as formulated and seen in terms of the internal representation" (Newell & Simon, 1972, p. 88). Then the method is applied. But what does it mean to say "the method is *applied*"? As Newell and Simon (1972) put it, the method "comes to control the behavior, both internal and external, of the problem solver" (p. 88). (I turn my attention to finding the telephone number I need; perhaps I visualize where I think I left it; I look in my appointment book, on the kitchen table, in the wastebasket. I look in the phone book but the number is unlisted.) There are now three possibilities open to me: try another method (I'll call a friend to get the number); reformulate the problem (I'll get the information tomorrow when I see this person); or, because the process can be stopped at any point, give up (I'm in a hurry; I'll manage without the information). It is in this way that researchers have sought to identify with precision the steps involved in attempting to solve a problem so that every aspect will be accounted for. The process may then be ready to be explained at other (e.g., the neurophysiological) levels.

Another facet of problem solving has to do with the familiarity of the problem solver with the domain of the problem. We have all observed that people who are "experts" in a particular area seem to solve problems in that area more easily, and certainly more quickly, than people to whom it is unfamiliar territory. A person's reaction to this observation might well be "But of course. It's obvious that's the way it would be!" However, if we wish really to understand the process of problem solving, we must always ask why. In this case, *why* does the "expert" have so much easier a time with problems in his field of expertise than the non-expert? That is, in precisely what ways are experts different from novices, and exactly what are the experts doing in the process that makes the solution so much easier and faster for them?

One element of the answer is found by examining what familiarity with the domain "buys" for the problem solver. Suppose, for example, that you accidentally drop a table knife down the drain of your kitchen sink. First of all, you need the knife; second, you know it will trap crumbs and such and may eventually cause a backup and a flood. That knife must come out of there. You reach down, but your fingers are not long enough. You look around for something to pry it out with. A fork? You try, but you can get no purchase on it. All you've accomplished is to push it down still further. Scissors? Longer and stronger, but with the wrong action. Further down goes your knife. Now what? You look under the sink and see an elbow pipe: That's where the knife is trapped. You could unscrew the pipe if you had the right tools, but you don't know what the right tools are, and even if you did you don't have them—and if you had them you'd ultimately have to put the system back together again, and without properly knowing how, you might be left with a leak. You look at your watch; you've been struggling with this problem for an hour and are no closer to solving it than you were at the beginning; in fact, you've made it worse. Finally you call the plumber, who goes immediately to the elbow pipe and has your knife out, and everything replaced and watertight, in 5 minutes.

Of course the plumber took one look and knew just what to do. "Seen it lots of times before. You'd be surprised what people drop down there." Experts working in their own domain are familiar with all aspects of it and don't have to stop to think what tools they need, whether physical or mental, to tackle a given problem within it. Their experience has allowed them in many cases to store representations of whole "chunks" of it so that they don't have to take it one step at a time as the novice must. They don't make false starts; they don't have to backtrack. They go straight to the point, directing their attention to what matters, without spending time or expending effort on irrelevant aspects of the problem. Their immediate awareness of what is relevant permits them to focus on these elements and transform or arrange them in such a way that they may reach their goal with the greatest efficiency.

An experiment carried out early in the annals of problem-solving research is still cited in the literature because it so beautifully captured the essence of the issues involved in "the structure and dynamics of problem-solving processes" (Duncker, 1945/1976). The researcher posed the problem thus:

> Given a human being with an inoperable stomach tumor, and rays which destroy organic tissue at sufficient intensity, by what procedure can one free him of the tumor by these rays and at the same time avoid destroying the healthy tissue which surrounds it? (Duncker, 1976, p. 1)

The experimenters found that subjects followed a series of hunches specifying concrete proposals, for example, altering the position of the tumor or causing the healthy tissue to adapt to the destructive force by successive weak applications of the rays. None of the proposed solutions was practicable, unless or until subjects arrived at one approaching the best solution. This in principle entails sending to the tumor several weak bundles of rays from different directions so that they do not damage the tissue en route but converge on the tumor with enough strength to destroy it. The suggestions made by the subjects focused at first on either the tumor or the surrounding tissue, but the solution required focusing instead on the rays, which were not at first perceived to be relevant. It did not occur to the subjects until they had made a number of false starts, from which they had to backtrack, that one might use more than one ray or that one might decrease the intensity of the rays. Their attempts at a solution were grounded in assumptions about what was "permitted," much as in the nine-dot problem we saw in Chapter 1, which many approach under the implicit assumption (termed "boundary bias" by Chute, 1994) that going outside the perimeter of the dots is not an option. As novices confronting this type of problem, the subjects did not proceed as the expert might have, by disregarding the irrelevant and going immediately to that aspect of the situation whose alteration would provide the solution.

Many more recent experiments, conducted in a variety of domains, support the conclusions that have been reached regarding the nature of problem solving. Experts focus on the relevant while having available whole "chunked" areas of information to bring to bear on the problem. For example, in a 1992 experiment within the domain of music, subjects were presented with a portion of a Bach chorale. Their task was to compose, within an hour, an appropriate concluding section. One of the subjects was an expert; the rest were students in music, but novices in composition. Only the expert was able to complete the task. From recorded "think-aloud" protocols and subsequent interviews, the researchers determined that the novices had concentrated on chord-by-chord solutions, consciously and rather laboriously noting the key signature and other technical details. The expert, working from a larger knowledge base and a larger repertoire of procedures, was able to consider a number of aspects of the task simultaneously—the rules of harmony and the shape of the work, for example—and even to take stylistic matters into account (Colley, Banton, Down, & Pither, 1992).

As with all of the topics involved in cognitive science, one field informs another. The field of artificial intelligence has refined our notions of what distinguishes the expert from the novice, for example, in the effort to program a computer to play chess—and to win. But before we return to this topic in our unit on artificial intelligence, we must turn our attention to the area on which all of our cognitive processes rely and without which there would be no learning, no possibility of categorizing, no way to use our representations—propositional or imagistic— and no development of expertise in problem solving. That area is memory.

Memory

In a column in the *The Wall Street Journal* in August 1997, Lee Berton wrote of a young man, Suleyman Gokyigit, who at 18 was already among the top computer technicians and programmers at a major software company. One wonders how he managed to arrive at this level of expertise while still a (straight-A, of course) student in computer-science engineering at the University of Toledo, Ohio. To be sure, young Mr. Gokyigit is something of a prodigy, even in an area in which the young seem to excel these days; but his achievements are all the more remarkable for the fact that he is blind.

How does he do it? Technology helps: Rather than relying on Braille screen displays, which he says "waste time," Mr. Gokyigit uses a voice-synthesizer turned up to high speed, which rattles off a mechanical-sounding reading of what is on the screen. When reading for oneself, one has the benefit of the page or the screen before one, with its material available for perusal as long as one may wish; but speech is ephemeral, and what is spoken, whether by human or machine, is gone as soon as it has been pronounced. The easy luxury of glancing back at a particular sentence or section of a program is denied the listener. In order to work as efficiently as he does, Mr. Gokyigit must simply *remember* what he has heard. And that is how he manages: He has a prodigious memory. As he works on a project, he remembers virtually everything on the successive computer screens as read to him by the voice-synthesizer. As Mr. Berton reports it, Mr. Gokyigit "mentally 'maps' the computer screen with numbered coordinates (such as three across, two down) and memorizes the location of each icon on the grid so he can call up files with his mouse" (Berton, 1997, p. B1). If you have ever seen the television game show *Concentration,* or have played the game yourself, you know how difficult it is to remember the location of objects hidden on a grid when you have seen them once or even several times. How much more difficult one would find it not only to have to remember them but also to use them in complex ways in order to progress through a task!

We marvel at the abilities of this young computer whiz, not the least of which is his amazing memory. Perhaps we do not stop to think how marvelous is our own everyday, common, "garden-variety" sort of memory, generally noticing only when it fails us. But memory surely lies at the heart of our cognitive abilities and has therefore stimulated a great deal of research in our quest to understand the nature of our uniquely human brand of intelligence. The burning questions, the motivation for the thrust of cognitive science, can in a very real sense be boiled down to *Who are we? What are we?* What, in fact, does it mean to be human? Questions about our make-up, our functioning, are, at the most fundamental level, motivated by a powerful wish to understand ourselves. This wish fuels our research into how we represent the world, how we learn, how we think, how we reason, how we solve problems, how we communicate. And *all* of this depends on how we store, retain, access, adapt to, and use the information brought to us by our senses, our language, our perception of the world. In short, it relies on the memory that underpins all these aspects of ourselves as human beings.

In recent years the wish to understand how memory works has received added impetus from a societal problem that grows greater as the segment of the population comprised of older people grows larger: the plight of those with **Alzheimer's disease** and other conditions that affect memory. In examining the nature of memory, whether to help address the losses experienced by the aging, or to understand remarkable memories like young Mr. Gokyigit's or the more ordinary version which is our own trusty or not-so-trusty memory, we note that it is not as simple as it may seem at first glance. In truth, memory has many aspects. There is the memory for information that we need only briefly, such as a phone number. This sort of information we are just as happy to discard once it has served our immediate purpose. Then there is the type of memory that lasts, perhaps for a lifetime. To this day I remember taking my place on line for an eye test in elementary school and fooling the tester, albeit unintentionally, by reciting correctly several lines of the eye chart. I was not seeing them clearly; I had learned them from hearing the recitation of the children ahead of me. (This was, I may point out, still another feat of memory—one that did not serve me particularly well, postponing for a year the eyeglasses I plainly needed.) Some of what we remember we have labored to retain, and some remains with us though the experience may have lasted but the briefest moment.

There is the memory of sights we have seen (the first time we looked up and saw the Concorde, perhaps) and sounds we have heard (the wooden spoon against the pot as Mother stirred chocolate pudding). There is the memory of tastes (the pudding as we licked it from the wooden spoon—mmm—or cod liver oil from the bottle—ugh!), and that of scents (the aftershave used by that boy in high school . . .), and of sensations on our skin (running into the icy ocean after sunning ourselves on the beach). These are memories of information and events perceived directly through our senses, as opposed to those we have acquired through the intervention of language, such as the letters on the eye chart someone else has recited or the sequence of U.S. presidents we learned in school. There is, in addition, the kind of memory we are consciously aware of, such as knowledge of our address or the store of grammatical information about a foreign language we are studying. This sort of memory is distinct from the sort that provides the backdrop against which we function. We call on knowledge stored unconsciously to permit us, for example, to participate in social situations, recognize friends and movie stars, and solve problems. Furthermore, there is our memory of *ourselves,* the continuous process of remembering who *we* are and what our own history has been (sometimes referred to as "autobiographical memory"), which results in what we call a "sense of self."

In what follows we shall examine ways in which human memory is studied by cognitive scientists. Several models of how it works have been proposed in their attempts to account for the phenomena of memory. We shall survey these phenomena and in the process note some of the models that have been influential in recent research.

Systems of Memory Storage

We often have a need to store information briefly. Every time we drive from one location to another, for instance, we must store the knowledge of where we have just been in order to know where to go next. When we read a book or converse with someone, we need to retain the information given in one sentence so that we may comprehend the one that immediately follows it. But when we have reached our destination, or when our conversation or book has come to an end, we may not need the specific and precise information any longer. Just as we may forget the long-sought phone number once the connection is made, we retain only an overall sense of what our conversation or book was about, without the details that interested us earlier. Memory that hangs on in this way is also essential. For example, without the storage of all those categories we considered earlier as so critical to our making sense of the world, where would we be? Both the kind of memory that is of the moment and that that remains indefinitely contribute crucially to our ability to function.

A question with which memory researchers have grappled is whether we are equipped with a separate memory system for each of these needs or whether one memory system can encompass both. Our description of human memory would in one sense be simpler, more parsimonious, if it did not require positing more than one system to account for remembering. A commonsense perspective, however, leads us immediately to hypothesize that there are indeed different memory systems involved in the different kinds of remembering that we do. For example, we observe that many people, as they age, can readily tell us stories of their youth but seem unable to remember that they have asked us the same question three times in the past 3 minutes. Their memory for things long past remains intact, but the memory for what they are currently doing works poorly or not at all. Therefore it is reasonable to assume that these two systems are separate. Another observation leading to the same conclusion is that the memory we use for briefly storing telephone numbers gets full rather quickly, but, whatever its limitations are, they do not affect the memories we retain over long periods. That is, no matter what "tricks" we may notice our memory playing on us, it is clear that we do not approach the limits of our long-term storage of memories. There's always room for more.

The Modal Model: A Multistore Approach

An important theoretical model for considering human memory is the information processing framework. Within this approach one of the most influential models is the **modal memory model** proposed some 30 years ago by Atkinson and Shiffrin (1968). Under this approach the memory system is characterized first by a distinction between the "permanent, structural features of the system [and the] control processes that can be readily modified or reprogrammed at the will of the subject" (Atkinson & Shiffrin, 1968, p. 90). The researchers liken the *permanent structure* (which includes the basic memory stores) to a computer being operated by a programmer at a remote console. The *control processes,* on the other hand, are likened in this model to the programs the programmer can write at the console, which specify what the computer is to do. In terms of human memory, these processes include procedures for coding information to be stored, means of searching the stores, and operations for keeping a memory "fresh," such as repeating or **rehearsing** information needed only temporarily.

   With the distinction between the permanent structure and the control processes drawn, Atkinson and Shiffrin proposed a system of the sort that has come to be referred to as a **multistore model** because it consists of several structural components. The first of these is the **sensory store,** or **register,** where incoming sensory information remains only very briefly before "decaying" and being completely lost. The second is the **short-term store,** where the work of the current moment is carried out. The researchers proposed that this component receives its input from the sensory register as well as from a **long-term store,** where material is retained over a long period, and which constitutes their third memory system component. Information in the short-term store is kept only briefly—30 seconds or so. The only way to retain this information longer is to keep rehearsing it until it is no longer needed. The reader has no doubt noticed, many times over, that only a limited amount of information can be kept in this way, and once one stops rehearsing it, it is gone.

Operating quite differently is the third component of memory, the long-term store. This is the component of the memory system to which information from the short-term store is transferred, or "copied," for fairly permanent storage, as one copies a computer file from a floppy disk to a hard drive—without removing it in the process from the short-term store.

The Sensory Store   The sensory register of course records information coming from all the senses. It stores the information after the stimulus has ceased, but only very briefly. The senses that have in this regard received the most attention so far are vision and hearing. In his 1967 book *Cognitive Psychology,* Ulrich Neisser refers to the "'persistence' of visual impressions [which] makes them available for processing even after the stimulus has terminated" (p. 15). Neisser contributed the term **iconic memory**, which has since been generally used to refer to this brief persistence of a visual impression. An example he gives of this phenomenon is the "streak of light which appears when a lighted cigarette is moved in a dark room" (p. 16). One's iconic memory apparently retains the perception of the spot of light at the beginning of the movement (and at each point thereafter) until the movement is completed, so that when processed, the movement is interpreted as a streak. Research indicates quite clearly that iconic memory lasts only about half a second (Sperling, 1960).

Neisser (1967) addressed the issue of memory of information perceived through hearing, suggesting that "since the auditory input is always extended over time, some kind of transient memory must preserve it long enough for the processes of speech perception to operate" (p. 199). That is, in order to understand what someone is saying, the listener must remember the beginning of a sentence until he or she has heard the end. It is not possible to process a whole sentence, to understand its meaning, until one has heard all of it. As we understand that the "streak of light" caused by the cigarette means that the cigarette has moved from one point to another, so we understand the idea of the sentence once having registered the whole of it, though each part of it is gone as soon as it has been uttered. This transient auditory memory Neisser termed **echoic memory**. A way of demonstrating your sensory memory for sound—your auditory sensory memory—is simply to clap your hands. You will notice that the sound remains present to you for a brief instant after the clap. You will also notice that the stored sight of the streak of light and sound of the clap vanish very rapidly.

The information perceived through the senses remains long enough, however, for you to pick out those aspects you need to process. After all, not every bit of what is happening at any given moment requires your attention. In fact, if you could not limit your focus to certain aspects of it, you would be swamped with information and unable to function. (Perhaps that is why many people, when trying to concentrate, cannot tolerate the television or the stereo at the same time. But how is it some are *not* bothered? Is there a cost for the effort required to ignore the distracting sensory information?) In any case, once elements of sensory information so briefly stored have been processed, according to this model, they pass into the **short-term memory**.

Short-Term/Working Memory   This component of the memory system also retains information only briefly—perhaps 30 seconds—as mentioned earlier. Surely we have all had the experience of leaving a room in search of some item, only to arrive in another room, having been somewhat distracted along the way, with no memory of what we had set out to look for. The explanation, according to this model, rests in the elapsed time between the beginning and the endpoint of our little journey, during which we have presumably not been rehearsing what we needed to remember, or upon our having been distracted from rehearsing it by events (even our own thoughts, triggered by some association or other) occurring during this time. The information concerning the purpose of our search never made it to our long-term memory, and it is only when we return to the first room that associations linked to what we had been doing there allow us to reconstitute the information—that is, to identify once again the item we had gone to look for.

This sort of occurrence happens fairly frequently in the normal run of events. But the effects of short-term memory loss that far exceed the norm can be devastating, as described by Oliver Sacks in his fascinating book *An Anthropologist on Mars* (1995). He tells of a young man, Greg F., whose brain was severely damaged by a large tumor. The damage to Greg's **hippocampus** (a region in the temporal lobe that has been associated with memory) and its adjacent cortex resulted in an extreme loss. Although older memories (for example, of the music and concerts of the rock group the Grateful Dead) remained accessible, Greg became incapable of transferring into his long-term store new perceptions and memories formed in the present. When given lists of words by Sacks, he could not remember any of them a minute later (Sacks, 1995, p. 47). Three minutes after an event has occurred, he has forgotten it.

This poignant example brings home not only the rapidity with which items stored in short-term memory vanish, but also what life must be like for one who is unable to transfer short-term memories to long-term memory, and for whom, therefore, no experience can add to a sense of the continuity of one's existence, and hence to a sense of one's self. Sacks (1995) comments that, having tested Greg's memory, he found the young man's "confinement, in effect, to a single moment—'the present'—uninformed by any sense of a past (or a future)." "Given this radical lack of connection and continuity in his inner life," Sacks continues,

> I got the feeling, indeed, that he might not *have* an inner life to speak of, that he lacked the constant dialogue of past and present, of experience and meaning, which constitutes consciousness and inner life for the rest of us. He seemed to have no sense of "next" and to lack that eager and anxious tension of anticipation, of intention, that normally drives us through life. (pp. 49–50)

Interestingly, Greg, like other patients reported in the literature, does become familiar in a general way with hospital routine and the individuals he encounters there frequently. This suggests that other sorts of memory continue to function, of which more shortly.

The model of memory proposed by Atkinson and Shiffrin is, as they themselves recognized, not the last word in accounting for all the phenomena involved in the functioning of human memory. Although the multimodal model they propose has become part of the repertoire of those involved in memory research, human memory is more complex than their original model suggested. We noted that the senses most studied with regard to the sensory register have been seeing and hearing. With respect to short-term memory as well, there is experimental evidence from these two modalities that it comprises at least two different forms. There is short-term memory that represents information in speechlike forms and short-term memory that represents information in visual forms. It would seem reasonable—and there is some evidence to support the hypothesis—that we also store on a short-term basis information we receive via our other senses in modes that are appropriate to those senses.

Another and more recent contribution to this area is the notion of "working memory." The idea here is that short-term memory is not just a repository for brief storage but is rather a system that also *manipulates* information as it is being stored and uses it to perform various tasks. According to this account, even this aspect of memory is not as simple as it may once have seemed. It consists of at least three components. One is concerned with perceived sounds (specifically those of speech), a second with visual and spatial information. The third is the "central executive," which supervises and integrates information from the first two as well as from information called out of the long-term store. (These concepts are developed in Baddeley, 1986, and Baddeley, 1992.)

To engage in any study under the rubric of cognitive science is constantly to raise new questions. So it is with the study of memory. If we accept the evidence that there are different modes of storing information for the short term, we face other questions. Are there really "separate neurological systems in the brain, like the multiple pathways that are clearly present in the visual system, that underlie the recovery and maintenance of information over the short versus the long term" (Nairne, 1996, p. 120)? One's entire working life could be spent delving into any *one* of the questions raised along the way!

Long-Term Memory   Having briefly considered the sensory register and short-term memory systems of this multimodal, information processing approach to human memory, we turn to the last component of the system: **long-term memory**. We take this for granted most of the time, so well does it serve us in most cases (though, as we can all attest, not well enough when it comes to people's names at a party or when we must reproduce information on an exam). Here again, though, there are myriad questions. We may speak casually about information "passing" from short-term to long-term memory, but what exactly does this mean? *How* does information pass into long-term memory? Atkinson and Shiffrin hold that information in the short-term store is constantly being transferred in some measure to the long-term store but that control processes the individual engages in affect the transfer. For instance, they propose that when someone is actively rehearsing information in the short-term store, the information is in a relatively weak state and rather easily interfered with. (Remember our trip from room to room in search of— what was it, now?) Of the various processes used in coding the information for storage, according to this account, some increase the strength of the information being transferred. An important example is **elaboration**, by which new information is linked to associations already in the long-term store. This is a process we often engage in consciously, as when we invent **mnemonic devices** to help us remember facts such as our code number for the ATM, which we relate to an important anniversary that we know we won't forget. In other words, we find ways of linking the new information with old, previously stored information. (The areas of artificial intelligence and neuroscience both contribute to our understanding of phenomena such as these, as computer programs that learn are developed and as researchers track down the biochemical processes by which storage and transfer take place.) Retrieving these established memories in order to link them to new information seems to strengthen them; the more often we retrieve a particular piece of information, the stronger its memory "traces" become.

It would seem reasonable to expect that information has to be held in short-term memory for some time in order for it to be transferred to the long-term store, but this does not seem to be the case. Although rehearsing information may result in the transfer of some of it, we all know that most of those dates so important to remember for a history test on Tuesday vanish, if not by Wednesday morning, then certainly before very long. On the other hand, material need not be held at all in short-term memory for it to achieve long-term storage. Experiments in which patients whose short-term verbal memory has been severely damaged show that they are nevertheless able to remember test items later on (Shallice & Warrington, 1970).

As Figure 2.9 illustrates, this model conceives of memory as operating serially. That is, the process is a series of steps, carried out one after the other: Information enters short-term memory (STM) and proceeds (if it is not lost) to long-term memory (LTM), from which it can be transferred again into STM. The process can be repeated as often as necessary. Because information does not have to enter STM before it can be sent to LTM, one might consider the two stores to be parallel. Another way of regarding the situation, however, is that STM is "a diverse collection of temporary capacities that are distributed across multiple, separate processing modules" (Squire, Knowlton, & Musen, 1993, p. 456). Similarly, it now appears that LTM "is not a single entity but is composed of several different components, which are mediated by separate brain systems" (p. 457), as indicated in Tulving's model, discussed next. The process of entering information into the long-term memory store is not, then, simply a question of registering it through a sensory modality, retaining it briefly in the short-term store, and passing it on. With regard to human cognition, nothing, it seems, is that straightforward.

Tulving's Model

An important contribution to memory research was Endel Tulving's proposal, put forward in the early 1970s, that contrasts two types of **declarative memory: semantic memory** and **episodic memory** (Tulving, 1972). The notion of semantic memory rests on the assumption that our LTM contains a complex structure—a network—that includes such components as concepts and words, enabling us to understand

FIGURE 2.9 Structure of the Memory System Represented as a Series of Steps in Which Information Is Transferred from One Step to Another

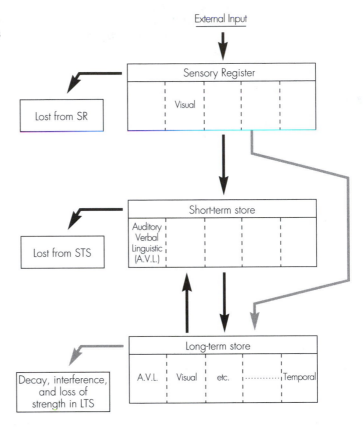

ideas, solve problems, and use language. Episodic memory, on the other hand, Tulving considers to be the memory that stores occurrences of events that are part of a series of events, yet each constituting a distinct event unto itself. Rather than being based on words,

> Episodic memory receives and stores information about temporally dated episodes or events, and temporal-spatial relations among these events. A perceptual event can be stored in the episodic system solely in terms of its perceptible properties or attributes, and it is always stored in terms of its autobiographical reference to the already existing contents of the episodic memory store. . . . Semantic memory is the memory necessary for the use of language. It is a mental thesaurus, organized knowledge a person possesses about words and other verbal symbols, their meaning and referents, about relations among them, and about rules, formulas, and **algorithms** [formulas] for the manipulation of these symbols, concepts, and relations. Semantic memory does not register perceptible properties of inputs, but rather cognitive referents of input signals. (Tulving, 1972, pp. 385–386)

In this framework, then, my memory of my late arrival to class one day constitutes one of my episodic memories, as does my memory of the event, a flat tire, that caused the delay. On the other hand, my knowledge of what "flat tire" means, and that it serves as an adequate excuse for lateness, derives from my semantic memory.

The two types of declarative memory were later contrasted with yet another sort, "procedural" memory. The reader will surely make the connection between the distinctions drawn in the present discussion of memory and the earlier discussion of knowledge representation, which is, after all, dependent on memory. It is no accident that the terms "declarative" and "procedural" surface in both discussions. The distinction is equally necessary in the context of memory because it seems clear that there are learned processes that are apparently not explainable in terms of either recall of episodes or knowledge of meanings. When I learn to tie my shoelaces, for example, or to play a Chopin nocturne on the piano, I am engaging in a process that is not precisely an event, nor is it language- or meaning-based. As described by Squire (1997), "Declarative memory is memory that is directly accessible to conscious recollection. It can be declared." This I can easily do with regard to the reason for my lateness to class. **Procedural memory**, on the other hand, "is memory that is contained within learned skills or modifiable cognitive operations" (p. 152). I cannot easily state just *how* I play that nocturne, nor can I describe a precise time when the event "I learned to play it" occurred. The distinction between declarative and procedural memory can be summed up as the distinction

> between conscious memory for facts and events and [on the other hand] various forms of unconscious memory, including skill and habit learning, simple classical conditioning, the phenomenon of priming, and other instances where memory is expressed by performance rather than by recollection. (Squire et al., 1993, p. 457)

Two of the major questions about memory that we would like to be able to answer are how and where our long-term declarative knowledge is stored. Is declarative memory mediated by a "distinct 'memory system,'" or is it, rather, more of a "kind of knowledge" or a "particular level of processing" (Eichenbaum, 1997, p. 548)? We *have* learned that "memory for an event, even memory for a single object, is stored in component parts and in distributed fashion across geographically separate parts of the brain" (Squire et al., 1993, p. 484). Furthermore,

> Although direct evidence is not available, permanent information storage is thought to occur in the same processing areas that are engaged during learning. By this view, long-term memory is stored as outcomes of processing operations and in the same cortical regions that are involved in the perception and analysis of the events and items to be remembered. (Squire et al., 1993, p. 484)

Research reported fairly recently has led to the suggestion that "declarative memory is mediated by a brain circuit composed of functionally distinct components in the cerebral cortex, parahippocampal region, and hippocampus" (Eichenbaum, 1997, p. 568).

One reason to hypothesize at least the two different types of memory we have been discussing is a need to explain the situation occurring in some patients with amnesia. Such patients may remember virtually nothing of their past lives, but they will still remember how to use the telephone or to ride a bicycle. If, after they have become amnesic, they are taught to play a new game or to find their way through a maze, they have no recollection afterward of having learned these skills. Nevertheless, they remain able to use them.

Constructive Memory

In addition to the sheer fascination the subject of human memory holds, memory research has many applications. These range from working with amnesia victims to developing and implementing more effective methods of teaching and studying, to treatment of the aging; there are even courtroom applications. Evidence from witnesses is often contradictory or inaccurate, and the controversial notion of "implanted memories" has recently surfaced. We are all familiar with media reports of court cases involving "repressed memories" of childhood abuse and with the scandals concerning day-care center personnel accused of abusing the children they are supposed to have been caring for. The prosecution may call as witnesses psychotherapists who testify that memories of traumatic abuse, repressed by the plaintiff for years, have finally surfaced. During the course of a trial in such cases, as in those involving child-care centers, many questions will have been put to the plaintiff or plaintiffs, who are usually either adults or children who are not very long out of day-care situations. These questions and the suggestions they raise may have an effect on the "memories" elicited in the individuals being questioned.

The defense in such cases often includes the notion of implanted or "constructed" memory. This is not simply a tricky legal response to the claims of the prosecution. Rather, it is based on a hypothesis that has been supported by recent research into the nature of memory. In a discussion of what is referred to as "the constructive nature of human memory," Schacter, Norman, and Koutsaal (1998) take note of the fact that memory consists of a collection of constituent elements distributed widely across different parts of the brain such that "no single location contains a complete record of the trace . . . of a specific experience. . . . Retrieval of a past experience involves a process of pattern completion . . . in which a subset of the features comprising a particular past experience are reactivated, and activation spreads to the rest of the constituent features of that experience" (p. 291). In the process, the features of a given episode or occurrence must be linked in a way that leads to a coherent representation. If this fails to happen, people may retrieve pieces of the episode without remembering how or when they acquired these pieces. In such a case, they may arrive at illusory or distorted memory. Studies have been carried out in which subjects view slides or a videotape of a sequence of events and are then asked questions about the events. Some of the questions refer to incidents that never actually happened, but which are subsequently "remembered." People evidently fail to remember whether the source of the memory was the videotape or slides, or the later discussion, and so confuse the two. "Insofar as thinking about an event frequently involves mentally picturing the event, mere contemplation of a suggested event can result in a vivid and detailed representation that is difficult to distinguish from stored representations of events that were actually perceived" (Schacter et al., 1998, p. 294).

There are other elements as well required for the construction of memory. One of these is retrieval cues, which may match more than one stored experience so that the target experience (i.e., the one at issue) gets muddled up with others. As the researchers point out, when the pattern completion process yields a match, then another process involved in retrieval must consider various elements, such as whether the information the individual retrieves is a memory of something that really happened, or whether it is merely a general idea of some such occurrence, or perhaps even a fantasy. Clues as to its source may come from its relative detail or vividness: If it is something that really happened, it may contain more detail or be more vivid than if it is not (Schacter et al., 1998)—though, as has been mentioned, even a thought-about "nonevent" may be filled in with such detail and vividness.

Difficulties in pinpointing the source of a memory are implicated in the "false memory" claims in the kinds of court cases I have mentioned. When events that have not in fact occurred are suggested, they may get mixed up with memories whose sources are not accurately remembered. There are various points in the process where slippage can occur. So wittingly or unwittingly, those who question adults or children about supposed instances of abuse, whether long ago or recent, may be contributing to the confusion of fact with nonfact. This confusion may then produce the false recognition that occurs because of the way cognitive mechanisms work as they form and retrieve memories.

Considering all of this, we can see that we are dealing with an extremely complex subject. In our daily lives we tend to regard memory as an either/or proposition: Either we remember something or we don't. But the moment we stop to think about it, simply by introspection we become aware that there are different types and different stores of memory. Myriad factors must be taken into account and have been addressed from many angles by much research. The phenomena are far too complex to be boiled down to a couple of easily stated distinctions that one may memorize and walk away from with a satisfied sense of "well, then, that's that."

But though we still have a long way to go in learning about the fundamental mechanisms serving memory, we are beginning to home in on them. In this area, as in all of those that underlie human intelligence, we are developing techniques that bring us closer to the explanations we seek. For instance, there have been studies making use of brain imaging to examine false recognition. We will return to this topic in Chapter 4, in the unit on neuroscience. Now it is time to proceed to that unit and an examination of the field that has in recent years supplied us with information about the physiological underpinnings of our increasing knowledge about human cognition.

Questions to Think About

1. Have you ever "observed" your own thought processes? Albert Einstein said that he thought in images not in words. Many of us think in words. People who are truly bilingual typically think in whichever language is salient at the

moment. What are the elements of your thoughts? Pictures? Words? Sounds? Something else entirely?

2. One way to study effectively is to find ways of classifying the information you need to master into meaningful and related concepts. When you study, you probably do this without thinking much about the process you are engaging in. What does this chapter tell you about the steps you take when you study? For example, do you look for examples? Do you relate what you are supposed to learn to your own experience? Do you relate one part of a chapter to another? Do you try to guess what the questions will be and then construct a prototypical answer?

3. It has been said that the present generation of people in their teens and early twenties is maturing in a culture that is quite different from their parents' and particularly from their grandparents' generation. Does the Sapir-Whorf hypothesis shed any light on such difficulties as you may have in communicating with older generations?

4. Some concepts are extremely difficult to define—*art,* for instance, or *game.* How helpful is the idea of "family resemblance" in assisting one to generate definitions of such concepts?

5. You sneeze and someone says, "God bless you." Is that a proposition? Why or why not? Are there any arguments in the statement? If so, what are they?

6. At this point in your study of cognitive science, do you think that the computer represents an apt metaphor for the human mind? Is a computer organized around nodes and links and spreading activation? Consider these questions again when you have read the material on artificial intelligence.

7. How might you go about "priming" yourself to retrieve a name that you have forgotten?

8. Describe any relationship that might exist among script, propositional network, and spreading activation. Are these concepts contradictory? Complementary? Unrelated?

9. The psychologist Wolfgang Köhler described chimpanzees who seemed to mull over a problem (reaching an out-of-reach banana) until they suddenly jumped up, piled up some crates, and climbed on the crates to reach the fruit. He described what he saw as an "Aha!" reaction. When you solve problems, do you go about it by some trial-and-error method, do you figure it out after lots of reflection, or does the answer suddenly come to you? You have probably experienced all of these methods. What approach are you most likely to use? Relate this to the concepts of comprehension, transformation, and arrangement discussed in the text. Is yours a different type of problem from these?

10. Are you "expert" in some domain in which your friends lack expertise? How did you become an expert, and what does your knowledge or skill enable you to do that your friends cannot do?

11. How do you understand the relationship between memory and identity? In patients with advanced Alzheimer's disease, all memory is lost. In what ways is the patient still, or no longer, "himself" or "herself"?

12. How do episodic and semantic memory, both aspects of declarative memory, differ from procedural memory? Can one learn a procedure for studying effectively, or must one rely on semantic (or episodic) memory in order to master the content of a course?

Exploring the Brain

In August 1997, *The New York Times* ran an article under the striking headline "Removing Half of Brain Improves Young Epileptics' Lives." The article concerned the unusual steps taken in the treatment of 54 children whose incapacitating epileptic seizures were not controllable by medication. (Epileptic seizures are brief mild to severe episodes in which a person experiences either involuntary movements of parts of the body or convulsions, often accompanied by loss of consciousness. They are triggered by electrical malfunction in an area of the brain.) The seizures experienced by these children interfered so with their lives that a radical procedure, called hemispherectomy, was invoked. Hemispherectomy is the removal of the entire hemisphere of the brain in which the seizures originate. As one might expect, the procedure is indeed effective in stopping the seizures. But one might also expect to pay such a heavy price in terms of loss of abilities that no one who had any alternative would voluntarily choose to undergo the procedure. What would happen to all the functions normally governed by that missing half of the brain? For instance, we tend to expect that language is, in most of us, a "left-brain" activity. What would happen to a person who has had half a brain removed? We might envision a child no longer suffering seizures, but also no longer able to understand or use language. What a trade-off!

But as it turns out, the human brain is far more "plastic" than we had imagined. That is, some of its functions seem to be transferable to areas of the brain not used for those functions under ordinary circumstances. The article describes the case of Alex, an 8-year-old with abnormalities in the left hemisphere that had left him mute, half-blind, half-paralyzed, and epileptic. Some time after a hemispherectomy was performed on Alex to remove the malfunctioning left hemisphere of his brain, he surprised everyone by beginning to speak—ultimately becoming fluent. This result was unanticipated. Everyone had assumed that Alex's language functions had been accomplished by his left hemisphere and that his right one was destined— programmed, as it were—for other, different functions (Zuger, 1997).

In February 1998, just 6 months after this article appeared in *The New York Times,* the magazine *Discover* carried a short piece on so-called phantom limbs. This expression refers to the phenomenon in which people who have had a limb or other body part amputated continue to feel the missing part. It may ache, it may tingle, it may swing, it may bend. It may feel the way it used to feel when it was still part of the body. But how can a person continue to "feel" a body part that isn't there? One hypothesis offered to explain how these feelings come about is that the brain fashions a kind of map based on the sensations one experiences while living with one's body. Part of the map remains, according to this hypothesis, even when a part of the body that contributed to producing it is lost.

But this article reported that people *born* without limbs, and therefore deprived of the daily experience of living with them, also "feel" them—an itching or a numb sensation, or a reaching-out impulse. One researcher cited in the *Discover* article suggests that the brain's map of body parts is not simply learned through experience. He proposes that it is innate, consisting of networks of neurons (individual nerve cells) laid down before birth. These networks link various regions of the brain, enabling us to sense where our limbs are, to feel pain, and to learn from our experiences (Melzack, 1990). In other words, the brain comes equipped with a kind of blueprint of where the body parts are going to be so that even if they fail to develop their "ghosts" continue to exist in the brain.

> It's as though the brain has a dual representation, one of the original body image laid down genetically and one on-going, up-to-date image that can incorporate subsequent changes. For some weird reason, [an] amputation disturbs the equilibrium and resurrects the original body image, which has always been competing for attention. (Ramachandran & Blakeslee, 1998, p. 58)

According to the article in *The New York Times,* when a *brain* is deprived of a crucial hemisphere, the remaining half manages to direct behavior it wasn't "designed" to handle. According to the *Discover* article, a *body* is deprived of a portion of itself, yet that portion continues to be represented in the brain and hence is "felt." Phenomena such as these pique our interest in the amazing organ we usually take for granted, an organ so designed that its attributes include the ability to change function midstream, as it were, and the ability to register sensations from nonexistent entities.

One of the most intriguing aspects of our study of the brain is that we have learned and continue to learn about the human brain by using it to study itself. This fact leads to an interesting speculation about how far our quest can take us: Can an entity confined to itself exceed its boundaries and grasp all there is to know about itself? Or does the very nature of the situation limit what we can know?

It will be best to reserve such questions for a later chapter, in which we will examine issues addressed by philosophers. In the present chapter we focus on early investigations of this organ, this amazing brain. We shall look at research that prepared the ground for the exciting developments of the late 20th century in the field of neuroscience.

Chapter 1 describes brain research carried out late in the 18th and early in the 19th centuries by such pioneers as Gall and Spurzheim. Having come to the conclusion that structure and function were related, these researchers tried to relate the structure of the brain to people's behavior. This effort led them to the "science" of phrenology. Although phrenology was later discredited, its theory of localization of function was a very important insight. The work of Broca and Wernicke on the language functions of the brain provided evidence for this theory, as did that of some later researchers, who are briefly referred to in that chapter. To understand what modern neuroscience is accomplishing, we need to devote some time to the object so actively under investigation—the brain itself—and then to take a closer look at the work of researchers working near the end of the 19th century and into the 20th. We may regard them as the immediate precursors to the field that flourishes at the beginning of the 21st century, a field we examine in Chapter 4.

The Brain Itself

Looking at a human brain (Figure 3.1), one would never suspect the wonders of which this rather odd-looking object is capable. But do not let its appearance fool

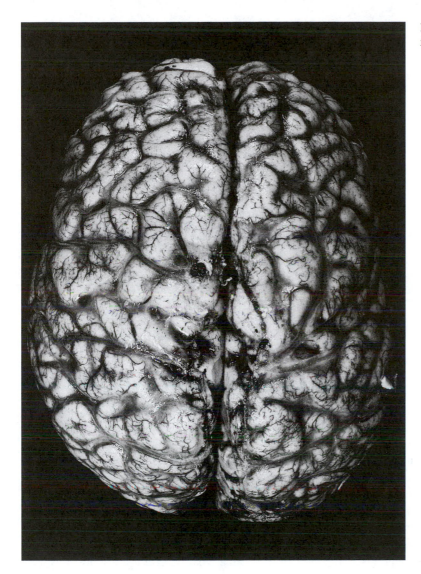

FIGURE 3.1 The Brain Viewed from Above

you. There are interesting observations to be made in the single nerve cell, in the many regions of the brain, and in the brain taken as a whole. We are going to be concerned primarily with the *cerebral cortex,* the outer layer that directs our motor and cognitive functions. But the cerebral cortex does not operate alone. Rather, it functions as part of a system. Like other animals, humans require a set of components that enable us to receive information from our environment and to respond to this information. To accomplish these tasks, we have a *nervous system.* In vertebrates, such as frogs, rats, and cats (all of them favorite experimental animals), as well as in humans, this nervous system consists of two parts. The first of these is the *peripheral nervous system.* It is made up of *afferent* nerve fibers, which carry signals

FIGURE 3.2 The Major Parts of
the Neuron

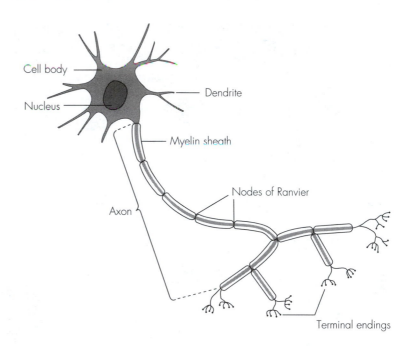

Cell body

Nucleus

Dendrite

Myelin sheath

Nodes of Ranvier

Axon

Terminal endings

from the senses *to* the brain, and of *efferent* nerve fibers, which carry messages *from* the brain to muscles and glands that tell them to move or to secrete. The second part is the *central nervous system,* which consists of the spinal cord and the brain.

The cells that make up the nervous system are called **neurons** (Figure 3.2). Neurons vary in size, from very small to perhaps 3 feet long, and are themselves made up of three parts: the cell body, or **soma**; branching systems of **dendrites**; and an **axon**. The soma contains the cell nucleus, which in turn contains the genetic material (**DNA** and **RNA**) of the neuron. Dendrites are thin "ribbons" that extend from the body itself, like strands of bubblegum pulled from the main mass. A membrane surrounding the soma receives information from other cells, and little "bumps," or *dendritic spines,* on the dendrites do the same. The axon is a single, longer branch that also originates in the soma. Near its end it branches into little *terminal boutons* or *end feet.* When neurons are not at rest, they are "firing," producing what are called "nerve impulses." These are electrical charges that travel along the axon to the axon terminals. The terminals are the transmitters of information to the membranes of other neurons, not in the course of touching them—because typically they don't—but rather across a small space or gap, called a *synaptic cleft.* The junction of the end foot of a transmitting neuron, the portion of the other neuron that receives its information, and the synaptic cleft is called a *synapse.* Chemicals, called neurotransmitters, are released across the synapse. It is these, when received by the next neuron in the chain, that are capable of initiating (or inhibiting) the impulse in it (Levinthal, 1983).

Although much is still unknown about how the human brain functions, a good deal *is* understood about it and the nervous system of which it is a part: the func-

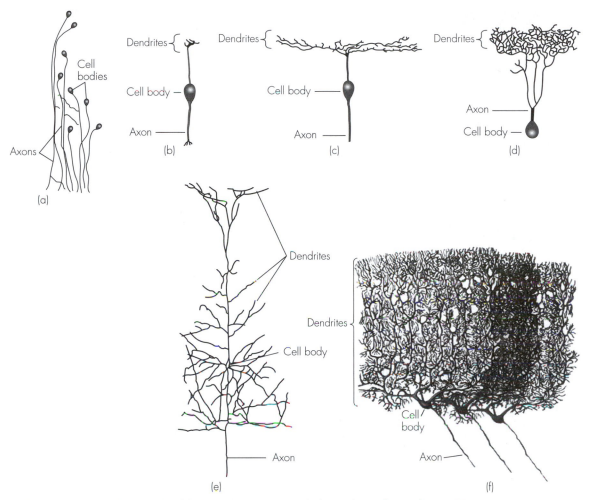

FIGURE 3.3 Various Nerve Cells. (a) Neurons in mesencephalic nucleus of cranial nerve V. (b) Retinal bipolar cell. (c) Retinal ganglion cell. (d) Retinal amacrine cell. (e) Cortical pyramidal cell. (f) Cerebellar Purkinje cell.

tioning of neurons and the roles and types of neurotransmitters in that functioning. Our understanding is increasing daily. We have only to open the newspaper, for instance, the science section of *The New York Times,* to be apprised virtually every Tuesday of new information being acquired by researchers in the field—so much information as to be quite overwhelming. It may even be fair to say that by the time an article is published it is out of date!

Some facts about the human brain we have known for some time, however. For example, it contains *billions* of neurons. Some of these have relatively few dendrites branching from the cell body, as illustrated in Figure 3.2; some, such as the Purkinje cell (Figure 3.3) are extremely complex, having a very large number of dendrites.

FIGURE 3.4 Cerebral Hemispheres, Side View

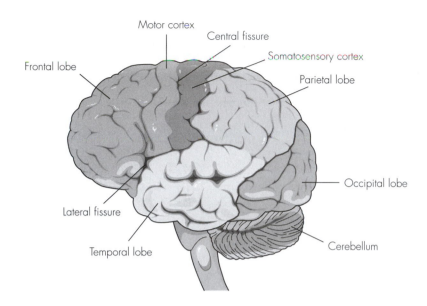

The huge number of these interacting neurons, with the innumerable possibilities they contain for interconnections, "makes the brain not only the most complex organ of the body but also the most complex structure of its size in the known universe" (Levinthal, 1983, p.15). The study of the functioning of the neurons of the brain is a fascinating one in itself, as is the study of the many components of the brain that humans have in common with other vertebrates. For our purposes, however, we turn to the cerebral cortex, that portion of the brain that is considered to have evolved most recently and that contains most of the elements serving our human intelligence.

The cerebral cortex is a layer of cells about 3 millimeters thick—and that is a very, very thin layer to contain the great number of cells required to allow us our "intelligent" behavior. The only way, in fact, that so many cells can be packed into such a thin layer is for that layer to be "scrunched up," folded in on itself enough so that a large surface area can be contained in a small space inside the skull. That is what those "convolutions" are that people refer to when talking about the human brain. Each convex (hill-like) portion is called a **gyrus**. The "valley" between two gyri is called a **sulcus**.

The cortex consists of four major sections, or lobes: the frontal, the parietal, the occipital, and the temporal (Figure 3.4). The whole is divided into halves, the cerebral hemispheres, which are connected by a thick bundle of fibers called the **corpus callosum**.

Two types of functional areas of the cortex were identified early on by researchers. The first consists of those areas that act as receiving stations for information arriving from the senses and as dispatching centers for commands to the muscles and glands. The visual area, for example, is located in the **occipital lobe**, and the area for hearing is located in the **temporal lobe**.

Most of the cortex is taken up not with these areas but rather with those involved in what we consider the "higher" mental functions, such as memory, language, and thought. Much of our information about these functions comes from individuals in whom damage to a particular area of the cortex is associated with loss of certain functions. Language is one of the most obvious of these functions. Studying the human brain is not an easy task, for ethical and for practical reasons. But the difficulty has not been insurmountable, and researchers have used their own considerable "brain power" to take advantage of opportunities presented to them and to devise ingenious new methods of inquiring into the mysteries of the brain.

The decade of the 1990s was designated the "decade of the brain" because of the intense international focus on the study of this fascinating entity. This world-wide effort has produced, in a short time, an immense explosion of knowledge (and, of course, many new questions). But a great deal of background work preceded that explosion. Let us now examine some of the important research that has enabled us to penetrate these mysteries to such an encouraging degree.

Brain Research in the Late 19th and Early 20th Centuries

Hughlings-Jackson, Fritsch and Hitzig, and Ferrier

The first researcher we shall consider is John Hughlings-Jackson (1835–1911), a clinician who worked with epileptic patients. Hughlings-Jackson's work is discussed in a book by his associate, neurologist David Ferrier (1843–1928). The book, titled *The Functions of the Brain,* originally published in 1876, was revised in 1886. Ferrier recounts how Hughlings-Jackson, having observed recurrent patterns of epileptic seizures in his patients, came to the conclusion that there are separate motor centers in the brain. He had carefully observed patients whose convulsions involved one side of the body and concluded that a stimulus event in specific areas of the left hemisphere of the brain triggered a certain muscular response on the right, or **contralateral** side of the body. Likewise, a stimulus event in analogous areas of the right hemisphere triggered a muscular response on the left side of the body.

Hughlings-Jackson had hit upon an important fact. His conclusion tied in nicely with what was beginning to be understood about the location of functions in the two hemispheres. The experimental techniques from which support for his ideas would derive came from the German researchers Gustav Fritsch (1838–1927) and Eduard Hitzig (1838–1907), who were experimenting with electrical stimulation of the brain. Hitzig had noticed that a patient whose cortex was being electrically stimulated produced certain eye movements. Until then, researchers had generally assumed that stimulating the brain tissue directly would *not* lead to bodily reactions. Fritsch and Hitzig tested this notion. But even in the 1870s, intrusive experiments on people's brains were not undertaken unless the patients were being operated on for a reason their doctors judged to be compelling. Even when this was the case, doctors did not want to place a patient at any greater risk than was required to cure or ameliorate a specific condition. So for their experiments, Fritsch and Hitzig used dogs.

Because I am mindful of the reaction of many people to descriptions, or even the notion, of experiments on animal species that feel pain much as we do, I will not dwell on that aspect of these experiments, which were often conducted without anesthesia. It is important, however, to be aware of the experiments and of their results in order to understand how they contributed to our knowledge of the brain.

Fritsch and Hitzig set up a delicate apparatus for electrical stimulation of the dogs' exposed brains. They adjusted the strength of the current so that a dog would react to it but not find it painful when it was applied to the dog's tongue via the wire leads. The wires, with this weak current switched on, were then guided to various areas of the dogs' exposed brains. When Fritsch and Hitzig stimulated the posterior (back) half of the brain, the stimulation produced no movements in the body. When they applied the current to some areas located in the anterior (front) half of a hemisphere, they found that it elicited muscular contractions *on the opposite side of the body*. This was real evidence supporting the initial theory of contralateral (opposite-side) control that Hughlings-Jackson had reached after observing his patients' convulsions.

Additionally, Fritsch and Hitzig were able to pinpoint specific areas that produced the muscular contractions, enabling them to assert that

> one part of the convexity of the **cerebrum** [the upper part of the brain] of the dog is motor and the other is not. . . . The motor area is generally more toward the front; the nonmotor area is more toward the back. In stimulating the motor area electrically, one elicits combined muscular contractions in the opposite half of the body. By using very weak current, one can localize these contractions exactly in narrowly delimited groups of muscle. If more intense current is used, other muscles—and indeed, also corresponding muscles in the [same] half of the body—immediately take part [in the reaction] as a result of the stimulation of the same or neighboring places. The possibility of isolated stimulation of a limited group of muscles is therefore limited to weak current on very small areas. For brevity's sake, we call these areas "centers." (Fritsch & Hitzig, 1870/1968, p. 231)

They also found that stimulation of areas of the brain's surface *between* centers did not evoke observable responses. The same weak current did not produce observable muscular contractions. Fritsch and Hitzig were thus able to demonstrate very precisely the location of the motor centers. And, being true scientists, they made sure to perform a large number of experiments to see whether the results were consistent (reliable); they were able to report that "most of [our experiments] agree even in the smallest details. With the exact description of our method . . . and with [certain] facts at hand, it is so easy to repeat our experiments that confirmations will soon appear" (Fritsch & Hitzig, 1870/1968, p. 231).

We can well imagine the excitement such results must have generated, especially as highly sophisticated methods of peering at the workings of the brain are generating just such excitement today. The point to note here is that for the first time *facts* about the workings of the brain were becoming available. Although these facts derived initially from the study of nonhuman species, techniques would soon be developed that could begin to provide answers to the questions we had— and have—about ourselves.

David Ferrier, who described Hughlings-Jackson's work in his book *The Functions of the Brain,* considered that "a new era in cerebral physiology was inaugurated by the discovery by Fritsch and Hitzig." His own studies confirmed theirs (Ferrier, 1886/1963). Operating on a number of species, including, in addition to dogs, monkeys, guinea pigs, fish, and frogs, he extended the results to these other species so that the phenomenon could be considered a general one. In a section of the book headed "Functions of the Cerebrum," Ferrier writes:

> The great and significant feature of the reactions produced by electrical excitement of the cortex is that they are definite and predictable, and vary with the position of the **electrodes** [devices for applying electric current]. . . . Areas in close proximity to each other, separated by only a few millimeters or less, react to the electrical current in a totally different manner. If there were no functional differentiation of the areas under stimulation the diverse effects would be absolutely incomprehensible. (Ferrier, 1886/1963, pp. 220–229)

If we think back to childhood, we may remember the way it felt when curiosity led us to take apart a toy, revealing its mechanism. "Oh, so *that's* what's in there! So *that's* how it works!" Fritsch and Hitzig, Ferrier, and the other early researchers into the workings of the brain were, in essence, playing with the most sophisticated, complex toy imaginable—and its mechanisms were beginning to reveal themselves.

Ferrier did not limit his investigations to "motor centers" but reported as well results of experiments having to do with what he called "sensory centers." Noting the effects on eye movements produced by electrical stimulation of specific areas of the cortex, he suspected that those areas were involved in vision. He followed these studies with experiments in which, among other techniques, he selectively destroyed those areas by ablation (surgical removal). The results convinced him that the structure of the brain has a significant influence on visual perception. In addition, localized destruction of another area of the cortex led, in monkeys, to deafness. Ferrier concluded that he had thus pinpointed the "center of hearing."

Convinced by the results of his many experiments that there were indeed areas in which functions were localized, Ferrier considered the implications of this fact with regard to cognition. He regarded as "beyond doubt" that the hemispheres of the brain "consist of a system of sensory and motor centers" and asserted what he called a "universally admitted axiom": that the brain is the organ of the mind. He stated further that

> we have . . . many grounds for believing that the frontal lobes, the cortical centers for the head and ocular movements, with their associated sensory centers, form the substrata of those psychical processes which lie at the foundation of the higher intellectual

operations. . . . Intelligence and will have no local habitation distinct from the sensory and motor substrata of the cortex generally. There are centers for special forms of sensation and ideation, and centers for special motor activities and acquisitions, in response to and in association with the activity of sensory centers. (Ferrier, 1886/1963, pp. 220–229)

The idea that the various functions of the brain are located in different areas of the brain has had a checkered history. We have seen how it lost credence and fell into disrepute by being taken to conclusions we now know to be incorrect and even, to our modern minds, absurd. We know that the traits of cautiousness, self-esteem, acquisitiveness, and mirthfulness, for example, as depicted in the phrenology head illustrated in Chapter 1, are not at all those that can be localized in the brain. But once the research of Fritsch, Hitzig, and Ferrier confirmed the insights of Hughlings-Jackson about the functioning of the brain, a revised theory of localization of function became reputable. Experiments were carried out within its framework, this time with psychologists taking up the banner.

Franz and Lashley

Until about 1900, knowledge about the brain had been advanced by techniques such as electrical stimulation and the surgical destruction or removal of specific areas. These techniques probed the organ itself in order to learn what areas were associated with which behavior. Exciting as all of this was, at the end of the 19th century there had not yet been a rigorous and systematic attempt to carefully observe and measure behaviors of experimental animals. Such efforts were necessary to complement the growing body of information about the brain itself. The picture was one-sided, incomplete. But it did not remain so. This other aspect of the task was undertaken by a new set of researchers—psychologists. Their interests included *measurement* of the motor and sensory capabilities of the animals they used in their experiments and these animals' ability to acquire habits and to retain them.

Among the first to tackle the job was the psychologist Sheperd Ivory Franz (1874–1933) who, in 1902, published the results of experiments that he had undertaken in order to "determine, if possible, the relation of the various so-called association areas . . . to simple mental processes" (Franz, 1902, p. 1). But Franz added a new ingredient to the recipe: In addition to the surgical procedures previously employed to study objectively and quantitatively the functions of the frontal lobes, he used objective and quantitative methods to study the *behavior* of the experimental animals. His experiments incorporated training the animals in new habits. Interestingly, he found that the new habits were lost after the removal of portions of both frontal lobes—but *old* habits were retained!

Franz also found that the animals could relearn the lost new habits, lose them again if additional portions of the frontal lobes were removed, and relearn them once again. The implication of these results was that it was *not* one specific location that was responsible for the learning of new habits. Therefore, the theory of localization of function, as espoused by researchers such as Fritsch, Hitzig, and

Ferrier, was open to question. In fact, as Franz continued with his experiments, the evidence convinced him that the theory was wrong. The publication of his results initiated a debate that lasted for years.

On one side of this debate were those who held that because various areas of the brain are demonstrably different from each other these areas must have different functions. On the other side were those who thought, like Franz, that this position was "the entering wedge for a more complete phrenology than has been advocated since the time of Gall" (Franz, 1912, p. 328). In 1923, even more convinced by the results of experiments in the intervening years, Franz published an analysis in which he drew attention to an error in thinking that had led to this "new phrenology." He pointed out that though an individual's loss of a cognitive ability is clearly *associated* with damage to the brain in a particular area—such as speech loss and Broca's area—the conclusion cannot rightly be drawn that language ability is *located* in that area. Evidence that it is not comes, for instance, from what Franz (1923) refers to as "functional restitution or reëducation after cerebral lesions" (p. 443). That is, since there are people who recover functions lost as a result of brain damage, the functions cannot have resided in the damaged area alone. He considers the nervous system in general to be "a great connecting system" and that "many parts of the brain function at one time, and so widely separated are those parts that we have right [sic] to say that the brain functions as a whole" (pp. 444–445).

In the next chapter we shall see that researchers are now largely agreed that although certain areas of the brain seem to be the locus of certain behaviors the brain does act as an integrated whole, its functions distributed in ways that are not yet fully understood. This must be an important part of the explanation of seemingly odd cases like the one that began this chapter, that of the mute boy who began to speak after the entire left hemisphere of his brain had been removed.

The neuropsychologist Karl Lashley (1890–1958) was another major figure in brain research. A bit younger than Franz, with whom he worked for a time, Lashley also came to the conclusion that the prevailing notions were not entirely correct. In a paper published in 1937, he wrote:

> It has been assumed that the properties of experience are represented at the level of some simple nervous activity or in single loci: sensation in the sensory area, volitional pattern in the motor regions or particular forms of intelligent behavior in restricted coordinating centers. Such conceptions of localization are oversimplified and must be abandoned. . . . The functions of every center are dependent on its relations to the rest of the intact nervous system. (pp. 375–376)

Lashley saw, of course, that the data we work with in "using our heads" come largely through our senses and must somehow be "registered" in our brains. He understood that although our movements rely on the motor capabilities provided by our brains there is clearly more to intelligence than that—in other species as well as in humans. Lashley (1929) was interested in the nature of the learning process and of intelligence; he considered that his findings "lend support to the theory which conceives intelligence as a general capacity" (p. 173) rather than an entity whose components can be strictly localized. These findings resulted from a set of experiments with white rats as subjects, by means of which he set about studying *learning* and through which he arrived at a new conclusion.

Lashley's experiments involved training rats—that is, having them learn—to find their way through mazes. Once they had learned the mazes, Lashley surgically removed portions of the rats' cerebral cortex. After recovering from the surgery, the rats were reintroduced to the mazes and demonstrated that they could no longer negotiate them. They also demonstrated that they were able to relearn the route. The amount of practice they needed in order to learn depended not on the *location* of the cortex that had been removed, but rather on the *amount*. In other words, Lashley found that unlike specific motor activity, learning—and retention of what has been learned (an aspect of intelligence, as we usually conceive it)—cannot be localized to a specific area of the cortex. It is, rather, a more global function. And because it was apparent that learning can recur after one location has been destroyed, provided enough cortex is left, Lashley concluded that the areas were not differentiated with regard to this function. Rather, their potential for fulfilling the function was equivalent. This conclusion is referred to as the *principle of equipotentiality* of parts. In his words:

> The term "equipotentiality" I have used to designate the apparent capacity of any intact part of a functional area to carry out, with or without reduction in efficiency, the functions which are lost by destruction of the whole. This capacity varies from one area to another and with the character of the functions involved. (Lashley 1929, p. 25)

When a functional area of the cortex is damaged, its ability to perform previously mastered complex functions may be lost in proportion to the extent of the injury. This Lashley called the *principle of mass action*.

The type of theorizing and the methods of experimentation Lashley employed have become so routine in scientific endeavor that it may not occur to us that this was not always the case. Krech (1963) calls these methods "revolutionary innovations." Indeed, they influenced for many years both the way researchers thought about the problem of localization of brain function and the experimental research they undertook.

The course of scientific discovery, however, runs no more smoothly than anything else in the area of human endeavor. This fact has its positive side: What is learned by researchers following a particular method of inquiry can be complemented or contradicted by others following a different path. Both Lashley's ideas and his methods were important in increasing our knowledge about brain function. The results of laboratory experiments in which rats were the subjects had very interesting implications for the capacities of the *human* brain. (It is always well to remember, though, that it is a considerable—and not always justifiable—leap from the rat to what we conclude about humans!) However, not every researcher interested in the subject was a laboratory researcher. There were still clinicians—surgeons like Broca and Wernicke a century earlier—who observed and wondered about the causes of the puzzling and fascinating symptoms and behaviors of their brain-injured human patients. Interestingly, as we shall see, the results of their research did not support Lashley's hypotheses, as embodied in his principles of equipotentiality of parts and mass action.

The research methods of these neurosurgeons differed crucially from those of experimentalists in the laboratory. Up to this point, neurosurgeons had not been able to design experiments addressing directly the relation of brain injury or damage to the behaviors of their patients. Research could not be allowed to dictate interference with human patients' brains as it did with the brains of dogs and rats. Because of this limitation, what we could learn about human brain function depended, until recently, largely on the serendipitous.

The Living Human Brain: The Neurosurgeons

Early Research: Bartholow and Cushing

In the past, the brains of patients suffering from brain malfunction or injury were not available for study until after the patients had died. Then their brains could be examined at autopsy. But the technique of electrical stimulation of the *living* brain developed by Fritsch and Hitzig opened new possibilities.

The first to exploit and report on these possibilities was Dr. Roberts Bartholow, an American physician and a professor at the Medical College of Ohio. Only a few years after Fritsch and Hitzig's work became known, Bartholow made use of a situation that chanced to come his way. In 1874 a young woman who had recently had surgery on her brain was brought to him. The surgery had left her with an opening in her skull through which it was possible, as Dr. Bartholow (1874) reported, to see the "pulsations of the brain." Because incisions had earlier been made in the brain for medical treatment, Bartholow reasoned that there would be no additional damage if he inserted fine needles at various points in the brain in order to direct a weak electrical current there. When he did so, he made some interesting discoveries. The patient was awake during the procedure, and when asked if she was feeling pain, she reported that she felt none! This was an important finding, for it meant that surgeons might take advantage of situations in which patients' brains were exposed during necessary surgical procedures in order to learn from these living and conscious patients more about the functions of the brain than had been possible before.

What Bartholow learned about the effects of applying weak electrical current was also important. As with Fritsch and Hitzig's experimental animals, stimulating localized areas of the human brain could produce specific muscular contractions—and furthermore, *human* patients could tell the surgeon what they were feeling during the procedure. Humans, unlike animals, could report sensations, thus opening another realm for inquiry. Stimulation of the left posterior lobe of the young woman's brain (through the opening in her skull) produced muscular contractions of the right arm and leg, as well as "a very strong and unpleasant feeling of tingling in both right extremities" (Bartholow, 1874).

As the possibilities opened up by Fritsch and Hitzig's experimental techniques had been seized upon by subsequent investigators of animal brain function, so

Bartholow's findings suggested opportunities for surgeons to study the living brains of conscious human patients, and they too seized these opportunities. Of course they did not all find convenient skull openings through which they could conduct their experiments. Rather, under local anesthesia, they performed a procedure called a **craniotomy**, cutting through the scalp and skull in order to reach the brain. Since the brain itself feels no pain, it is for the craniotomy that anesthesia is required, for the scalp and skull certainly feel pain—as you know if you have ever bumped your head. Because the anesthesia is local, the patient may remain awake and conscious. The surgeons then induced motor responses by stimulating areas of the brain with weak electrical current and thereby confirmed for human subjects the findings of earlier animal experimenters. In 1909 Harvey Cushing, of the Johns Hopkins Hospital, located by means of this technique areas in the brains of two patients that, when stimulated, produced sensation—but this time without producing muscular movements in the body (Cushing, 1909). Unlike animals, these human patients were able to report the sensations they experienced during the procedure. Now it became possible actually to *map* brain areas; that is, one could trace in the brain the locations associated with specific bodily *movements* and those associated with specific bodily *sensations*.

Mid-20th-Century Research: Penfield and Hebb

All of these developments laid the groundwork for the research of Wilder Penfield (1891–1976), probably the best known of the new "surgeon-experimenters." In 1950 Penfield, Professor of Neurology and Neurosurgery at McGill University in Canada, published *The Cerebral Cortex of Man* (Penfield & Rasmussen, 1950). In this book he reported on his findings and conclusions derived from 19 years of treating patients and investigating the human brain.

Penfield's information came from more than 400 operations on the brain that he performed under local anesthesia. Of course these operations were not undertaken for the purpose of brain research but rather to treat various conditions, such as severe epileptic seizures and brain tumors. However, as Bartholow, Cushing, and others had done, Penfield (1958) made use of the opportunity to learn what he could about localization of brain function when, as he put it, "conditions present themselves which would satisfy the most exacting requirements of a critical investigator" (p. ix).

As we saw earlier in this chapter, all human brains are initially constructed along the same general lines. However, as with human characteristics in general, they vary somewhat from person to person. In addition, the environment in which each individual develops is unique, and in response to its environment each brain develops uniquely. Therefore, it is not possible to make the surgeon's task easier by plotting out a single brain "map" that will accurately represent everyone's brain (as the phrenologists had endeavored to do). No neurosurgeon would want to risk operating on a patient without specific knowledge of the effects the surgery might have on areas surrounding the affected one. So it is necessary for brain surgeons to "map" each brain individually.

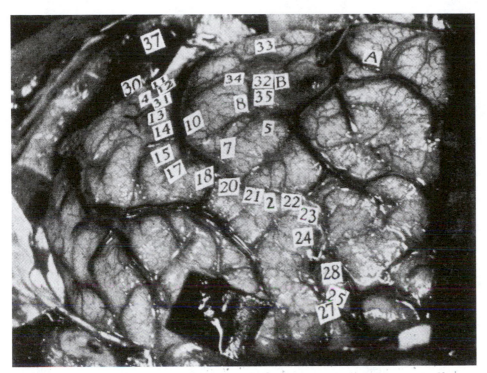

FIGURE 3.5 Numbered Tickets on Exposed Cortex. The numbered tickets identified areas of the brain where stimulation produced a response, providing a map to guide Penfield during surgery.

In *The Cerebral Cortex of Man,* Penfield describes how he used the technique of electrical stimulation to map areas of the brain. In one case, for example, he operated on an 18-year-old boy who suffered from epileptic seizures. When Penfield exposed the boy's brain, he found a small tumor that needed to be removed. The boy was awake and reported his sensations as the current was directed at different spots on his brain. A secretary, separated from the operating room by glass, recorded the effects of the stimulation. Where there was no reaction, she simply recorded this fact. When there was a reaction, she recorded it and Penfield placed a little numbered ticket directly on the relevant site on the brain. Penfield notes in his book a few of the positive responses to stimulation; some are simply sensations: a tingling in the upper part of the left leg, a sensation in the left lower lip, a sensation in the tip of the tongue. Others are sensations with movements, such as contraction of the left hand and arm, with movement in both; and still others are reports of contraction (in a leg, for example) with no accompanying movement. When all the stimulated areas had been numbered by means of the little tickets placed directly on the brain at the appropriate spots, photographs were taken of the brain with all the numbers in place (Penfield & Rasmussen, 1950). Penfield thus had a map to guide him in the surgery and to help him avoid damaging crucial areas as he removed the tumor (Figure 3.5).

The information about localization of motor and sensory brain functions that Penfield's technique afforded was of great interest, but there was an even more exciting aspect to it: Conscious patients undergoing electrical stimulation of the brain reported *mental* phenomena as well. Imagine for a moment that you are a neurosurgeon performing the delicate mapping procedure Penfield described. Your patient is a woman who has no idea of when or where you are stimulating her exposed brain with the electrode. You stimulate one spot and are not surprised when her body reacts and she reports the reaction to you—a muscular contraction in her right hand and arm. You carefully note both the reaction and the area that, when stimulated, produced it. You switch the current to another location and again are not surprised when your patient reports a tingling sensation in her right foot.

Now you move the stimulator to a spot on the right temporal lobe, and suddenly she tells you that she hears an orchestra playing a popular tune. You remove the electrode and she says the music stops. You stimulate the same spot again, and again the orchestra plays the tune. You ask her to hum it, and she does. The music is so real to her that she thinks you are playing a record in the operating room. No matter how many times you repeat the process, the result is still an evocation of the same tune being played by the same orchestra, beginning at the same place and continuing as it would exactly as if it were actually occurring. The muscular contractions the patient reported earlier are of the sort you had been expecting, based on similar experiments with animals. The tingling and other sensations she reported are reactions you can imagine occurring in other animals as well, although they lack the means to report them to you. But this report of a *mental* happening is something you did not expect.

It is, in fact, precisely what Penfield found in D. F., one of the patients whose cases he reports in his 1959 paper titled "The Interpretive Cortex." Penfield's paper begins

> There is an area of the surface of the human brain where local electrical stimulation can call back a sequence of past experience. An epileptic irritation in this area may do the same. It is as though a wire recorder, or a strip of cinematographic film with sound track, had been set in motion within the brain. The sights and sounds, and the thoughts, of a former day pass through the man's mind again. (p. 1719)

The electrifying effect was not only on the patient. Suddenly neurosurgeons seemed able to tap memory (or what patients experienced as memory) directly. And that was not all. Stimulation of certain areas in the temporal lobe produces interpretive responses: The patient interprets what he or she is experiencing, noting for example that it seems familiar, while realizing nevertheless that it has in fact *not* been experienced before. Or a patient may report what Penfield calls "psychical states"— feelings of fear or of loneliness or "as though he were observing himself at a distance" (Penfield, 1959, p. 1720). Penfield pointed out that such psychical states are experienced not only during brain surgery, but that people interpret the ordinary present in this way as well. Furthermore, they use such interpretations in deciding how to act or react to real situations. He reasoned that if the interpretations were to be helpful they must be accurate, based on similar experiences that people have already had. Therefore, both the remembering and the interpretive response to it may come about by a mechanism all humans share, a "common inclusive mechanism of reflex recognition or interpretation" (Penfield, 1959, p. 1720).

In a practical sense, understanding the mechanisms of this interpretive cortex can be of great use. Penfield (1959) pointed out that in epileptics certain psychical states (often referred to as "auras"), such as dreaminess, frequently herald a seizure. Hughlings-Jackson had found that the anterior and deep portions of the temporal lobes were the areas where these states would be produced at the onset of an epileptic seizure. Penfield identified this area with the interpretive cortex. If, by electrical stimulation, the neurosurgeon could trigger the psychical state that initiated the seizures, and if mapping indicated that it could be spared, the area of cortex responsible for initiating the seizures could be removed.

Practical reasons provide the incentive for medical research. But there is also the simple desire to know, to understand. We accept gratefully that aspirin will take away our headache and perhaps be helpful in avoiding heart attacks, but we would still like to know *why*. Pinpointing the area of the interpretive cortex responsible for a patient's epileptic seizures may be of great benefit to the patient, but we would still like to understand the function of the interpretive cortex. It might have seemed, when specific spots of recall were activated, that it was the seat of memory. But, as Penfield (1959) says,

> We may say that the interpretive cortex has something to do with a mechanism that can reactivate the vivid record of the past. It has also something to do with a mechanism that can present to consciousness a reflex interpretation of the present. To conclude that here is the mechanism of memory would be an unjustified assumption. It would be too simple. . . . A vast amount of work remains to be done before the mechanisms of memory, and how and where the recording takes place, are understood. This record is not laid down in the interpretive cortex, but it is kept in a part of the brain that is intimately connected with it. (p. 1724)

Penfield makes this assertion because even when large areas of the interpretive cortex are removed the ability to remember recent events is not always destroyed. Other areas are involved in recording recent events, and still others handle the storage of long-term memory. Penfield's very important paper was published in 1959, and a great deal of the "vast amount of work" he speaks of has been accomplished in the 40 years since that publication. We know considerably more today about the mechanisms of memory than we did then; this new knowledge will be discussed in the next chapter.

While Penfield was engaged in the clinical work on the cortex that he reported in his 1959 paper, a somewhat younger colleague of his was making a different sort of contribution to knowledge of the workings of the brain. McGill neuropsychologist Donald O. Hebb (1904–1985) was addressing the problem of integrating mental (i.e., psychological) and brain (i.e., physiological) processes.

Hebb called attention to the fact that when a portion of the cortex is removed from a person's brain the effect on that person's intelligence may be very small, perhaps not detectable. As he states in his 1949 book *Organization of Behavior,*

"Intelligence must be affected by any large brain injury—yet sometimes it seems not to be" (p. 1). He cites instances in which people who have had a great deal of brain removed—even an entire right hemisphere—nevertheless achieve very high scores on intelligence tests. (We shall later see evidence that people who have had such extensive removal of or damage to their brains show effects that bear upon certain aspects of their intelligence that are not tapped by such tests.) According to Hebb (1949), "The effect of a clear-cut removal of cortex outside the speech area is often astonishingly small; at times no effect whatsoever can be found" (p. 1). (Perhaps there *is* loss of intelligence that goes along with aphasia, a condition that results from damage to the area associated with speech; but Hebb notes that if so that still leaves unexplained the cases in which damage elsewhere in the brain seems to have no effect on intelligence.)

If functions that are usually considered crucial elements of intelligence, such as the ability to learn and to remember, are not necessarily affected by loss of cortex, then those functions clearly cannot reside only in specific locations in the cortex. If not only rats, but humans as well, can continue to learn under such circumstances, the explanation must lie in the ability of the brain to achieve new learning, to lay down new memories. Hebb's theory of *cell assemblies* and *phase sequences* proved a major insight, suggesting productive directions for research into how such learning and remembering occur.

Today we are comfortable with the notion that *neural circuits* are the under-pinnings of cognitive processes; it was Hebb who presented the first testable the-ory of how these neural circuits work. This theory rests on the idea that "any two cells or systems of cells that are repeatedly active at the same time will tend to become 'associated,' so that activity in one facilitates activity in the other" (Hebb, 1949, p. 70). Hebb (1959) suggests that many repetitions of sensory events, such as exposure to a particular speech sound (a vowel, perhaps) or "a particular pat-tern of pressure in a small area of skin" or "the common property ('hardness') of a series of tactual stimulations as the infant's hand touches a rattle" (p. 628), will lead to the gradual building up of a set of perhaps 25 to 100 neurons, which Hebb terms a **cell assembly**. This is

> a brain process which corresponds to a particular sensory event, or a common aspect of a number of sensory events. This assembly is a closed system in which activity can "reverberate" and thus continue after the sensory event which started it has ceased. Also, one assembly will form connections with others, and it may therefore be made active by one of them in the total absence of the adequate stimulus. In short, the assembly activity is the simplest case of an *image* or an *idea*: a representative process. The formation of connections between assemblies is the mechanism of association. (Hebb, 1959, p. 628)

The connections are established, Hebb suggests, because

> the persistence or repetition of a reverberatory activity (or trace) tends to induce last-ing cellular changes that add to its stability. The assumption can be precisely stated as follows: *When an axon of cell A is near enough to excite a cell B and repeatedly or persistently takes part in firing it, some growth process or metabolic change takes place*

in one or both cells such that A's efficiency, as one of the cells firing B, is increased.
(Hebb, 1949, p. 62)

Thus changes in the connections (synapses) between neurons allow the neurons in a cell assembly to act together. As they develop into the assembly (i.e., as learning takes place), the connections are strengthened, leading to activation of a neuron even when the signal from another in the assembly is weak. If one neuron in the set fires, then they all fire. "This notion of a 'Hebbian synapse' is central to much of modern neuroscience" (Posner & Raichle, 1994, p. 7).

Hebb's presentation of the theory of cell assemblies was grounded in visual perception (about which more was known than was known about other areas of perception), but it is clear that this theory applies outside that domain as well. It is extended ultimately to help explain mental activity in general. As part of his account of this process, Hebb suggested the manner of organization of cell assemblies. At the outset, he proposed, they are involved in aspects of a perceived experience; his example is assemblies constructed from visually perceiving (having in the center of one's field of vision) the corners of a triangle. This establishes "three diffuse, irregular cell-assemblies, each of which is capable of acting momentarily as a closed system" (Hebb, 1949, p. 86). These are eventually integrated into a perception of the whole (in this case, the entire triangle).

Thus mental activity begins as a localized process, involving a behavioral pattern such as visual perception, dependent on specific neurons or groups of neurons. But the process does not stop there. Over time more complex perceptions and behaviors are formed from sets of these cell assemblies; these sets Hebb termed *phase sequences*. Phase sequences spread out, involving cell assemblies from areas of the brain that may be separated by quite some distance and many intervening, uninvolved neurons, so that the resulting network is diffuse. Following one after another, phase sequences constitute what he called—and we have been calling—a "train of thought." Thus, Hebb was proposing a schema not only for perception but for thought processes in general. William James, in his 1890 *Principles,* described thought in terms of a "stream of consciousness" by which one thought or perception leads to another, which in turn stimulates a third, and so on. Hebb's model describes an analogous physiological process.

One can readily see implications of this schema: A given function will not be dependent on one set of cells located in one area of the brain and hence subject to total destruction if that area is damaged. Rather, when such damage occurs, the remainder of the diffuse network involved in that function will still be working and the function will be retained—though perhaps not at the same level of effectiveness as before. The influence of Hebb's theory, as presented in *The Organization of Behavior,* was far-reaching and provides a basis for current research.

When perusing the literature in this field, one has the sense of a process gathering speed, as a train does on leaving its station. The background to today's burgeoning knowledge involves the contributions of many researchers, each one or each group uncovering individual pieces of one of the most intriguing puzzles we can imagine. Unlike the jigsaw puzzles we play with on rainy days, however, this puzzle lacks a correct theoretical framework at the outset, and there are no convenient straight edges to help identify it. For example, are brain functions localized, or are they diffuse—or perhaps a little of both? The framework one chooses determines how and where one looks for answers. When we examine the "brain-puzzle," as each piece is fitted into place the picture grows more and more complex. This fact, however, does not deter those eager to assemble the whole picture. We continue our account with a brief look at the important directions this research took in the 1960s, 70s, and early 80s—before we turn our attention to the breakthroughs that fueled the research of the 1990s, the "decade of the brain."

The 1960s and Beyond: Hubel, Wiesel, and Sperry

Three names jump immediately from the pages of the history of this endeavor, those of neurobiologists Torsten Wiesel (b. 1924) and David Hubel (b. 1926) and physiological psychologist Roger Sperry (1913–1994). Hubel and Wiesel, who worked together for more than 20 years, shared with Sperry the 1981 Nobel Prize for Medicine or Physiology. Hubel and Wiesel worked on the visual system; research into the effects of severing the connection between the hemispheres of the brain led to Sperry's award.

The Visual System   In 1959, Hubel and Wiesel began collaborating on research into visual "receptive fields." At any given moment there is an area that is visible to you while your eyes are not moving (for example, as you gaze out the window at a daffodil in a row of daffodils); this is called the **visual field**. The area of the visual field that will produce a response in a given cell is referred to as its **receptive field**. It was already known from earlier experiments with frogs and certain other species that, at least in those species, there are neurons sensitive to only certain aspects of a visual image. In the optic nerve of frogs, for example, there are "bug detectors"—cells that respond only to small, dark objects that move in "bug-like" ways (Lettvin, Maturana, McCulloch, & Pitts, 1959). These neurons are more formally referred to as **feature detectors**. Now the primary visual area of the human brain, the striate cortex, contains a great many cells—on the order of a hundred million—and before the award-winning work of these two researchers, it was not clear that recording the activities of individual cells among them would tell us much about the workings of the whole.

Hubel and Wiesel pursued this line, however. They inserted a tiny single-cell recording electrode into the brain of an anesthetized but conscious cat. "It was exciting to be able to record from a single cell in the cortex of a cat that was looking around and purring," Hubel reports (1981, p. 1). What they learned from their experiments was that different types of cortical cells of the cat detect different features. They noted "simple cells," which respond to features such as orientation of the stimulus—a vertical line but not a slanted line, for example—and to features such as whether the stimulus is lighter or darker than the background. They distinguished these simple cells from "complex cells," which receive input from many simple cells and react to specific images anywhere in the receptive field as they sweep across it. And they found cells that receive input from complex cells and respond to patterns; these they called "hypercomplex cells." Data indicate that questions remain about the nature of and the relationship between these two types of cells, and the research continues today.

Among Hubel and Wiesel's contributions to knowledge about the visual system was another important piece of the puzzle. They demonstrated that in depriving a kitten of the use of one eye for a period, by closing its eyelid, the connections that the eye would otherwise make to the cortical neurons are permanently disrupted (Wiesel & Hubel, 1963). If one deprives a kitten of normal access to the stimuli provided by the world around it, the process of development in the area of the brain involved in the perception of those stimuli is impeded.

Split-Brain Research Hubel and Wiesel were pioneers, taking a direction soon followed by other researchers, who added to the picture yet more puzzle pieces. Still others were taking a different route. One of these was Roger Sperry, whose own pioneering research was directed toward the role played by each of the two hemispheres of the human brain.

The background to this work included years of research into the relation of nerve circuits to the functional networks that produce motor behavior. Much about vision is well understood. For example, there is a nerve, the *optic nerve,* that links the eyes to the brain. Chains of neurons projecting from half of each eye (the half nearer the nose) cross to the opposite hemisphere (at a point called the *optic chiasm*). Lateral projections (from the side of the eyes nearer the ears) don't cross over. This arrangement ensures that information from both eyes goes to both sides of the brain. (A benefit of this structure is that if a person loses one eye information gathered by the remaining eye will still be projected to both hemispheres.) When this crossover pathway was cut in such a way that each eye led to only one cerebral hemisphere, Sperry and his colleagues found that a memory of a visual pattern was nevertheless transferred between the hemispheres. However, when the corpus callosum, the large bridge of fibers between the hemispheres, was severed, this transfer did not take place. Figure 3.6 illustrates the crossover pathway linking the eye to the brain.

The research including severing of the corpus callosum has been referred to ever since as "split-brain research." Later, Sperry and his associates extended this work to monkeys, observing them (once they had recovered from surgery) in ordinary sorts of situations, where, the researchers noted, the monkeys behaved quite normally.

It occurred to the researchers that, since the monkeys seemed to suffer no drastic alterations in their behavior or abilities, the procedure might be safely employed with human patients who suffered from intractable and debilitating epileptic seizures involving electrical discharges across the corpus callosum (which in humans is made up of about 200 million nerve fibers). If this bridge were severed, the discharges responsible for the seizures could not cross from the hemisphere in which they originated to the other one. In the late 1950s and early 1960s this procedure was carried out on a group of patients. The procedure was successful,

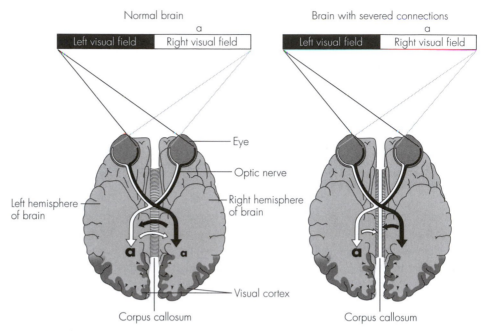

FIGURE 3.6 Diagram of Optic Crossover

allowing patients a more normal life than the seizures had permitted. The bonus to researchers was that systematic psychological testing of these patients after their recovery from the split-brain surgery provided a good deal of new information with regard to the functional specializations of the two hemispheres. It is for this research that Sperry won the Nobel Prize.

Consider the opportunity presented for research by the appearance on the scene of a group of people whose cerebral hemispheres had no means of communicating with one another. It meant that each hemisphere could be tested separately, without either "knowing" what the other was engaged in. Sperry, with his then student Michael Gazzaniga (a major figure today in this area) designed experiments to investigate the issue. In the now famous 1968 experiment, Sperry relied on the fact that objects seen to the left of a central fixation point (i.e., objects in the left visual field of each eye) are projected to the right cerebral hemisphere and that objects in the right visual field are projected to the left hemisphere. Figure 3.7 illustrates an apparatus used in split-brain research. In this experiment, he asked a subject (M. G.) to stare at a black dot in the center of a screen. Then, to either the right or the left of the dot, he flashed a picture of a spoon for less than a second. Sperry then asked the patient "What did you see?" When the picture appeared in the right visual field (and was thus transmitted to the left hemisphere), M. G. said she saw a spoon. But when the picture was flashed in the left visual field, which transmits to the right hemisphere, and M. G. was asked what she saw, she couldn't say. What an interesting result! How was it that one half of the brain could respond to the question and the other could not?

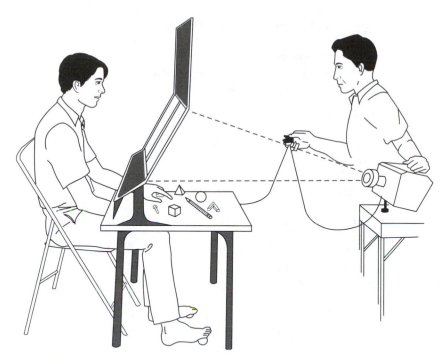

FIGURE 3.7 Diagram of Apparatus for Studying Lateralization of Visual, Tactual, Lingual, and Associated Functions in the Surgically Separated Hemispheres

Apparently what was happening was that the left hemisphere, already known to be involved in speech, on receiving information from the screen was able to convert that information immediately into speech. The right hemisphere, receiving the same information, was not able to process the information into speech. Did that mean that the right hemisphere did not *have* the information? To answer that question, Sperry hid objects such as a pencil and a key, as well as a spoon, behind a screen and asked the subject to touch them with her left hand. When he asked her "Which of these objects did you see before?" she chose the spoon. The information received by her left visual field, and sent to her right hemisphere, was indeed there; but her right hemisphere was not equipped to put that information into language.

Other experiments carried out by groups of researchers under Sperry's direction yielded similar results. The activity of the hemispheres is not symmetrical, and when the connection between them is severed, they no longer function together. Many everyday activities can be carried out without noticeable difference after such surgery, but the normal activity of the *mind* is altered in that the two hemispheres now function independently. Tests involving the auditory mode, for example, indicate the same outcome. Just as there is a "separate existence of two visual inner worlds" (Sperry, 1968, p. 725), so there appear to be two distinct auditory inner worlds, and so forth.

Interesting questions arise from these demonstrations. If our two separate brain hemispheres, which normally work together to give us our sense of consciousness, are disconnected, do we have two minds? Two types of awareness? Two consciousnesses? Sperry (1968) summarizes the situation as

> an apparent doubling in most of the realms of conscious awareness. Instead of the normally unified single stream of consciousness, these patients behave in many ways as if they have two independent streams of conscious awareness, one in each hemisphere, each of which is cut off from and out of contact with the mental experiences of the other. In other words, each hemisphere seems to have its own separate and private sensations; its own perceptions; its own concepts; and its own impulses to act, with related volitional, cognitive, and learning experiences. Following the surgery, each hemisphere also has thereafter its own separate chain of memories that are rendered inaccessible to the recall processes of the other. (p. 724)

Sperry recognized the significance of these findings not only for the neuroscientific world but also for our understanding of the nature of consciousness. This issue has long been a focus not only of that world and of the world of cognitive psychology but for philosophers as well. We have not yet really considered here the question of the nature of human consciousness, which is characterized by *self*-awareness, a feature perhaps not shared by other species. One is aware, for example, not only of what is occurring at the moment (such as the fact that one is reading a book on cognitive science), but in a flash one can also be aware of this awareness and aware of the awareness of this awareness. . . . I may think about what I am reading, then notice that I am thinking about it, then think about the fact that I am noticing that I am thinking about it—and then think about the fact that I am thinking about the fact that I am noticing that I am thinking about it! We have all experienced this sort of chain of awareness from time to time; this capacity has always been one of the mysteries of our make-up. The subject of human consciousness is a thread that winds through every aspect of our cognitive capacity; we will return to it when we consider the field of artificial intelligence and again when we turn our attention to the contribution of philosophy to cognitive science.

For now we continue with our account of some of the important research in the field of neuroscience that, following the path of development we have been tracing, has added much to our understanding of the functioning of the human brain. We have truly come a long way from notions such as those expounded by phrenologists in the 19th century and even from the first real evidence that specific areas in the brain control motor activity. We have been able to resolve some of the issues in the debate between the notion of localization of function—sparked by such evidence—and Lashley's principle of equipotentiality. We have even acquired understanding beyond that provided by later 20th century researchers such as the Nobel Prize winners Hubel, Wiesel, and Sperry.

The understanding we have achieved through the journey to this point has depended largely on intrusive techniques. In the case of experimental animals, these techniques involved interfering surgically with the brains of rats, cats, and monkeys, among others and, in the case of humans, using the opportunities provided when conditions such as epilepsy mandated treatment that involved exposing the brain.

Today we have added to our store of techniques some wonderful, new, very sophisticated methods for observing the living brain in action. We shall examine these in the next chapter.

Questions to Think About

1. If you suffered from neurological symptoms of a sort that caused your doctor to propose severing your corpus callosum, what concerns would you have in deciding whether to have the surgery? Are there functions or abilities you would fear losing?

2. Does it make sense to you that humans will be able someday to understand the brain by using it with great effectiveness? Or is that a logical impossibility in your view?

3. In your view, does the work of Hughlings-Jackson and Fritsch and Hitzig represent a real advance over the work of Gall and Spurzheim, or is the difference really just superficial? Explain your answer.

4. What is a principal advantage of research of the sort done by Fritsch and Hitzig over that of Hughlings-Jackson?

5. If it is true that the brains of men and women differ in aspects of brain structure, does this lead you to conclude that they differ as well in brain functioning? Why or why not?

6. How do you understand the similarities and differences in research techniques of physicians, biologists, and psychologists?

7. Given the fact that his subjects were rats, how persuasive is Lashley's support of the "theory which conceives intelligence as a general capacity"?

8. Does it seem to you that there is a conflict of interest for physicians who use their patients as research subjects? Were Bartholow and Penfield justified in what they did?

9. The text makes much of the theoretical importance of Hebb's work. Why are theories so important? What is their role in the work of science?

10. A split-brain patient cannot name an object exposed to her right hemisphere, but if she is asked to use her left hand, she can *write* the very name she cannot utter. How can you account for this?

4

Modern Technology and Research

As a rule, young children probably do not really enjoy shopping for shoes. They probably prefer running around in their old ones to sitting still while a salesperson brings out box after box and urges their feet into pair after pair of new and unfamiliar-feeling shoes. Eventually, though, after pressing the toes of the shoes to see how much room there is for comfort and for growth, the salesperson deems a pair to be the right size, the child deems it a satisfactory fit, and the parent deems it time to pay and go home.

When I was a small child, however, a visit to the shoe store held a special attraction for me. First of all, there was a viewing machine through which, as I turned a crank, I could watch a brief filmed story. But that pleasure paled beside the really exciting picture the salesperson would show me when my turn came to be fitted. As I stood on a platform, placing my newly shod feet in little foot diagrams outlined on it, a switch would be thrown, a light would go on, and *I would look down and see through the shoes, skin, and flesh of my feet to my very bones!* There they were, my toe bones, wiggling inside the stiff shoes. More exciting even than television, which was making its way into our neighborhood and later into our own living room, was this entrée into my own body.

I remember too another magic machine, this one in the doctor's office. If I stood quite still despite the cold of the plate being pressed against my chest, the doctor could see through it, through the barrier my skin presented to mere eyes—clear through to my skeleton. This magic machine and the one in the shoe store were **fluoroscopes.** They used invisible (and hence apparently magical) electromagnetic radiation, which today I know by the name of **X rays**, waves that penetrate the body and are absorbed to different degrees by different anatomical structures within it. The unabsorbed radiation passes through the body and registers on a photographic plate or, in the case of the fluoroscope, on a fluorescent screen. By virtue of the continuous flow of X rays through my feet or my chest, they provided a moving image of what was normally hidden from view.

The fluoroscope eventually disappeared from both shoe store and doctor's office because the continued exposure to radiation they required was found to be unsafe. Taking its place, at least for medical purposes, is the X ray we are now familiar with. We have all waited for the picture of a portion of our insides taken in a brief moment by the doctor's or dentist's machine and developed on the spot, the picture that will assist him or her to diagnose what ails our teeth or our shoulder or our lungs and to decide on the appropriate treatment—or, if we are lucky, to give us a clean bill of health. This very brief exposure to X rays is safer than the continuous exposure needed for the fluoroscope. But the static black and gray picture it produces does not evoke the excitement of that luminous green moving image of our own wiggling toe bones.

It is of course not only our teeth and our bones, and organs such as our lungs, that practitioners of the various fields of medicine and surgery examine. The pathways neurosurgeons now have into our brains yield information that contributes enormously to the practical goal of curing, or at least treating, what ails us. A significant bonus is that, in the process, we are approaching answers to some of the questions that have been asked for hundreds, for thousands, of years about what makes humans "tick."

In the preceding chapter we reviewed the major methods used in the past in following these pathways and some of the difficulties they presented. The mapping of the brain Penfield achieved, for example, with the aid of electrodes and cameras, could not be carried out on just anybody; it required patients whose brains were exposed in preparation for surgery. A researcher could not simply devise an experiment and have a ready population of, say, left-handers, female adolescents, non-Alzheimer's-afflicted senior citizens, or identical twins. The living brains that were studied at the time of surgical procedures belonged to all sorts of individuals with perhaps little in common save something amiss in their brains—that something differing as well from patient to patient. Very important, too, is the fact that patients with exposed brains are in a very restricted situation, unable for the moment to engage in ordinary activities such as reading a book, subtracting an expenditure from a checkbook balance, or trying to solve a problem. Furthermore, the information obtained, like a photograph—like the X ray—is frozen in time, unlike the moving view beneath the skin made possible by the fluoroscope. Examining the information reveals nothing of its dynamics.

The methods available today for peering into the living brain make possible many of the inquiries older methods precluded. It is now possible for researchers to present tasks to selected populations of healthy individuals as well as those in need of treatment, and to observe both the location and the intensity of activity in their brains as they carry out these tasks. The computer and other technological developments have made it possible to capture the brain in action. In this chapter we will examine the techniques and some representative examples of the many experiments that are contributing to our ability not only to treat various types of brain damage and disease but also (ultimately more significant, for our purposes at least) to approach a better understanding of the organ that distinguishes humans from all other species.

Brain Mapping: Structure Versus Function

From the time of Fritsch and Hitzig until the research of today, **brain mapping** has become more and more precise, and the effectiveness of the methods employed has been enhanced by developments in computer technology. An important goal of brain mapping is to achieve a three-dimensional map of the brain, as a globe is a three-dimensional rendition of the earth. But a geographic globe represents only what is on the surface, revealing nothing of the contents enclosed within that surface. Our map of the brain must represent both what lies on the surface and the structures within. Further, it must address not only the *structure* of the mechanism —where its components are located in space—but also the *functions* performed over time by the various components of that structure as they act and interact to receive and integrate information and to produce behavior.

Structural mapping of the brain by **electrophysiological** means yields information about the neural "hardware," that is, the connections that link one part of the brain to other parts and the principles according to which these links are ordered. A part of the system is stimulated, and a response (usually electrical activity) is recorded from another part of the neural circuit (Cheney, 1996). (Recall the electrical stimulation employed by Fritsch and Hitzig on dogs and by Penfield during the course of surgery on human patients.) This process allows the location of different functions to be mapped with great accuracy, because techniques are now available to tap the activity of individual neurons. The information about such locations is given in very fine detail. The process also permits the recording of extremely short-lived bits of activity, capturing changes so rapid they are countable in milliseconds (Cheney, 1996). As described in Chapter 3, this method lends itself particularly well to the mapping of sensory and motor locations. But because it is directed at individual cells of a vast system of neurons, it is a very time-consuming process. To put together a complete map, it may be necessary to observe the properties of thousands of thousands of neurons. Such sensory maps of the entire body surface have in fact been made, not of humans but of a particular species of monkey, by mapping areas in the brains of several individuals and then combining the maps (Figure 4.1).

This is not a practical procedure to employ with humans when the only brains available for mapping are those of patients on the operating table. The advantage to the method is of course the precision it allows, the clarity of the picture it yields. (There is an important point to bear in mind with regard to the usefulness of information gained from brains stimulated for purposes of study during surgery. The operations are performed because of abnormalities in the brain, such as epilepsy or brain tumors. Patients may have been suffering from the condition or tumor for a long time, and changes may therefore have occurred in their brains to compensate for the losses produced by the abnormality. These brains may thus not be representative of the normal condition [Mazziotta, 1996].)

Brain Mapping Techniques: Structural

Several methods for mapping the structure of the brain have been developed. These are described in the following sections.

X-Ray Techniques

The following are techniques that employ X-ray methodologies in exploring aspects of brain structure.

Cerebral Angiography   A method of imaging the living brain, called cerebral **angiography**, has been useful in detecting certain disorders associated with abnormalities in the arteries in the brain. If, for example, there is a malformation of one of these arteries, a **hemorrhage** (heavy bleeding) may occur, resulting in a

FIGURE 4.1 Brain of Monkey as
Mapped Following Systematic
Electrode Penetration

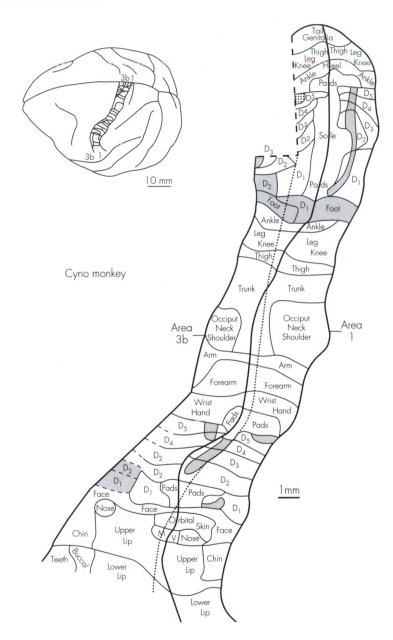

disrupted blood flow. When this happens, there is a loss of oxygen to the associated
area of the brain and hence damage to that area. In cerebral angiography, a dye
injected into the vertebral artery or the **carotid artery** in the neck is carried to the
arteries in the brain (Figure 4.2). Because the paths of these arteries reflect the
anatomy of the surrounding brain tissue, it is possible, using X rays of the skull, to
locate the malfunctioning artery and thus the damaged area (Gazzaniga, Ivry, &

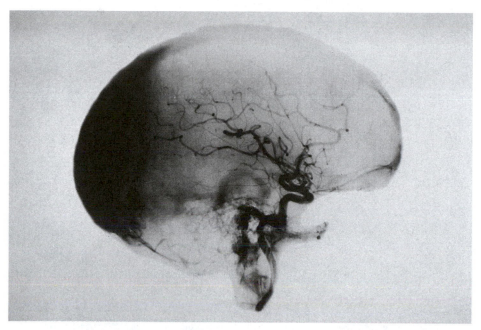

FIGURE 4.2 Angiogram. This type of image is useful in locating damaged arteries. This in turn allows the location of associated damaged brain areas.

Mangun, 1998; Springer & Deutsch, 1997). Techniques of brain mapping are very useful for such purposes.

Computed Tomography   For those of us whose experience of X-ray pictures is limited to the occasional examples we see when we visit the dentist or doctor, it may seem almost like magic that he or she is able readily to identify the elements in it, such as the bone—and the place on it—that require treatment. To the untrained, the picture is blurry, the shadows of structures above and beneath it providing too much interference for us to recognize what we are looking at. The blurring oc- curs because the picture we are seeing is a two-dimensional rendition of a three- dimensional body. In order to eliminate the visual "noise" surrounding the portion we wish to image, that one plane, or "slice," is the one in focus, while the surround- ing structures are blurred. To obtain the whole picture, we would have to X-ray many such slices, exposing the patient to the full dose of radiation for each one.

Computer Axial Tomography (CAT)   In the early 1970s a procedure called **axial tomography** was developed. A fan-shaped X-ray beam is rotated around a single cross section, or slice, exposing the body to much less radiation than traditional X rays. The word *tomography* was coined from the Greek *tomos* "cut" or "section" and *graphein* "to write"; it simply means "representation of a section," and a *tomograph* is an image slice through an organ, without the interference of all the layers of tissue present in X-ray images. Like any other procedure for imaging the

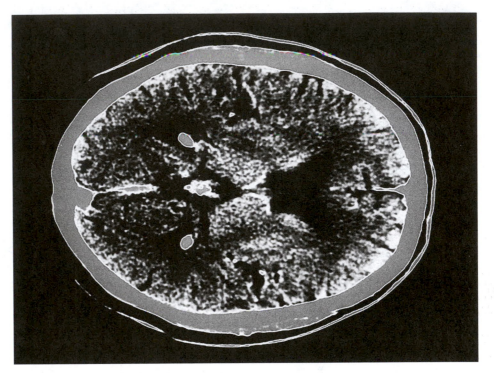

FIGURE 4.3 CAT Image of a Human Brain

body internally, tomography has its blurring problems, but computer technology was developed at the time that made it possible both to "deblur" the picture and to reconstruct a complete image from the multiple views provided by the rotating beam. The procedure is called **computer axial tomography**—familiarly, "**CAT** scan." It has been used primarily to image bone; further developments lent themselves more readily to the imaging of organs, such as the liver—and the brain (Figure 4.3)—which are made of soft tissue. But with the development of computer axial tomography, the process of imaging internal structures was becoming safer, more precise—and, equally important, three-dimensional.

Magnetic Resonance Imaging (MRI)

In the mid-1980s a new method of **neuroimaging** came on the scene. Called **magnetic resonance imaging**, or **MRI**, this technique makes use of the fact that, in the presence of a magnetic field, many atoms behave like little bar magnets. These atoms can be lined up in much the same way as the needle of a compass lines up in the earth's magnetic field. If radio-wave pulses are applied to atoms that are lined up in this fashion, detectable radio signals are emitted that differ according to the particular atoms involved and their chemical environment. For purposes of imaging human anatomy, researchers use protons, of which there are very many in the human body. Using the radio signals emitted by these protons, MRI provides more detailed information than that resulting from CAT scans, without subjecting the body to the radioactivity of X rays or introducing into the body **radioactive isotopes** (atoms emitting radiation) as is done with the technique known as PET, discussed later in this chapter (Posner & Raichle, 1994).

Although there is no evidence that there are long-term effects of the MRI procedure, it is not without effect on the body:

> The MRI is for all intents and purposes a mild microwave. You create an electromagnetic field that vibrates every cell—actually every molecule—in your body, and a radio-like receiver measures the amount of vibrations. This magnet is so powerful that they [the medical center] had to move the MRI imaging center back from the road that it was near because during use it was causing semis to swerve toward the edge of the road. . . . My subjects who had nose studs and eyebrow rings that could not be removed couldn't participate due to the metal arcing. [This indicates] the degree to which this machine puts your whole body into a level of resonance. (J. Alexander, personal communication, August 30, 1999)

The reader may know from experience, or may have heard through reports of friends who have undergone MRI, that as the procedure is carried out the subject is ordinarily required to lie quite still, in a rather narrow tube. The process is painless, but subjects who experience a claustrophobic reaction to being in a small space may find the confinement disconcerting. (Recently, centers specializing in MRI have begun to offer "open MRI," using a less confining apparatus, to reduce stress for such subjects.) In any case, for most subjects—and certainly for the neurologist treating patients and the researcher seeking to comprehend the brain—the results are well worth the discomfort. In addition to the fact that there is no need to inject a radioactive substance into the subject's body, the resolution of the image is much sharper. On the other hand, the MRI technique is slow, so an image generated at a given time will depict a situation that is no longer precisely as it was at the time of the imaging.

There is, however, another important advantage to the MRI technique: its flexibility. It is possible to use different sequences of pulses to image different types of biological substances. That is, MRI allows the researcher to distinguish among, for instance, the gray matter, the white matter, and the **cerebrospinal fluid** that fills in the cavities in the brain so that any of these can be examined without interference from the others. Unlike CAT, which provides images of tissue that can be clouded by nearby bone, the image yielded by MRI is clear, as Figure 4.4 illustrates (Krasuski, Horwitz, & Rumsey, 1996).

Brain Mapping Techniques: Functional

Functional mapping reveals where reactions are taking place in the brain as parts of the body move or external events such as a light in the visual field affect it (Cheney, 1996). Although this type of mapping does not provide the high resolution provided by techniques that record the activity of specific neurons, ideally it

FIGURE 4.4 Image of Human Brain Obtained with Magnetic Resonance Imaging (MRI)

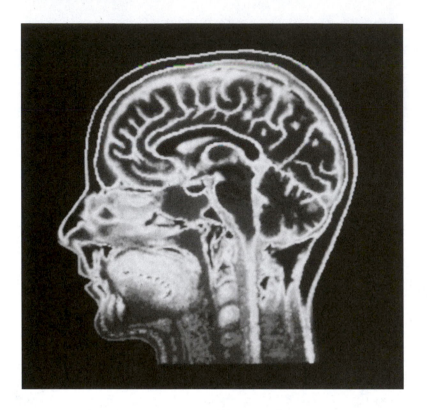

has the advantage of providing a complete picture of the brain, and it allows the identification of regions involved in particular functions, such as reading or solving a problem. Functional brain mapping is a major direction being taken by contemporary neuroscientific research. In this section, we will examine briefly the major tools currently used to advance this research.

Electrophysiological Techniques

Among the functional brain mapping techniques are several that employ electrophysiological methods. We will look at each of these in turn.

Electroencephalography   In 1929 an important paper was published in Jena, Germany, by the neurologist and psychologist Hans Berger (1873–1941). It was the first of a series describing a new technique for imaging the activity in the brain. The technique, called **electroencephalography**, involves first attaching electrodes to the scalp with a paste or liquid that enhances the conducting of electricity. Then the changes in voltage from each electrode are amplified and recorded as line tracings on paper. These tracings, called **electroencephalograms**, or **EEGs**, are recordings of patterns of electrical activity in the brain. They give a fine-tuned reading of rapidly occurring changes, which MRI cannot do because it is too slow.

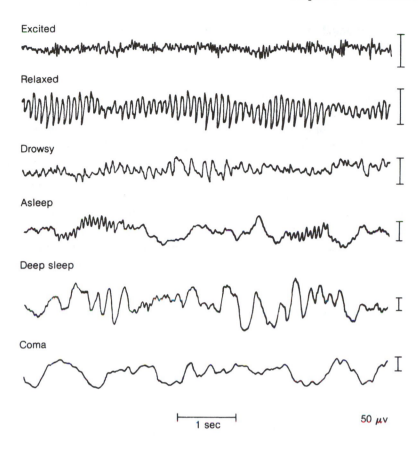

Excited

Relaxed

Drowsy

Asleep

Deep sleep

Coma

1 sec

50 μv

FIGURE 4.5 Characteristic EEG Recording During Various Behavioral States in Humans

Berger's series of papers described "nearly all the main EEG findings of cerebral diseases and the EEG alterations of normal subjects during attention, sleep, and **narcosis** [deep unconsciousness]" (Jung & Berger, 1979, p. 279). His innovation "increased the range of diagnostic techniques available for a series of brain diseases and revolutionized the study of epilepsy. . . . It remains an indispensable instrument of neurophysiological diagnosis, especially in its capacity as a 'seismograph' of the brain" (Karbowski, 1990, p. 170).

A major advantage of electroencephalography, in addition to its ability to trace rapid changes in neural activity, is that it does not rely on the risky, invasive surgical exposure of the brain that previous work, such as Penfield's, required. In addition to avoiding the risks inherent in the surgical procedure, another significant advantage of this method is that it can be used to record activation in the brains of people who are *fully conscious* and engaged in various activities in a natural environment (Gevins, 1996). See Figure 4.5.

While appreciating the noninvasiveness of the technique, it is important to be aware that the "invasiveness" of a procedure is relative. Any substance that is applied to the body or introduced into the system may have its effects on that system, and the disturbance thus produced may affect the validity of the data to some degree. This is but one of the many factors that researchers take into consideration when designing their experiments and evaluating their data (Mazziotta, 1996).

Along with the advantages of EEGs, there are also certain disadvantages. One is that a certain amount of "noise"—interference from the subject's movements or even heartbeats, for example, or from the equipment itself—can blur the reading, and methods must be devised to correct or eliminate such interference. Another difficulty is that since the sampling is taken at sites only on the surface, the electrical activity occurring below cannot be determined directly. Furthermore, because the technique has been used largely for detecting the site of malfunctions in the brains of patients, in most cases electrodes have been attached at a relatively small number of sites spread on the scalp. These are generally enough to detect signs of such malfunctions, which often originate in specific areas. But the complex human cognitive processes such as remembering, using language, and thinking in general depend on the activity of hundreds of thousands of neural connections, spread out over many areas. Therefore, we need a picture of the brain with much higher resolution in order to capture its activity during these processes. It has recently become possible to attach, instead of single widely spaced electrodes, high-density electrode arrays. The resulting images may then be enhanced by means of computer processing so that the amount of detail available for study is increased. This means of recording activity in the brain is, therefore, becoming more useful, especially when combined with more recent neuroimaging techniques (Gevins, 1996).

Event-Related Potentials (ERPs)   I mentioned that interference from a variety of sources can blur the EEG reading. This difficulty has been largely resolved by the introduction of another technique, the use of what used to be called "evoked potentials," or EPs, now more accurately referred to as **event-related potentials**, or **ERPs**. The technique, illustrated in Figure 4.6, works roughly as follows. During the process of obtaining an EEG from a human subject, researchers can present the subject with a stimulus, for example, a sound. A specific period can be established around the stimulus, say, 100 milliseconds (ms) before the onset of the stimulus to 1000 ms after it ends. Voltage changes recorded during this period that are specifically related to the brain's response to the event constitute the event-related potential, the ERP (Coles & Rugg, 1995).

The voltage changes are typically very small in relation to the EEG **waveform** in which they are embedded. Therefore, the signal has to be extracted from the noise around it. This is done by recording a number of repetitions of the event, keeping the time period in which it occurs the same over all repetitions. The EEG values obtained in this way are then averaged. Unrelated EEG activity forms the "background" against which the ERP signal must be detected. This activity is assumed to vary randomly across the time periods, tending to average to zero. That is, the noise fluctuations vary in different directions and tend to neutralize each other. Therefore, what is left should be largely the activity representing the ERP (Coles & Rugg, 1995). The responses evoked by stimuli in ERP studies provide a precise record of the underlying neural activity. The evoked response provides a picture of neural activity changing over time as the brain processes information.

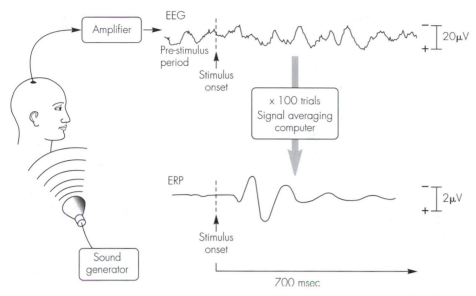

FIGURE 4.6 Event-Related Potential. The diagram indicates the process, beginning with the presentation of a sound stimulus. Next, recordings are made of the voltage changes related to the brain's responses to the stimulus; these are then averaged over 100 trials.

Neural activity is very rapid. The advantage of EEG/ERP is that it is capable of the speed needed to capture and record this activity. Best of all would be a technique combining this capability with the spatial resolution provided by, for example, MRI.

Blood-Flow Techniques

In addition to the electrophysiological techniques just described, blood-flow techniques have been developed. We examine these next.

Positron Emission Tomography (PET)   Earlier we examined the structural imaging technique known as computer axial tomography, or CAT. In the 1980s another tomographic technique for imaging body structures was developed. **Positron emission tomography,** or **PET,** is a method of measuring cerebral blood flow while a subject is carrying out certain cognitive tasks. It makes use not of X rays but of radioactive isotopes—in this case, positrons. These are incorporated into tracer molecules of various sorts and injected into the body, where they are carried along with the blood to the brain. Like the other types of brain imaging, PET scans present their own requirements and their own difficulties.

A requirement of this type of imaging is that a **cyclotron,** a very expensive piece of equipment, be available to provide the radioactive isotopes used in the procedure. Because these cannot be stored for long periods, they must be produced each day. A difficulty involved in this procedure is that the images it produces,

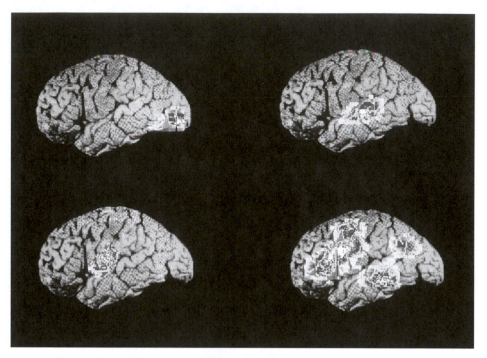

FIGURE 4.7 Left-Hemisphere Images, Showing the Results of a Hierarchical Series of PET Scans of Regional Cerebral Blood Flow

like those of X-ray images, are somewhat blurred. They can, however, be made more accurate by comparing successive scans so that blood-flow activity in the brain can be pinpointed within a range of a few millimeters. This is very useful information because, when people are engaged in the cognitive tasks that characterize their thinking, visualizing, reading, and so on, the blood-flow activity in their brains increases in the specific areas involved in those tasks (Figure 4.7). PET scans are not, however, as sensitive to changes over milliseconds as are the electrophysiological techniques described earlier, so they are not as precise as one might wish for use in analyzing those cognitive tasks that involve changes within a span of milliseconds. Combining the two sorts of studies provides a better picture than does either one alone (Krasuski et al., 1996; Posner & Rothbart, 1994).

In the early days of PET, most subjects were studied at rest. In some studies subjects' eyes were covered and in some they were uncovered; in some studies subjects' ears were plugged and in some they were not. In all of the early studies, subjects were placed in a quiet, dark room so that there would be as little interference from sensory stimulation as possible. Today, many PET studies involve tasks that depend on cognitive activity, such as listening to musical pitches or looking at written musical notes. Researchers learn in this way about the functions of various brain regions and how they interact in complex networks. When subjects are not so stimulated, these brain regions and interactions may not be active (Krasuski et al., 1996).

Single Photon Emission Computed Tomography (SPECT)   Somewhat earlier, in the 1950s and 1960s, another tomographic technique for imaging body structures had been developed: **single photon emission computed tomography**, or, more simply, **SPECT**. As with PET, this technique relies on introducing into the bloodstream a radioactive entity that can be traced; in the case of SPECT, the entity that makes this possible is the photon rather than the positron used in PET. Certain biochemicals are labeled with radioactive compounds that are injected into or inhaled by subjects. These enter the bloodstream and make their way to the brain, where, as they decay, they emit the high-energy photons (Purves et al., 1997). Detectors that have been placed or rotated around the head of a subject pick up the emissions. Computer programs then

> "reconstruct" what the distribution of the labeled substance must have been to generate the pattern of emissions sensed by the detectors. So far, SPECT procedures have been used to measure cerebral blood flow and blood volume in three-dimensional cross sections of the brain. (Springer & Deutsch, 1997, p. 67)

An advantage of this technique is that it allows investigators to "lock in" the brain activity state at the time the labeled substance is introduced into the body. So, for example, it becomes possible to capture the blood flow during an epileptic seizure by injecting the substance during the seizure and scanning the patient later. From the scans, it is possible to detect the place in the brain where the seizure started, as shown in Figure 4.8 (Springer & Deutsch, 1997). It is also possible to discover the location of activity in the brain when a subject is engaged in a particular mental exercise, such as a memory task.

Another advantage of SPECT imaging is that, although not as flexible or accurate as PET imaging, it can use commercially available **radioprobes**. Thus there is no need for an expensive on-site cyclotron, as with PET (Purves et al., 1997).

Functional Magnetic Resonance Imaging (fMRI)   Since the development of structural MRI, the techniques involved in this method of brain mapping have been modified so that, in addition to information about brain *structures,* it can provide information about brain *function.* Because of this capability, the technique is now generally referred to as **functional magnetic resonance imaging**, or **fMRI**. Functional MRI—also known as real-time or dynamic MRI—became available in the 1990s. It uses MRI scanners with fast imaging techniques to detect the changes occurring in the magnetic state of the blood. These changes depend on the amount of oxygen in the blood flowing to activated tissues of the brain. As subjects perform various tasks involving memory, mental imagery, calculation, and so forth, the imaging equipment registers changes in oxygen level and blood flow in various locations in their brains. The images it provides of these changes allow researchers to infer which locations are involved in specific activities.

The development of fMRI contributed greatly to progress in neuroscience in the 1990s, the "decade of the brain," and was a major factor in the establishment, in 1995, of an annual International Conference on Functional Mapping of the Human Brain. Researchers from all over the world come to this conference, held in

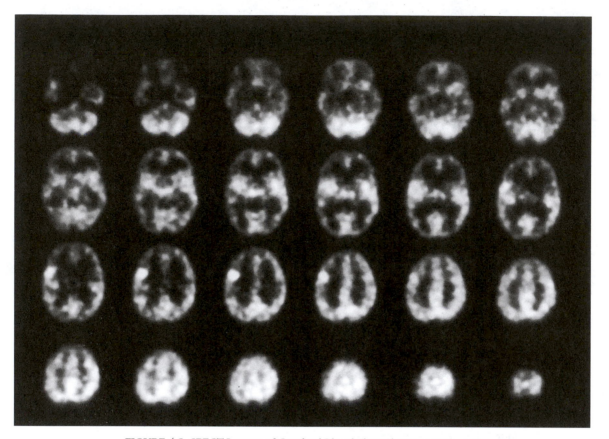

FIGURE 4.8 SPECT Images of Cerebral Blood Flow Showing Seizure Onset

a different country each year. They present results of research they have been conducting using the various methods of brain imaging, and they learn about the findings of those in other areas of research. The mood of these meetings is one of tremendous excitement, as participants sense that they are in the midst of an explosion of knowledge that promises greater understanding of ourselves as human beings than has ever before been possible. In a speech at the 1997 Functional Mapping Conference in Copenhagen, Denmark, Endel Tulving, a leading authority on human memory function, summed up his expectations for the future in this regard. Given current methods and anticipated improvements in sophistication of technologies to come, he predicted that "the sky's the limit—the next five years will be unbelievable!"

Many of the aspects of human cognition discussed in the preceding chapters are being explored via the imaging technologies I have described. In the next section of *this* chapter, we will look at some of the research that has employed these technologies and at what the results tell us about the areas of the brain involved in very specific types of behavior.

Brain Mapping Research

Literally thousands of studies have been carried out making use of the various techniques of brain mapping we have been reviewing. Before looking at some representative examples, we should note that each technique measures a very specific activity: electrical, oxygenation, blood flow, or glucose. Some techniques have the advantage of rapid sampling of neuronal activity but poor spatial resolution (EEG/ERP), and some, much slower, have better spatial resolution (MRI, fMRI). Another point to bear in mind is that when an individual performs a cognitive task (perhaps a memorization task or a math problem) many cognitive behaviors are invoked. Thus while we are—justifiably—congratulating ourselves on the long way we have come in developing neuroimaging techniques, we must also recognize that the scanning procedures we have developed do not report the associated behavior in as much detail as we could wish:

> Having someone . . . do math problems nonstop for five minutes during a scan is not a good enough piece of behavioral evidence. Too many cognitive behaviors come together during [such a] gross behavioral task to allow us to conclude much of anything! (J. Alexander, personal communication, August 30, 1999)

Having noted these points, let us look at some examples of the research that has been conducted in recent years making use of the new techniques.

Language

Of all the human cognitive functions, conscious and unconscious, in which we humans engage—those involved in, for example, thinking, remembering, solving problems, playing games, seeing, hearing, dreaming, speaking—language is perhaps the most accessible to us. It surrounds us; we engage in it constantly and overtly. It comes as no surprise, then, that many of us wonder about what is really involved in the process as our brains produce and understand language. In the next unit we will examine something of its structure and some of the ways researchers have studied its development in babies and children as they acquire language or fail to do so. We will see some of the effects on language of damage to the brain and, stemming from these, some early hypotheses as to its "location" in the brain. At this point let us look at some of the kinds of evidence regarding the language function that have recently been gleaned from experiments using the imaging techniques we have been discussing.

The issues neuroscientists are addressing in this domain run the gamut from brain activity during speaking to the way words and their meanings are accessed in the brain during reading; from the effects on the brain of language training after a stroke to sex differences in the way the brain is organized for language. For example, in the April 1998 issue of *Trends in Cognitive Sciences* (one of the newer journals designed to provide a forum for the information now accumulating so rapidly), researchers report that the neural organization of language is quite similar for language learned in the ordinary way—through hearing and speaking it—and for signed language acquired by deaf individuals. The evidence comes from experiments involving aphasia in signers (Hickok, Bellugi, & Klima, 1998).

Recall Broca's and Wernicke's 19th-century findings that loss of speech function and loss of comprehension function resulted from damage to the lower back part of the left frontal lobe and the upper back part of the left temporal lobe, respectively—the areas commonly referred to as **Broca's area** and **Wernicke's area**. Although we know today that locating the language function in the brain is not as simple as it then seemed, we can ask whether Broca's area plays a role in the production of sign language as well as of spoken language. Of course the first step must be to determine whether Broca's hypothesis is supported by evidence from imaging studies. To this end, researchers obtained fMRI images of the neural activity occurring in non-brain-damaged hearing speakers of English as they read English sentences and in deaf signers as they viewed **American Sign Language (ASL)** sentences. These images indicate that Broca's area, and Wernicke's area as well, are indeed involved in such activity, though they are not the *only* ones (Figure 4.9). Broca's and Wernicke's 19th-century hypotheses were based on examination *after death* of the damaged brains of individuals who had while living exhibited certain language deficits. Their hypotheses *are* supported by evidence gathered from 20th-century fMRI of *living* subjects engaged in speaking or signing respectively (Bavelier et al., 1998).

In another fMRI experiment, in which deaf native users of ASL (those for whom ASL is a first language) were asked to produce ASL signs, the results were similar: Subjects did exhibit activation in Broca's area during this task. Interestingly, in another fMRI study, researchers also found neural activation in Broca's area in deaf native signers when they *perceived* ASL sentences. This evidence contradicts the 19th-century assumption that Broca's area involved only speech *production* (Hickok et al., 1998).

Whether subjects used spoken English or ASL in these studies, researchers were addressing a question involving their use of only one language. But linguists and cognitive psychologists have long been interested in the situation in which an individual speaks two languages (such a person is known as a **bilingual**) or more than two languages (a **polyglot**). A question they ask is whether the languages of such a person involve the same or different areas of the brain. Because it has been observed that occasionally a bilingual or polyglot who has suffered brain damage will exhibit aphasia in only one language (Paradis, 1995), it may be inferred that different areas are involved in each language. Experiments using electrical stimulation of the cortex have also suggested that this is the case. Yet the picture that emerged was unclear; results of earlier brain imaging studies produced varying results. Now that fMRI is available, researchers can use it to help clarify the issue.

In fact, Dehaene et al. (1997) have done just that in a study involving 8 male students, all of them native speakers of French who had learned English after the age of 7 and who were not very proficient in it. A native speaker of French read short stories to them in French; a native speaker of English did the same using stories in English. The results coincided with those of the PET studies, confirming that understanding one's native language

English: Hearing

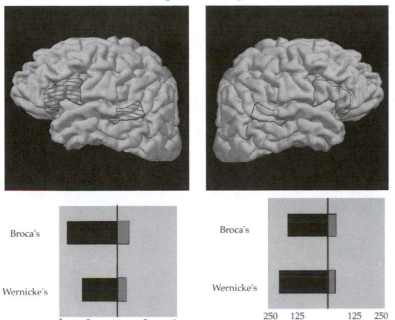

FIGURE 4.9 Average fMRIs indicate that Broca's and Wernicke's areas are much involved in language activity in deaf signers as well as in hearers.

American Sign Language: Deaf

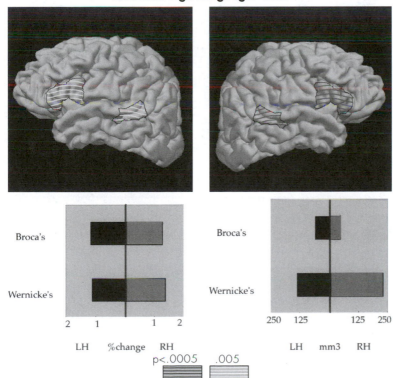

relies on a reproducible cerebral network, mostly in the left temporal lobe. Listening to [the second language], however, activated widely different areas for different subjects, suggesting that in late learners with low proficiency, the primary language network ceases to be available for acquiring a second language. (Dehaene et al., 1997, p. 57)

Another issue that has interested cognitive scientists is that of **brain plasticity**. Think of the boy described early in Chapter 3, who, seemingly miraculously, regained language fluency after surgical removal of his malfunctioning left cerebral hemisphere. His accomplishment makes it clear that the right hemisphere can, if necessary, perform tasks it was not initially required—or slated—to do. Following another path, the issue of brain plasticity was recently investigated by means of PET imaging (Musso et al., 1997). In this study, the subjects were 23 German-speaking patients, each of whom had suffered a stroke resulting in **Wernicke's aphasia** (that form of aphasia in which patients' language may sound fluent, but it lacks meaning). The researchers provided rehabilitation training to improve the subjects' language ability. Their hypothesis was that since the lesion was in the left hemisphere, improvement during this training would involve activation in the right hemisphere. They found that in Wernicke's aphasia patients, "even short-term training improves language comprehension" and that "specific training leads to a shift from left hemisphere to homologous [corresponding] right hemisphere language zones, corresponding to a measurable improvement of lost language function" (Musso et al., 1997, p. 60).

Not only do these findings have implications for our greater understanding of brain functions and brain capabilities, but they can also lead to practical benefits. If up to now clinicians and therapists have inferred from patients' behavior the usefulness of language training after stroke, at this point there is evidence from neuroimaging studies that whatever degree of success patients achieve in regaining language results from actual changes in the brain. This confirmation that training is warranted, and that it can produce valuable results, is encouraging news for patients and for those who care for and about them.

A final example in the domain of language will help to illustrate the different kinds of information researchers are seeking by means of the new brain imaging techniques. The issue in question concerns the processing in the brain of different types of words—in this instance, concrete nouns and so-called function words. These are words that do not themselves have a meaning in the sense that a noun or a verb does but that derive their meaning from the functions they perform in sentences (words that sequence, such as *and* and *or,* and words that link, such as *from* and *to*). They are the words performing the grammatical task of "tying a sentence together." The question is whether different regions of the brain are involved in processing words with concrete meaning (which presumably have rich semantic and perhaps visual representations and many associations in the brain) and words whose function is, rather, grammatical.

The researchers obtained fMRI images spanning most of the cerebrum during tasks addressed to processing word meanings and also tasks that focused on the sounds of the subjects' language (English) and their **articulation** (the way in which the vocal organs produce the sounds). The areas of activation observed on the images when subjects were identifying the concrete nouns were similar to those found in the earlier tasks focusing on meaning. The brain regions involved in identifying function words were consistent with those imaged in the tasks emphasizing the speech sounds and their articulation (Nobre, Price, Turner, & Friston, 1997). Studies like this one provide information about which areas of the brain are involved in very specific aspects of language. The situation is complex, but answers are coming in.

Memory

Understanding memory function is crucial to understanding all the other cognitive functions, because they all rest on it. In an earlier chapter we noted some of the hypotheses proposed by cognitive psychologists concerning the structure of memory. We saw that examination of behaviors dependent on memory led to concepts such as short-term or working memory and long-term memory. Described next are some of the imaging experiments that have been carried out to investigate these hypotheses—to determine whether different brain regions are in fact activated when people work at tasks designed to call on the different components of memory that researchers have postulated.

Working Memory   It has been known for some time, from the results of injury to the medial-temporal lobe, that this area of the brain is essential to memory, specifically to working memory—that is, to those functions that enable us to process new events and facts. Damage to this area makes it impossible for an individual to remember new information. In April 1997, a study was reported that sought to determine whether different portions of the medial-temporal lobe are active in the functioning of various types of working memory (Gabrieli, Brewer, Desmond, & Glover, 1997). Six non-brain-damaged individuals served as volunteer subjects in an experiment that required them to perform two memory tasks. The first was a retrieval task in which the subjects were shown achromatic (black-and-white) line drawings of common objects and animals and asked to remember them. Then, during fMRI scanning of their brains, they were shown words in two different conditions. In one condition, the words consisted mostly of names of the line drawings they had seen; in the other condition, the words consisted mostly of names of drawings they had *not* seen. Their task was to judge whether each word was or was not the name of one of the drawings they had seen.

The second task was an encoding task, that is, a task involving the entering of information into memory. The subjects in this experiment were shown, during scanning, color pictures of complex indoor and outdoor scenes. They were asked to judge whether each depicted an indoor scene or an outdoor scene and to remember the pictures for a memory test later. Here again there were two conditions: In one, subjects saw pictures for the first time, and in the other they saw the same pictures over and over. In this way, it was possible to contrast fMRI images of the encoding into memory of new scenes with the encoding of familiar ones.

The object of the experiment was not to see how well the subjects performed these tasks. (Neuroimaging would not be necessary for that.) Rather, it was to determine which areas of the brain were active during the retrieval and encoding processes. An interesting fact about human brains is, of course, that no two are identical. Therefore, it came as no surprise to these researchers that the findings were not identical for all the subjects. However, 5 of the 6 did show greater activation in a particular location in the front portion of the middle of the temporal lobe when viewing words that named drawings they had studied, as opposed to words that named drawings they hadn't seen before. Five of the 6 subjects also showed greater activation in a particular location in the *posterior* (rear) medial-temporal lobe when they were encoding new pictures than when they were encoding familiar ones. In both cases the activation in the particular locations occurred in both hemispheres of the brain.

By means of these tests, and others of a similar nature that confirmed the results, the researchers were able to show quite clearly that these two distinct functions of working memory are performed in different locations within the area of the brain with which working memory has been associated (Gabrieli et al., 1997). Figure 4.10 shows the locations of eight "slices" of the brain, each of which yielded an image of that particular cross section. The bracketed lines indicate those regions where activity involved in retrieval and encoding occurs.

Clues to areas of the brain likely to be involved in specific functions are gleaned from research on those functions in monkeys. For example, if an area in monkeys' brains can be shown to be involved in a particular aspect of working memory, such as memory for faces or memory for location of objects in space, then it makes sense to look for activity in analogous areas in the brains of human subjects as they perform tasks involving those functions. That is, in fact, what a team of researchers did recently. Courtney et al. (1998) used fMRI scanning to study an area of the human prefrontal cortex that in monkeys has been implicated in working memory for spatial locations. They also examined an adjacent area that in monkeys had been shown to be activated when calling on their working memory for patterns, colors, objects, and faces.

In this study the researchers used several criteria to determine whether the superior (upper) **frontal sulcus** (a groove between the frontal lobes of the brain) has a role in spatial working memory. One criterion was that the area must show sustained activity while spatial working memory was being employed; a second was that this activity must be greater during this time than during other kinds of working memory tasks. The task that was used involved working memory for faces. Functional MRI scans were obtained while the subjects in this experiment looked at a series of three faces for 2 seconds each, then waited during a 9-second delay, after which they saw a single face in a particular location. In some tests they were to remember the *locations* of the faces on the screen; in other tests they were to try to remember the *identities* of the faces. After viewing the initial set, they waited through the 9-second delay. Then the test face was pre-

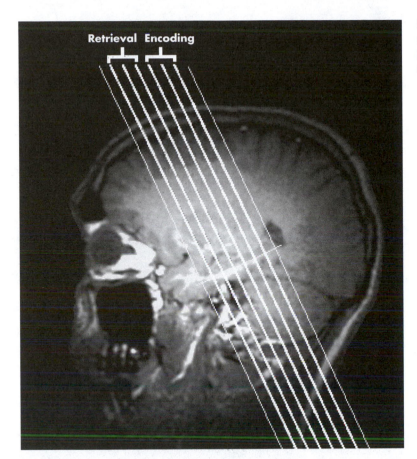

Retrieval Encoding

FIGURE 4.10 Lines Indicating the Cross Sections of the Brain Shown by fMRI to Be Active in Retrieval and Encoding

sented to them. For the *spatial memory test,* they were to press a button indicating whether the test face was in the same location as one of the three faces in the memory set. For the *face memory test,* they were asked to press a button indicating whether the test face was the same as one of the three they had seen in the memory set.

The result was clear: All the subjects showed continued activity in the dorsal (upper) frontal cortex during the 9-second delay in the spatial working memory test. During the face working memory test, on the other hand, the activity was more in the left inferior (lower) frontal cortex. The different regions involved in these two memory tasks indicate that the working memory area is not just a generalized one. Rather, different sorts of working memory processes call for quite specific regions (Courtney et al., 1998). See Figure 4.11 for an illustration of the regions involved in spatial and face working memory.

PET—The Role of the Hippocampus   In another experiment aimed at discovering the role of different areas of the brain in memory, the scanning technique used

FIGURE 4.11 Areas Specialized for Spatial and Face Working Memory in Human Frontal Cortex

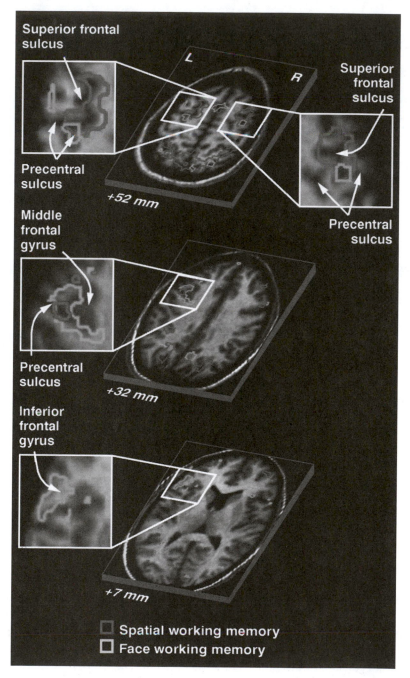

was not fMRI but PET (Schacter, Alpert, Savage, Rauch, & Albert, 1996). In this study, researchers focused on the **hippocampus**, a region in the temporal lobe that has been associated with memory. They examined the role of the hippocampus in both explicit and implicit memory of events—i.e., recollection that is conscious and recollection that is not conscious. Volunteers were asked to study a list of familiar words under conditions that would make it either easy or difficult for them to remember them. In one condition 20 words were presented four times each, and the subjects were asked for judgments about their *meanings*. (They were asked to count the number of meanings associated with each word. The assumption that associating meaning with list items makes them easier to recall is based on results of many experiments.) In the other condition 20 words were presented only once, and the subjects were asked for judgments about their *appearance*. (They were asked to count the number of times the horizontal line crosses the vertical in the letter *t*, a task that distracts attention from the words of which the *t* is a part). The first condition was referred to as High Recall, and the second as Low Recall.

The subjects were then given three-letter word beginnings. For each they were asked either to respond with the first word that came to mind beginning with those three letters, or to try specifically to recall the word on the list that began with those letters. The first of these tasks addressed **implicit** memory, memory for what they were not at the moment conscious of. The second addressed **explicit** memory, memory for what they were conscious of because they had been studying it.

PET images were obtained as the subjects carried out the tasks. The results indicated first of all that the hippocampus was not activated during implicit memory tasks—that is, when the subjects were to respond with whatever word they thought of first that began with those three letters. If you were given the letters *str,* you might think of *street, strength, strike, straight,* and so on. This task would involve words you had stored but were not at the moment consciously thinking of. The results of this study indicate that the hippocampus is *not* involved in retrieval of one of these words. With regard to explicit memory, when the subjects were to think of a *particular* word they had studied beginning with three letters, in the High Recall condition blood-flow increases *were* observed in the hippocampal region. When the subjects were trying to recall words that had been presented in the Low Recall condition, a task that requires greater effort, blood-flow increases were observed in the frontal regions but not in the hippocampal region (Schacter et al., 1996). Figure 4.12 shows the areas of activation involved in these different conditions.

Results of this study suggest several possibilities. One is that studying (or "priming," as discussed in Chapter 2) is carried out in regions other than the hippocampus, depending instead "on brain systems involved with the perceptual representation of words and objects" (Schacter et al., 1998, p. 324). Another possibility is that activation within the hippocampus is associated more with the actual recollection of an event than with the effort involved in trying to remember it. The researchers point out that in addition to information about the role of the hippocampus in memory, their results also provide information about the prefrontal cortex. This area seems to play a significant role in explicit memory—the conscious effort to retrieve information about a past event. A complete understanding of the role of the various regions in the brain is still far off, but studies such as this contribute important pieces to the puzzle.

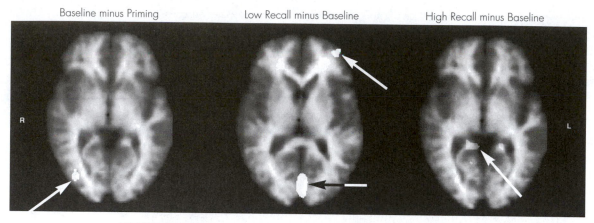

FIGURE 4.12 PET Statistical Maps Showing Territories of Activation Superimposed Over Averaged Magnetic Resonance Images. The Baseline minus Priming image shows a region of significantly decreased blood flow associated with priming in right visual association cortex. The Low Recall minus Baseline image shows regions of significantly increased blood flow associated with high effort and low explicit recall (35% accuracy) in the left prefrontal cortex and secondary visual cortex. The High Recall minus Baseline image shows regions of significantly increased blood flow associated with high levels of explicit recall (79% accuracy) in bilateral hippocampal regions.

In a 1997 fMRI study (Cohen et al., 1997), researchers examined brain activation during a working memory task that was designed to reveal whether the *amount* of memory load (information that must be remembered) affects which areas are involved. A series of memory tasks was presented to 10 volunteers. In some cases they had to decide whether a letter they were shown was the same as the preceding one. In other cases the issue was whether it was the same as a letter two or three back from the preceding one. In this way brain activation could be scanned under different conditions of memory load. (More is required of memory when we must keep two or three letters in mind than when we need remember only one.) The results provided evidence supporting the researchers' prediction (Figure 4.13). There was greater activation at higher levels of load. Also supported was their prediction that the areas involved would be of two types: Those involved in actively maintaining memory show continuing activation; areas having to do with time-limited processes, such as decision processes and updating the contents of working memory, are activated only briefly. But the activation reaches higher levels and lasts longer if the memory load is higher.

Long-Term Memory   Lest the reader assume that working memory is the only type of memory of interest to researchers, consider a 1997 study that used PET to study an aspect of *long-term* memory, in this case, long-term memory related to vision (Rosier et al., 1997). Twelve volunteers participated in this experiment. Long-term visual memory performance was impaired in one of two ways. One type of interference was designed to interfere with the *acquisition* of visual information.

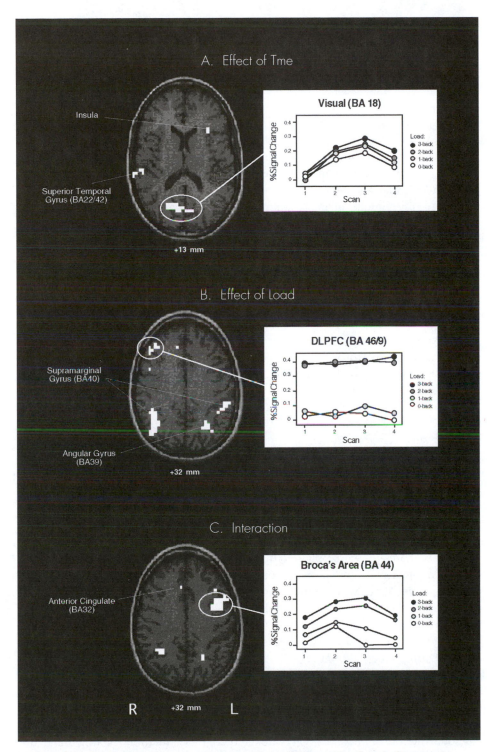

FIGURE 4.13 Regions of Activation Showing Effect of Time, of Load, and of Interaction Between Time and Load

FIGURE 4.14 Three Examples of
Abstract Stimuli

It employed a drug, diazepam (popularly known as Valium). The other type of impairment, intended to interfere with visual *recognition* of a stimulus, involved a sensory challenge. This challenge consisted of a stimulus, presented during a recognition task, that was intended to interfere with the task. The researchers termed this interfering stimulus a "mask" stimulus; it was a shape made up of a combination of eight shapes superimposed on each other.

The task was arranged as follows: The subjects were shown, several times very briefly, pairs of stimuli consisting of outlined abstract shapes that did not suggest anything in particular (Figure 4.14). They were instructed to memorize the shapes, regardless of their size or the order or position in which they were shown. Two types of test followed: recognition tests and detection tests. These were performed both with and without the interference of the drug or the mask stimulus.

In the standard recognition task, carried out *without* interference, subjects were shown, very rapidly (for 1,700 milliseconds), pairs of stimuli (shapes). They had to signal the appearance of the "old" (i.e., previously learned) shape by pressing a key on the same side as that shape. Correct responses would be evidence of recognition. In another task, subjects had to indicate by pressing the appropriate keys whether the two shapes were the same or different. In the third task, termed a detection task, the subjects were shown random pairs of shapes. They had to indicate, by pressing both keys at the same time, the moment at which they saw each pair.

When the recognition tasks were carried out with the interference of the mask shape, the stimuli to be recognized were presented for an even shorter time than they were in the tasks without interference (75 milliseconds—a very short time indeed). Subjects were then shown the mask stimulus for 1⅝ seconds (1,625 milliseconds).

PET scan images were obtained during task performance, under conditions of both nonimpairment and impairment. These images indicate that when visual memory is impaired, whether by a drug or by a mask, there are changes in the long-term memory network employed when recognition of abstract visual shapes is called for later on (Rosier et al., 1997). Both the drug and the sensory memory challenge are associated with a decrease in activation in a particular area of the left cortex. During recognition, these challenges enhance the activation in the posterior **thalamus** (the principal gateway for most sensory input). This suggests that the subjects are engaging in stronger or more frequent efforts to reactivate the stored information.

In another study (Swick & Knight, 1999), the technique of ERP was used to elucidate the role of the prefrontal cortex in recognition memory. Noting that many recent functional neuroimaging studies have linked the prefrontal cortex to re-trieval of information from either semantic or episodic memory, the researchers sought to test this conclusion by obtaining evidence from an ERP study. They chose ERP in part because PET, used in some other studies, has limited temporal resolution: It is just not fast enough to establish whether frontal activations reflect processes that precede the retrieval of memory or evaluative processes that fol-low retrieval.

In this experiment, stroke patients with lesions in one hemisphere of the pre-frontal cortex, and a set of control subjects, were given a continuous recognition task. They were presented with stimuli, on a screen, consisting of words and pronounceable nonwords four to eight letters long. (The nonwords were created by changing one to three letters in real words or by rearranging the letters of real words.) In each block of items there were 22 or 23 words and the same number of nonwords. Each of these was repeated once, so that the first time they were seen they were new; the second time they were not. There were three different lengths of delay between the first and second presentations of items: 3 seconds (no items in between); 6–12 seconds (3 items in between); and 30–60 seconds (9–19 items in between). The two shorter delays assessed short-term memory performance, and the longest delay tested long-term memory. By pressing different buttons, the participants indicated their recognition of the distinction among new words, non-words, and old ones.

Using electrodes strategically placed on the subjects' and controls' scalps, the experimenters obtained electrophysiological readings, from which they computed ERP averages for each type of stimulus: word/nonword and the different delay times. Then they computed grand ERP averages of both groups of participants (Figure 4.15).

Analysis of the results indicated that the patients with frontal lesions were not slower or less accurate than the controls at recognizing repeated words. But they *were* slower in responding to new words, and they were more likely to identify incorrectly new items as old ones. These results were compared with results from another, smaller group of patients who had damage not to the frontal region but to the hippocampus. This group performed quite differently, having a very low rate of misidentifying new items as old ones and in demonstrating a rapid decline in the rate of recognizing old words in the longest delay condition.

The experimenters interpreted these findings as suggesting that, whereas the patients with hippocampal damage demonstrated difficulty in remembering, those with frontal damage did not have an impaired recognition memory. Rather, their deficit is more likely one of "strategic processing or postretrieval monitoring" (Swick & Knight, 1999, p. 155).

These examples of the type of memory research being carried out will convey some idea of the complex thinking researchers engage in and the clever designs of experiments that provide promising answers to some of their questions about the functioning of memory.

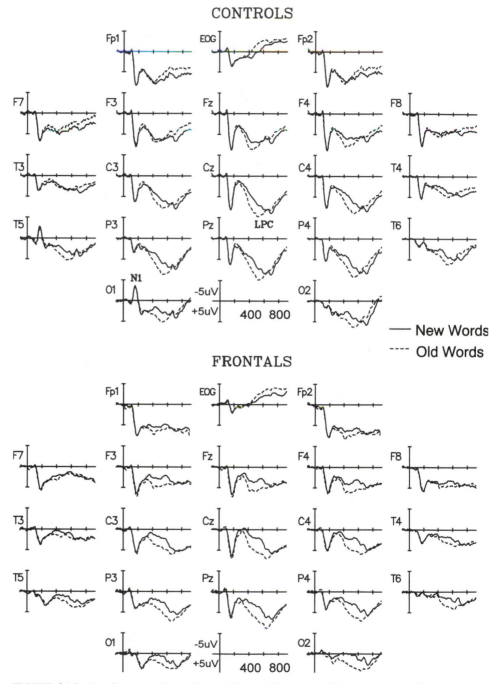

FIGURE 4.15 Grand Average Event-Related Potentials Recorded from Controls (Top) and Frontal Patients (Bottom) in a Recognition Memory Task

Concepts and Categories

Another fundamental aspect of human cognition, discussed at length in Chapter 2, concerns how we form and use concepts and categories, without which our world would be a hopeless jumble. How can neuroimaging techniques help to unravel this particular mystery? The aspect of cognition we refer to when we use the term "memory" is fairly clear to us. But concepts and categories are, for many, I suspect, somewhat fuzzier, a part of what we mean by "thinking"—a concept itself not altogether transparent. Perhaps a few examples of current studies in this area will help to illuminate the matter.

PET Studies of Category-Specific Knowledge   In Chapter 2 an experiment is described involving categories of manufactured and natural items. We revisit such categories now, in a study making use of neuroimaging. We know from individuals who have suffered brain damage that, depending on the location of the damage, there may be a selective loss of knowledge about a particular category. The loss may involve, for example, objects created by humans, such as tools. In a PET study reported in February 1996, Martin et al. sought neural correlates of this kind of category-specific knowledge. Sixteen volunteers participated. During PET scanning, the participants were shown a variety of line drawings, some of animals, some of tools, and some of nonsense objects. The participants were asked to identify the drawings of animals and tools. The reason these particular categories were selected is that the way people tend to distinguish among their members is different for each category. What people notice about animals is differences in physical features such as their form, color, and size, whereas what they tend to notice about tools is differences in their functions—the way they are used.

As the subjects named the drawings, a pattern of brain activation became clear. First of all, identifying real objects (as opposed to the nonsense objects) activated the primary visual cortex. But what is especially interesting is that apart from this the areas activated when naming animals and when naming objects were quite different (Figure 4.16). Although identifying both was associated with increased cerebral blood flow in the ventral region of the temporal lobes and in Broca's area, when naming tools the activation extended into the middle temporal gyrus and the left premotor area. This did not happen when subjects named animals. When naming animals, the left medial occipital lobe was activated. It was not activated when naming tools.

Researchers seek not only the basic data yielded by their experiments; they also try to interpret, or explain, these data. In this study, when subjects were asked to name animals, the activation in the occipital lobe, which controls vision, suggested to the researchers that naming animals places demands on the early stages of visual processing. This may be because the differences in this case are fairly subtle. This is especially true of line drawings, which lack the size and color cues that normally help to distinguish one species from another.

The significance of this study is that it pinpoints areas of the brain that evince increased cerebral blood flow during tasks that require categorization and that different areas are activated depending on the nature of the categorization task.

FIGURE 4.16 Regions of Increased Cerebral Blood Flow When Subjects Silently Named Drawings of Animals Compared to Viewing Nonsense Objects

A. Animals - Nonsense Objects

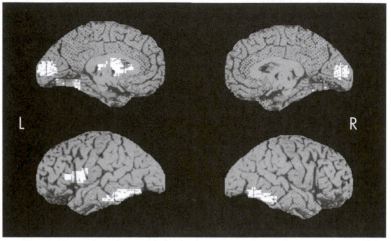

B. Tools - Nonsense Objects

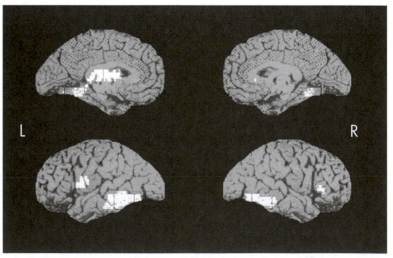

Two parallel studies involving **lexical retrieval** (word finding) were reported in April 1996 (Damasio, Grabowski, Tranel, Hichwa, & Damasio, 1996). These, too, addressed the neurology of concepts and categories. The researchers used PET to determine the regions of the brain participating in the normal process of retrieving from memory words that denote concrete entities. Their hypothesis was that the retrieval of words referring to members of distinct conceptual categories depends on distinct regions in the left temporal lobe. This hypothesis would be supported if they could demonstrate that activity occurred in different regions of this lobe when tasks involved different types of categories.

One of the studies investigating this hypothesis involved lexical retrieval in 127 adults with single, stable lesions in the brain (Damasio et al., 1996). These lesions affected both hemispheres, within and outside the temporal region. The subjects were to name 327 items that were shown to them. The first type of item consisted of photographs of well-known people, each of whom is a unique member of the category *male or female human.* The second type of item consisted of photos of animals, and the third consisted of photos of tools. *Animals* and *tools,* like *male or female human,* are superordinate categories. That is, they are the categories to which the specific tools (e.g., wrench, screwdriver, hammer) and animals (e.g., lion, bear, fox) belong. The researchers hypothesized that for all three categories disruption in the ability to retrieve words would be correlated with damage to regions in the left hemisphere only, and that for each category the disruption of word retrieval would be correlated with separate neural sites *within a particular area* of the temporal region.

The subjects were classified according to whether their task performance was normal. (A "normal" response to a task item means that the subject's response was the same as that of normal controls who were matched with the subjects for age and education.) Of the 30 subjects whose performance on the task was *abnormal,* all but one had left-hemisphere damage so that the first hypothesis was in fact supported. (The reader might note that, as in this case, results are rarely "perfect"; but the fact that 29 out of 30 subjects behaved consistently with the prediction counts as pretty persuasive supporting evidence.) As for the second prediction, the study indicated that abnormal retrieval of words for animals was correlated with damage in one particular area of the left temporal lobe, whereas abnormal retrieval of words for tools was associated with damage in another. See Figures 4.17 and 4.18.

The second, related study focused on lexical retrieval in normal (non-brain-damaged) subjects. They were presented with the same tasks used in the previous study. All subjects indicated, through increased cerebral blood flow, activation in the anticipated areas of the left hemisphere. And as the findings of the previous study had led them to expect, Damasio et al. (1996) found one region activated in person naming but not in tool or animal naming, and differing patterns of activation for each category in the regions involved in tool naming and animal naming.

A very important result of these studies is that they confirm the findings of other researchers who conducted both electrophysiological imaging and fMRI. They indicate that it is not Broca's area alone that is responsible for name finding. Other regions of the cortex are involved in semantic associations. Name finding

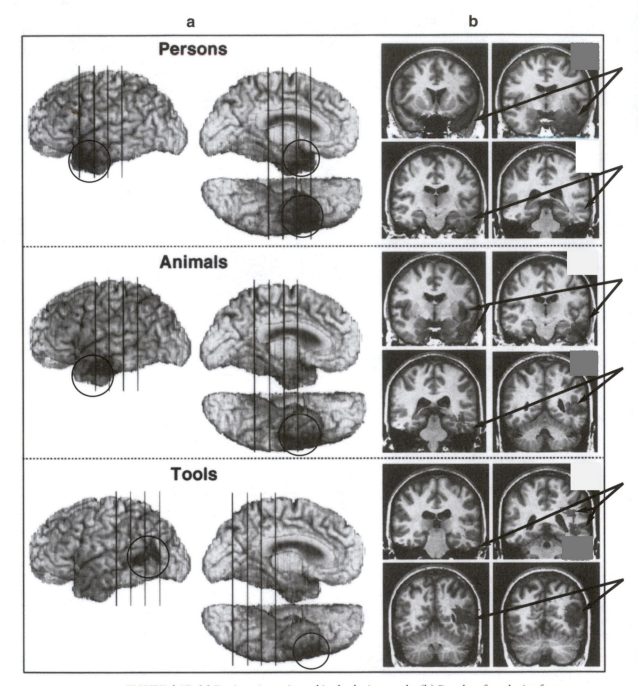

FIGURE 4.17 (a) Regions investigated in the lesion study. (b) Results of analysis of magnetic resonance or computed tomography scans showing regions of the brain involved in the retrieval of words for persons, animals, and tools.

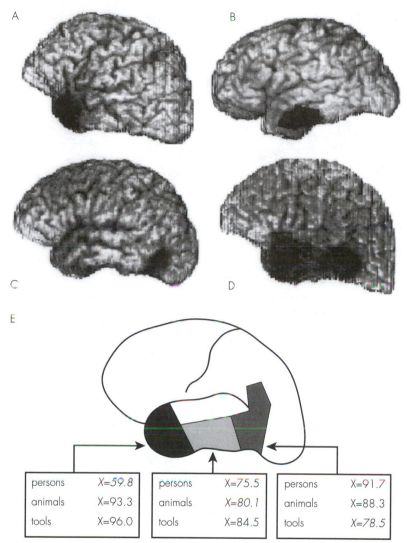

FIGURE 4.18 Reconstructed brains showing locations of defects in word retrieval for (a) people, (b) animals, (c) tools, and (d) all of these categories.

persons	X=59.8
animals	X=93.3
tools	X=96.0

persons	X=75.5
animals	X=80.1
tools	X=84.5

persons	X=91.7
animals	X=88.3
tools	X=78.5

depends not simply on some specific "name finder" function in a restricted area but rather is part of a complex concept/categorization system that has neural components in various regions of the cortex.

We have seen that much of our information about brain function has come from damaged brains—often depending on associating behavior exhibited while a patient was alive with brain lesions observed after the patient's death. In the study just described, PET made it possible first to obtain information gleaned from living brain-lesioned patients engaged in cognitive tasks and then to compare it with information garnered from people with undamaged brains engaged in the same tasks.

Although today we have developed modes of discovery different from those of earlier periods, we are still using all the techniques and evidence at our disposal to learn about the functions of the brain. An area still rich in information waiting to be tapped is that of disorders of the brain, which we can also observe much more directly than ever before. We conclude this unit, then, with a few recent studies that illustrate ways in which this vein is being mined.

Disorders

Bipolar and Unipolar Disorder   We hear a great deal today about so-called mood disorders. Years ago, if a person was unhappy or "depressed," the mood might be attributed either to an external event, such as the death of a loved one, or to the individual's general "make-up" or personality. The first of these notions is, at a certain level, a kind of explanation: Something tragic happens and we know from observation that such occurrences generally produce unhappiness or depression. The effect is so common that it does not surprise us; in fact, we find it remarkable when it does *not* occur. Furthermore, if we prescribe an antidote, it is often in the form of advice to "get away for a bit—a change of scene will help you to feel better." Or it may be in the form of soothing platitudes such as "Time heals all wounds," because it has also been observed that most people do not remain forever in that sad state.

But such an emotional state may continue for a protracted period in the absence of an evident cause, leading some to conclude that it is simply attributable to the individual's personality. This explanation offers no particular cause; it is the equivalent of saying "So-and-so is that way because that's the way she is." Yet the development of antidepressant medications (e.g., Prozac and Zoloft) that can "cure" or ameliorate the condition indicates that this "explanation" is more apt than one might have assumed. A more complete explanation is now possible, one involving events at the chemical level. We are beginning to grasp the role neurotransmitters play in many aspects of people's make-up, including their moods. And physicians can now provide substitutes, Prozac, for example, for missing or deficient substances. Of course our solutions to the many problems caused by such deficiencies are not perfect, but we seem to be well on the road to greater successes.

Still, we would like to understand fully the various ills—depression, bipolar disorder, schizophrenia, autism, dyslexia, to name a few—that beset our species by virtue of something amiss in the brain's functioning. And here again the techniques of brain imaging constitute another set of arrows in our quiver. Let us look at a few studies recently addressing these particular ailments to see what kinds of information they yield.

In a study reported in April 1997, the researchers provide the setting for their study as follows:

Pathological disturbances of mood may follow a "**bipolar**" course, in which normal moods alternate with both depression and mania [a state of extremely heightened excitement and activity], or a "**unipolar**" course, in which only depression occurs. Both bipolar and unipolar disorders can be heritable illnesses associated with neurochemical, **neuroendocrine** [brain/endocrine system] and autonomic abnormalities. The neurobiological basis for these abnormalities has not been established. (Drevets et al., 1997, p. 824)

The study made use first of PET images of cerebral blood flow from depressives who were not taking any medication for the disorder. There were two groups of these, each paired with a control group of subjects who did not suffer from the disorder. In the first group, a particular area of the prefrontal cortex showed a 7.7% decrease in blood flow in the depressives relative to the controls. From these results, the researchers hypothesized that blood flow in this region is abnormal in bipolar depression; the 6.6% decrease in blood flow in the same region found in a comparison study using the second group confirmed their hypothesis. Because they wanted to localize the region of abnormality more precisely, they used a higher resolution camera and looked this time also at glucose metabolism images (which tell a story similar to that of blood flow images), using yet a third set of unmedicated bipolar depressives and controls. From the images obtained in this test, they found that relative to the controls the blood flow in the same region was decreased by 18.5% and the metabolism by 16.3% in the bipolar depressives.

The next phase of the study was to obtain, by the same high-resolution PET methods, images of brain activity of unipolar depressives whose family history was of pure depressive disease (that is, with no occurrence of mania). The images of the region under investigation obtained from these subjects showed a pattern similar to that of the bipolar depressives—a decrease in metabolism of 12.2% in the same region relative to the controls.

Next the researchers examined PET images obtained from bipolar subjects in the manic phase, and, interestingly—but not surprisingly—these images showed an *increased* metabolism relative to the controls. Images obtained from a single subject of the same region of the prefrontal cortex showed an increase in metabolism in the manic phase over the depressive phase measured 8 weeks later.

From these and related results there appears to be a pattern of reduction and increase in blood flow and metabolism in a particular region of the brain in bipolar and unipolar depressives. Many questions remain to be answered. PET and MRI scans have contributed some of the what and where, but not the why or the how, of what has gone wrong in the victims of depressive disorder (Drevets et al., 1997).

Schizophrenia   Forty years ago behaviorists tried to identify lucid periods in the lives of schizophrenics by tracking their behavior under various schedules of reinforcement for simple motor activities. Now brain scans can provide such information more directly. Scans are also helpful in *treating* patients suffering from **schizophrenia**, a severe mental disorder involving, for example, hallucinations and delusions. For example, it is possible to track the changes occurring in the course of treatment by periodic brain scanning. From this information, on the one hand, clinicians can determine the effects the treatment has on the brain, and on the other, they can learn more about brain function.

In a systematic brain MRI study, researchers examined patients with childhood-onset schizophrenia (Frazier et al., 1996). Background to this study included MRI studies of adults with schizophrenia, whose brains were found to have enlarged **basal ganglia**. (The basal ganglia are masses of gray matter that are embedded in the white matter of the brain. They are associated with the control of movement.) Although it is not clear whether the ailment or certain treatments were responsible for this phenomenon, it is interesting that in the present study researchers found a similar condition, along with other similarities to the brains of adults with schizophrenia, including smaller brain volume. The children in this study were being treated with a medication called clozapine. As part of a treatment trial, 8 patients and 8 matched comparison subjects had 2-year follow-up MRI scans to detect changes in their basal ganglia. The researchers hypothesized that the volume of the basal ganglia would decrease during the period of treatment. At the outset, the only statistically significant difference between the patients and the comparison subjects was in the size of the **caudate** (a portion of the basal ganglia): In the schizophrenics it was significantly larger. When scans were obtained at the end of the 2-year study, there was no difference in the volume of the caudate between the two groups. Admittedly this was a small-scale study, but the results are suggestive, though it remains for a different level of explanation to determine *why* this treatment has these effects. But what has been learned from the imaging technique is that the benefits of this medication to schizophrenic patients are associated with specific (and observable) effects in the brains of patients to whom it is administered.

The preceding study was concerned with structural matters, and MRI, a structural imaging technique, was appropriate. But for functional matters, such as the processing of language in schizophrenia, researchers may turn to ERP. Such is the case in the next study (Niznikiewicz et al., 1997), in which the issue is the *cause* of the language abnormalities exhibited in schizophrenia—specifically, whether they are due to a dysfunction in the language system or to a general cognitive dysfunction.

Some of the traits of the language of schizophrenics are incoherence and a tendency to produce loose and irrelevant associations (sometimes described as "word salad"). These associations have been attributed by some to overaction of semantic networks; that is, there is not the control over the priming effect (the activation of nodes in the semantic network) that is evident in normal language use.

In this study, researchers relied on a particular waveform generated when electrophysiological readings are taken of the electrical activity in the brain during language processing. This waveform is referred to as N400, because it reaches its peak about 400 ms after a written or spoken word is presented to a subject at the beginning of a sentence. The N400 responds differently to words that occur frequently than to words that occur more rarely: the less frequent the occurrence of the word, the larger the N400. But the story is different when the word, no matter how common or uncommon, occurs at the *end* of a sentence. In this case, the amplitude of the N400 has been shown to depend on how well the word fits the context.

These characteristics of the N400 make it a good candidate for a measure of language dysfunction in schizophrenia. In the study we are now considering, researchers were seeking to learn whether N400 differences in the *visual* modality that had been found between normal participants and schizophrenic participants exist also when the modality is *auditory*. The language abnormalities in schizophrenic subjects might be related to a dysfunction in a language system regardless of the modality in which the language was perceived. If so, the difference between their responses and those of the controls would be similar whether the words presented were seen or heard. But if the impairment for language-related stimuli was similar to that found for *non*-language-related stimuli (for example, simple tones, where impairments in processing involve hearing, not seeing), then the researchers would expect that the processing for sentences *heard* would be more impaired than for sentences *seen*.

After their scalps were fitted with the necessary electrodes, the participants were presented with two sets of sentences, one to look at and the other to hear. In each set, half of the sentences ended in words that made sense (such as "Alice has gone to the store") and half ended in words that didn't fit the context (such as "Harry thought he should eat his hat").

One of the interesting findings was that the N400 response was greater in the schizophrenic patients than in the controls in both the visual and the auditory modality. This was true for both sentence types. Another interesting finding was that the schizophrenic patients' N400 waveforms were similar for both sentence types. This was not the case for the normal controls.

The fact that the *visual* language processing difficulties that had previously been found in schizophrenic patients exist in the *auditory* modality as well suggests that their language difficulties are related to a language system independent of the modality in which the language is perceived. Furthermore, their N400 waveforms indicate that they did not distinguish, as the normal controls did, between sentences that made sense and those that didn't. In view of these results, the researchers suggest that a deficit in the processing ability of schizophrenic patients with regard to context integration may be a factor in their language dysfunction.

The value of ERP in adding to our understanding of the brain should be clear from this as from the earlier example (regarding memory function) of research that makes use of it.

Autism   Like other disorders incomprehensible at various times in history, **autism** was once thought to result from environmental factors, perhaps poor parenting. (Parents were blamed for schizophrenia too; many families were devastated by the widespread assumption that bad parenting led to this disorder, which is now viewed as largely a chemical matter.) Parents of autistic children are faced with a behavioral syndrome that for a long time was inexplicable except by assigning blame—it was surely someone's "fault." Although the level of intelligence of autistic children varies from one individual to another—some functioning at a high intellectual level and some, for all practical purposes, barely functioning—they do share certain characteristics. Among the most difficult for them and for their parents are their social and communication deficits. They do not seem to relate emotionally to others but remain largely in a kind of isolation marked by repetitive behaviors such as rocking and head banging and a rejection of physical and emotional closeness.

Many attempts have been made to explain autism. Although it is not yet clearly understood, there is now a general recognition that something in the neurobiology of autistic individuals produces the disorder. Studies of the brains of autistic individuals have revealed a number of abnormalities, but a clear picture has yet to emerge. MRI offers the possibility of increasing knowledge in this area, and a 1995 study employing this technique (Piven et al., 1995) has contributed some interesting findings. These researchers sought detailed measurements of the volume of the brains of autistic individuals. Twenty-two male autistic subjects and 20 male volunteer comparison subjects participated in this study in which detailed MRI images were taken. "The results of this study suggest that the volume of the brain is larger in male subjects with autism and that enlargement of the total brain volume occurs as a result of enlargement of both the volume of the brain tissue and the volume of the lateral **ventricles** [spaces in the brain generally filled with protective fluid]" (Piven et al., 1995, p. 1147).

How does this happen? And why? Piven et al. note that there are three possible developmental causes for the greater brain volume in these autistic subjects: It may be that there is an increased production of neurons; it may be that neurons don't die off in as great numbers as they do in the normal course of development; and, finally, it may be that there is an increased production of nonneural brain tissue such as blood vessels. Further research is needed to determine whether any of these, or some combination of them, is the cause of the greater brain volume found in victims of this disorder. In addition, this study points to the need for other types of research. Do genes play a role in the development of these larger brains, and if so, what sort of role? Neuroimaging plays a part, then, in indicating directions for new research initiatives. Indeed, one of the lures of science for the scientist is the fact that research *always* raises more questions than it answers.

Dyslexia   More widespread distress in recent times is experienced by parents and children confronting the difficulties of **dyslexia**. In earlier societies, in which reading and writing played little if any part, dyslexia, which we now classify as a disorder, would not have caused trouble for anyone. It would not have been noticed. But in the modern world, being able to read and write well is a prerequisite to success in virtually every pursuit. A problem in this arena affects people's lives from an early age. Children who are competent—even superior—learners in other areas often suffer when they fall behind in this one. Instead of the approval of their teachers, parents, and classmates, they suffer the (often voiced) conviction that they are lazy, that they do not try hard enough, even that they are stupid. As more has been learned about dyslexia, it has become clear that it is an impairment for which its sufferers are not responsible and that, like autism, it is unrelated to what is usually meant by "intelligence."

Enter neuroimaging, which holds out the promise of explanation. In March 1998 a study was reported (Shaywitz et al., 1998) in which researchers used fMRI to obtain images of the brains of dyslexic subjects as they performed various tasks associated with reading. They sought to discover which functions of the brain were impaired. As will be elaborated in Chapter 5, the indefinitely numerous words in any language are constructed of a small number of phonological segments, or phonemes (sounds that make a difference to meaning, such as the *n* and *t* in *nap* and *tap*). Reading requires the association of a set of symbols, an alphabet, with these phonemes. It is the awareness of speakers that all words can be broken down into these segments that allows most of us to make these associations and thus to read. Contributing to the rationale of the study in question are earlier studies that indicate that this awareness is missing in dyslexic individuals. An effective means of testing for dyslexia has been the task of reading nonsense words that are phonologically possible words in the language of the speaker. (A phonologically possible word makes use of combinations of sounds permitted in the language, such as *st* or *pl,* which occur in the meaningful words *store* and *plank.* The meaningless words *strank* and *plore,* which also use these combinations, are thus *phonologically* legal.) Because such words are possible—though not actual—words, they are read with ease by most people. But someone who has difficulty decomposing words into phonologic segments will have difficulty reading them (words like these cannot be recognized by their familiar pattern, a potential aid to reading). Such an individual may well be dyslexic. The aim of this study was to

> develop a set of hierarchically structured tasks that control the kind of language-relevant coding required, including especially the demand on phonologic analysis, and then to compare the performance and brain activation patterns (as measured by functional MRI) of dyslexic . . . and nonimpaired . . . readers. (Shaywitz et al., 1998, p. 2636)

The subjects were asked to perform a series of judgment tasks that made demands on a set of increasingly complex functions involved in reading.

The researchers designed the following tasks: The least complex level in the hierarchy is the judgment regarding line orientation, for example, "Do [\\\ /] and [\\\ /] match?" This task is intended to tap only visual-spatial processing, not to involve anything having to do with spelling. A letter-case judgment is next, for example, "Do [bbBb] and [bbBb] match in the pattern of upper- and lowercase letters?" This task involves a spelling processing demand, but not a phonological one, because the string of letters consists of only consonants and therefore cannot be a word. In the third task, subjects are asked to make judgments about whether letter names rhyme ("Do the letters [T] and [V] rhyme?"). This task is intended to involve phonological processing, because it presumably requires that subjects encode the letters, which are elements of spelling, into phonological structures that must then be analyzed to determine whether or not they rhyme. A fourth task presents subjects with nonwords and requires that they decide whether these rhyme ("Do [leat] and [jete] rhyme?"). These are more complex structures to analyze than are single letters or phonemes. The final task is one that requires the subjects to make a judgment about the semantic category of words ("Are [corn] and [rice] in the same category?"). This sort of judgment requires moving from the printed word to the word as a phonological and semantic entity. Thus it requires activation of the representations in the reader's mental store of words and their meanings.

Analysis of the results of the five tasks showed that the reading performance of the dyslexic subjects was significantly impaired, most strikingly in the nonword rhyming task. This task is considered by the researchers to provide the clearest indication of decoding ability (or inability), because no one would be familiar with the letter patterns. Thus they could not influence anyone's response.

As the participants (29 of them dyslexic readers and 32 nonimpaired controls) performed these tasks, fMRI images were obtained, focusing on several brain regions that earlier studies had indicated were involved in reading and language. A posterior cortical system adapted for reading including, among other regions, Wernicke's area, had been hypothesized; the fMRI images obtained in this study supported the hypothesis. At the sites involved, the nonimpaired subjects showed a systematic increase in activation as the complexity of the tasks placed increased demands on the spelling and phonological components of reading. The dyslexic subjects, however, showed no such systematic changes in activation as the task demands increased.

The nature of this sort of experimentation requires that nonimpaired controls serve to permit comparisons with the impaired readers. In the process of seeking the cause of the impairment, much is learned about the normal state as well. In this case, for nonimpaired readers, the data "provide functional evidence of a widely distributed computational system for reading" (Shaywitz et al., 1998, p. 2639). Within the system, activation varies from region to region depending on the task. For dyslexic readers, the data indicate "a functional disruption in an extensive system in posterior cortex encompassing both traditional visual and traditional language regions and a portion of association cortex" (p. 2639). This last (the association cortex) is considered essential to the more complex integrations required by reading, for example, converting what is perceived as print into the phonologic structures of the language.

The studies about which you have just read are only a small sample of the work employing PET and fMRI imaging techniques. From studies such as these, designed to shed light on both normal and impaired conditions, researchers are piecing together a picture that is leading us toward an ever better understanding of the brain. From the perspective of the final years of the 20th century, we can see what a long way we have come in 150 years of this endeavor. The technologies described in this chapter are fulfilling the promise of the early attempts examined in the preceding one; the new millennium holds further promise. A map is in the process of being assembled, one which holds for us the possibility of charting the cerebral course of human cognition. With pleasure and excitement like that of a child watching the bones of his toes respond to his brain's command to wiggle, the human species, now standing on the more powerful platform provided by present and yet-to-be-developed technologies, will watch the unfolding of more and more of the mysteries of its own brain.

Questions to Think About

1. The people involved in research on brain mapping are very excited about their work. They feel themselves to be at "the frontier of knowledge." What does that mean to you? Have you ever discovered something on your own?

2. Most of us accept at face value what we are told by "experts." We file it away, perhaps in our long-term memory, without asking "How does this person *know* this?" Only a few people ask "Is there some other explanation for this finding?" Consider one of the studies described in this chapter and ask these questions of yourself. Can you come up with any ideas for a follow-up study? Can you propose a hypothesis that, if tested, might help answer one of your questions?

3. The distinction between structure and function is extremely significant. If you had to make a choice between pursuing study of the structure and pursuing study of the function of, say, the human brain, which would you choose? Why?

4. Distinguish among the following: CAT, MRI, EEG, fMRI, PET and SPECT. What does each contribute to the study of the human brain? If you were a neuroscientist, which of these techniques would you find most interesting to work with? Why?

5. Is the research described in this chapter important in its own right, or is it worthwhile only if it is applied to problems of real people suffering from depression, schizophrenia, autism, or dyslexia? Explain why you think so. In which case, if either, should the research be supported by government funds? Why?

What Linguistics Is About

We acquired Rex, some sort of terrier, from a person who had trained him well. My father would say "Rex, beg!" And Rex would get up on his hind paws and hold up his front ones in a begging gesture. But then, after praising him and encouraging him to come down from that position, my father would say "Rex, eat soup!" And Rex would beg. If my father instead said "Rex, lie down!" Rex would again beg. No matter what words my father substituted in his command, Rex would respond obligingly—by begging.

Jennifer was another story. At 2½ she was interested in the flowers outside her house. The colorful tulips never failed to draw her attention as her mother exclaimed each time they passed them, "Oh, look at the pretty tulips!" One day, at the end of tulip season, there was only one blossom left. "Look, Mommy," said Jennifer, "one lip!"

Both Rex and Jennifer were behaving in ways that amused the people around them, and the behavior in both cases involved language. But Rex's indicated that his response did not depend on the actual sentence he heard; rather, it was a learned response, apparently to a particular tone of voice. He did not beg when my father said, in an affectionate tone, "Good dog, Rex," nor when someone summoned him by calling his name. In themselves, neither the words nor their particular arrangement seemed to convey anything to him.

Jennifer, on the other hand, was clearly sensitive to the words themselves; furthermore, as early as age 2½ she was able to do something with them that Rex would never approach—something very complex indeed. She had recognized the "tu" in "tulip;" it was a sequence of sounds she had heard before, in other contexts, having a meaning she understood quite well. Now she *interpreted* this sequence as meaning what it meant all the other times she had heard it; then she invested the other half of the word (that is, the "lip" that her mother knew to be simply part of the flower name) with a meaning of its own. This done, she went on to create a new sentence, one she had not heard before, using her new word. All of this Jennifer did in a split second, without having been explicitly taught to and without being aware of the marvelously complicated feat it represented.

Jennifer was a very bright little girl. But her accomplishment at the age of 2½, though perhaps somewhat precocious, was not unique; all children born with normally functioning brains and hearing arrive at the ability to manipulate the stuff of language by, or not very much past, the age Jennifer was when this incident occurred. No member of Rex's species, on the other hand, no matter how long or how closely associated with humans, has ever learned by exposure, nor ever been taught, to do what Jennifer did so spontaneously, so early—and so effortlessly.

We readily fall into the habit of thought that if something comes easily to us it must *be* easy. In a real sense, it was easy for Jennifer to engage in the behavior I have described. Why? Because Jennifer, like you who are reading this now, was *born* equipped to learn language simply from having it used around her, as Rex was born equipped to react to moving objects by chasing them.

But when you examine human language—any language: yours, your great-great-grandmother's, your Japanese or Greek or Hungarian pen pal's—you find it characterized by a great deal of complexity. Think of the difficulties we encounter in attempting, after childhood, to learn a foreign language. No matter how many rules we absorb, we may never be satisfied with our achievement, because we still have to stop, at least sometimes, to think about whether or not we are following those rules. Even when we succeed in putting the words together into flawless sentences, someone may ask us where we are from, indicating by the question that something is still not quite right in the way we speak the language. These are difficulties we did not encounter the first time around, when we learned to speak our native language or languages.

The data—the information on which all of our questions about language rest and with which linguists grapple—are anywhere and everywhere people are found, in all the statements they make, the questions they ask, the many ways in which they express themselves in language. What do these data indicate about the nature of the activity itself—the very structure of language? Of what does its complexity consist? "Doing" language, acquiring and using it, must be possible because some commensurately complex mechanism in our brain exists to support this activity. What sort of mechanism can this be? We are not born with a particular language already in there and prepared to go to work for us. What exactly is it that we *are* born with? How does it work to allow us to catch on to the meanings and organization inherent in the language or languages we are exposed to from birth? Where has this ability gone when we need it, later on, to learn a foreign language? What is the relation of our language capacity to thinking, as we humans experience it?

These are some of the questions linguists pose, and the information they gather and the understanding they achieve in the course of their research into individual languages have implications for these basic questions. As we have already noted, they are not alone in the quest. Their concerns overlap with those of the other fields comprising cognitive science. Linguistics figures importantly in the quest because language, as a behavior unique to humans, can teach us much about the human brain.

The Uniqueness of Human Language

Anyone who stops to consider the phenomenon of language is aware that humans are the only species to engage in this behavior that we take so for granted. (For this reason, when I use the term "language," I will be referring only to human language, the spontaneously developing system that human children absorb from their environment and produce early and without specific instruction.) Yes, members of other species communicate with each other (and often with us) by means of bodily displays. Think of a cat arching its back and appearing larger than it normally does by virtue of its fur standing on end, or a peacock fanning out its tail to reveal a magnificent color display. They communicate by gestures, as the grimacing and chest pounding of the gorilla, for example, or the complex "dance" of honeybees. They communicate as well by vocalizations, as in the songs of birds and of whales, and the barking, growling, and whining of dogs. Students of these various types of communication have been able to describe and classify many of them and have observed their consistent pairing with certain behaviors so that we can be quite sure of their purpose. It is of course always possible that we, probing with our human faculties, are missing something in these communicative manifestations—that we simply do not understand complexities that it takes a bird's mind, or a gorilla's, to appreciate. But science requires evidence before hypotheses are considered confirmed, and we have no hard evidence to support the notion that any other species is capable of just the sort of complex system of communication that enabled Jennifer to produce her "one lip" invention.

You may be wondering at this point what the real difference is between what these other species are doing and what Jennifer did in talking about the flowers— what we humans do all the time, whether the communication is carried out in English or in Swahili or in Urdu. After all, the various systems of communication employed by other species serve them perfectly well. The cat with the arched back manages to scare off an intrusive neighbor cat, and the bird singing so sweetly generally succeeds in attracting a mate. What we have observed about the communication of other species—often called their "language"—is that each manifestation, whether of bodily display, of gesture, or of vocalization, pairs with a specific and consistent meaning. That is, a particular tail swish of your kitten or a particular utterance of a vervet monkey or a particular cry of the crow in the tree outside your window will occur under the same circumstance every time. The kitten will not swish its tail just that way to indicate anything but readiness to pounce. The vervet monkey will produce just that sound to alert other vervet monkeys that there is a snake in the grass. The crow will caw in just that fashion always and only to warn intruders to keep out of its territory. The display or gesture or sound will be inseparable from the given situation.

You, on the other hand, can separate your vocalization from a given situation. For instance, you can communicate something about the future: You can tell the friend who calls to invite you to lunch that you can't go because you have to finish this book on cognitive science, when what you really have in mind is a nice nap. Not only are you expressing something about the future, but what you are saying isn't even true. Your language affords you as much freedom in what you express by means of it as your conscience allows. The bee that communicates the location of food to its hivemates does not produce movements that will lead them to fly south for a certain distance and then when they get there produce movements that communicate "ha, ha, just kidding." There is something quite different in the process we are engaging in when we use our language from what bees are doing when using theirs. One of the unique and telling aspects of this difference is the fact that we are able to separate what we express from the requirements of the moment, to convey concepts ranging from the factual and true ("I'm on my way to work/class") to speculations about what would happen if the situation were different ("What if I were to hang out in the mall instead?") to out-and-out lies ("I'm really sorry I didn't come in yesterday, but I wasn't feeling well"). This ability makes possible our use of language for the large and varied set of intellectual, aesthetic, emotional, and social purposes characteristic of human behavior, ranging from the straightforward transfer of information to the exploration of ideas, from poetry to deception, from sarcasm to joking and play.

Characteristics of Human Language

Although the differences among languages spoken in different parts of the world fairly jump out at us, these languages are in fact far more similar than we generally perceive. That this is so is not surprising, for all human languages—those known only through historical documents and comparative studies as well as those currently spoken—reflect the linguistic capacity of the human brain.

The fact that it is possible for us to express so much that other species cannot has to do with the way our language is constructed. We are not limited to a specific utterance to express a given meaning, though there are utterances that do this: "Ow," for example. Nor are we limited to a number of stock expressions, though we have those, too, such as "How do you do?" Our language is not made up simply of a set of expressions like these, wrenched from us or trotted out for social purposes. Rather, it is constructed of a fairly small set of sounds, known as **phonemes** (about 40 in English), that most often have no meaning in themselves: *nnn, eee*. These we string together one after the other to form meaningful bits and pieces: *morphemes* (*ex-, -ism*) and *words* (*needle*). The number of words made from phonemes is large—about 600,000 in English—but finite.

Except for a small set of words exhibiting **onomatopoeia** (*meow, clang*), the strings of sounds making up our words and parts of words bear no necessary or logical relation to their meaning. Think for a moment of the way English refers to one of our favorite pets, the dog. *Dog*. French calls it *chien,* and in German it is *Hund*. These words sound entirely different from one another, yet they all mean the same thing. There cannot then be anything necessarily "dog-ish" about any of these words. It's just that members of each language community, for historical reasons, agree that the word they use refers to that animal and nothing else. The fact that the sounds of words are not logically or necessarily tied to the meanings, a characteristic often referred to as the **arbitrariness of the sign**, is one of the reasons for the flexibility of human language. It can express virtually anything speakers want or need to express.

Before we look any further at the structure of language, let us consider for a moment one of the words I have just been using, a word we use all the time without giving it any thought because the concept it expresses is so obvious. Or is it? The word I mean (there I go using it again) is *mean,* or *meaning*. The question of the meaning of *meaning* is a profound one that has been with us for a long time. But even what seems to us most simple and obvious may in fact be quite complex, defying easy definition. Sound sequences may be associated arbitrarily with meanings, but the two are bound together in the linguistic structures we create in a way that is anything but simple, and the way in which meaning is expressed by language is anything but obvious.

In order to express meaning linguistically, once we have organized the sound sequences of a language into words, we must arrange them, again in sequence, into sentences. Sentences tend to express complete thoughts. (Here is another word whose meaning I have just assumed. Take a moment, if you will, to define *sentence* for yourself, without simply reciting what you may have been taught in school. Does a sentence express a complete thought? Must it do so explicitly in order to be a sentence? What about expressions like "Leave!" or "No!"?)

Although the number of words at any time in a given language is large, it is, as I said, finite. Yet the number of sentences that can be constructed out of these words is infinite. That's why "I learned a new word today" is a reasonable thing to say, but you would get some strange looks if you said "I learned a new sentence today." An unabridged dictionary will give you some idea of the number of words in English at the time the dictionary was compiled (words are being dropped from and added to the language all the time), but see what happens when you try to count the number of sentences you can make out of a simple one such as "Amy likes Stan:"

> *I think that Amy likes Stan.*
> *You know that I think that Amy likes Stan.*
> *I think that you know that I think that Amy likes Stan.*
> *You're sure that I think that you know that I think that Amy likes Stan.*

You will soon see the impossibility of the task. (I know that you will soon see the impossibility of the task. You realize that I know that you will soon see the impossibility of the task . . .).

The interesting property of human language embodied in these sentences is called **recursion**. It is this property of allowing one sentence to be contained, or embedded, within another that causes the number of sentences in any language to be infinite—for all languages are capable of such embedding. Embedding turns up in nursery games; perhaps you remember "the house that Jack built." It begins with a quite ordinary sentence:

> *This is the house that Jack built.*

What you undoubtedly never stopped to notice if you, as a child, uttered this sentence was that it expresses two different ideas about the house, two separate thoughts, really:

> *This is the house*
> and
> *Jack built this house.*

The single sentence "This is the house that Jack built" is in fact a compression of these two separate thoughts into one sentence. So far, it looks easy. Then the sentence is expanded, including yet another idea, to

> *This is the cheese that lay in the house that Jack built*

and then to another

> *This is the rat that ate the cheese that lay in the house that Jack built*

and still another

> *This is the cat that chased the rat that ate the cheese that lay in the house that Jack built.*

By the time the game ends, memory is taxed: The players are hard put to remember all the steps. They are aided, of course, by the fact that a story is implicit in these steps, a story that follows a logical progression. It turns out not to be so difficult after all.

But when sentences with multiple embeddings are produced that are not based on a simple story pattern, what happens?

> *The dog chased the boy.*
> *The boy the dog chased got lost.*
> *The boy the dog the man trained chased got lost.*
> *The boy the dog the man the book belonged to trained chased got lost.*

How long did it take *you* to get lost? Even as adults, we soon do. Why? Because such a sentence is too involved to follow, let alone remember. Therefore, we don't usually create sentences like these. It's hard to follow them, to keep track of what's happening, and once you've gotten some distance into one of them, it's hard to keep in mind all of its earlier components. "Keeping track" is a part of the processing function of the brain, as "keeping in mind" is the function of its memory capability. But the fact is we can create such sentences, even though our processing and memory limitations lead us to avoid them. This property of language—that sentences can readily be placed one inside the other and that the process can in principle be infinitely continued—is characteristic of all human languages. Like the arbitrariness of the sign, it is another of the properties that make our sort of language unique. These properties lead us to puzzle over and marvel at the nature of a brain that is capable of producing such sentences but then, because of its limitations in other domains, has difficulty in managing them. As we are led to considerations like this, we see how it is that linguistics relates to other areas of cognitive science—in this particular case, cognitive psychology and neuroscience, areas we examined in Parts 1 and 2.

The Rules of Language

I have pointed out some of the building blocks of language: sounds, meaningless in themselves, that combine in a linear order to make meaningful units (prefixes, suffixes, words); combinations of words, also in a linear order, making sentences; sentences that fit inside one another, demonstrating that their nature is one of infiniteness. But these building blocks by themselves are not enough to constitute language. How do we know the order in which to put them? How do we know that one sound is English (*mm,* as in *me*) and another is not (that French *r,* for example, that we have such difficulty pronouncing)? How do we know that one combination of sounds is English (*tr,* as in *track,* for instance), and another is not? (Try *nl.* Is *nlack* an English word? Could it be? Why not?) How do we know that one ordering of words is a "real" sentence ("I think that Amy likes Stan") and another, using the very same words, is not ("Think likes I Stan that Amy")?

It cannot be that we have learned each instance individually, because the possibilities, at least for sentences, are infinite. But the brain that accomplishes all of this is not infinite. Although it contains a very large number of neurons that enable us to "do" language, that number is finite. The elements used in doing language *must* be finite—because the resources of the finite brain suffice to learn them. The answer is that there is a finite set of rules that we have learned, rules that enable us to put together the sounds, words, and sentences of our language and to recognize when they are not being followed.

But each answer to a question leads to more questions. If we know the rules, how did we learn them? We may have tried out the sequence *nnnlll* when we were babies. No one told us that English does not contain this combination of sounds at the beginning of a word (we did hear it *inside* of words [*only, unless*]), but we know it's not English to have it at the beginning. No one explained that *un-* must go at the beginning of a word and nowhere else, yet if you were told to put it on a new adjective, one you'd never heard before—say, *winky*—you'd immediately choose *unwinky,* not *winkyun.* Likewise, you know the rules that allow you to produce a sentence about Amy's feeling for Stan without scrambling it.

Grammar

What sort of rules are these? They are not the sort you learn from teachers, who tell you how you are supposed—and not supposed—to say what you wish to express. Rules of that sort, called **prescriptive rules,** take the form "Don't split infinitives," "Say 'yes,' not 'yeah,'" "Say 'I don't want any,' not 'I don't want none,'" "A pronoun must agree in gender and number with the noun to which it refers," and the like. These are prescriptions for speaking the language in the manner educated people consider "correct." Prescriptive rules may need to be taught. In the case of learning a foreign language in school, they certainly need to be taught.

But the rules linguists focus on when they are concerned with a speaker's implicit knowledge of linguistic systems are the rules *inherent* in the language or dialect. They *describe* these rules—they do not *prescribe* them. For this reason the endeavor is known as ***descriptive*** linguistics. Research has demonstrated the vast number and complexity of these rules in all of the many languages that have been studied, yet these are the rules children absorb unconsciously, as their language is spoken around them. They are not taught—indeed they cannot be taught, for most speakers are generally unaware that they know them and could not necessarily articulate them if they wanted to. (What are often taught are the exceptions to the rules, for example: The way to make *sheep* plural is not to add *s* but to add nothing; the way to speak of *swim* in the past is not *swimmed* but *swam.*)

Our ability to use our language, what we know about it even if we do not know that we know it, is referred to by linguists as our **linguistic competence**. This contains the rules pertaining to every component of the language: the **phonology** (the rules pertaining to the sound system), the **morphology** (the rules governing word structure), the **syntax** (the rules governing the structure of sentences), and **semantics** (the rules concerning meaning). Taken together, all of these comprise the **grammar** of the language, and linguistic competence is the (largely unconscious) knowledge of that grammar. (Note that this is not the meaning of "grammar" as we commonly use it, which is to refer specifically to what they teach in school—the rules of syntax. A linguist may use the term "grammar" in a number of ways. One of these ways is as I have done here: to refer to the entire set of rules of the language that an individual has internalized. But the term may also refer to the linguist's hypothesis about what this consists of.)

The rules that underlie our linguistic competence can be deduced or inferred by studying the patterns observable in a language as it is actually spoken by a given population. In the little demonstration that follows you will see that, though you are generally unaware of knowing these rules, you in fact know them well and, with some guidance, can bring them to consciousness. A favorite example of linguists for demonstrating phonological rules most people are unaware of knowing is one that concerns the pronunciation of the **plural marker**—the sound added to nouns to make them plural. This sound, as you all know, is spelled *s*. The following are two short lists of nouns to which may be added this plural marker:

A	B
ship	tub
nap	lab
cat	bud
nut	lid
park	rag
wick	wig

Try adding the plural as you say each of the words in column A, listening carefully to the sound you make in doing so. Then do the same for the words in column B. If you are indeed listening carefully, you will surely hear the difference. To the words in the first column, you have added the sound *s*, as you expected to. But to the words in the second column, you have added the sound *z*. Now if you examine the words in column A and those in column B, you will notice that all of them end in a consonant. What you may not observe right away is that there is a small but significant difference between final consonants in the two sets. The final consonants in the column A words are articulated *without* the voice, whereas those in the column B words are articulated *with* the voice. Putting a finger on your larynx (your "Adam's apple") as you say the words will enable you to feel the vibration of your vocal cords; it is this vibration that makes voice happen. You will notice that when you finish saying the vowel sounds in the column A words, the vibration stops. The final sound in each word is not accompanied by vibration. Notice the way you say the plural of each of these words; there is no vibration on the final *s* sound either.

If you now try the same experiment with the words in column B, you will notice that the consonant at the end of each *is* accompanied by vibration and voice. And so is the plural sound you attach to them; that's why it sounds like *z*. You quite automatically put the voiced sound on the words that end with a voiced sound, and you put the sound without voice on the end of the words that end with an unvoiced sound. You can test this by adding the plural to, for example, *talp* and *torb,* which you have no doubt never come across before. Because they are not words of English, you have not heard anyone say them, either in the singular or in the plural. Yet if you treat these nonsense words—and any others you make up— as real ones, and make them plural, you will unfailingly attach the version that follows the rule.

And this rule you have just discovered can be simply stated: When forming the plural of nouns, add the voiceless version of the plural marker to words ending in voiceless consonants, and add the voiced version to words ending in voiced consonants. No one taught you this rule, and you were in all probability unaware that you knew it. You have acquired many such rules, which function in all the aspects of your linguistic competence. Although the rules differ from one language to another (the one we have just examined is a rule specifically of English), all languages have such rules and all speakers learn them as you did this one: effortlessly and usually without awareness.

Additional aspects of our linguistic competence concern certain other abilities that we also tend to take for granted, that is, until it is pointed out to us that they are really pretty impressive. For example, we are immediately able to know when an utterance is "all right"—that it accords with our notion of obeying the rules of the language—and when it is not. In this sense it is all right to say, for instance,

Hildegarde left home this morning without her keys.

But it is not all right to say

Left morning home this her without keys Hildegarde.

The words are all there, but they are in the wrong order. As you have internalized the rule for the pronunciation of the plural of nouns, so you have also internalized the rules for ordering the words of English into sentences that feel right—that are, in other words, grammatical.

We are also able to understand utterances even when parts are left out. "Stop it!" is an example. Complete sentences always have a subject, a person or thing or idea that the sentence is about. "You stop it!" expresses this subject: It is *you.* But we routinely leave this part out of commands, knowing somehow that the subject of a command is always *you.*

There are still other rather amazing abilities that we possess with regard to language. We are able to recognize—and create—sentences that have more than one meaning: We call these **ambiguous sentences**. It is clear that we know there are two meanings to a sentence such as the following:

Andrew saw the girl with binoculars.

What is not clear is who has the binoculars—Andrew or the girl. Has Andrew seen her through them, or has Andrew seen her and perceived that she has them? Or take a sentence such as

The zoo contained young llamas and anteaters.

Are both the llamas and the anteaters young, or just the llamas?

As we are able to recognize and create ambiguous sentences, so are we able to recognize and generate sentences that *paraphrase* each other. These are sentences that take a different form but have the *same* meaning. You will recognize the common meaning within each pair of the following sentences:

Ernest ate a sandwich.
A sandwich was eaten by Ernest.
Sally is climbing the tallest tree in the yard.
The tallest tree in the yard is being climbed by Sally.

You know the pairs constitute paraphrases; in the first, the one who is eating and that which is eaten remain the same. In the second pair, it is always Sally doing the climbing and the tree that is being climbed. That is, the **grammatical relations** remain constant—and somehow we are equipped to know this, though we are taught in school that the subject of these sentences changes as we change their form from active to passive.

Nor is this all our linguistic competence allows us. At its most fundamental level, language is constructed of sounds strung together, one after another, in a linear order. Some of our basic abilities concern the sounds and sound combinations that make up the words of our language. When a native speaker of a language other than yours speaks to you in your language, you notice immediately that he or she produces sounds that do not strike your ear as you expect. When an adult native speaker of Hungarian says the English word *bad,* it may be pronounced *bed,* because Hungarian lacks the vowel sound in *bad.* When an adult native speaker of French says the English word *something,* it may sound like *somesing,* because French does not have the *th* sound English has.

I'm sure you have also observed that utterances in an unfamiliar language seem less like sequences of words than like a steady, undifferentiated stream of sound. Where does one word end and the next begin? Without instruction, how can you figure it out? Yet this is precisely what you *did* do as a baby, when you began to learn your own language. Quite efficiently, and in a remarkably short time, you figured out which sounds, among all those assailing your ears, were the ones to pay attention to; where to assume boundaries between individual words; how to manipulate the words so that when you yourself began to utter them they came out in the right order and got you what you needed more than anything else:

to be understood. And you did virtually all of this *on your own,* because a lot of what was said to you was incomplete and simplified, if not downright babytalk (*Tommy want his blankee? Bye bye doggie.*).

If all of this is not impressive, I don't know what is. What linguists seek to do is to account for, to explain these wonderful abilities that characterize our species.

Approaches in the Field of Linguistics

Early Approaches: Pānini and Grimm

The notion of linguistic competence introduced previously rests on the assumption of unconscious knowledge and unconscious cognitive activity. This is not a new assumption; it underlies, for example, the work of the grammarian Pānini, who carried out his research in India sometime between the fifth and seventh centuries B.C.E. Pānini sought to capture the underlying patterns of the Sanskrit he spoke and, in this fashion, to describe the whole of the language. The few examples presented in the previous section indicate something of the nature of the rules that a language rests on. How vast a task it would be to try to describe it all: rules affecting the sounds and their variants, rules for forming words, rules for generating all the possible sentences. Pānini approached this monumental task by formulating detailed, highly condensed rules. Their nature was not prescriptive but rather descriptive. As such, they reflect the unconscious knowledge of speakers of the language rather than rules that might have been explicitly taught. They capture so much detail of the language so tersely that expanding and understanding them has required the work of many scholars and much time. Since Pānini, no one has accomplished so impressive a description of any language.

The work of Pānini, and of other Indian linguists of his time and earlier, was not known in the West until the 19th century. Linguistics scholars of the 1800s had observed many similarities among the languages of Europe and sought to trace their history, engaging in comparative studies of these related languages and projecting backward to arrive at a "reconstruction" of the ancestral language, or group of dialects, from which they derived. One of the most famous of these scholars was Jacob Grimm (1785–1863), of fairy-tale fame. Grimm's contribution to the understanding of certain important consonant shifts among the Indo-European languages (many of the languages most familiar to us, including English) is a staple of historical-comparative study, known to all linguistics students and scholars as **Grimm's law.** This law, which aids in the process of linguistic reconstruction, explains for example the historical relation between Latin *p* (as in *pater*) and English *f* (as in *father*), both of which derive from the same source, a language spoken some thousands of years ago and referred to today as **Indo-European.**

Linguistics scholars engaged in reconstructing early languages of which there is no written record made educated guesses as to what the earlier forms were based on evidence from all aspects of these languages—from the vocabulary they contained to the kinds of change exhibited over time in their sound systems and in their grammatical structures. This type of comparative-historical research contributed a great deal to our understanding of the processes languages undergo on their evolving paths. Access to information about Sanskrit played an important role in this endeavor.

Edward Sapir and Benjamin Lee Whorf

In line with this type of research was research carried out into this century by scholars who sought to learn what processes underlay the many languages spoken by Native American tribes. In the process, they encountered ways of thinking quite different from those of the Western European culture, which had up to then provided the background for their studies. These scholars drew attention to the many different possibilities inherent in languages for expressing perceptions and experiences common to humankind. Edward Sapir, the American linguist and anthropologist mentioned in Chapter 2, made many contributions to the field, among them important technical studies in Native American, Indo-European, Semitic, and African languages. With this wide basis, he was able to provide the field with cogent analyses of the relation of language and culture. His interest in this aspect of linguistics extended to the relation of language and thought. He and his student, Benjamin Lee Whorf, expounded a view that had great influence on linguists and other scholars in the middle decades of the 20th century. Known as the Sapir-Whorf hypothesis, it was articulated thus by Whorf in 1940:

> We dissect nature along lines laid down by our native languages. The categories and types that we isolate from the world of phenomena we do not find there because they stare every observer in the face; on the contrary, the world is presented in a kaleidoscopic flux of impressions which has to be organized by our minds—and this means largely by the linguistic systems in our minds. We cut nature up, organize it into concepts, and ascribe significances as we do, largely because we are parties to an agreement to organize it in this way—an agreement that holds throughout our speech community and is codified in the patterns of our language. The agreement is, of course, an implicit and unstated one, *but its terms are absolutely obligatory*; we cannot talk at all except by subscribing to the organization and classification of data which the agreement decrees. (in Carroll, 1956, pp. 213–214)

Whorf had held, for example, that the Hopi language reflects a different conception of time from that of English. He claimed that Hopi has no linguistic means of referring directly to time, as English does, no word for "past" or "future." If he was correct, then, according to some, the Hopi could not distinguish past from future. Whorf's point was that the Hopi language reflects a different worldview—one that our own language lacks the means of expressing.

The strong version of the Sapir-Whorf hypothesis holds first that our language determines the way we think (**linguistic determinism**) and, second, that the distinctions found in a given language will not be the same as those in any other language (**linguistic relativity**). The basic principle follows from the observation, through study of the languages of different peoples, that populations "carve up" in many different ways the natural world they experience. An instance is found in Whorf's paper "Science and Linguistics." After describing some of the characteristics that distinguish the worldview of speakers of the Hopi language from our own, Whorf says

> What surprises most is to find that various grand generalizations of the Western world, such as time, velocity, and matter, are not essential to the construction of a consistent picture of the universe. The psychic experiences that we class under these headings are, of course, not destroyed; rather, categories derived from other kinds of experiences take over the rulership of the cosmology and seem to function just as well. Hopi may be called a timeless language. It recognizes psychological time. . . but this "time" is quite unlike the mathematical time T, used by our physicists. Among the peculiar properties of Hopi time are that it varies with each observer, does not permit of simultaneity, and has zero dimensions; i.e., it cannot be given a number greater than one. The Hopi do not say, "I stayed five days," but "I left on the fifth day." (in Carroll, 1956, p. 216)

Whorf's description of the Hopi conception of time seems to indicate that for the Hopi time exists as a series of points rather than as a continuous flow. This conception relates interestingly to Kant's discussion of time, in which he argues that "all appearances of succession in time are one and all only *alterations . . . all change (succession) of appearances is merely alteration*" (Kant, 1781/1965, p. 218). That is, we only recognize time by the sequential changes that we observe. A flow, or passage, of time, as we are accustomed to conceiving of it, and which seems to us the natural way of conceiving of it, is equally naturally perceived as a sequence of events, each one different from the preceding one. The Hopi's "I left on the fifth day" seems to accord with this conception of time better than our own characterization of the situation "I stayed five days": "The fifth day" marks one of a series of days, whereas "five days" combines them into a whole.

The notion that language serves not only to express thought but also to filter it leads easily to the idea embodied in the Sapir-Whorf hypothesis that language serves to *shape* thought. This view was subsequently interpreted to mean that we cannot—and cannot learn to—think in any way but the way in which our language dictates. Because many felt this interpretation was incorrect—and was threatening to groups that might be politically affected by it—the hypothesis was rejected by the establishment. In fact, there was a strong reaction against it, because it seemed to predict that if one's language lacked some forms of expression its speakers were incapable of conceptualizing what such expressions express. Consider, for example, the construction that is second nature to English speakers: "If I were you. . . ." Of course I know perfectly well that I am not you. That is precisely why I put it in this way, using an *if* construction, paired with the special form *were* of the verb *to be*. There are languages that lack a construction of this sort, called a **counterfactual**, as it is counter to what is in fact so.

A weaker version of the hypothesis was somewhat more acceptable, namely, that the constructions of language make it relatively easier or more difficult to think in certain ways. But consideration of the effect of language on thought was for a period a topic many were unwilling to engage in.

More recently, scholars such as Alfred Bloom have returned to this issue, as we will in the next chapter.

Ferdinand de Saussure

Another approach to the field of linguistics was that introduced early in the 20th century, when attention turned from the focus on historical-comparative studies to the principles governing the structure of languages still being spoken. The theoretical ideas introduced at this time by the Swiss linguist Ferdinand de Saussure (1857–1913) were extremely influential, essentially redefining the field. These ideas were based on the observation by scholars going all the way back to Pānini's time (and perhaps even before then) that when people actually speak they often produce sounds and constructions that they themselves would report as somehow being not "really right," but which are understood anyway. For example, if, around lunchtime, a friend called out to you, asking *"Jeet jet?"* your response would probably not be "Huh?" but either "Yeah" or *"No, joo?"* What surfaces as *Jeet jet?* and *No, joo?* is clearly understood by both of you as "Did you eat yet?" "No, did you?" You could at any time "translate" the rapid form of these questions into the complete version you produce when slowing down and enunciating carefully. By means of rules specific to your language, a conversion takes place between what you know is the real underlying form of the utterance and what you actually say. All of this is part of the unconscious knowledge we have been calling your linguistic competence.

Pānini's work on the rules underlying the language of speakers of his form of Sanskrit leads to a recognition of the distinction between those rules and the language they generate. The notion that something underlies the forms we actually produce is the important insight here, one that has been brought out at other times in the history of linguistics. Contemporary scholars such as Noam Chomsky (discussed later) give credit to, for example, René Descartes and to the authors of the volume *Grammaire générale et raisonnée,* published in France in 1660 (usually referred to as the Port-Royal Grammar), for reintroducing such insights from which much of modern-day linguistics has benefited.

More recently, Ferdinand de Saussure, working near the beginning of the 20th century, distinguished between **langue,** the linguistic *system* internalized by speakers of a language, and **parole,** the *act* of speaking. This distinction implies a tacit assumption that underlying the actual utterances of speakers of a given language is a shared structure, absorbed by speakers when very young and remaining largely below the level of consciousness. This implicit structure enables them to judge, for example, when one utterance is correctly formed, another is not, and a third is all right when speaking (especially quickly) but is not really the way it is "supposed to be," as our *Jeet jet?* example. Put more succinctly, the distinction is between what you know about your language (your *linguistic competence,* unconscious though it may be) and what you actually say, which linguists refer to as your **linguistic performance.**

Behaviorism: John B. Watson and B. F. Skinner

Saussure's work has had great influence on contemporary linguistics. But the direction taken by the field was altered for a time, despite the insights he provided and developed. With the advent of the "behavioristic" paradigm, the "mentalistic" approach to the study of language was abandoned. The American psychologist John B. Watson (1878–1958) struck out in a new direction, becoming the founder of the school known as **behaviorism**. Behaviorism operates on the principle that what goes on in the mind that is not directly observable or measurable is not an appropriate and useful subject of research. The only appropriate subject matter of psychology, according to the behaviorists, is *behavior*. Behavior is all that we can hope to treat objectively, because it is all we can *measure*. This approach leaves no place for study, linguistic or otherwise, based on unconscious knowledge. The insights of scholars over a very long period were abandoned as linguists attempted a stimulus-response account of language.

B. F. Skinner (1904–1990) is today probably the best-known proponent of the behaviorist approach. Among his many works was the 1957 book *Verbal Behavior*, in which he sought to interpret and explain the major aspects of linguistic behavior within the behaviorist framework. In 1959 the American linguist Noam Chomsky (b. 1928) published a review of *Verbal Behavior* in which he refuted Skinner's premise that it is possible to account for linguistic behavior within this framework. He systematically discussed each concept introduced by Skinner in order to show "that, in each case, if we take his terms in their literal meaning, the description covers almost no aspect of verbal behavior, and if we take them metaphorically, the description offers no improvement over various traditional formulations" (Chomsky, 1964, p. 574). This review sparked a period of debate and called attention to the beginning of a new phase in linguistics, in which Chomsky has figured prominently.

The Return of the Cognitive: Contemporary Linguistics

Noam Chomsky

The impetus that set the field of linguistics on its current path came from the publication of Chomsky's *Syntactic Structures* (1957) and *Aspects of the Theory of Syntax* (1965). These works ignited a revolution in linguistics, placing it squarely back into the domain of the mind and determining the direction it has followed ever since.

What Chomsky contributed initially was a shift of focus to the (vast and largely unconscious) set of rules he hypothesized must exist in the minds of speakers and hearers in order for them to produce and understand their native language or languages. Like Pāṇini, he was concerned with discovering, isolating, and pinpointing these rules, to make their formulation precise and predictive. But, as a 20th-century researcher, he was working within the contemporary framework of science. Scientific effort requires abandoning vagueness in favor of focusing on the observable specifics, which alone lead to productive hypotheses. But unlike the behaviorists, Chomsky based his hypothesis on the assumption of a capacity in the brain that functions without the conscious awareness of the person in whom this functioning is taking place, and which it is indeed possible and profitable to study. The data provided by language permit us to infer what must be taking place as language is produced. In the process, Chomsky proposed a method of formalizing the rules of the components of language. In view of the impact on and pervasiveness of this approach in linguistic research in the second half of the 20th century, a brief introduction is in order.

The first component of language Chomsky addressed was the syntactic component—the portion of one's linguistic competence that handles the arrangement of words into sentences. A simple sentence serves as an example of what formal rules must contain if they are to be capable of generating such a sentence:

The cat chased a mouse.

This sentence contains five separate words, some of which—*the cat, a mouse*—"feel" as though, when taken together, they form a somewhat larger unit. The words in each grouping must occur in this order: *cat the* and *mouse a* are not permissible English combinations. (The asterisk preceding each such formulation is, by convention, a sign that what follows is not grammatical in the language.) It is also true that in English one or the other of these combinations may come first and the verb, in this case *chased,* must come between them. The following ordering would also be fine for English, though it expresses a somewhat unusual situation:

A mouse chased the cat.

Also perfectly good sentences of English are these two:

A cat chased the mouse.
The mouse chased a cat.

A rule that would specify that these four orderings are just those that are permitted for this set of words would have to refer to the part of speech each word represents. These sentences demonstrate that nouns may occur both before verbs and after verbs and that **articles**, when present, must be placed before the nouns they refer to. But the rules would also make clear that not all sentences contain nouns that are preceded by an article:

Babies cry

is a perfectly good English sentence, yet there is no *the* or *a* before *babies.* Nor, for that matter, is there a noun after the verb. So the rules would specify that a verb need not be followed by a noun.

The rules Chomsky formulated making all of this explicit are written, in their most basic form for the simplest of sentences, as follows: Letting S stand for the sentence, N for nouns, V for verbs, and Art for articles, and an arrow, →, for the way in which S can be expanded to include its elements,

S → (Art) N V (Art) (N).

S can be rewritten or expanded as (i.e., the sentence contains) an article followed by a noun followed by a verb followed by an article followed by a noun—*in that order.* Articles and the noun following the verb are placed in parentheses to indicate that they may or may not be present in the sentence. The first noun, which serves as the subject of the sentence, must be present, as must the verb.

A slightly more complicated sentence might contain another element:

The white cat chased a frightened mouse.
A brave mouse chased the small cat.

Now we must accommodate adjectives. In English, when an adjective is associated with a noun, it occurs before the noun. Modifying our rule to allow for this, we can write

S → (Art) (Adj) N V (Art) (Adj) (N).

But we know that a noun may have more than one adjective associated with it. Therefore, we need a symbol to indicate that indefinitely many adjectives may occur before a noun. To make this clear we place an asterisk after Adj: Adj*. (A moment's thought will suffice to convince you that there can be only one article preceding a noun.) Our rule now looks like this:

S → (Art) (Adj*) N V (Art) (Adj*) (N).

This is not a very economical formulation, because it repeats so many of the elements. It may be condensed, because in principle a noun will *always* have the possibility of a preceding article and indefinitely many adjectives. If we call this combination a *noun phrase,* and abbreviate it **NP**, we can write our rule this way:

S → NP V (NP).

Now we must write a rule that expands NP:

NP → (Art) (Adj*) N.

A sentence can be divided up intuitively much as a noun phrase can, into components that seem to "go together." *The white cat* forms one part of the sentence, that which is being spoken about—the subject. *Chased a frightened mouse* forms the other part of the sentence, that which is being said about the subject—the predicate.

The white cat chased a frightened mouse at high speed into the grassy yard.

To capture the intuition that the sentence breaks into two major parts, we can recognize the status of the second part by calling it a *verb phrase,* or **VP.** The rule that produces, or generates, sentences can now be stated in the condensed form

S → NP VP.

Our latest sentence now contains two additional phrases, *at high speed* and *into the grassy yard*. Each of these, as you can see, contains a **preposition**, abbreviated Prep (*at, into*), followed by a noun phrase. This we can categorize as a prepositional phrase, abbreviated **PP**, which we formulate as follows and add to our list of rules:

PP ⟶ Prep NP.

As the sentence indicates, there is the possibility for an indefinite number of prepositional phrases following the verb.

Each part of our rule for generating sentences can be expanded by writing the rules we have formulated for each element, giving us the following set:

S ⟶ NP VP.
NP ⟶ (Art) (Adj*) N.
VP ⟶ V (NP) (PP*).
PP ⟶ Prep NP.

The NP in this last rule can of course be expanded by means of the already stated NP rule.

It must be understood, of course, that these particular rules apply to English sentences only. The rules for generating the sentences of other languages would require a different formulation. German, for example, would require the verb to occur as the last element in the verb phrase.

So far we have formulated only four rules. Now, having formulated the rules, we must include the words themselves in order to generate the sentence. Each category they involve—nouns, verbs, articles, prepositions—can be further expanded to include the words that constitute that category. Thus:

N ⟶ [cat, mouse, speed, yard . . .]
V ⟶ [chased . . .]
Art ⟶ [a(n), the]
Adj ⟶ [white, frightened, high, small, grassy . . .]
Prep ⟶ [at, into . . .]

You can easily see that a very great number of English sentences can be generated by means of this small set of rules, using the many other words that fit into the categories N, V, Adj, and Prep. (The category Art is different; there are only two articles in English—*an* being a variant of *a*.) However, if you consider sentences such as the following, you will also see that there is much more that must be accounted for in English sentences:

Whose mittens are these?
I disagree entirely.
I don't want you to go out tonight.
Get lost!

Let's see the crossword puzzle you have just finished.

Kenny told the girl who came to pick up the books that she couldn't have them because he wasn't finished reading them yet.

This will give you some idea of the vastness of the task of formulating the syntactic rules of a language—and we haven't even mentioned the rules for making the words *sound* right for the language or for constructing the words or for deriving "*Jeet jet?*" and "*No, joo?*" from "Did you eat yet?" and "No, did you?"!

Let us look briefly at an example of unconscious rules of the sort Chomsky sought to formalize, drawn from the phonological component of your linguistic competence, that portion that deals with the sound system of your language. One example will suffice to indicate that the phonological component is also vast and complex. Sounds of a language that are identified by its speakers as being "the same," such as the two instances of the sound *p* in the English word *paper,* are in fact pronounced in a somewhat different manner and thus sound somewhat different. You can demonstrate this yourself quite easily. Hold a sheet of paper up to your lips as you pronounce the word *paper;* you will find that the first *p* carries with it a puff of air that blows the paper away from your lips, whereas the second *p* is said without this puff of air. Linguists refer to the puff of air as **aspiration**, calling the first *p* "aspirated" and the second one "unaspirated." The variation in their articulation depends on their position in the word: The sound *p* becomes aspirated when it occurs at the beginning of a syllable and is immediately followed by a stressed vowel (as in the first syllable of *paper*). When it is in any other position, it does not. Native English speakers never make the mistake of using one version where the other belongs. Yet they are generally unaware that they are using two versions of the sound. Thus we can speak of an *underlying* notion of the sound, which is stored in the speaker's brain as part of the pattern of speech sounds of his or her language. Just as water can exist as liquid (water), solid (ice), or gas (steam), so too are many of the sounds of language manifested differently in different environments, as the two versions of *p* in *paper* clearly show. The variants of a given sound, taken together, constitute a phoneme. A phoneme, then, is a kind of abstraction.

The sounds *t* and *k* are articulated in very much the same way as *p*—that is, without voice and by closing off the passageway in the mouth that allows the sound to be uttered on the expelled breath. (*P* does this at the lips, *t* with the tip of the tongue behind the top teeth, and *k* with the back part of the tongue touching the roof of the mouth. This can easily be demonstrated by simply saying the sounds.) All three of these sounds behave the same way, following the same rule with respect to aspiration. Following a convention that indicates aspiration by means of a superscript ^{h}, it is possible to write a rule that expresses this situation:

p, t, k become p^h, t^h, k^h when they occur at the beginning of a syllable and are immediately followed by a stressed vowel.

By means of a set of symbols and terms that capture the commonalities among the three sounds, the conditions under which the rule is applied, and the result of its application, a very economical formal rule can be written. (To explain all the complications involved in arriving at such rules would require a course in linguistics. My purpose here is merely to suggest their complexity.)

The Relevance of the Rules to Cognitive Science

Perhaps your head is spinning from this discussion of the formalization of rules of English. Perhaps you are wondering why it was included. There are several reasons. First, to appreciate what was involved in the new linguistics of the 20th century, it is necessary to have at least some understanding of the turn it took in the direction of scientific inquiry and method. Second, establishing a formal means of encoding the rules of language enables important generalizations to be grasped (such as the one that extends the effect of the aspiration rule from one sound to all sounds made in the same manner). If we can capture in this way the rules that characterize languages, we can compare them to see what types of rules characterize human languages in general. From there we can proceed to a greater understanding of what the human brain is equipped with that enables it to "do" language.

Another reason for making the rules explicit is to increase our understanding of the way children learn their first language. If it is indeed by means of acquiring such rules (however they are represented in the brain), we can more readily understand how it is possible for them to do it in the short time it actually takes.

Still another important reason to formalize the rules of language has to do with the capabilities we are developing, via the computer, to model aspects of human intelligence. Computer programs require very precise and unambiguous instructions. The formalization of the rules of language has enabled computer scientists involved in artificial intelligence to attempt to model human language on the computer, as will be discussed in Part 4.

Identifying and formalizing the rules of language rests on the assumption that they have been internalized, represented in some fashion in the brain—that they are in fact *in there,* somewhere. Regarding the issue from this perspective requires that we consider how it is possible for an infant to begin to acquire these rules, on the assumption that it is born not knowing them. This assumption is reasonable, because babies will learn to speak the languages spoken in their environment. (If a child is adopted by a family of a different culture from that of the biological parents, where a different language is spoken, the child learns the language of the adoptive culture.) We wonder, of course, how it is possible for the linguistic system of a given language to be absorbed, as it demonstrably is, early in childhood. Is the capacity to "do" language a specialized one, residing in brain functions evolved just for that purpose? Or is it rather, as some have proposed, one among many abilities that arise from certain general cognitive abilities, such as the ability to categorize experiences of our environment (this is a chair; that is a person; this word is a potential sentence subject, but that word can only designate an action)?

Chomsky's hypothesis was that the inborn linguistic capacity of humans is sensitive to just those rules that occur in human languages—and in no other sorts of language or system. In other words, something quite specific to language has evolved in the human brain, something that enables the steady stream of language sounds to be perceived by the infant as distinct in an important way from other sounds and that also enables the infant to begin to break down the flow of this stream into meaningful parts, arranged, as the infant somehow recognizes, in a systematic way. Chomsky likened this capacity to the capacity to walk, in the sense that it is a behavior in which humans naturally engage, without the need for special instruction, as soon as they are developmentally ready—provided the environment permits. That is, walking proceeds if the toddler has undergone maturation sufficient for growth of bones and muscles, and language development occurs if the environment provides exposure to language. Both are part of our biological endowment. It is thus no accident that there are many similarities among languages: The many systems, or grammars, that underlie them are ultimately generated by the human brain.

That there are as many different grammars as there are languages is evident. But linguists cannot discover the grammar of any one of them without careful study of the actual language as it is spoken. At the outset one might propose any number of possible grammars to account for the speech heard in a given language. How many sets of rules might one be able to think up that would generate the things people say? Think for a moment about how many explanations one might propose for how a machine—say, a car—works, in the absence of actually looking inside to see the components and what drives their operation. One might come up with many explanations, ranging from "There are forty little guys in there pedaling for all they're worth" to very complicated schemes for having one element move another, which would then move another . . . something like a **Rube Goldberg contraption**. Someone might even hit on the correct explanation, and we who actually *know* how the car works know that there is only one correct explanation.

So it is with language. There are many possible grammars that would serve to produce a given language. But if we adults cannot peer inside the mechanism and learn which is the correct one, how on earth does a small child find it on his or her own? Even if we are willing to assume, with Chomsky, that what the child brings to bear is an innate capacity to project the right grammar on the language spoken in the environment, we might not wish to endow—to overburden—this child with all the grammars to select from that would be necessary for all languages. But if babies do not know in advance which language they will be confronted with at birth, how else could they possibly find the right grammar?

The hypothesis proposed to answer this question is that despite their surface differences all human languages share a fundamental structure, and what is common to them all has come to be known as **universal grammar**. Innate in all of us, according to this hypothesis, is the ability to apply this universal grammar to whatever languages we are faced with at birth. This explanation is not universally accepted; some have maintained, for example, that the human capacity for language is not richly specified in the brain but is rather a special function of the general cognitive abilities humans possess.

Chomsky's early hypotheses regarding the nature of the human linguistic capacity date from the mid-1950s. During the next 20 years or so, researchers following that line of thinking worked with the kind of explanation discussed earlier in this chapter—that is, that each of us is endowed with an innate capacity to respond to rules of language of the sort I have described. But there are so many languages, and each has its own set of rules. How is it possible for a brain to possess *innately* a system adequate to the task?

The approach then taken by Chomsky and others was to attempt to "factor out" general *principles* that hold for all languages, principles that govern application of the rules of languages. Under this new **principles and parameters** formulation, which crystallized around 1980, it is these that constitute the universal grammar. Variation in languages results from the ways in which these principles apply. There is a finite set of ways in which the principles may apply; these are the *parameters* (Chomsky, 1995). The parameters have been likened to a set of switches, each having a fixed range of potential settings. The actual language the learner is exposed to provides the data that trigger the setting of the switches. Under the principles and parameters hypothesis, learning the syntax of one's first language is a matter of setting these switches; acquiring language is a process of fixing the parameters in one of the permissible ways. With no requirement that the innate component specify all manner of language-specific rules of the sort described previously, the hypothesized innate machinery of language can be reduced.

Whichever way one looks at it, some of the questions we find ourselves asking regarding the language capacity of humans are:

> How is language organized in the brain?
>
> How does it work?
>
> If a person speaks more than one language, how are these languages stored?
>
> Once the rules of a given language have been internalized by the child, how and where are they represented in the brain?

We cannot take the direct path and look inside for the answers, because even when the brain is exposed to view for medical reasons, as in Penfield's work, one sees neither rules such as VP → V (NP) (PP*) nor principles and parameters lurking there in some recognizable form. But the recently developed sophisticated methods of scanning the brain, as we saw in the preceding chapter, allow us to observe brain activity during the performance of language-related tasks, among others. Nonetheless, we see no rule hopping about the cortex clamoring to be recognized.

There are, however, experiments that do provide us with information. Brain-damaged patients can serve as subjects of such experiments (Damasio & Tranel, 1993). These experiments indicate that certain brain structures link areas of knowledge about traits, sounds, and movements of birds, for example, with the nouns and verbs associated with them. Subjects in the experiments could describe, using verbs, what was taking place in pictures of activities involving birds, but did much worse than non-brain-damaged controls in using the appropriate nouns, such as duck, ostrich, and other bird names. Another conclusion to be drawn, according to the experimenters, is that areas of the brain that handle nouns are not the same as those that handle verbs.

In the next chapter we will turn to the sorts of experiments that have been carried out in recent attempts to understand the acquisition and functioning of language in our species. Chapter 6 presents the ways in which linguistics relates to the other disciplines participating in the cognitive science endeavor.

Questions to Think About

1. What are some of the things you are able to express in your language that your pet or your friend's pet can't? Why can't it? Why can *you?*

2. Consider the sentence

   I just finished reading this chapter.

   Is it possible for you to write down all the other sentences you can think of in which this sentence might be placed? Why or why not?

3. Linguists talk about ***prescriptive* rules** and ***descriptive* rules** of language. Can you see a need for this distinction? If not, why not? If so, what is the need?

4. The chapter describes the phonological rule of English that causes the suffix *-s* (added to a noun to make it plural) to sound like *z* if the noun ends in a voiced sound (*door,* for example). But if the noun ends in an unvoiced sound (as in *cat*), the unvoiced sound *s* is added instead. Consider the suffix *-ed,* which is added to verbs when they express the past tense. How is it affected by the voiced or unvoiced quality of the last sound in the verb it is attached to?

5. Try to find examples from your own speech or that of your friends that illustrate the difference between your linguistic competence and your linguistic performance.

6. If you speak or have studied a language other than English, can you think of any words or expressions that occur in it that cannot be accurately rendered in English? How about the other way around? Is there anything you would like to be able to express in language that you cannot? If so, what sort of thing is it? How might it be expressed?

6

The Role of Linguistics in Cognitive Science

Linguistics and Cognitive Psychology

Linguists search for the underlying commonalities among languages. Some reconstruct rules of languages no longer spoken, and some focus on the rules of languages currently spoken. The data they describe contribute to our knowledge of the types of rules and principles underlying languages. From these data we can infer much about the functioning of the cognitive processes that produce them. As you read in Part 1, cognitive psychology attempts to understand the processes our minds engage in, the "cognitive architecture" that makes it all possible. Thus language is of great interest to those of us in the field of cognitive psychology, concerned as we are with issues of learning and of the representation of knowledge in the brain. The following is a brief look at some of the areas in cognitive psychology in which language plays a major role and where the overlap with linguistics is plain.

Language and Thought

A fundamental question, one that has long been asked, is "What is the relation of language to thought?" Once having acquired at least one language, we find it difficult to imagine how we would be able to think—at least to engage in the kind of thinking you are now engaging in as you read this—*without* language. The kind of thinking required here is abstract. The very notion of thinking is abstract; we can't see it, though facial expressions may give us a clue that it is occurring. It would be hard to represent it as a picture, though one might draw or paint a person seemingly engaged in doing it.

An object—a Honda Civic, like the one mentioned in the preface, for instance—is, on the contrary, concrete. Our reaction to the notion of such a concrete object may very well be to see one in our mind's eye. The particular one we conjure up in this manner will of course be influenced by many factors, one being the particular Honda Civics we have encountered in the past. Your experience of your friend's gray 1988 model may differ in detail from my experience of my neighbor's 1990 blue one, but the way it would be represented in the thoughts of both of us might be as a "mental image." (Mental imagery is examined in greater detail in Chapter 2.) But how, without the possibility of a concrete mental image to represent it, do we manage to think about something abstract, such as sincerity or friendship—or thinking itself?

It seems likely that the capacity for abstract thought depends on the capacity for language. It may be, as some think, that these two human abilities evolved interdependently, that the type of thinking that characterizes humans and, as far as we know, no other species, was simply not possible until the development of language gave it a medium in which to grow. An important question in this regard concerns the sort of language in which our thoughts are encoded. Do we think in ordinary language? From a number of very common and familiar types of occurrence, it would seem not. For example, how often has it happened to you that you sought a word to express an idea, knowing you "had" the word somewhere, that it was on the tip of your tongue, but you just couldn't find it? Or what of the times your thoughts were "racing faster than you could put them into words"? And haven't you, when asked to define a word, sometimes found yourself saying "I know what it means; I just don't know how to explain it"? Then you demonstrated that you knew the meaning by using the word correctly in a sentence. Consider too the fact that we "have" concepts that are separate before being combined into a single sentence, such as the two ideas referred to in Chapter 5 in our discussion of the sentence "This is the house that Jack built."

Another example is one that readers will recall from Chapter 2, when I told of a situation in which I responded to a question without realizing until afterward that it had been asked in French. Apparently, the *meaning* of the question was primary, being understood and eliciting a response not only instantaneously but without conscious effort on my part to clothe it in words. The actual language used to express the meaning, or the concept, was secondary; any language at my command would do.

Our impression from such instances is that thoughts that are ultimately expressed in language exist somehow in advance of their being so expressed. We have already encountered, in the unit on cognitive psychology, the notion of propositional representation, in which sentence-like structures (propositions) are hypothesized that are related but not identical to the form they take when they are ultimately uttered. The relation of this aspect of the discipline to that of linguistics is clear, and the consideration of language inevitably leads us to the broader question of the representation of knowledge in the brain.

Language Acquisition

First-Language Acquisition

We have also raised the question of how it is possible for human infants to acquire their first language (or languages, for many learn more than one in the environment in which they are raised). The word *infant* itself indicates this state of affairs: Its meaning in Latin, from which we borrowed it, is "not speaking." How are you accustomed to judge when an infant has become no-longer-an-infant? Probably you consider key elements in this judgment to be whether the child walks and talks. In an important sense, Jennifer-of-the-tulips was no longer an infant when she produced her creation of "one lip," an utterance that gave evidence of her command of the subtleties of English. Other examples of the creative use of language in very young children can be observed virtually every day, such as this construction produced by Matthew, a 3-year-old boy, on noticing for the first time an adjustable side-view mirror of a car: "Does this go downer and downer, or is that the only far it can go?"

The branch of linguistics concerned with the current approach to the issue of **first-language acquisition** is **developmental psycholinguistics**. This approach had its origins in the late 1960s and early 1970s, following the initial period of ferment occasioned by the 1957 publication of Chomsky's *Syntactic Structures*. It was then that researchers began systematic studies of the linguistic development of individual children, collecting their utterances and attempting to explain how these were achieved. The old notion that children learn language solely by imitation had to be abandoned, because it was abundantly clear that children often produce sentences they have not heard before; think of Jennifer's novel production "one lip." It also became clear that direct teaching and correcting of their grammar could not account for children's utterances either, because the rules children were unconsciously acquiring were largely buried in the unconscious of the adults around them, as we saw in the preceding chapter.

Rules such as the one that causes us to add an *s* plural sound to words ending in voiceless consonants and a *z* plural sound to those ending in voiced consonants are not taught because the adults who have acquired them and use them correctly all the time are not aware of them. The mistakes children make are likely not to be in *failing* to follow the rules but rather in *applying those rules where they should not*: to the exceptional forms that violate the rules. The little girl who says "I rided my bike around the corner" is demonstrating that she has in fact learned the rule for forming the past tense of verbs, that the way to do it is by putting a particular ending on the verb. (Of course she does not think of it in these terms; she does not think of it at all, until teachers at school point it out and teach it as a prescriptive rule.) It happens that the verb *ride* doesn't follow that rule, and such exceptions—fortunately not intimidatingly many—do have to be learned individually. Correcting a child old enough to assimilate the correction is a way of teaching, in cases like this. But think of how much of their language children already know before they can even make such a mistake.

Complicating the issue of how the child is able to learn a first language is the readily observable fact that in communicating with very young children adults do not even use the complete version of the language: "Susie want blankee . . . ?" "All gone cookie." Of course children hear language spoken *around* them as well as *to* them, but even the adult language is often incomplete: "Wanna go?" "Can't." Even though they are not exposed to the entire linguistic system, children nevertheless master its rules very early.

Experiments carried out by developmental psycholinguists provide support for the claim that children in the process of acquiring their first language or languages are in fact learning the underlying rules. In a famous experiment carried out in 1958 by psycholinguist Jean Berko, children were shown sets of pictures, the best known being one of a small creature the children were told was a "wug" (Figure 6.1). Underneath the wug was a picture of two more. The experimenter read the instructions to the children, who were to fill in the missing word in the sentence "There are two ____ ." A response of "wugs" was taken to indicate that a child had learned the plural rule; a response of "wug" was taken as an indication that the child had not.

The linguistic capabilities of even younger children—infants, in fact—is another fruitful area of experimentation. In recent years, experiments have been carried out in which linguistic material of various sorts has been presented to them

FIGURE 6.1 Item from the "Wug"
Test

This is a wug.

Now there is another one.
There are two of them.
There are two ____ .

in an attempt to identify the elements of language they employ while acquiring their first one. In some cases, the subjects in the experiments are young enough to cause us to think some of these elements they appear already to possess may be innate. Some experiments involve recognition of the sounds of a language. We have already noted that speakers of a given language perceive certain sounds as "belonging" in that language, whereas other sounds, quite natural in some other languages, do not.

In the January 1992 issue of the journal *Science,* researchers reported experiments that found that 6-month-old infants were already distinguishing not just the *sounds* of their own language but the *categories* to which groups of sounds belong. Recall the discussion in the preceding chapter of the sound *p* and the rule of aspiration that applies to it. English speakers regularly ignore—don't even notice— the different pronunciations of *p,* regarding them all as instances of the same sound (phoneme). In the experiments with 6-month-olds, the babies were first exposed to prototype sounds of English, representing the phonemes, such as unaspirated *p*. When these were followed by variants of the sounds, researchers reported, the babies reacted as adults do: They perceived the prototype as identical to the variants. They had apparently already begun to use phonemes as categories into which they sorted the sounds of the language (Kuhl, Williams, Lacerda, Stevens, & Lindblom, 1992). Long before they will produce *any* utterance in their native language, that language has begun to shape the way their brains organize it.

Other studies using even younger subjects, 1- and 2-month-old infants, suggest that even at that age infants can differentiate among speech sounds occurring in different languages of the world (Eimas, 1975). It begins to look as though people are born with this ability—one that seems to disappear as they get older. (Part of the difficulty adults have in learning how to pronounce words in a foreign language results from the fact that some sounds native speakers classify as different sound the same to the adult learners.)

More recent experimental results bear out this finding. The researchers wanted to "explore the age at which experience first begins to influence phonemic perception and the mechanisms that might be responsible for this change" (Werker & Desjardins, 1995, p. 77). Some of the subjects were 6- to 12-month-old infants; the others were children aged 6, 8, and 12 years. One challenge was to determine whether the infants in fact recognize phonemes from languages other than their own better than adults do. To determine this, they had to devise tasks that could be adapted to both infants and adults so that the groups' results could be compared.

The procedure chosen was one in which the subjects were exposed to a continuous background of syllables beginning with a consonant of one phonemic category (e.g., a *b* sound, as in the syllable *ba*). The subjects were to indicate when the stimuli changed to a different category (e.g., a *d* sound as in *da*). Older subjects pressed a button to indicate the change in the stimulus category; they were rewarded by a flash of light. The infants, sitting in their parents' laps, were rewarded by seeing moving toy animals and being praised when they turned their heads to the sound source on noticing a change. The sounds the subjects were exposed to were from their native English and from Hindi, a language spoken in India.

Results of a series of experiments of this sort indicate that the infants do indeed recognize sounds in languages other than those spoken around them not only better than adults but better than the 6- to 12-year-olds. Even 4-year-olds perform like adults in this regard. Infants of 6 months, who can already distinguish the phonemes of their own language, are also already beginning to lose the ability to distinguish those of other languages.

Stages in First-Language Acquisition   Let us assume, then, that infants start off at birth with certain linguistic abilities that enable them to progress through the stages of language learning. You have no doubt observed children as they passed through these stages, perhaps without realizing that both early "cooing" and later misapplication of rules to irregular forms, for example, represent specific stages on the route to mastery of their language. These stages are, of course, achieved at different ages by different children; however, they do seem always to occur in the order described here. Developmental psycholinguists have sought to describe these stages and to characterize the grammar that underlies the children's linguistic competence at each step. (The earliest stages, which do not involve entities recognizable as language, do not lend themselves to such a project, at least given the present state of our knowledge.) The description of the stages is by far the easier task. **Longitudinal studies** (careful and detailed observation and recording of the linguistic behavior of numbers of children as they progress from one level of development to the next) provide data from which generalizations can be drawn.

The stages of language acquisition that can readily be characterized may be summarized very generally as follows. At some time early in the first year, babies begin to utter sounds distinguishable from the crying sounds and other vocalizations that occur from birth and indicate various kinds of feelings and needs. These sounds are the same in all babies, regardless of which languages are spoken around them. Researchers sometimes refer to the period of this behavior as the "cooing" stage. The infants are now beginning to use their vocal apparatus—their tongues, their lips, their vocal cords—in ways that develop into the motor gestures that will eventually produce speech.

This stage is followed by the "babbling" stage, in which a smaller set of sounds is used, organized a good deal of the time into repeated consonant-vowel pairs: *baba, mama*. The intonational patterns of language also begin to develop in this

FIGURE 6.2 An Intonation Diagram of the Sentence "Shall I Wash the Dishes or Will You Do It?"

stage so that though few or none of the utterances are real words, they follow typical "music" of the language—the intonation of its sentences. This often makes them sound like real sentences. See Figure 6.2 for an example of the intonation pattern of a sentence of English. It is this type of rise and fall of the voice that babies produce early, even before they begin to produce words.

When words do begin to appear in the infant's inventory of utterances, it is only one at a time: *doggie, blankee*. Next come two-word utterances: *see doggie, more juice*. Finally, longer strings of words are produced: *Mommy see doggie, truck go bye-bye*.

The complexity of these utterances develops over time until the basic structure of the language has been acquired. Some constructions, which are apparently more complex, take longer to understand and to produce. The passive construction is an example: "The street was crossed by the boy" is acquired later than "The boy crossed the street." Think once again of the complexity of 2½-year-old Jennifer's "Look, Mommy, one lip!" and the difficult construction Matthew was trying out when he asked "Does this go downer and downer, or is that the only far it can go?"

Characterizing the grammar that underlies these stages is more difficult. We hope eventually to gain insight into what is going on in the children's linguistic competence that enables them to produce utterances like those. One way linguists determine what is going on under the surface of a person's language is to pose questions about whether the sample sentences are grammatical or not. Much of the grammar of a language may be inferred from grammaticality judgments— judgments about "rightness" or "wrongness"—that native speakers render about a given phonological entity or syntactic construction. Large collections of such data reveal to the phonologist and the syntactician underlying rules of that language, like those we looked at in Chapter 5. Clever experiments have been devised to ascertain whether a particular rule has been acquired by very young children (remember the "wugs"). But it is more difficult (though not necessarily impossible) to elicit judgments about grammaticality from children than from adults.

Bilingualism   The fact that some children acquire more than one "first" language raises some interesting questions. Are the languages in fact learned equally? That is, is the individual equally fluent, equally comfortable in all aspects of both (or all)? Do the languages that are being learned simultaneously affect each other, and if so, how? Where and how are they stored in the brain? Are patterns of cerebral organization different in bilinguals from those in **monolinguals**, and if so, how do they differ? Is the rate of learning affected when two or more languages are being acquired at the same time? Is the child hindered or aided in any way in other aspects of development by learning more than one first language? What can be learned about the organization of language in the brain from studies of language loss in bilinguals? The questions are legion, and some are in the process of being answered. For example, researchers have noted that children learning two first languages tend to use words from both languages in their sentences when they are around 2 years old. The habit of combining vocabulary declines rapidly over the course of about a year so that it occurs only infrequently by the time they are about 3. It may also be the case that children use only one system of rules for both languages, taking time to develop two separate grammars, two sets of rules. The research being conducted in this area will surely prove important to our understanding of human language.

Second-Language Acquisition

Just as accounting for the acquisition of first languages is a clear concern of the field, the acquisition of subsequent languages is also a major area of research. **Second-language acquisition** involves the learning of a language or languages *after* one has acquired a first language. I have remarked on what an impressive job little children do in mastering their first language as quickly, as early, and apparently as effortlessly as they do. This apparent effortlessness is highlighted every time we try, as adults, to learn another language. We may study French year after year in school only to find, upon arriving in Paris, that we cannot make ourselves understood. And even if, by dint of great effort, we manage to convey a wish, a need, or even a greeting, we are unable to understand the response we elicit. Adding insult to injury is the fact that a 2- or 3-year-old Parisian Jennifer is rattling off sentences, and producing those impossible sounds, without any difficulty at all!

We have also noted that there must be some innate mechanism that enables us to learn our first language or languages. It now seems that maturation figures in the process as well. We usually think of maturation in terms of not being able to do something until we are older, such as not walking until our muscles have developed sufficiently to allow us to, or making inept judgments before we acquire enough experience of the world to make better ones. But as experiments have shown, the infant's brain goes to work immediately to acquire language. After a time, maturational effects cause this capacity to *decrease* to the point where we experience the difficulties and frustration with which most of us are familiar in learning a new language.

An interesting study was reported in 1989 by Johnson and Newport. They sought to determine the level of grammatical competence in English of adults who had learned it as a second language. The subjects were native speakers of either Chinese or Korean. They were of similar socioeconomic backgrounds and had all been in the United States about 10 years. At the time of the study, they were all students or faculty at the University of Illinois, thus ensuring other important similarities, such as the amount of their exposure to English. What differed among them was the age at which they had come to the United States and become immersed in English. This ranged from age 3 to 39. They were given two types of sentences: grammatically correct ones and sentences identical to these except for a single grammatical error in each. Twelve types of rules were involved. The subjects were asked to judge whether each of the sentences, both correct and incorrect ones, was acceptable. The results indicated a strong (statistically significant) relationship between their age of arrival in the United States and their performance on the test, with performance declining as the age of arrival increased (Figure 6.3). The researchers hypothesize that there are maturational constraints on language acquisition, for which at least two types of mechanisms are possible explanations. One is that there is a **language acquisition device**, a special language faculty that is sensitive to the types of structures that occur in human languages and that changes may occur as children mature that lead

> the older language learner to less success in inducing the linguistic systems to which she is exposed. A second possibility is that at least some of the constraints crucial to success in language acquisition are nonlinguistic, and that the maturational changes which lead to more difficulty in language learning occur in these nonlinguistic constraints on perception and memory. (Newport, 1990, p. 27)

The Critical Period   What exactly are the maturational effects that have occurred between the time we accomplished the task of learning our first language and now, when we feel so frustratingly incapable? As the study just described suggests, bilinguals who have acquired their second language after having acquired the first, if young enough when exposed to the second language, do not experience the difficulties they would have encountered at a later age. The question is "Why?" We need to explain not only how our language acquisition device works but also why its efficiency eventually declines. Interference from our first language may provide part of the answer. So may a difference in the process of learning a subsequent language, a difference caused by our already having done it once. (A question still to be answered is "To what extent is the learning of a second language after the acquisition of the first a different process from that of learning that first language?" After all, the knowledge of one language and the effects on the brain of having learned it may cause the starting point to be quite different.)

Most important, we need to examine the hypothesis that there is a developmental change in the language acquisition mechanism as we mature. There is apparently a stage during which language learning takes place as a matter of course, and if this stage, known as the **critical period**, has passed, the task becomes quite different. Where should we look for answers to our questions about the

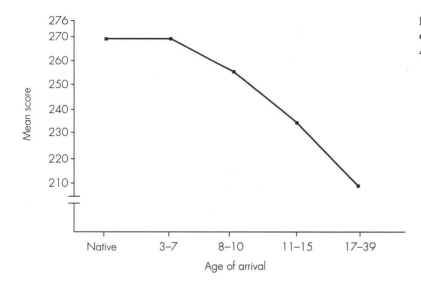

FIGURE 6.3 Total Score on a Test of English Grammar in Relation to Age of Arrival in the United States

nature of the critical period? One thing we may not do is hold back language in order to introduce it when a child has reached a certain age, say 10 or 14, to determine just when the critical period has passed. We may, however, and do, design and carry out benign experiments on infants that can yield interesting results. Two such experiments were described earlier, in which evidence was presented that an ability infants were apparently born with had disappeared very early on.

It is interesting that this loss parallels a loss observed in experiments using other species, such as certain species of birds. Researchers have reared birds in an environment in which they varied the time when the song of the species was introduced. The results indicate that the birds have an innate capacity to acquire their species' basic song pattern, but only while they are very young. They must hear the song during their first few months. If it is absent from their environment during this period, they are no longer able to acquire it. That the innate acquisition capacity lasts only a short time indicates the existence of a critical period in these species.

A good example of the interrelationship of participating disciplines in cognitive science is that neuroscientific research provides us with a basis for understanding the results of experiments like these. We learn from such research that neural differentiation occurs in the parts of the cortex involved in various behaviors as these behaviors develop. That is, areas of the brain that handle different aspects of our behavior—for example, language—develop their different potentials by increasing the numbers of synapses (connections) among nerve cells that are stimulated by interaction with the environment. The periods of differentiation correspond to the critical periods for the behaviors. The proliferation of synapses leads to the brain plasticity discussed in Part 2—the ability to tailor the portion of the cortex to the developing behavior. So it is the content of the environment in conjunction with the developing brain that appears to set the limits. If the environmental stimulus, such as birdsong or language, is missing during the normal period of development of a behavior— singing the song of one's species or speaking the language of one's environment, for example—the capacity for that behavior is impaired or lost. (We have seen another example of this in Wiesel and Hubel's work with vision in kittens in Chapter 3.)

Language Deprivation

Occasionally situations arise that out of common humanity we would not have wished for, but that, once presented to us, we may study in our quest for understanding. We sometimes come across children who, through abuse or abandonment, have been deprived of normal exposure to language as they developed. Children who are born deaf or with severe hearing loss constitute another example. These children may grow up lacking the amount of exposure to language the environment normally provides. From both sorts of situation we may be able to glean some evidence concerning the existence of the critical period.

Other sources of information that may have a bearing on the critical period derive from new imaging techniques. One interesting recent example concerns brain development in musicians. Magnetic images of the brains of violinists show differences between older learners and those who began their training in the violin early (before the age of 12): The latter exhibit larger and more complex neuron circuits.

Language Acquisition in Abused or Feral Children

Cases of so-called wild, or **feral**, children have been reported throughout history and have always aroused interest. Victor, the "wild boy of Aveyron," caught the imagination of the public and the interest of scientists in France at the turn of the 19th century. Found in the woods at about 11 or 12 years of age, having survived on his own apparently since early childhood, Victor appeared entirely unsocialized. Among the effects that apparently stemmed from his long isolation from human contact was his inability to understand or use language.

Victor became the ward of Dr. Jean-Marc-Gaspard Itard (1775–1838), a physician who studied him carefully over a period of years. Itard wanted to determine the abilities Victor possessed despite his deprivations. Success in this effort would have provided a means of approaching the larger question of what the mind contains innately, before it is subjected to the social environment. Itard left detailed records of the time he spent with Victor, describing the work he did with the boy in an attempt to socialize him and encourage his language development (Itard, 1894/1962). Although he made at least some progress at first, his efforts to teach Victor to use language failed. It is not possible to be sure, given all the unknowns of his background before he was found, what abilities were innate in Victor. Nor can the effects of subsequent damage be stated with certainty. A degree of mental retardation is surmised nowadays by researchers, based on behaviors described by Itard. This may account for some of the difficulties and dead-ends Itard experienced during his work with Victor. But intellectual deficits rarely preclude acquiring language. It is tempting, therefore, to ascribe Victor's inability to use language to its absence in his environment during the critical period. However, the many unknowables surrounding his situation make it impossible to be certain.

There are other cases in the literature that are interesting (if distressing) to read. A more recent one came to light in 1970. Genie, a 13-year-old girl, had lived all her life in nearly total isolation in her own home. She had suffered various kinds of abuse, from restrictions on her physical movements to an almost complete lack of environmental stimulation, including a lack of exposure to language. When Genie was brought out of this environment she, like Victor, was an unsocialized creature, unable to communicate by means of language. Again like Victor, Genie became an object of study, this time by modern-day psychologists and psycholinguists. They detailed both her condition soon after she was found and her linguistic progress once language was available to her. Psychological tests showed Genie to be of normal intelligence, but she never achieved full mastery of language. Indeed, she was able to learn only a fraction of what children of her age absorb easily under normal conditions.

We cannot rely on cases such as Victor's and Genie's for evidence of a critical period for language acquisition. It is not possible to separate out all the factors that brought these unfortunate children to the condition in which they were found. Physical and emotional damage are influential to an unknowable degree. Nevertheless, it is interesting and suggestive that these children, deprived of society until adolescence or near-adolescence, fail to acquire language in the normal fashion or to a normal degree even when they are finally exposed to it.

A somewhat different sort of case sheds some light on the question, however. Called Isabelle to protect her privacy, this little girl was described in a 1947 article in the *American Journal of Sociology*. Isabelle experienced an upbringing similar to Genie's in its isolation and language deprivation. But Isabelle was found not at 13, as Genie was, but at the age of 6. At that point her cognitive development appeared to be less advanced than that of a normal 2-year-old. Most significant for our discussion is the fact that she demonstrated no knowledge of language. However, presented with a normal environment, Isabelle caught up. She progressed through the same stages of learning that occur in normal language development during a child's first 6 years—but far more quickly. It took her little more than 2 months from the time she began to speak until she began combining words into sentences (Davis, 1947). Within a year Isabelle had acquired the degree of language of other 7-year-olds, and tests indicated that her general cognitive development was at a normal level, allowing her to go to school with others of her age. This fact may well be evidence for the existence of a critical period in humans for language acquisition, as in some species of birds for the acquisition of song. There are, in addition, still other types of evidence that it is instructive to examine.

Another population that has contributed to our understanding of the child's acquisition of language is comprised of those who, whether from genetic causes or environmental factors in early childhood, have grown up deprived of all or much of their hearing. These are not situations in which the child suffers emotional damage from abuse or abandonment. These children may have loving and concerned parents who do their best for them. Not being able to hear the language spoken around them, however, constitutes a major loss of environmental input to their development.

Language Acquisition in the Deaf and Hearing Impaired

Studies reported by Newport (1990) bear on the question of the critical period. Thirty subjects ranging in age from 35 to 70 participated in these studies. All had been born deaf or had become deaf before they had acquired language, and all had had at least 30 years of exposure to American Sign Language (ASL). Their background was such that they formed a homogeneous group—except for the age at which they had first been exposed to ASL. In this respect they fell into three categories: The first group, the *native* learners, were those who had been exposed to ASL from birth by deaf signing parents. These had, between the ages of 4 and 6, begun to attend a school for the deaf where ASL exposure was continued. The second group, classified as *early* learners, had received their first exposure to ASL between the ages of 4 and 6, when they entered the same school as the first group. The third group, categorized as *late* learners, had not been exposed to ASL until after the age of 12. When Newport tested the subjects in these three groups on many aspects of their ASL grammar, she found that only those who had been exposed to the language before age 6 showed native fluency in it. The group exposed to ASL after 6 but before 12 were not as fluent, and the grammar of those not exposed until 12 or thereafter showed significant deficits.

Such results have implications for our understanding of the language development of children who are born deaf or hearing impaired or who become so early on. The development of language skills in this population is at risk: If the impairment is great enough so that it interferes with adequate exposure to language during the critical period, these language skills may not develop as they should. To the extent that other cognitive processes (e.g., thought) depend on language, they too may be at risk.

The study of sign language has been a fruitful approach to our understanding not just of the critical period but of the nature of human language in general. Sign language was for a long time widely regarded as a mode of communication inferior to spoken language. It was thought by many to lack the resources for subtleties spoken language relies on and, furthermore, not to make use of the same type of "brain power" required by spoken language. It used to be commonly accepted that a deaf or hearing-impaired person's best road into society lay in lipreading. But lipreading presents a significant problem: The articulations enacted behind the lips are difficult—and many are impossible—to see. When you press your lips together to utter the first sound in "mommy," for instance, anyone looking at your face can observe this action. The articulation of the first sound in "lolly" is somewhat visible, though not as visible as that of the m in "mommy." But the way the first sound in "cookie" is made is completely hidden from the observer. You can, in fact, say "cookie" without visibly moving your mouth at all. The invisibility of so much of the articulation of speech places severe limitations on the amount of an utterance that the lip-reader perceives.

But studies of sign languages, such as ASL, have convincingly demonstrated that these are indeed languages in the same sense that spoken language is. Linguistic analysis of the signs, sign combinations, and sign sequences clearly shows the parallels: ASL is constructed of a finite number of signs that combine to allow the production of an infinite number of sentences. The system, though expressed in a mode employing sight and movement in space rather than speaking and hearing, is thus the same in fundamental respects as that of spoken language. The imaging techniques described in Chapter 4 support this conclusion. They have provided images that clearly show activity in the same areas of the brain whether the individual is engaged in signing or speaking.

Given the fact that ASL is a fully developed linguistic system, albeit one carried out in a different mode from the usual, we now know that being exposed to *spoken* language is not the only means to normal linguistic development. This knowledge encourages us to enrich the environment of deaf and hearing-impaired children by including complete access to language, allowing them to develop their cognitive abilities much as they would have had they been able to hear. This has been an important practical development resulting from cognitive psychological, linguistic, and neuroscientific research.

Language Loss (Language Attrition)

Causes of Language Loss

An important avenue to understanding both the nature of language and the functions of the brain in which language figures is language loss. Language loss may occur in a variety of situations, for example, among immigrants who marry into a family of speakers of the language of the country they now live in and who work at jobs in which they must use this new language. It may also occur when a person who started out bilingual finds him- or herself at some point having to use one of the languages much more extensively than the other. The language used significantly less may become less available to the individual. A loss of the individual's native language is referred to as **first-language attrition**; the loss of a language acquired subsequent to one's native language is known as **second-language attrition**. Many of us encounter this sort of loss when a language we have studied in school, but failed to use after we have left school, seems to evaporate.

As we saw earlier, *first-language acquisition* occurs through a series of stages in which more and more of the elements and rules of the language are added to the child's linguistic competence, from the sounds and sound combinations, to the words and the way they are structured, to their organization into sentences. The study of first-language attrition, occurring in normal individuals with no brain damage, is useful in our quest for knowledge about the workings of the brain in much the same way that the study of first-language acquisition is: It may give us clues to the way language is organized in the brain. For example, studies have addressed the question of which aspects of the grammar of a first language are the most readily lost under conditions in which speakers are conducting most of their lives in a second language.

Language loss also occurs in people who have suffered brain damage either through disease, such as Alzheimer's disease or a brain tumor, or through trauma, such as a stroke or a blow to the head. The condition these people exhibit is known as **aphasia**. Like *infant,* this term means "lacking speech." As an infant is one who has not yet developed a linguistic system, an aphasic is one who, through brain damage, has lost some or all of the linguistic system he or she once had in fully developed form.

Aphasia

Many of us have had experience with people who can't seem to come up with the words they need to complete a sentence. I don't mean the ordinary searching for a name that you know you know but can't think of now ("You know who I mean, the guy on television last night") and that you may suddenly find at 1 a.m. ("Oh, yes, JAY LENO!")—when the person you were talking to has long since gone home. Nor am I referring to the temporary inability to remember the word that the crossword puzzle definition calls for or the term for the dress design you are describing to your sister. These are annoyances we are all subject to in the normal course of events. The condition I am referring to is one in which the inability to remember words, to produce grammatical or complete sentences, or to understand what is being said is severe enough to interfere with one's ability to communicate and hence to function in the world.

If the aphasia results from a degenerative disease, it generally progresses along with the physical deterioration brought about by the disease, until the language loss is so severe that there is not enough left to study. In cases involving trauma, there may be at least a partial recovery; in any case, there is often no further deterioration. Investigating the language loss in individuals whose condition remains relatively stable has proven a fruitful line of research, as we seek to understand how language is organized in the brain. Early aphasia research focused on describing and classifying the manifestations in different patients, which led to an interesting if confusing picture. Some patients could talk but not read; some could understand but not talk; some could construct sentences but had difficulty with finding nouns. Some lost the ability to repeat what they heard, and some could sing words but not speak them. Clearly, different aspects of language that normally interact with each other can be specifically affected, depending on where the damage is.

More recently, psycholinguists have been able to take advantage of the linguistic theory that began to develop in the late 1950s. To explain how one aspect of grammar can be disrupted while others remain intact, there must be a clear notion of the grammatical structure and relations that were once part of a person's linguistic competence but that have now been so affected as to seem no longer to be there. A theory of grammar that explains the kinds of underlying rules that generate, for example, passive sentences will enable us to identify that aspect of an individual's grammar as one that has been disrupted. Some cases of aphasia are characterized by a loss of words (or of the ability to access them). In many cases the loss does not stop there but is manifested in a failure to produce grammatical sentences. Such speech is marked by the omission of grammatical pieces. Some of these are **inflectional suffixes**—endings that give information about number (the plural -*s*, for instance) or tense (the past tense marker -*ed*). If syntactic rules are the basis for our sentences, then the aphasics' inability to produce grammatical sentences (**agrammatic aphasia**) can be viewed as a deficit in the syntactic component of their linguistic competence.

Another possibility suggested to account for agrammatic aphasia is that there is a mechanism in people with normal language ability that acts very quickly, enabling them to tell the difference between grammatical elements in a sentence, such as plural or past tense endings, and vocabulary items like "bird" or "jump." Under this assumption, aphasics who omit the grammatical elements may not have access to this mechanism so that they process these elements slowly. This explanation suggests that the difficulty is not a deficit in the syntactic component, because the grammatical elements may in fact be represented in the aphasics' linguistic competence. Rather, it is a difficulty (a slowness) in processing sentences.

Our discussion has focused on some of the ways the field of linguistics intersects with cognitive psychology. Aphasia research points us now to the ways in which linguistics relates to neuroscience.

Linguistics and Neuroscience

As we saw in Part 2, some of the many studies using brain imaging techniques involve language-related abilities. Studies cited there were concerned with Broca's area and Wernicke's area and with brain function in signing. These are but a few of the areas targeted in language-oriented neuroscientific research. To broaden the picture a bit, it may be helpful to mention a few other studies before returning to the subject of aphasia. Experiments conducted with three brain-damaged men have been reported, indicating that interconnected groups of neurons in the brain function as separate "information processing streams" that handle either nouns or verbs, as well as the general concepts that underlie them (Damasio & Tranel, 1993). Another study, using fMRI to image brain activity in 19 male and 19 female subjects, suggests that the brains of men and women typically differ in the responses of their brains to a task in which they must understand sounds that correspond to written letters. The researchers claim clear evidence for a sex difference in the functional organization of the brain for a specific component of language—the phonological component (Shaywitz et al., 1995). And studies using positron emission tomography indicate that "the normal process of retrieving words that denote concrete entities depends in part on multiple regions of the left cerebral hemisphere, located outside the classic language areas. Moreover, anatomically separable regions tend to process words for distinct kinds of items" (Damasio et al., 1996, p. 499). From these examples and the ones cited earlier, you can get an idea of the range of activity under way in the neuroscientific community with regard to the study of language-related phenomena.

Aphasia Revisited

The extent and location of the damage to the brain determine the aphasic patient's language deficits—the decrease in language abilities the patient possessed before suffering the damage but that are now impaired. There are about as many different manifestations of aphasia as there are patients, because damage to the brain is not uniform among them: A blow to the head or a stroke will likely not injure the identical area in any two people. Some clusters of symptoms appear together regularly enough, however, so that researchers in the 19th century were able to identify two major types of aphasia. The first of these, known as **Broca's aphasia**, was described by the French surgeon and physical anthropologist Paul Broca, mentioned in Chapter 1. From his clinical observation of patients, coupled with examination of their brains during autopsy, Broca drew the connection between a particular form of aphasia and a portion of the left frontal hemisphere of the brain, now referred to as "Broca's area." Patients with Broca's aphasia speak haltingly, omit grammatical elements of sentences, and demonstrate difficulty in "getting the thought out." They do not necessarily exhibit the same difficulty in comprehension, however, and many recognize when the sentence they are trying so hard to produce is rendered correctly by the listener. (More recently we have learned, through presenting rather complex constructions, that though comprehension difficulties may not be apparent in ordinary conversation with these patients more subtle ones do indeed exist [Goodglass, 1993].)

Broca's aphasia, at first referred to as "expressive aphasia," is now known by the clearer and more descriptive term **nonfluent aphasia**. A patient exhibiting this type of difficulty produced the following, in response to the question "What happened?":

> I had . . . a stroke. We'd just . . . finished . . . ah . . . patrol. And the . . . ah . . . We had . . . debris. I didn't go . . . because . . . I was . . . well . . . I had a stroke . . . in the middle . . . of the night. And bring me . . . to the hospital. The go here . . . to get . . . therapy. (Helm-Estabrooks & Albert, 1991, p. 3)

The second major type of aphasia, involving damage to a posterior portion of the left hemisphere, was described by the German neuropsychiatrist Carl Wernicke (1848-1905). The speech in patients exhibiting "Wernicke's aphasia" flows with relative ease but is disordered and contains many wrong words; it is also characterized by an impairment in the understanding of speech. Wernicke's aphasia, earlier called "sensory aphasia," is now known as **fluent aphasia**. A patient afflicted with this type of disorder responded in the following way when asked "What happened to you?":

On Sunday I get up. I feel fine, but on Monday . . . I have as many to . . . A man who
believes to me and I am talking to him about what I am doing and this man is a new
man and he says . . . "Al . . . You're doing . . . I have your stuff on reddin' in ere . . . but
you cannot talk to me today. I cannot take your . . . I do not know what you're saying
to me well. I want you to do with one of the girls to your doctor and go him on Monday
and the girl takes me in her car to doctors." (Helm-Estabrooks & Albert, 1991, p. 3)

Understanding what has happened to the linguistic system of an aphasic depends on understanding what constitutes language, and this effort ordinarily begins with the linguist. Devising the tests that will divulge the nature of the deficit is
part of the task of clinical psychologists, psycholinguists, and neuropsychologists,
who along with other neuroscientists engage in clinical observation and testing of
patients. Neuroscientists also study the activities associated with various brain
structures, using both neuroimaging techniques and examination of these structures either in living patients during surgery undertaken due to medical necessity
or during autopsies performed on the brains of aphasic patients who have died.
The intersecting approaches to the study of aphasia thus bring together linguistics,
cognitive psychology, and neuroscience.

Linguistics and Philosophy

As will be explained more fully in Part 5, when we explore the relation of philosophy to the cognitive science endeavor, the connection between philosophy and
the study of language as a human function is a complicated one, because

> the history of philosophical thinking about language is not easily separated from
> the . . . entire history of philosophy. There is no division between thought about the
> major philosophical categories—knowledge, truth, meaning, reason—and thought
> about the language used to express those categories. . . . There is . . . no major philos-
> opher or school that has not had some doctrine about the relationship between mind
> and language, and language and the world. (Blackburn, 1995, p. 454)

Consciousness

For now, let us turn first—and briefly—to one of the important concerns of philosophy and of cognitive science, the subject of consciousness. (We return to this
topic in Part 5.) How does the area of language relate to consciousness? Think back
to our earlier discussion of the set of largely unconscious rules that have been
hypothesized to make up our linguistic competence—what we know about our
language without necessarily being aware we know it. Remember that these rules
are supposed by many modern linguists to have been acquired by the child, coming into the world knowing nothing of the language(s) he or she will learn so
quickly. Something that is *in there before the infant has experience of the world*
responds to that experience selectively; otherwise, how would we know to latch
onto the important aspects of the stream of sounds issuing from the mouths of
those around us, to ultimately make sense of them? In this notion of the way

language is acquired we hear echoes of the French philosopher René Descartes (1596–1650), who proposed the notion of the innateness of ideas, and the later German philosopher Immanuel Kant (1724–1804), who argued for "a priori" categories and the mind as the only sources of knowledge. The ideas of both will surface again in Part 5.

Language and Thought Revisited

In our earlier discussion of cognitive psychology and language, we considered the relation of language and thought. In Chapter 5, we reconsidered it from the perspective of linguistics. Not surprisingly, given what we are coming to expect about the interrelatedness of the subject matter within the various fields of cognitive science, we find ourselves returning to this topic, this time via the discipline of philosophy. Strange as it may seem, an increase in the ease of travel early in the 20th century leads us to it. As people began to travel more readily, they came into contact with previously unknown or little-known populations. In the process they encountered "exotic" languages, hitherto unknown to scholars. Many such languages were observed even among the different peoples living across the United States, as the work of Sapir and Whorf indicates. The so-called linguistic turn taken by philosophy at the beginning of the 20th century was influenced both by what linguists found in studying these languages and by the earlier thinking of Kant.

The relevance to language of Kant's notion of **a priori** or **innate knowledge**, which shapes what we know of the world, is that the linguistic structures we acquire in the process of learning our first language(s) also contribute to the way we experience the world. The categories of kinship, for example, as expressed in language, give us insight into how different cultures organize their worlds. Even a culture as close to our own as that of Scandinavia places a different emphasis on family organization. English speakers categorize grandparents as "grandmother" and "grandfather," making no distinction in the terminology between those on the father's side and those on the mother's side. Danish-speaking children have, along with the general terms *bedstemoder* and *bedstefader,* two other sets of terms: *mormor, morfar, farmor,* and *farfar* "mother's mother, mother's father, father's mother, father's father." Thus the vocabulary of their language draws a distinction that is not made in the vocabulary of English. As people became aware of differences such as these (and some that are far more profound), they became aware also that language serves as a filter of thought.

In the preceding chapter, I pointed out that some languages lack the counterfactual construction—the grammatical forms for indicating a situation that is contrary to fact (e.g., *if I were you*). In his study *The Linguistic Shaping of Thought: A Study in the Impact of Language on Thinking in China and the West* (1981), Alfred Bloom considers the fact that Chinese lacks this construction. His research addresses the question raised by the Sapir-Whorf hypothesis: What effect does the lack of certain constructions in a given language have on the way speakers of this language think? Are speakers of Chinese in fact incapable of having a counterfactual thought? Although the answer to this question seems quite clearly to be "no"—of course such speakers can think of situations that are contrary to fact—it may also be the case that the availability of constructions facilitates thinking in certain ways. We do not yet know all there is to be known about how our cognitive abilities develop in response to the environment in which we develop.

The Hopi concept of time, the Chinese approach to the concept embodied in counterfactuals—these are also the stuff of philosophy. Even in a short discussion such as this, it is possible to see the very close relation between philosophy and linguistics, a relation that goes back a long way. In their treatment of their subject matter, the two disciplines clearly complement and nourish one another.

Linguistics and Artificial Intelligence

So far we have been considering questions that spring from our awareness of ourselves. We wonder about how we think, how we acquire and use language, what effects language has on our thought processes, and what examining our brains can tell us about how they work. We yearn to understand the essence of being human—the crucial differences between ourselves and every other species. We know we are animals, but animals, it seems, like no others: animals of a certain kind of intelligence, animals with a complex and sophisticated sort of language, animals that *think*.

The development of the computer has presented us with a new route to travel in our quest to understand this distinction. The first focus in the development of modern computers was on getting them to do some of our work for us, especially the work we find boring and/or time consuming, such as keeping track of vast amounts information or performing computations that would take us forever to do by hand. But interesting ideas arose in the process. Computers were doing some of the things we could in fact do ourselves. Indeed, they can be regarded as extensions of ourselves. They are not the same sort of extensions as other tools, which extend our strength, the range of our voice, or our speed in going from place to place. But, fundamentally, the strength and range and distance that computers enable us to extend are of our *minds,* because it is the work of our minds that they further.

True, early computers could perform only those tasks we specifically programmed them to perform. True, we perform with ease tasks they could not at first even approach: recognizing someone's voice, abstracting the essential elements of a category, being able to learn, using language of the sort *we* use with mastery even as small children. Nevertheless, the fact that computers could perform some of the activities we had thought only we were capable of was suggestive. Could we somehow get them to do more? And if so, would they ever reach a stage we would consider intelligent in the way we think ourselves to be? In recent decades we have explored this issue with increasing sophistication and capability, made possible by our development of increasingly sophisticated and capable computers. But if we are to achieve intelligence in machines, as we endeavor to build into them our own abilities, we must have a firm sense of what *human* intelligence is.

So it is that the attempt to create intelligent machines, by researchers in the field of artificial intelligence, or AI (so named to distinguish it from our own, presumably natural, sort), has led us to refine our own notions about what constitutes intelligence and to seek a more profound understanding of our own intellectual functioning. As computers became able to perform more and more of the tasks we assumed require intelligence, even to the point of being able to learn (as we shall see in Part 4), we kept raising the ante. All right, we say, the computer can do *this*—but can it do *that?*

Machine Translation

One of the touchstones of intelligence is language. So, in their enthusiastic experimentation with this new machine, those working with computers attempted, in the early 1960s, to get them to do what they thought of as a simple linguistic task: automatic translation. Feed in a passage from one language, the "source language," as input, and receive as output a passage in the "target language" that is the equivalent of the original. This might be accomplished by storing in the memory of the computer a dictionary of words of the source language and an equivalent dictionary from the target language. But it turns out that translation is not so easy after all.

Have you ever tried to assemble a piece of equipment or an item of furniture, dutifully and carefully following the accompanying printed directions? Many such items are produced in countries in which English is not the native language. The directions we try so hard to follow are often translations into English from the language of the country where the item was made. A recent experience of mine along these lines concerned a cuckoo clock that needed assembling. Although the procedure was a fairly simple one, some of the instructions were bewildering: "Mind that the clock is suspended on the wall straightly and its ticking proportionable . . . push the pendulum-disc a little down, is the clock slow a little up." Although our difficulty sometimes arises out of our own ineptitude, it may also derive from, or be compounded by, translation errors such as these.

Think too of those signs on establishments addressing English speakers, signs that contain clear attempts to translate from another language, like this one posted on a restaurant in Greece: "Utmost of chicken with smashed pot" (Fromkin & Rodman, 1993, p. 473).

What often happens in translation is that the meaning selected for a given word from among its several possible meanings, although correct in one sentence, makes no sense at all in another. Meaning is crucial to translation; selecting the wrong sense of a word can lead to garble. Meaning also requires detailed knowledge of the world. To understand the meaning of a sentence such as "I stopped for lunch near the bank this afternoon," you need to understand the context as being either a shopping district or proximity to a river. To translate a passage without that knowledge may lead to an unexpected and useless result.

Furthermore, there are sentences in a given language that express concepts (counterfactuals, for instance) for which there is no ready translation in another. That's why speakers of two languages, when holding a conversation in one of the two, often resort to words from the other to express what they wish to express. When enthusiastic workers in the field first attempted to use computers to translate from one human language into another, they did not take into account the complexity introduced by the varying shades of meaning of a given word or the many different meanings one word may have or the fact that some words or phrases may not have equivalents at all in another language, such as the French expressions *joie de vivre* and *déjà vu*.

An additional difficulty faced by machine translation is the fact that different languages may make use of different word ordering in their sentences. English, for example, requires the subject (S) to occur first in a simple sentence, then the verb (V), and finally the object (O) of the verb. Linguists refer to English, then, as an SVO language. German, on the other hand, is an SOV language, ordering its sentences with the subject first, then the object of the verb, and finally the verb. An automatic translation of the sort projected at first would require a point-for-point correspondence between sentences of the source language and those of the target language. In English and German, a point-for-point correspondence is not possible.

All of this is an indication of the difficulty of translation. If it is so difficult for us, it is obviously not an easy job to program a computer to do it. Machine translation requires a much more sophisticated approach than was at first realized. What we might term the "Jabberwocky condition" will not do. Lewis Carroll's famous poem "Jabberwocky," from *Alice in Wonderland,* is syntactically completely correct: The words are all recognizable as nouns, verbs, adjectives, and so on, and they are arranged entirely correctly according to the rules of English—yet many of them are empty of meaning ("Twas brillig and the slithy toves / did gyre and gimble in the wabe"). Therefore, the poem itself lacks adequate meaning. It is not enough to supply the computer with the syntactic framework, anymore than it is enough for us. Translation, like comprehension of a poem, depends crucially on meaning.

As researchers in AI have fully recognized the requirements of translation with regard to meaning (and other aspects of language), they have made progress. So far, though, machine translation works best when the vocabulary involved is limited to that of a very specific domain. According to computer scientists Russell and Norvig (1995),

> Although there has been no fundamental breakthrough in machine translation, there has been real progress, to the point that there are now dozens of machine translation systems in everyday use that save money over fully manual techniques. One of the most successful is the TAUM-METEO system, developed by the University of Montreal, which translates weather reports from English to French. It works because the language used in these government weather reports is highly stylized and regular. . . . In more open domains, the results are less impressive. (p. 692)

Natural Language Processing

Another area in which linguistics and artificial intelligence are interdependent is natural language processing. Early in their attempt to find ways for computers to handle human natural language, computer scientists designed programs in which sentence pattern frames were stored as data. The program could both recognize sentences constructed of these frames and produce such sentences itself. The most well known of these programs, ELIZA (Weizenbaum, 1965), allows a dialogue to be carried on between itself and a user, ELIZA acting as a "psychiatrist" and the user as a "patient." Moyne (1985, p. 277) provides the following example, using dashes to represent slots in the frames into which words or phrases can be inserted:

"Patient"	"Doctor"
My __1__ is __2__ .	How long has your __1__ been __2__ ?
__1__ thinks I am __2__ .	Do you think you are __2__ ?

The "patient" provides the input and the "doctor" the output. The numbers indicate the correspondence between them. When there is a match between input and a stored pattern, ELIZA produces a corresponding response:

HUMAN: My mother is hateful.

ELIZA: HOW LONG HAS YOUR MOTHER BEEN HATEFUL?

HUMAN: My father thinks I am crazy.

ELIZA: DO YOU THINK YOU ARE CRAZY?

An example from ELIZA's creator, Joseph Weizenbaum, gives an additional indication of how this works. Here the conversation is between a young woman and ELIZA, with the computer's responses to the young woman's input in capitals:

Men are all alike.

IN WHAT WAY

They're always bugging us about something or other.

CAN YOU THINK OF A SPECIFIC EXAMPLE

Well, my boyfriend made me come here.

YOUR BOYFRIEND MADE YOU COME HERE

He says I'm depressed much of the time.

I AM SORRY TO HEAR YOU ARE DEPRESSED . . .

You are not very aggressive, but I think you don't want me to notice that.

WHAT MAKES YOU THINK I AM NOT VERY AGGRESSIVE

You don't argue with me.

WHY DO YOU THINK I DON'T ARGUE WITH YOU

(Weizenbaum, 1976, pp. 3–4)

When the program contains no match for a particular input, ELIZA simply produces an all-purpose response, such as "Why do you think . . . ?" or "Can you think of a specific example?"

ELIZA contains more complexities than these examples demonstrate, but because the design is fundamentally one of matching input to fixed patterns, its limitations are clear. ELIZA is not "understanding" the input in any way resembling our own notion of understanding; nor is the program capable of stepping outside the fixed framework to create a novel response. No constructing "one lip" from "tulip" for ELIZA!

Programs built on this model, no matter how complex they may become, do not resemble human natural language. But in recent years an attempt has been made, with an encouraging degree of success, to design computer programs that "understand" passages of a given natural language such as English. This they do by means of **parsers**, which assign categories—parts of speech—to the words in a sentence and group them into phrases. The formalization of the underlying rules of a language, discussed earlier, has been important to this project, because it is precisely such very specific, very unambiguous instructions the computer requires. Given categories and phrase groupings, and a set of rules for combining them, a program comes much closer to doing what humans do when they manipulate language.

But all is not smooth sailing here either. Sentences exist in our own language that are perfectly legitimate, having been generated by our internalized rules, but that are not readily understood. An example familiar to all students of linguistics is this one, framed by Bever in 1970:

> *The horse raced past the barn fell.* (p. 316)

The problem here is not with the words. It is, rather, with the fact that as we process this sentence, we understand it (or think we do) readily enough as far as the word *barn,* but then we stop, puzzled by the presence of *fell.* It seems to make nonsense of a sentence we thought we were understanding. Having come to the end of the sentence, we have to go back and reinterpret it. At this point, we realize that the problem lies in the fact that because *raced* occurs immediately after the subject (*the horse*) we at first took it to be the main verb of the sentence. In reality, it modifies *the horse,* having been reduced from the phrase *which was raced,* as in

> *The horse <u>which was</u> raced past the barn fell.*

How can we "instruct" a machine to engage in this process? Both the human's linguistic competence and the computer's parser, in a first pass, after assigning the category NP (noun phrase) to *the horse* will then assign the expected VP (verb phrase) category to the rest, with the verb leading off. Think of the sort of knowledge we must have about our language to be able to look again from the beginning and reassign categories so that *raced* is removed from, and *fell* is correctly placed in, the category *verb.* The enormous complexity of the task of programming a computer to "do" human language reflects the vast complexity of human language.

Other Language-Related Tasks

Because computers are so well suited to storing and retrieving large amounts of data, there are many tasks that they can perform that would be daunting for a human to undertake but that are of importance to researchers and scholars. Tasks of this nature exist in all fields, among them those that are language-related.

The computer can be used to produce a **concordance**, a frequency count of all the words (and phrases and sentence constructions, if such information is wanted) in a given text, along with their exact location(s) within the text. To scholars seeking to determine the creator of a particular literary work of which the authorship is in dispute, a concordance is a valuable tool. One may count the occurrences of certain words in an author's works, or certain phrases, or certain sentence constructions, and compare the results with those of a similar count based on the disputed work. If the two differ significantly, it is probable that they were not written by the same author.

Concordances were once produced by hand. It is easy to imagine how much time and effort must have been expended in such a project. Think of the drudgery in counting all those items! An appropriate computer program, designed to recognize words, phrases, and constructions—linguistic devices employed by a given author—can do it much more rapidly than human scholars can, and with far less stress. This is an example of a practical application of computer technology in the area of language, one that does not depend on providing the computer with abilities we think of as peculiarly human or as particularly "intelligent" (though in the earlier days of the development of computers it might have been so regarded).

More in line with abilities associated with human intelligence are the attempts to program computers to comprehend and produce speech. From our earlier discussion, you will recall that one of the most difficult tasks we face when confronted with a new language is learning how to separate a steady stream of speech, in which there are few helpful pauses, into meaningful units. The way humans accomplish this feat is not yet completely understood. Yet AI researchers have been able to program computers to some extent to recognize speech and its component sounds and words and to "comprehend," or interpret, it. The amount of speech a computer may be programmed to recognize, interpret, or utter (via speech synthesis) is as yet severely limited. And although even very young children can decide for themselves what they are going to say and how they are going to say it, recent advances in programming computers to produce reasonably good synthetic speech still do not equip the computer to speak freely on any topic it wishes. Some of the developments predicted by early enthusiasts within the field of artificial intelligence have as yet not materialized. Nevertheless, even in the realm of language the accomplishments are impressive.

Having provided a glimpse of artificial intelligence, via its interrelationship with linguistics, I turn now to a fuller discussion.

Questions to Think About

1. Why is *mama* generally among babies' first words? Has it anything to do with the way the sounds in the word are articulated?

2. If you have studied a language other than your native language, what have you found to be the most difficult aspects of the new language? Why do you think these aspects have been particularly difficult?

3. This chapter discusses the fact that the capacity to learn to speak new languages as easily and well as one learned one's native language(s) seems to deteriorate as one matures. What hypothesis or hypotheses can you suggest regarding why this should be so?

4. The idea that communicating in a sign language like American Sign Language was bad for deaf individuals used to be quite prevalent. Why do you think people thought it would do them more harm than good? Having read this chapter, what are your thoughts on this topic?

5. It is pretty clear that language reflects thought. A subject that has engendered much debate is whether language *influences* thought. After reading about the Sapir-Whorf hypothesis and some of the research that produced it and resulted from it, what conclusion have you come to?

6. You have read about the difficulties experienced by AI researchers in developing machine translation. Why do you think a computer program might have difficulty in translating the following sentence?

Would you rather a friend helped you or your brother?

7

Setting the Stage for Artificial Intelligence

My parents were writers, and my earliest memories include the tapping of typewriter keys after I had been tucked into bed and was drifting off to sleep. In the 1940s, 50s, and 60s, when my parents were working most fruitfully, the sound of their typewriters was a constant in our home. Much thought went into each correction and revision: how to say this more clearly, how to express that most felicitously. The human faculties of logic, reason, imagination, sensitivity to linguistic nuance—all of these were called into play for every sentence, every paragraph, every page produced. Manuscript sheets piled up as stories, books, and articles underwent revision after revision because each revision required retyping a whole section or chapter. The writer did it all, from finding the initial idea through choosing the appropriate format (story, novel, essay, article, poem) to spinning out the sentences or lines, and even to the refashioning of the product, as the old manuscript was revised and discarded and a new one produced.

By the 1970s, when I was writing my doctoral dissertation, nothing much about this process had changed: All the mental activity was mine, but so also was the tedium involved in revising. Each time I made a mistake or had a new thought or a better way of expressing an old one, the section I had already laboriously tapped out had to be retyped.

To today's students, such reminiscences must seem like those of the father who is fond of telling his children about his 4-mile trek to school (in the snow, of course)—and how they should therefore appreciate how easy things are for them! When it comes to typing (admittedly a less strenuous activity), it is true that the development of the word processor has made the task of those who write considerably easier and less tedious. Today's writers and students delete errors, substitute corrections, move paragraphs around, insert new material, alter a document in any way they wish—even include illustrations—all without ever having to actually retype a word. Time that used to be spent on this drudgery can now be used for revising and polishing our words and, in the process, for clarifying and refining the thoughts we are using them to express.

But even here the machine can now help. We can ask it to check our spelling and even our grammar. It is thus possible to relegate to the machine some portion of linguistic tasks that were once strictly the domain of the human being. Are not human and machine in a sense, then, thinking together?

Another innovation, the handheld electronic calculator, was developed in the late 1960s. This invention prompted a certain amount of concern as it became, in the 1970s, widely available and increasingly affordable. At that time there was considerable discussion about the wisdom of allowing students to use these calculators, either in the classroom or while doing their homework. Adults had had to learn, in their day, the times table and many arithmetic and algebraic techniques (just as they had had to walk to school through the snow . . .). Some worried that letting the machine substitute for mental processes would cause a "mental laziness" detrimental to students' development. Their misgivings notwithstanding, the convenience and speed of calculators won the day. Today, at the beginning of the 21st century, we take both the word processor and the handheld calculator for granted, in general regarding them as expanders and enhancers of our own "brainpower."

The functions of word processor and calculator now combine, along with many other functions, in a complex machine we call the computer, which sits upon our desk or in our lap—or, more recently, in the palm of our hand. Like inventions such as the washing machine and the television, the computer enables us to move beyond our human limitations. The washing machine and the television enabled us only to move beyond our physical limitations (the one to wash many items of clothing at once in little time and the other to see events occurring beyond our range of vision), but the computer enables us in addition to extend abilities we think of as part of our intelligence. In so doing, it also plays a role in helping us to understand this intelligence. As we ask it to do more and more of what has been our own domain, we must clarify how *we* accomplish what we wish *it* to accomplish. Chapter 6 discusses attempts to have it "do" human language, for example. These attempts necessarily involve analyzing the components of the process. Through our analysis, we see that the task of "doing" language, which seems to us so natural and therefore easy, is in fact enormously complex. The attempt to create a machine that can accomplish this task leads us to examine our own linguistic processes in a new way. So it is with each component of our cognitive processes. The endeavor has fed our understanding of ourselves, which in turn leads us to regard the task of implementing those processes in the machine differently than ever before.

If we are successful in constructing a machine that can engage in activities we consider to require intelligence when we ourselves engage in them, then how shall we characterize what the machine is doing? When we add or subtract or check the grammar of a sentence we have written, we consider these tasks to involve thinking. Chapter 2 opens with a conversation I had with my young friend Amy, in which we referred to an unanticipated pause in her computer's functioning as "thinking." Implicit in our mutual understanding was that we were just kidding; of course the computer can't think!

Or can it? Some find this suggestion disturbing. To them, it may seem as though sharing that capacity, which presumably distinguishes humans from all other species, poses a threat to our uniqueness—and our cherished "superiority." To others it is an exciting idea; playing with it has produced many very interesting works of science fiction—one of the best known being Arthur C. Clarke's *2001: A Space Odyssey.* Some of what was science fiction, or only an unpublicized—and far-fetched—idea a generation ago, is now reality. Just this morning I heard a radio commercial for a computer program that will, from the laptop in the car seat next to you, respond to your spoken questions about the route to your destination. When you inquire of it how far you are from the left turn it has advised, it pauses, then tells you the distance. How shall we describe what it was *doing* during that pause?

What has already come to pass, along with what may be envisioned for the future, thus provides a springboard for philosophical discussion (see, for example, Stork's *Hal's Legacy: 2001's Computer as Dream and Reality,* 1997). In his book *Darwin Among the Machines,* George B. Dyson (1997) writes, "Philosophers and mathematicians have made limited progress at deconstructing the firmament of mind from the top down, while a grand, bottom-up experiment at building intelligence from elemental bits of addition and subtraction has been advancing by leaps and bounds" (p. 7). Postponing consideration of philosophical issues until later in this chapter, let us examine the background of this **bottom-up** experiment that is the current state of what we call "artificial intelligence."

The Beginnings

Setting the Stage

The name "artificial intelligence" (AI) was given, in the 1950s, to the newly emerging field whose concern was as I have described: machines that perform tasks that seem to us to require intelligence (or some facet of intelligence) when performed by humans. Alhough computers with which we are familiar today go some distance in this direction, like the program that gives us directions as we drive, they are still a far cry from *2001*'s Hal. (Readers who have seen the film will remember that Hal exhibited some pretty sophisticated behavior. He was capable of true emotion—a characteristic of no real machine so far. He could carry on sustained conversation with humans. And, very impressive—not to mention chilling—he was capable of deceit.) Some work in the field of artificial intelligence is concerned with accomplishing even more along these lines, bringing us closer to a machine with Hal-like capabilities. Its researchers seek to understand and build intelligent entities. Others in the field see the goal of AI as designing machines that can perform tasks that people can, or try to, perform. In their comprehensive 1995 volume, Russell and Norvig introduce the issue thus:

> AI addresses one of the ultimate puzzles. How is it possible for a slow, tiny brain, whether biological or electronic, to perceive, understand, predict, and manipulate a world far larger and more complicated than itself? How do we go about making something with those properties? These are hard questions, but unlike the search for faster-than-light travel or an antigravity device, the researcher in AI has solid evidence that the quest is possible. All the researcher has to do is look in the mirror to see an example of an intelligent system. (p. 3)

The first of these questions—how something as small as the human brain can perform the tasks that it does in fact perform—has long tantalized possessors of these brains and fueled research in fields that investigate human intelligence. The second, dealing with the actual creation of an intelligent entity, could not be adequately addressed (outside of fiction) until the necessary technological underpinnings became available. To create an intelligent entity, we need the technology we began developing only in the second half of the 20th century.

As we note in other parts of this book, there is not total agreement among researchers in human intelligence about exactly what constitutes the object of their research. But whatever working definitions underlie the research in these fields, whatever arguments may be brought to bear and whatever clashes may occur among their proponents, it is clear that if you seek to build an intelligent entity—one by definition *artificial*—you need a clear idea of what you are trying to build.

Russell and Norvig (1995) point out that researchers in the field generally define artificial intelligence along one of four dimensions, which fall into two major categories. The first of these categories is *thought processes and reasoning,* and the second is *behavior.*

Within the first of these, thought processes and reasoning, researchers focus either on systems that think rationally or on systems that think like humans. Systems that think *rationally* are those that function by the rules, as we humans do often, but certainly not all the time. A system that functions by the rules all the time does not make mistakes; if the rules are followed, mistakes cannot occur. Logical thinking, for example, when based on premises that are correct, will necessarily lead to correct conclusions. As we all know, humans do not always base their thinking on correct premises, nor, because they are subject to interruptions, distractions, and emotions, do they always follow the steps involved in logical reasoning. Human thinking and the conclusions humans draw are filled with error. But one might well engineer a system in which the premises, or rules, and instructions for following them correctly are built in. Correct answers will always then result. A machine that thinks rationally is, in this system, an intelligent machine.

On the other hand, if one has in mind building a system that thinks like humans, one must begin with a theory of human thought processes, and then, as Russell and Norvig put it, "express the theory as a computer program. If the program's input/output timing behavior matches human behavior, that is evidence that some of the program's mechanisms may also be operating in humans" (Russell & Norvig, 1995, p. 6). Under this definition of intelligence, if the system is thinking *like humans,* the machine is intelligent.

In behavior-based AI, rather than focusing on endowing machines with the ability to think like humans, some researchers are trying to get machines to act like humans, to do what we do, without necessarily being concerned with whether the machines are doing it *in the same way* we do it. In other words, for these researchers, if the machine can do what we do—however it does it—it is intelligent. Hal could carry on conversations, but it was not necessary, for purposes of the film, to explain his language processing system. In real life, we would like a machine to be able to converse with us. Imagine dictating a term paper to your computer (the technology already exists for this) and having it make suggestions as you go along (no way to do this yet). Would it matter to you *how* the feat was accomplished? Or would it be enough that it *was?*

Other researchers taking this direction focus on building a machine that acts *rationally.* "Acting rationally means acting so as to achieve one's goals, given one's beliefs. An **agent** is just something that perceives and acts. . . . In this approach, AI is viewed as the study and construction of rational agents" (Russell & Norvig, 1995, p. 7). An advantage of this approach is that it does not have to take into account the components of human behavior (or human thought), which are notoriously difficult to quantify, and thus difficult to re-create in a program. In this approach, a machine that acts rationally is an intelligent machine. It will be well to keep these categories, thought and behavior, in mind as a frame of reference as we examine some of the salient aspects of the background of AI.

FIGURE 7.1 A Russian Schoty Set at the Number 123

We might begin an investigation of the development of artificial intelligence by discussing the devices, such as fingers or the abacus, employed by people since they began keeping track of more numbers and number operations than they could readily hold in working memory. Such devices, whether parts of our bodies or machines invented for the purpose, facilitate or expand our ability to function in this realm of human thinking. All that we can now accomplish along these lines by means of machines has its roots in older techniques, older ideas. Our fingers have always been there, of course, and even the abacus originated in prehistoric times. Interestingly, the abacus proved such a useful tool that a version of it was used by the British Treasury into the 18th century (Pullan, 1969). "Counting frames" were still used routinely in elementary schools well into this century, and simple ones can still occasionally be found in the classroom. Figure 7.1 illustrates the **schoty**, a version of the counting frame still in use in Russia. That it was not supplanted for so long highlights the fact that a viable modern replacement was not developed until recently. The family tree of "computing machines" contains interesting early branches. Our purpose here, however, dictates that we jump some millennia to centuries not so distant from our own, to examine some of the developments that led to the current state of the art.

In 1623 Wilhelm Schickard (1592–1635), a German professor of astronomy, mathematics, and Hebrew (this was before the days of narrow specialization), designed and built a machine that could add and subtract completely automatically, and multiply and divide partially automatically. We know of this machine only from letters discovered in this century, in which the machine is described;

Schickard's half-finished model was destroyed in a fire. A somewhat later mechanical device for adding and subtracting, which did come to public attention, was built in 1642 by the French mathematician and philosopher Blaise Pascal (1623–1662). In 1694 the German mathematician and philosopher Gottfried Leibniz (1646–1716) produced an improvement upon it, a machine capable of automatic multiplication and division as well as addition and subtraction (Goldstine, 1972). After these inventions, the idea waited until the mid-19th century before it was picked up again and carried forward by Charles Babbage.

Historical Background: 19th Century

The Jacquard Loom

Before we arrive at Babbage's contribution, an interesting and important invention deserves mention here, as it played a significant role in the development of Babbage's machine and those that followed it. It serves, as well, to indicate the varied sources from which concepts derive and the ways in which ideas from one realm may be adapted for use in another. The reader may have heard of a particular weave called "Jacquard weave." This is a process in which a fabric acquires an intricate design not by means of dye but by causing the design to be actually woven into the fabric. The process takes its name from Joseph Marie Jacquard (1752–1834), a French weaver who, in the very first years of the 19th century, invented a device for the loom that allowed this process to be automated (Figure 7.2).

The patterning of fabric woven by this device is accomplished by means of a program that dictates, for any given pattern, which threads of the lengthwise strands (the warp) the crossways strands (the weft) should go over and which it should go under as it is directed by the shuttle. (The shuttle is the instrument that conveys the crossways strands over and under the lengthwise strands.) The program also dictates when the basic pattern is to be repeated. As with mathematical processes, human skill is useful up to a point. But as we know, very complex problems, which would take more years to solve than humans can give to them, are today more efficiently addressed by machine. Weaving a very complicated pattern is also best accomplished by automation. Jacquard's ingenious automated device made use of a set of cards with holes in them arranged in the desired pattern. When the cards were placed in the loom, hooks came up through the holes to pull down threads of the warp, allowing the shuttle, on its journey, to go over certain specific threads and under others.

Punched cards of this sort may be familiar to some readers. They were given out in the 1960s at toll booths, for example, or distributed to students registering at universities. They bore the caution "Do not bend, fold, spindle, or mutilate." Like Jacquard's punched cards, these had particular patterns of holes punched in them; but the holes on *these* cards allowed the cards to be "read" by a computer rather than by a loom. (Hence the caution; computers were no happier with bent cards than are vending machines with scrunched dollar bills.) The system invented by

FIGURE 7.2 Jacquard Loom for Weaving Patterned Cloth

Jacquard to allow any pattern, no matter how complex, to be automatically woven into fabric had been adapted to a totally new purpose, and the person who saw the possibilities afforded by the concept was the British mathematician and engineer Charles Babbage.

Charles Babbage and His Analytical Engine

Charles Babbage (1791–1871) was a polymath, a person whose interests and areas of learning are very varied. An aspect of Babbage's interest in mathematics was mathematical tables, which at the time people computed laboriously by hand. Hence they were subject to human error. Society depends on many types of tables: abstract mathematical tables such as squares and square roots; tables involved in concerns of business; actuarial tables affecting life insurance; tables having to do with computing interest on loans—all manner of tables. These had tremendous potential for error as people performed the calculations and wrote down (and made copies of) the results. Mistakes could lead to nasty results. Errors in navigational tables, for instance, could—and did—sometimes lead to shipwrecks. Computing and printing such tables mechanically would prevent the errors produced when this process is carried out by hand (Hyman, 1982).

Babbage had in mind a machine that would perform mathematical tasks very quickly. He had in mind, in fact, what we now recognize as the precursor to the computer of the 20th century. Babbage's machine, which he called the "Difference Engine No. 2," or the "**Analytical Engine**," was to be a "general-purpose programmable computing machine," which could add, subtract, multiply, and divide (Babbage, 1864/1968). (Although today we understand "engine" as that which drives a machine, in Babbage's day it simply meant "machine.") There was even a printer component to the design, because printing the results directly by machine would avoid human errors of transcription.

This machine was designed to operate using cards much like Jacquard's. Babbage saw that the concept of the "program" embodied in these cards exactly suited the purposes of a program to be used in a computing machine. As he explained it, the manufacturer of the fabric has a choice. He or she can implement the design dictated by the pattern of holes on the cards using threads all of one color, in which case the pattern will be realized as a kind of damask, woven into the fabric but undifferentiated as to color. Or the manufacturer may choose threads of different colors to implement the same design, using the same cards but in this case differently colored threads. The form of the pattern will remain the same, but the pattern will be represented as some arrangement of colors (Babbage, 1864/1968).

Babbage drew the analogy to the Analytical Engine, which would contain a "store" and a "mill." The store would contain the variables to be operated on and the results of the operations; the mill would be where the quantities to be operated on are brought. (Today we know these as the *memory* and the *processor*.) In this machine several sets of cards are used. One of the two major sets directs the operations, and the other directs the variables on which the operation cards must operate. When the machine is to compute, operation cards containing the series of operations needed are strung together in the appropriate order. Similarly, variable cards are strung together in the order in which the variables must be acted on. Each set will then be available to perform its calculation on whichever numerical values are inserted.

> The Analytical Engine is therefore a machine of the most general nature. Whatever formula it is required to develop, the law of its development must be communicated to it by two sets of cards. When these have been placed, the engine is special for that particular formula. The numerical value of its constants must then be put on the col-

FIGURE 7.3 Portion of Babbage's Analytical Engine

umns of wheels below them, and on setting the Engine in motion it will calculate and print the numerical results of that formula.

Every set of cards made for any formula will at any future time recalculate that formula with whatever constants may be required. (Babbage, 1864/1968, pp. 118–119)

See Figure 7.3 for a picture of the only portion of the Analytical Engine that was assembled in his lifetime (shortly before he died in 1871). Babbage's formulation remained the principle for a long time. In the much more recent period of those punch cards I mentioned, a typical program deck would consist of cards containing the program code followed by the cards containing the data. If the program didn't work because of a mistake, the programmer would have to go through the deck card by card to find the error.)

Babbage was aided in his project by Lady Ada Lovelace (1816–1852), the daughter of the poet Lord Byron and a competent mathematician in her own right. Lady Lovelace's contribution included notes interpreting Babbage's work. Because no other source about his ideas exists today that researchers might study, her notes are particularly valuable. Babbage's machine "was the first artifact possessing the characteristics necessary for universal computation" (Russell & Norvig, 1995, p. 15). The mechanism he designed for this machine was very complex and required a new sort of notation in which to encode its instructions. Therefore,

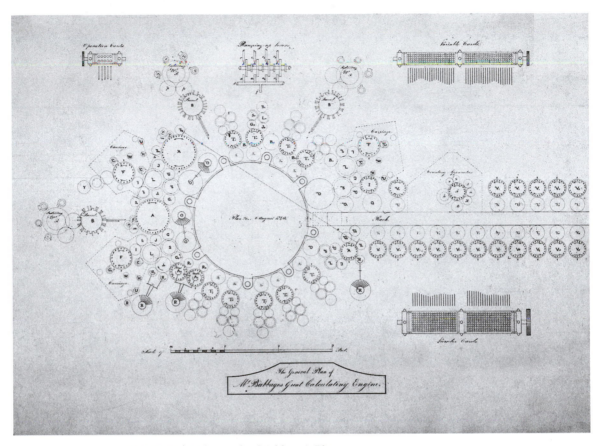

FIGURE 7.4 Lithograph of Babbage's Plans

Babbage invented a "mechanical notation" for this purpose. He also anticipated the formal programming languages that would be used in the future, when the machinery advanced beyond the mechanical structures he designed for his early machine.

As it happens, this wonderful Analytical Engine was never completely built—at least not until some contemporary engineers, taking as their mission to prove that Babbage's engines were "logically and practically sound," undertook to construct it. Fortunately, Babbage left hundreds of drawings of his ingenious and complex machine. In 1991 the engineers involved in the project completed a working model, using Babbage's drawings and only those techniques and devices that had been available to him in the 19th century (Swade, 1993). Figure 7.4 is a lithograph of one of Babbage's own general plans of the whole Analytical Engine.

An interesting aspect of Babbage's work is that he and Lady Lovelace also speculated on the Analytical Engine's ability to perform functions beyond those for which it was originally designed. These included playing chess and composing music, both of which have been realized today by the computer. What is additionally interesting to us is an issue that has received much attention in recent years, as the field of artificial intelligence leads us to think ever more deeply about our own cognitive processes: To what extent is our *own* thinking "computational"?

The question is not a new one; in fact it antedates Babbage and his Analytical Engine by at least 200 years. The 17th-century philosopher Thomas Hobbes (1588–1679) suggested that ratiocination, that is, the reasoning process in which our minds engage, *consists* in computation:

> By *ratiocination,* I mean *computation.* Now to compute, is either to collect the sum of many things that are added together, or to know what remains when one thing is taken out of another. Ratiocination, therefore is the same with *Addition* or *Substraction* [sic]; and if any man adde *Multiplication* and *Division,* I will not be against it, seeing Multiplication is nothing but Addition of equals one to another, and Division nothing but a substraction of equals one from another, as often as is possible. So that all Ratiocination is comprehended in these two operations of the minde, Addition and Substraction. (Hobbes, 1656, pp. 2–3)

Thus, Hobbes described (human) reason as consisting of mathematical functions. But it is fair to ask, as some have, "Could one represent all things under the sun through a set of symbols? Could thought result from the manipulation of these symbols according to a set of predefined rules? And if so, what should the rules and symbols be? . . . Such questions found their echoes in early AI efforts" (Crevier, 1993, p. 14). If, as Hobbes and many others since his time have suggested, thinking is (at least in part) computational, then a machine that computes—a "computer"—is a machine that thinks. Two centuries later, Babbage designed a machine that could perform such functions. Now, four and a half centuries after Hobbes, and a hundred years after Babbage, we have produced extremely sophisticated machines that perform these computational functions vastly more quickly, and probably more accurately, than we do ourselves. In the framework I mentioned earlier, such a device falls within the category of machines that think like humans—and is, therefore, "intelligent."

It is time now to move into 20th-century developments in AI and to consider a figure whose ideas were crucial to the development of the field as we know it today.

Historical Background: 20th Century

Alan Turing

It is often the case that mathematicians do their most significant work when they are young. This was certainly true of British mathematician Alan Mathison Turing (1912–1954), whose name is immediately cited when the subject of the history of artificial intelligence is raised. Turing's accomplishments in mathematics and computer science began while he was still in his twenties. He is also known for his work for the British military as a cryptanalyst, or "code cracker," during World War

II, when he contributed to the war effort by helping to decipher German coded signals produced by a machine called "Enigma."

Turing was, "to the extent that any single person can claim to have been so, the inventor of the 'computer'" (Britton, 1992, p. vii). In 1946 Turing presented to the National Physical Laboratory (NPL) in Teddington, England, his seminal "Proposal for Development in the Mathematics Division of an Automatic Computing Engine (ACE)." In this proposal he presented in detail the essential aspects of the computer. Among these he included erasable memory; converters from the binary form of calculations to the decimal form of input and output; logical control ("to interpret the instructions and give them effect"); a central arithmetic part to carry out the fundamental arithmetic processes; and means of selecting the information required at any given time (Turing, 1946/1986, pp. 21ff). He also indicated advantages to an ACE: speed (it would not have the limitations of human operators), avoidance of human fallibility (though he was astute enough to recognize that this might well be replaced by mechanical fallibility), and the ability to carry out "very much more complicated processes . . . than could easily be dealt with by human labour" (Turing, 1946/1986, p. 20).

The "Turing Machine"   Another of the contributions for which Turing is particularly known is his invention of the hypothetical **Turing machine**. In a sense this was the descendant of Babbage's Analytical Engine (and, like Babbage's invention, it was never built). Unlike the Analytical Engine, though, the Turing machine is in principle very simple. It would, nevertheless, be impossibly inefficient for practical purposes. Its value was as an abstraction that served to present the possibilities of artificial intelligence.

One critical aspect of human intelligence is the ability to solve problems, and a machine, to be considered intelligent, must also be able to solve problems. Turing's hypothetical machine is a very powerful device: It has the ability to perform *any computational process that can be performed*. Thus, if a problem can be solved by a set of precise instructions or rules (an **algorithm**), the Turing machine can solve it. (Bear in mind, though, that although we humans can and do solve many problems by following explicit instructions, we also often have recourse to what we call intuition and insight, and the solutions these produce are not necessarily arrived at by means of precise rules or sets of procedures.)

To understand the principle of the Turing machine, imagine a device that consists of a long tape with squares (or cells) on it, each one either blank or containing a symbol (0 or 1). The length of this tape is not specified; in principle it is infinitely long or, to put it more practically, as long as it needs to be in order to compute the solution to a given problem. All the machine is capable of is reading the tape, moving it forward or backward one cell at a time, and either printing new symbols in the cells or erasing the ones already there.

Any machine for performing computations has to keep track of intermediate steps in the process, and for this it relies on *memory*. At each point, a computing machine is in a "state," in which part of the computation has been performed and the results stored. Because such machines have a finite number of symbols, of

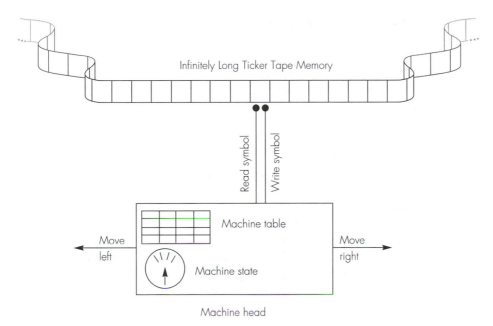

FIGURE 7.5 The Basic Properties of a Turing Machine

instructions, and of states of memory they can be in, they are called **finite-state machines**. A combination lock is one such machine, albeit a simple one. It is typically programmed to "remember" a particular sequence of 3 numbers out of perhaps 35 and to open when the correct sequence has been entered. Not all machines are that simple; nevertheless, there are limits to the amount of memory real machines have, and thus there are limits to the number of computations they can handle.

The hypothetical Turing machine is more powerful than a real machine because it has *unlimited* memory. The tape serves to feed in the data at the starting point, to feed out the end results, and to store the intermediate results. With infinite tape, there is no limit to the amount the machine can store; that is, there is no limit to what it can remember. The simple functions with which Turing endowed it permit it to compute anything that can be computed, no matter how complex the computation. Figure 7.5 illustrates the basic properties of a Turing machine.

From our perspective today, we can see the similarity of the Turing machine to a computer running a particular program. We may have one such computer on our desk or lap, performing its computation by following its set of instructions, coded in binary terms (in terms of 0 and 1). On someone else's desk or lap we may have another computer, performing its computation, following its own set of instructions. If one constructed a Turing machine that could simulate the operations of any and all Turing machines, each of which is devoted to solving a particular problem, one would have what Turing called a **universal machine**—in effect, just what today's computer is: a machine that carries out any program it is equipped to read (Johnson-Laird, 1988).

The "Turing Test"   Another of Turing's contributions appeared in 1950. In a paper titled "Computing Machinery and Intelligence," Turing set forth his ideas on machine intelligence. The criterion he proposed for deciding whether or not a machine is intelligent has come to be called the **Turing test**. The ideas presented in the 1950 paper have sparked a great deal of discussion and debate, and anyone interested in the question of machine intelligence must be familiar with the early operational definition it provides.

The idea of the Turing test fits the behavioral approach described earlier: A machine is considered intelligent if it *behaves* like humans. In pondering the question "Can machines think?" Turing observes that the definitions of "machine" and "think" are problematic. Therefore, he proposes a different approach to the question: an "imitation game." The game is played with three people: a man (A), a woman (B), and an interrogator (C). The interrogator, in a different room from the others, asks them questions to try to determine which is the man and which is the woman. One of them (let's say A) is supposed to try to lead the interrogator to guess wrong, and the other (B) is supposed to help the interrogator come to the correct conclusion. (Arrangements are of course made so that there are no helpful hints, such as voice quality. For example, the answers can be typed.) Turing poses the questions in this way:

C: Will A please tell me the length of his or her hair?

If A is the man, A answers with a statement designed to mislead:

A: My hair is shingled, and the longest strands are about 9 inches long.

It might be best for B, who is supposed to help C, to tell the truth and add to her answers statements such as "I am the woman, don't listen to him!" But A, who wants to hinder, can make such statements too, so B can't really help much in that way.

Turing (1950) then wonders what will happen when a *machine* takes the part of A. "Will the interrogator decide wrongly as often when the game is played like this as he does when the game is played between a man and a woman? These questions replace our original 'Can machines think?'" (p. 34).

If its cognitive skills are adequate to fool a human, the computer passes the test (that is, it is intelligent). What we must ask then is "What cognitive skills must the computer possess in order to pass the test?" Clearly it needs to be able to process human language, at least the language of the interrogator. (We have already noted, in Part 3, just how vast a task *that* is.) It also needs to have a means of storing the information it has been given before the test and that it acquires during the test. Furthermore, it must be able to use that information in answering the questions it is asked and to figure out who is who. It must, in addition, be able to *learn*. A mechanism that indicates by its conclusions that it has not learned from its experience will not fool a human for long.

In addition to cognitive skills, if a machine is really to fool a human, we should probably endow it with the ability to perceive objects and the ability to move them. The first of these is called computer vision; the second involves robotics. Both of these, as well as aspects of the cognitive skills mentioned previously, are capacities that have by now been built into machines, though not all into the same machines—and not for the purpose of fooling people. But more of that in the next chapter.

We will return, in the discussion on philosophy, to the question of whether a machine that embodies such "human" capabilities as these can be said to be "thinking." For now, let me just mention one related aspect of this issue, to which we shall also return. My constant reference to the *machine* keeps firmly in our minds that the object is built of parts that do not in any way resemble our own. The machine is made of metal or plastic or glass or all of these and more; but it is not made of flesh, of bone, of neurons . . . One current point of view is that the material of which the potentially "thinking" machine is made is of no consequence. It does not matter how the object is achieved, by what mechanisms. If the computer acts like a human being to the extent that a human being cannot distinguish it from a human being, it is thinking. The question of whether, if it is thinking, it possesses *consciousness* is a controversial one to which we shall also return. For now we continue our examination of the background of contemporary AI.

John von Neumann

Some rather successful attempts at building computers were made in the early 1940s in Germany, England, and the United States more or less simultaneously (Copeland, 1993, p. 4). Of particular relevance to our story here, however, is the mathematician John von Neumann (1903–1957), whose contributions were crucial to the direction computers, and hence AI, were to take. Born in Hungary, later an American citizen, von Neumann was a somewhat older contemporary of Turing.

Babbage's inventions had been stimulated by the needs of his day, such as speed and accuracy in constructing tables crucial to many areas of life. World War II (and subsequently the cold war) provided the incentive for the development of the machines on which both Turing and von Neumann worked. George B. Dyson (1997) compares Turing and von Neumann thus:

> Alan Turing and his colleagues at Bletchley Park [where they worked for Allied intelligence during World War II] were chess players at heart, pitting their combined intelligence against Hitler for the duration of the war and then returning as quickly as possible to civilian life. John von Neumann . . . was a warrior who joined the game for life. The von Neumann era saw digital computers advance from breaking ciphers to guiding missiles and building bombs. The advent of the cold war was closely associated with the origins of high-speed electronic computers, whereby the power of new weapons could be proved by calculation instead of by lighting a fuse and getting out of the way. (p. 75)

The ENIAC   The particular World War II project on which von Neumann worked was the Electronic Numeral Integrator and Calculator, called the ENIAC (Figure 7.6). Like the Jacquard loom and Babbage's Analytical Engine, this large and complex device made use of punched cards. Just how large and complex it was is

FIGURE 7.6 Portion of the ENIAC

demonstrated by the following facts: It consisted of about 18,000 vacuum tubes, 70,000 resistors, and 10,000 capacitors. It weighed about 30 tons and took up a whole room (Sankaran, 1995).

The ENIAC was developed and built, in the early 1940s, largely by the efforts of John W. Mauchly, whose design was stimulated by work on electronic computation in the 1930s, and the electronic engineer John P. Eckert (Goldstine, 1972). It was to be used to calculate artillery tables that would make it possible to aim artillery at specific targets. The problem faced by the military was that the targets they needed to hit, that is, enemy aircraft, were far away and in motion. Further, they needed to drop bombs from their own moving aircraft. The calculations required for the firing tables used in these operations depend on many complex and interdependent factors, including, for example, atmospheric conditions and temperature (Dyson, 1997). To provide such a great number of calculations was a job for a machine that could produce them much faster than human beings are able to. This was what the ENIAC, which became operational in 1945, was designed to do. Although the war ended before it could be pressed into service, the ENIAC demonstrated its capabilities in 1946 by computing "a shell trajectory in twenty seconds—ten seconds faster than the flight of the shell and a thousand times faster than the methods it replaced" (Dyson, 1997, p. 81).

The size of this monster machine may surprise some readers, who are accustomed to the small footprint of their desktop computers, or the smaller space taken up by their laptops or the very mini-sized palmtops that became available in the 1990s. As soon as a model smaller, faster, and more powerful than last year's becomes available, we become impatient with the models we already have, taking their enormous capabilities and small size entirely for granted. But even much more recently than 1945 very large machines were still state-of-the-art. In 1981, when I first came to the university where I teach, I was given a tour of the computing facilities, of which the university was justly proud. I remember walking through a large room, on a raised floor under which was an air-conditioning system to cool the two mainframe units—a VAX and an IBM 438. These, along with tape drives and all the other necessary components, lined the walls of the room and performed all the computing functions of this large organization. It was an impressive sight. (Of course even though today's desktop computers may be as powerful as such large models, organizations the size of a university still require a mainframe computer to be the repository of the shared data on which the organization depends. There is power on your desk, but the memory store is sufficient only for local purposes.)

EDVAC and the "von Neumann Architecture"   The computer as we know it owes the design of its basic architecture, which has become known as the "von Neumann architecture," to von Neumann and those with whom he worked on the ENIAC. Von Neumann "enunciated the fundamental architectural principles to which subsequent generations of computers have adhered" (Copeland, 1993, p. 7). It remained for the next generation of computers to implement this architecture fully. The machine that succeeded the ENIAC was the much smaller (only 5,000 vacuum tubes!) Electronic Discrete Variable Computer, or EDVAC. Crucial to this advance was the distinction between a computer's memory and its central processing unit (CPU), and the realization that the instructions for operations to be performed (that is, the *program*) can be stored in the computer's memory just as the data on which they operate are stored. The computer then carries out its operations in cycles; in each cycle the data and the instructions feed from the memory into the CPU. The CPU carries out the operations according to the instructions and stores the results in the memory. If one could provide a von Neumann computer with infinite memory and a program to carry out the required formal operations, one would in effect have a universal Turing machine (Bechtel, Abrahamsen, & Graham, 1998).

Turing had pondered the question of whether machines could be intelligent and proposed that a machine that could fool a person into thinking it too was a person could indeed be considered intelligent. Others expressed the conviction that a machine that can perform functions such as handling information and making choices is a machine that can think. Von Neumann

saw digital computers as mathematical tools. That they were members of a more general class of automata that include nervous systems and brains did not imply that they could think. . . . Von Neumann knew that a structure vastly more complicated, flexible, and *unpredictable* than a computer was required before any electrons might leap the wide and fuzzy distinction between arithmetic and mind. (Dyson, 1997, pp. 108–109)

An idea may be around for a long time—hundreds of years or more—before the technology exists to implement it, to make it a reality. Beginning with the creation of the general-purpose, electronic, digital computer that was the ENIAC, and with the improvements represented by the EDVAC, computers sprang up at many locations. The second half of the 20th century saw enormous progress in the engineering of the computer. Every 18 months its power has doubled, its speed increasing to an astonishing degree, as its size and cost decrease. Thus the possibilities for AI that the computer raises have begun to be realized.

Another element in the development of AI was the JOHNNIAC, a sophisticated computer designed by von Neumann, on which was run an early AI program known as the Logic Theorist. It may be somewhat arbitrary to make this the point where we leave the background to AI (this chapter) and begin to explore the field of AI proper (Chapter 8). The progression is not as clear-cut as doing so may make it appear. However, the point at which the subject of computer *design* begins to give way to the subject of the computer *program* seems an appropriate place to stop, step out of these waters and take a breath, before entering the current again. We return in the next chapter to the Logic Theorist and move on to the other aspects of AI that have eddied around our feet, creating such turbulence and excitement, and inspiring so much debate, since the mid-20th century.

Questions to Think About

1. What will be some consequences for researchers of the fact that most manuscripts today are composed on word processors and leave no signs of corrections or editing?

2. Under what circumstances might it be unwise to rely on a computer to check one's spelling? One's grammar?

3. Do you think computers make most people's jobs easier, or do they make them more demanding?

4. Would you ever ask a machine "What do *you* think?" Why or why not?

5. What are your feelings (or thoughts) about the statement "If the machine can do what we do—however it does it—it is intelligent"?

6. If most people can be trained to use an abacus, and the abacus is inexpensive and can solve most people's everyday math problems efficiently, why does one need an expensive computer?

7. Do you envision a day in which humans will be employed to make *computers'* lives easier? Is it possible that that day has already come?

CHAPTER 8

The Machine Performs

In February 1996, newspapers carried the story of a chess match between Gary Kasparov, world champion chess player, and Deep Blue, a computer. To the surprise of many, Kasparov lost the opening game of the match! He did win the next game, but the third and fourth each ended in a draw. Games five and six—and thus the match—went to Kasparov. The result demonstrated that humanity, represented by Gary Kasparov, was still king of the chessboard.

At the same time, it had not been a rout; Deep Blue had given humanity a run for its money. How long before humanity, in the person of the grand master and world champion, would succumb to the power of the computer, surrender its crown, and be removed from the board?

It took a scant 15 months. On Sunday, May 11, 1997, Kasparov and Deep Blue again made chess news—and chess history. In fact, more than *chess* history, because the winner this time was not the man but the machine. A domain that had been considered to belong to human intelligence alone had been conquered by the computer's "artificial" intelligence.

Less than a year and a half later, in October 1998, came the report of another sort of intelligent device: the spacecraft known as Deep Space 1. This device is designed to test a variety of new technologies, among them software that will "take care of itself, navigating through space on its own and occasionally calling home to let people on Earth know how it is doing" (Leary, 1998). It will use information from pictures it takes of stars and asteroids, adjusting its own course with reference to these and deciding how close it will come to them. Every so often it will use one of a repertoire of tones to signal controllers on Earth to apprise them that it is doing fine or that it may need help or perhaps that it has a problem that urgently requires their assistance (Leary, 1998).

These examples are realities today—and indications of what tomorrow holds. Deep Blue is a machine that, in playing chess, performs an activity we assume takes intelligence when performed by a person. If defining one's own goals and figuring out how to achieve them are also aspects of our human intelligence, then to the extent that Deep Space accomplishes them, it too qualifies as intelligent.

But as amazing as these programs are, they do not fulfill the expectations aroused at the midpoint of the 20th century, when there was tremendous excitement about the promise of artificial intelligence. And they have been longer in coming than was originally anticipated. When it became clear that miracles of machine intelligence were not immediately forthcoming, excitement yielded to a certain amount of disappointment as each small success brought home the complexity of what the human brain accomplishes with little apparent effort. Nevertheless, the disparity between our own abilities and the limited capacity of machines only seemed to spur the AI effort to close the gap. Thus, at the end of the 20th century, although AI has certainly not fulfilled early exaggerated hopes, it has come encouragingly nearer to meeting them. As the gap shrinks, the philosophical issue of the relation of human to machine intelligence engenders intense debate and has resulted in a number of books that have engaged the public interest. This issue, which is very much with us at the beginning of the new century—and millennium—is addressed in Chapter 10. In order to appreciate it fully, we must examine the progress that has been made in particular areas of AI research. This research is based on the development of the computer as not merely a speedy number-cruncher but rather as a processor of symbols in various domains. As such, it can be programmed to exhibit behavior we regard as intelligent, such as planning, problem solving, and deduction. It is also based on the creation of machines that learn and embodied mobile machines (i.e., machines housed in moving mechanisms, or "bodies") that employ all of these means to engage in intelligent behavior.

Intelligent Machines: Early Programs

Logic and the Logic Theorist

If not always as perfectly as a machine, we humans routinely follow logical steps as one approach to solving problems. Take for example the problem of shoveling last night's snow from our front steps. If this is the first time we have shoveled (and have never had to sweep) stairs, we might stop to consider how to go about the task. Our line of reasoning would probably go as follows: "If I start from the bottom step, when I shovel the next one up snow from it will fall onto the bottom step again and I'll have to shovel it twice. Then, if there is another step above the second one and I shovel *it* next, I will have to shovel step number two twice and the bottom step three times. What a waste of energy! I'd better start at the top." Reasoning of this sort is so natural to us (and so rapidly accomplished) that we hardly notice we are doing it, regarding it as "only common sense." We certainly notice, however, when someone *fails* to do it: Imagine a film clip in which Charlie Chaplin or Mr. Bean is shoveling snow from steps, starting from the bottom. The ensuing bit of business would make us laugh. We might mentally address the shoveler, clearly a silly fool, thus: "That's stupid! Why don't you start at the logical place?"

This type of reasoning is clearly one of the capabilities that we consider an aspect of human intelligence. If we stop to consider the information on which this ability rests, we note immediately that all manner of knowledge is called into play, such as the fact that when pushed off the steps, snow will fall down, not rise up. The human world is vast and complex, comprising many domains of knowledge. The computer will not at the outset have the wealth of information humans draw on for a task such as logical reasoning. So, if we want to program the computer to engage in this task, a first step might be to simplify its world. Our best bet might be to limit our project to very explicit information in a very restricted domain. Such a domain is pure logic, which relies on specific premises, or theorems, from which conclusions may be drawn.

In the 1950s, Newell, Shaw, and Simon followed this path when they attempted to program a computer to search in a logical way for proofs of the theorems of logic. In 1956 their program, the Logic Theorist, tackled the theorems presented in Alfred North Whitehead and Bertrand Russell's 1910 book *Principia*

Mathematica. In this book Whitehead and Russell had systematized and codified the central areas of pure logic, which consists of theorems such as

given that either X or Y is true, and given further that Y is in fact false, it follows that X is true.

The Logic Theorist program succeeded in proving 38 of the first 52 of Russell and Whitehead's theorems. For the first time, a computer program "did not simply crunch numbers, but teased out proofs of abstract statements. In a microscopic way, the Logic Theorist could reason" (Copeland, 1993, p. 7).

The General Problem Solver

The success of their project led Newell, Shaw, and Simon to take another step: programming the computer to approach problem solving the way humans do. This attempt resulted in what is known as the General Problem Solver, or GPS. Developing through a series of versions, the GPS was ultimately able to solve a variety of problems. Now it must be understood that its name, General Problem Solver, does not imply that this program can be expected to solve *any* sort of problem you may give it. Even people are not expected to do that. For instance, if you had a physics problem you wished to solve, you would be ill advised to give it to *me*. But certain types of problems, whose solutions lend themselves to a very explicit and clear set of steps, can be formulated for the GPS, which can indeed follow those steps to arrive at a solution.

The notion behind the GPS and its precursors was that, when one sets out to solve a problem, the mental activity being devoted to the task occurs within a cognitive *problem space* (Newell & Simon, 1972). A set of "operators," beginning at what is called the *initial state* (the beginning condition), moves the process along step by step, from state to state, until the problem reaches a solution (Waldrop, 1988). One example of the sort of problem that was tested on this system, and that it was able to solve, is the "Tower of Hanoi" problem. The goal of this problem is to move all the disks from the start peg to the finish peg. Difficulties arise because the rules are that only one disk may be moved at a time and that a larger disk may not be placed on a smaller one (Figure 8.1).

By 1969 the GPS had been modified a number of times and was able to solve, among other sorts of problems, the kind we call "brain teasers." You must have come across problems like these and enjoyed (or hated!) puzzling them out. Take for example the one about the father and two sons who want to cross a river. The only way they can do so is by means of a small boat, which all of them are capable of operating. The difficulty is that the boat can carry a maximum of only 200 pounds. Because the father weighs in at the maximum, and each son weighs 100 pounds, they have a real problem. How are they to get across? If you try to solve this problem, chances are the way you go about it is by trying a series of possible crossings one at a time and, if one does not work, going back and trying another. That is, first you may send the two sons together. But then how does the boat get back to pick up the father? So you think of sending one son with the father. But the

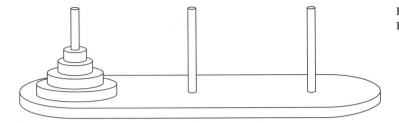

FIGURE 8.1 Tower of Hanoi Problem

boat cannot carry 300 pounds. Ah, but if you send the sons together and then send one back with the boat, the father can make the next crossing by himself. The son he leaves behind can then be picked up by the other one after *he* takes the boat back alone.

In solving such problems, the GPS followed a pattern similar to that which you probably use: searching among and following a series of elementary reasoning steps. But unlike us, the GPS does not have at its command the amount of information required to solve problems in domains wider than that of the simple and clearly defined sort just described. Its success in following the process was necessarily limited to problems of this sort. Those that humans must solve, however, are not usually so limited or so clearly defined. Our success in solving them relies on the knowledge we store automatically. If we try to identify all the pieces of information we must have in order to solve a problem, we are immediately struck by the vastness of this store. Furthermore, the problems we encounter in the course of a day arise in all manner of domains. For instance, suppose you lock your keys in the car. One way to solve the problem of getting to your next appointment on time (or at all) is to retrieve information about whom to call in this situation: who has either spare keys or a means of sliding past the window and reaching the inside lock. If that individual is not available, you try it yourself with an implement you judge capable of fitting through the small slit between the window and the door frame. In this case you rely on your knowledge of, for example, the physical properties of materials: You need to know how thin such an implement must be, how strong it must be, how flexible it must be. You also need to know where to look for or how to fashion such a tool.

This is but a trivial example of the sorts of information humans store, which comes from an astonishingly large number of disparate areas. These include physical properties, behaviors, and effects of substances; socially acceptable deportment in groups (both our own and those outside); word meanings and usages; the tools of our various trades; indications of tomorrow's probable weather; the next line of music in a song or a symphony. The list seems almost infinite. We humans are, of course, general problem solvers par excellence, and if AI researchers are to succeed in developing intelligent machines, these machines will have to behave more like us in this regard. To be considered really intelligent, a "general" problem solver will have to be more general than was this early GPS. In fact, this obstacle would eventually be addressed, as we shall see. But first let us look at another direction taken by AI researchers, one that was to figure in the improvements on the GPS: expert systems.

Expert Systems

In addition to the vast store of general knowledge most of us acquire simply in living, there are some people who have deliberately and consciously set about to acquire a large store of information in a particular area—plumbing or paleontology, masonry or medicine, for example. They can use this knowledge to make decisions and to solve problems within the area. We consider such individuals "experts" in their domains, and we turn to them to help us install our kitchens and bathrooms or to diagnose and treat our illnesses.

Unlike us, the computer program does not absorb information "out of the air" as we seem to from the moment we are born, nor can it decide on its own to develop an area of expertise. So AI researchers decided it for them: They began to implement what became known as knowledge-based systems. These are created by entering into the system a great number of pieces of information—data—within a particular narrow field. Such a program might become an "expert" in this single domain; one must, after all, start somewhere. An expert system has been defined as "a knowledge-based system whose performance is intended to rival that of human experts" (Duda & Shortliffe, 1983, p. 267). That is, it is intended to provide expert-level solutions to complex problems, to be understandable, and to be flexible enough to accommodate new knowledge easily (Buchanan & Shortliffe, 1985).

Expert systems are comprised of two main parts: a knowledge base and an engine, also called an *inference mechanism*. Such a mechanism is necessary because the system is specifically designed *not* to run through all possibilities. Rather, like a human, it must "know" when it has enough data to make a decision. Thus, like us, it must be able to make inferences from what it "knows." If the VCR clock is flashing, we infer an earlier power outage; if the child is flushed and very warm to the touch, yet complains of chills, she has a fever. Figure 8.2 illustrates in diagrammatic form the major parts of an expert system.

An early example of an expert system is the DENDRAL program, whose domain is organic chemistry. Begun in the mid-1960s, DENDRAL was the first AI program that stressed specialized knowledge rather than general problem solving. It was designed to suggest the chemical structure of unknown compounds. To do so, it made use of a large number of special-purpose rules. Within 10 years or so, DENDRAL became a collection of programs that interacted to help organic chemists explain molecular structures (Buchanan, Sutherland, & Feigenbaum, 1969).

There are many areas in which humans may choose to become expert. A given individual may be an expert mechanic; another may be an expert in the field of forensic anthropology; still another may be an expert in diagnostic medicine. As it happens, this last was the area that provided much of the foundation for the subsequent development of expert systems. It did so by means of the program known as MYCIN.

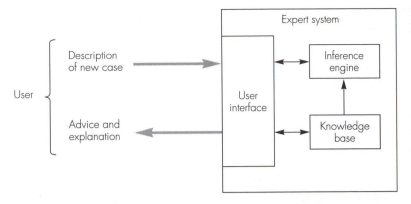

FIGURE 8.2 Major Parts of an Expert System

MYCIN

Making use of the knowledge gained from the DENDRAL project and techniques developed in implementing it, AI researchers in the mid-1970s designed MYCIN to help physicians choose appropriate antibiotics for patients with severe bacterial infections. A very important decision in designing a program like this concerns how its knowledge base is to be represented. In the case of MYCIN, it was decided that it should be represented as a set of conditional statements, or *inference rules,* of an if-then sort. That is,

> IF: There is evidence that A and B are true,
> THEN: Conclude that there is evidence that C is true.
> (Buchanan et al., 1969, p. 4)

In the MYCIN program, about 500 such rules are entered into the database, which represents knowledge on the diseases meningitis (infection in the cerebrospinal fluid) and bacteremia (bacteria in the blood). These rules are then "expressed in a stylized form that simplifies computer interpretation and facilitates their translation into English for human examination" (Duda & Shortliffe, 1983, p. 262). The following is what such a rule looks like, expressed in English:

> If (i) the infection is meningitis and (ii) organisms were not seen in the stain of the culture and (iii) the type of infection may be bacterial and (iv) the patient has been seriously burned, then there is suggestive evidence that *Pseudomonas aeruginosa* is one of the organisms that might be causing the infection. (Duda & Shortliffe, 1983, p. 262)

To employ a rule like this one, MYCIN clearly has to have certain information about the patient. For instance, if it knows that the condition is not meningitis, it will not apply this rule. If it doesn't have such information, it can ask for it, or it can infer the answer from other data it has. It gathers all the rules that might apply to the infection and attempts to apply them. Every time one is applied, a new fact is gleaned and entered into the database to be used in applying subsequent rules.

As MYCIN attempts to apply rules, it asks questions, and the user responds to the questions with facts or the response "unknown" or sometimes the question "why?" MYCIN responds to this question with the reason for the question and the rule it was trying to apply. If the user asks "why" repeatedly, he or she can trace back through the program's chain of reasoning and have the process explained. After the program arrives at a diagnosis, it provides the user with advice as to therapy: which medications to administer and what further steps should be taken. MYCIN thus serves as a consultant to the physician (Duda & Shortliffe, 1983).

The practical benefits of expert programs that interface with the user in this way are obvious. The system can store knowledge gleaned from many human sources, potentially very much more knowledge than any individual source can supply. It can then quickly search its knowledge base to suggest possibilities and treatments. These functions can be enormously helpful to physicians who, no matter how good their memory and their diagnostic ability, will not always have the necessary relevant information at their command. And, of course, in approaching the task of developing such systems, AI researchers refine our understanding of how *human* experts function.

Chess: Deep Blue Shows Its Mettle

A domain of AI that has also received much attention is games. Game programs that can be pitted against and even "outplay" humans constitute another instance of expert systems. The much publicized program Deep Blue defeated the human world chess champion Gary Kasparov. How was this possible? To answer this question, one must first understand what is involved in playing a game in which rules are specified and adversaries take turns making "moves" allowed within these specifications. (Some readers may be surprised to learn that *game theory* is a major area of mathematical analysis, contributing to our understanding of "games" such as business and war.) In a game like Tic-Tac-Toe, the rules are simple, and to think through all the possible moves and their consequences is not a complex project. One may lay them out as a kind of tree structure, a **game tree** that depicts all the possible moves and their consequences (Figure 8.3). The game is short, its game tree relatively short and straightforward. It is not difficult, therefore, to follow the moves in this tree from the initial one through all the possible choices, to the final result of each choice. Once you know these results, you possess the "trick" to winning. Given the opening move, you follow the path dictated by the result you seek, and you win. Once you know the trick, the game becomes boring.

Like Tic-Tac-Toe, the game of chess is predicated on rules, but these are more complex, and the possibilities held out by any given move are many times more numerous than those in Tic-Tac-Toe. An expert human chess player has mastered more than just the rules governing the moves (quite the simplest aspect of the game). The expert has also mastered, from experience, a large set of configurations that the pieces may assume on the chessboard and a large number of sequences

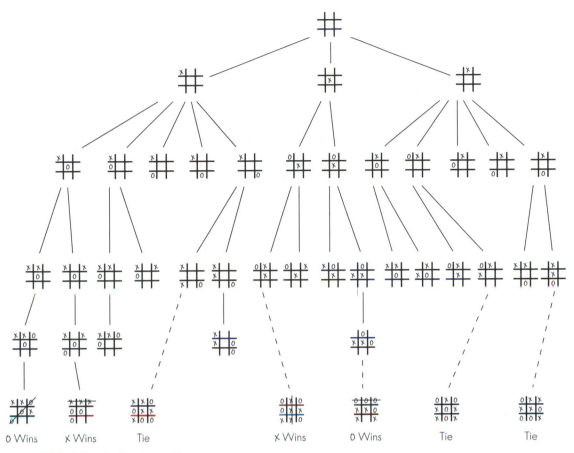

FIGURE 8.3 A Tic-Tac-Toe Game Tree

that can be played out beginning with these configurations. Human chess players do *not* simply run through all of these possibilities in their heads before making a move. Even if it were possible, doing so would drag out the game interminably; in fact, it might never end. We simply do not think that fast.

But a computer does. That is, it has the capacity to run through hundreds of thousands of possibilities in virtually no time. Even before the development of Deep Blue, a chess program called Hitech was able to examine about 175,000 positions per second (Copeland, 1993). Deep Blue improved on this to the tune of examining one *billion* positions per second (100–200 billion per move; Russell & Norvig, 1995). Another way of saying this is that its components function, like those of the human brain, *in parallel*. In developing a program that involves all that a chess program requires, it was necessary to include such **parallel processing**. That is, a single processor, operating in a serial manner (performing one function after another) cannot carry out all the functions necessary to play chess at the desired level—no matter how rapidly it does so. It cannot examine all the possibilities that these programs actually handle. Parallel processing harnesses the capabilities of many units simultaneously so that all the necessary functions can be carried out in the required time. Given parallel processing capacity and the rapid functioning it allows, in a thinking race in which number crunching is the key, the computer wins hands down.

Why then was there ever a question as to whether human or machine is the better chess player? The answer lies partially in the fact that examination of moves (following the game tree) is not by itself the most efficient way to play chess. That much is obvious from the fact that, until recently, humans continued to beat machines at the game. They must have been doing something better than simply examining moves. If we think about the problem for a moment, we realize that a crucial aspect of a game is *evaluating* moves. We need an efficient decision-making function that will select from among all the possible moves those that are useful. Human chess players must employ a system that enables them to choose not only moves, but also *good* moves—those that will advance their positions in the game. Like a human player, a computer chess program must incorporate this function along with its examination function.

> Deep Blue doesn't consult a historical game data-base or use AI techniques like pattern recognition. . . . [It] can recognize (in hardware) approximately 6,000 chess-specific features. . . . Human chess players evaluate their current positions by counting their material advantages ("I'm down a pawn") or weighing their control of the board ("I have control of the center"). These kinds of insights translate to computers. . . . Evaluation functions have become increasingly sophisticated, especially as computers have become more powerful. (Hamilton & Garber, 1997, p. 30)

Deep Blue's ability to beat the human world champion chess master Gary Kasparov was partly the result of its stored evaluation features (say, a knight's control of the center) and its ability to examine its current situation on the board and adjust the weights (i.e., take account of the importance) of these features. Deep Blue was thus designed to perform in a manner analogous to the human player.

I have included games under the heading of expert systems because programs have been developed specifically to be expert at playing a complex game. But we should keep in mind that becoming an expert in a game like chess is different from becoming an expert in, say, choosing appropriate antibiotics for patients. It involves a kind of problem solving. Choosing from among possible moves constitutes a problem, the steps of which must be considered and evaluated. But there is even more to the human approach to problem solving than this. There are still other concepts that must be taken into account by AI researchers as they work to design computer programs to engage in what humans consider intelligent behavior.

A program is an algorithm, a set of instructions. Humans frequently operate by following algorithms. A set of directions for getting from your house to the Department of Motor Vehicles is an algorithm; a recipe for stir-fry vegetables is an algorithm; the sequence of steps to follow in performing the Macarena is an algorithm; the formula for figuring out time/rate/distance problems is an algorithm.

For humans, arriving at a desired solution or goal by following an algorithm may be only one part of the process. The truth is, we don't always simply follow directions. We may "see" a way of getting from here to there without going through all the steps in an algorithm. Or the goal may not be achievable by such direct means, and we have to figure out a roundabout way of getting there. It is also true that there may not be a "best" (surest) way of achieving our goal. It may be that we could in fact find a sure way but it would be too tedious or time-consuming to bother with (running through all the possible chess moves, for instance). We might prefer a way that is approximate or even a bit risky. It may not be the "best" way, but solutions don't necessarily have to be perfect—just good enough. A solution that is "good enough" may save us a great deal of time and/or boredom. Such methods are called *heuristics,* and we humans are very good at them.

It must not be assumed that heuristics are random, however. One way of thinking of them is as rules of thumb. An example that readers will surely recognize concerns the placement of commas in a sentence. There are a number of specific comma rules: "separate dependent from independent clauses with commas," "use a comma before a coordinating conjunction," and the like. A rule of thumb, or **heuristic**, regarding commas is "place a comma at the point of a natural pause." The rule is not foolproof: Different readings of a given sentence may yield—and different readers may perceive—different pause points. But often the heuristic will work well enough; the commas will be in the right places most of the time.

All along AI researchers have appreciated—and exploited—the fact that machines don't get tired in the way we do. It's okay for a set of parallel processors to spend all day and all night running through steps; they won't feel fatigue or resentment. They won't even get bored. But even for a machine, as for a human, this process may not be the most practical. And apart from considerations of practicality, AI researchers who are interested in, for example, pitting machine against human chess master, may try to design their programs to function in at least some respects the way the chess master does. Trying to build human cognitive abilities into a machine entails the quest for an ever deeper understanding of these human abilities. One aspect of these, as exemplified by the human chess champion's performance, is heuristics—and it is possible, instead of relying simply on number crunching, to build useful heuristics into a computer program.

From the very beginning of AI research, various goals have been set for the computer that, once achieved, would constrain us, however grudgingly, to consider the machine "intelligent." But each time such a goal has been realized, we have upped the ante. Okay, we say, the machine can do X. But it isn't really intelligent until it can do Y. Oh, it has done Y? But wait—before we'll agree that it is intelligent, it must do Z! Yet it is becoming increasingly difficult to withhold that judgment, as the achievement of Deep Blue attests. And the same process is occurring in other areas of AI, in which particular cognitive abilities are at issue. Before going further in this direction, now that we have some understanding of the expert system approach to AI, let us go back for a brief look at the problem of the general problem solver (GPS) and, in the light of the work in expert systems, see how an attempt at resolving it was approached.

The Soar Project

So far, our consideration of machine intelligence has focused on problem solving and on expert systems as distinct aspects of intelligence, not as aspects of an integrated system. Human intelligence, on the other hand, both solves problems and gains expertise from its experience in a domain. In fact, it uses the knowledge or expertise it gains from experience to solve new problems. With our wonderful, complex brain, we somehow manage to do it all. Modeling human cognition would have to attempt to bring the aspects of problem solving and expertise together into a single entity. Even more ambitious was one of the goals set for the cognitive science initiative: "striving to develop a unified theory of cognition that spans the space of intelligent systems, both natural and artificial" (Rosenbloom, 1991, p. 309). Pursuing this goal of a unified theory of cognition in the mid-1980s, research led by Allen Newell of Carnegie-Mellon University resulted in a system known as Project Soar (for State, Operator, and Result).

In Soar, as in the earlier GPS, goals were set for solving problems, using a system in which encoded knowledge was represented by a set of if-then rules. Consider for a moment an ordinary sort of problem human beings may set for themselves, say, hanging a picture on a wall. The rules to get to the end state (the picture is hanging on the wall) might include these: IF you have the hammer and the nail, THEN place the nail against the appropriate spot on the wall. Having the hammer and the nail is one state of the situation. The rule has moved you along to the state of placing the nail where you need it. IF the nail is in position, THEN strike it with the hammer. IF the nail is stuck in the wall, THEN place the picture wire over it. Eventually, these rules have moved you to the end state, and the picture is hung. As in expert systems (recall MYCIN's if-then representations), Soar has stored many many rules of this sort. But only one rule can "rule" at any given time. If many "fire" at once, there may be a conflict or an impasse. What Soar does each time this happens is set up a new problem, a problem that may be characterized as "solve this impasse." Soar then stores the results as new if-then rules, in a process called **chunking** (Miller, 1956; Newell & Rosenbloom, 1981). Later, each time an impasse arises, it can use preferred ways of resolving it by recourse to a stored "chunk." Unlike expert systems whose information has been supplied by the programmers, Soar adds to its own memory, moving from novice to expert all by itself.

When, in 1993, the entire collection of papers relating to Project Soar was published in one two-volume collection (Rosenbloom, Laird, & Newell), it attested to the evolution of a very powerful and impressive system. However, lest you think that all problems entailed in achieving a unified theory of cognition and of modeling human cognition had been solved, I hasten to assure you that they had not. For one thing, the range of problems that Project Soar solves is by no means as great as the range of problems constantly confronting and being solved by human intelligence. Furthermore, it has been pointed out that in many respects a program that can reason logically to achieve a well-defined solution for a complex problem is, by virtue of that very fact, not behaving like a human being (Moray, 1996).

Those who wish for an artificial intelligence that truly models our own must address the kinds of situations *we* face, in which "even the answers are not well-defined, and the nature of problem solving is on-line, real-time, and continuously adaptive, without any certainty from moment to moment that an apparent solution will remain acceptable" (Moray, 1996, p. 165).

A new direction in this endeavor is currently under way in projects that attempt to build "embodied" robots that will act in real-world situations. Before we examine this direction, however, let us turn our attention to two important areas of human cognition that will have to be incorporated in an artificial intelligence that is capable of confronting such real-world situations: language and learning.

The Language Challenge: Natural Language Processing

Chapter 6 of this book discusses a number of the ways in which the field of linguistics interconnects with the other component fields of cognitive science, including some of the directions pursued by AI research. One such direction mentioned in that chapter is the usefulness of the computer in preparing concordances—counts of the frequency of occurrence and exact locations of all the words, phrases, and sentence constructions in a given text. Concordances are of great value in particular areas of study, but it is not machine "intelligence" that makes them possible. Rather, they derive from the particular capacity of the computer to store and access data more quickly than we can. They do not demand of the machine that it perform any of the cognitive functions of humans.

A function that *is* of this sort is computer translation from one human natural language to another. Attempts at machine translation can teach us much about the general properties of human language. Such translation would also be of practical value, in view of the benefits in having ready access to technical and cultural material produced in different parts of the world. (See Chapter 6 for some of the difficulties associated with machine translation.) Briefly restated, attempts to program the computer to translate from, say, Chinese or Russian or French into English made it clear that translation is not simply a point-for-point correspondence between the words of one language and those of another. It involves—crucially—*understanding*. The reader knows, for instance, that *He let me down* means either "He disappointed me by not doing what I wanted/needed/expected," *or* "Holding the end of the rope to which I was fastened, he allowed the rope to lengthen slowly as I made my perilous way down into the cavern." Context and metaphor are both among the determiners of meaning. Without understanding them translation is not really possible.

Browsing the Internet in January 1999, I located the Web site of a company currently advertising products that reveal the state of the art at this time. One such product is Easy Translator, which is described as enabling the user to communicate internationally, translating Web pages and e-mail. The program accomplishes this feat thus: It "doesn't just substitute words, it breaks down complex sentence structures, identifies parts of speech, resolves ambiguities, and synthesizes the information into the components and structure of the new language." Under the heading "How good is the translation?" the company informs the potential user that computers

> can't always produce perfect translations. Sometimes computer translations are awkward or even humorous. But for casual documents and for getting the gist of text in other languages, Easy Translator translates with the accuracy and quality you need. (www.transparent.com)

Perhaps it is impossible to do more. Certainly some researchers in the field have not been overly optimistic:

> The limitations on the formalization of contextual meaning make it impossible at present—and conceivably forever—to design computer programs that come close to full mimicry of human language understanding. (Winograd, 1984, p. 142)

ELIZA Revisited

Readers of Chapter 6 will recall another early and well-known approach to the problem of natural language processing: Weizenbaum's 1965 program ELIZA. This program makes use of key words. As a "patient" types in statements, ELIZA, playing the role of psychotherapist, responds to those words that it recognizes. It recognizes them by virtue of their matching words and sentence patterns, or "frames," previously stored as data. But the user doubtless notices in short order just how limited ELIZA's responses are, because the program cannot process any statements or questions whose key words or frames have not been stored. In matching input to fixed patterns, ELIZA is able to "mirror" the responses of the "patients" and thus to mimic part of the technique of some forms of psychotherapy. The program cannot, however, get beyond its patterns to produce any novel responses. It in no way *understands* what it is doing and thus cannot modify its linguistic behavior as human beings do constantly. ELIZA was successful in that its limitations served to clarify what needed to be done if a program were ever to use human language in a fashion more closely approaching that of humans. As a "therapist," however, it was a flop. It would not take a person sitting at ELIZA's keyboard more than a few minutes to realize that ELIZA's knowledge base, though impressive for a computer in 1965, was no match for a live therapist, who could readily pursue any number of avenues in response to a patient's "input."

Understanding Language

An attempt to address the limitations of programs such as ELIZA resulted in the creation of **parsers**, programs that assign grammatical categories (parts of speech) to the words in a sentence and group them into phrases. It is possible to do this because one of the contributions of contemporary linguistics is partial sets of formalized rules for many languages. Such unambiguous instructions lend themselves to computer programming. If a computer program contains categories and phrase groupings instead of mere sentence frames, and a set of rules for combining them, one may say that it is handling language somewhat more as we do than is a program like ELIZA. The achievement of this triumph in natural language processing, however, again pointed to its limitations, in view of the complexity of what humans do when they "do" language. There are many sentences that humans have no difficulty in comprehending but that resist such a simple parsing process (see Chapter 6). Further developments in the AI/language scene involve more capable parsers in combination with other capacities necessary for human language, as SHRDLU, a subsequent and very well known program, will illustrate.

Semantic Information Processing: SHRDLU

Early attempts at natural language processing lacked crucial capacities: the ability to learn, to reason, to plan—in some sense to understand why a particular course of action is taken. This was certainly true of the ELIZA program. A new development, the program called SHRDLU, seemed quite amazing in this regard when it appeared in 1972. SHRDLU's designer, Terry Winograd, had taken into account more than the parsing and storage functions humans exercise when engaging in language behavior. His design also included other cognitive functions crucial to understanding and using natural language:

> When a person sees or hears a sentence, he makes full use of his knowledge and intelligence to understand it. This includes not only grammar, but also his knowledge about words, the context of the sentence, and most important, his understanding of the subject matter. To model this language understanding process in a computer, we need a program which combines grammar, semantics, and reasoning in an intimate way, concentrating on their interaction. (Winograd, 1972, pp. 1–2)

In implementing a program that would function in this manner, Winograd followed a path similar to that taken by the designers of expert systems: He limited its world. Humans may come onto the scene equipped to deal with a complex environment all at once, but experience had shown that the most impressive computer programs of the day could handle but a small domain. So Winograd created in SHRDLU a (simulated, or virtual) simple robot, one endowed with a hand and an eye and the ability to manipulate toy blocks on a table. A person at the keyboard communicates with the virtual on-screen robot by typing commands, which the robot then carries out. The robot also types out answers to questions and accepts information for later use in reasoning.

Winograd had several goals in mind in designing this project. An important one was the creation of a system with the capacity to *understand* language. The language programs with which SHRDLU understood and communicated about its blocks world would not be limited to this simple world but were to be of greater generality, capable of being adapted to other systems. Another goal of the project was to gain a better understanding of what language *is*. Attempting to model a human cognitive capacity always contributes to our understanding of that capacity. A further goal of this focus on language, as humanity's very special and enormously complex cognitive system, was to increase our understanding of human intelligence in general—and of how we might emulate it in the computer.

FIGURE 8.4 Diagram of a Portion
of SHRDLU

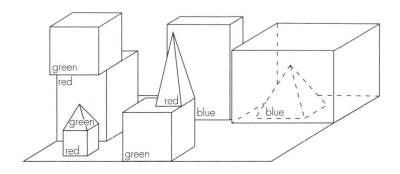

Winograd's program for understanding language is complex. It includes a dictionary containing information about both syntax (how words are arranged into sentences) and semantics (information about word meanings); a grammar that handles the basic units of English (such as clauses and noun phrases); a parser; and a set of programs to control the responses SHRDLU will make (remembering the discourse and taking it into account in making its responses). Other components are a program that deals with the typed input by looking up words in its dictionary and analyzing them to see how they fit into the syntax; and a component that contains the system's knowledge both of the physical properties of blocks and of the way to achieve goals in its limited world. This list of the programs that make up SHRDLU, although not exhaustive, nevertheless gives some idea of the complexity of the task.

Equipped with all of this, SHRDLU performs tasks involving a set of blocks on a table, as illustrated by Figure 8.4 and the following sample dialogue. The boldface lines in lowercase were typed in by a person, and the uppercase lines are the computer's response. Other lines are comments describing some of the features being exhibited.

1. **pick up a big red block.**
OK.
The system answers "OK" when it carries out a command. In order to pick up the red block, it had to clear it [the block] off by finding a space for the green one and moving the green one away.
2. **grasp the pyramid.**
I DON'T UNDERSTAND WHICH PYRAMID YOU MEAN.
There are three pyramids in the scene, so the program does nothing.
3. **find a block which is taller than the one you are holding and put it into the box.**
The system has to figure out what is meant by "one" and "it," as well as using deduction to decide which block it is holding.
BY "IT", I ASSUME YOU MEAN THE BLOCK WHICH IS TALLER THAN THE ONE I AM HOLDING.
Printed out to keep us informed.
OK. . . .
4. **what does the box contain?**
THE BLUE PYRAMID AND THE BLUE BLOCK.

5. what is the pyramid supported by?

Earlier the system responded to "the pyramid" by saying "I don't understand which pyramid you mean." Now, it assumes that we mean the one just mentioned.

THE BOX.

6. How many blocks are not in the box?

FOUR OF THEM.

7. Is at least one of them narrower than the one which I told you to pick up?

The phrase "at least one of them" must be analyzed to refer back to the previous question, and "the one which . . ." must also refer to blocks. Noun groups can have complicated numbers such as "at least one," "more than three," "exactly seven," etc. The memory of past events is used to deduce which block is "the one which I told you to pick up." Notice the complicated syntactic structure in which "the one" is actually the object of a clause embedded two levels deeper.

YES. THE RED CUBE. (Winograd, 1972, pp. 8–10)

This small sample gives some indication of the kind of response and reasoning of which SHRDLU is capable. It also indicates the narrowness of the "microworld" within which it functions. What remains to be made clear is that in storing a set of items and the possible relationships among them, SHRDLU cannot truly be said to *understand* them. And this is the crux of an issue still being hotly debated: Can a machine *think*? We will return to this question in Part 5. For now, let us examine some other approaches to the issue of natural language understanding and then proceed to other topics under investigation within AI.

Knowledge Representation: The Notion of Frames

As dazzling as the SHRDLU achievement was, it eventually evoked the same reaction as other attempts to implement aspects of human intelligence in a machine: disappointment. It fell short of the mark. Again, the predictions and hopes of many in the field—that a computer intelligence to rival that of humans was just around the corner—were proven overly optimistic. A crucial difference between programs such as MYCIN, Deep Blue, ELIZA, and SHRDLU on the one hand, and human intelligence on the other, is that all of the former are restricted to domains in which relevant aspects of the game or the knowledge base or the conversation or the "microworld" are decided *in advance*. "The difference between areas in which relevance has been decided beforehand . . . and areas in which determining what is relevant is precisely the problem" (Dreyfus, 1992, p. 33). This is the problem of knowledge representation: All the background knowledge humans have at their command is called into play when a problem is to be solved. The particular knowledge required to solve that problem is not a given, as it has been in computer programs. Computer programs simply do not have represented within their boundaries the amount of knowledge necessary to solve the types of problems humans confront and solve every day. One may even argue that the restricted "world" of a given program is not properly a world at all, because

a world is an organized body of objects, purposes, skills, and practices in terms of which human activities have meaning or make sense. It follows that although there is a children's world in which, among other things, there are blocks, there is no such thing as a blocks world. (Dreyfus, 1992, p. 13)

But perhaps a world may be developed by accretion. That is, if we add knowledge of one domain to knowledge of another, and another, and still another, we may arrive at an adequate—or at least a more complete—representation than heretofore. We have seen (Chapter 6) that the vast job of learning a first language is simplified—even rendered possible—by acquiring rules so that each piece of the language process does not have to be learned as an individual element. We have seen (Chapter 4) that we may store information not only as individual bits (such as the individual digits in a telephone number), but we may store chunks of information (such as the 1-800 before the telephone number) and thereby not have to remember as many different items as would otherwise be necessary.

In an analogous manner, one way of conceiving of people's background knowledge is as consisting not just of stored individual elements but rather as stored complex sequences, or data-structures. These complex sequences are known as **frames**. "A frame is a data-structure for representing a stereotyped situation, like being in a certain kind of living room, or going to a child's birthday party" (Minsky, 1975, p. 212). At the top level of a frame are those elements that are always true about a particular situation. At lower levels, there are "slots" to be filled by the specific instances of the situation. In other words, there is an invariant background that we have stored as a complex whole so that when we experience a given situation we already have a "frame" within which to comprehend it. The only problems to be solved are those presented by the specific details of the current situation.

Readers of Chapter 2 will be familiar with the version of this notion to which Schank and Abelson (1977) gave the name of *scripts*. Their discussion hinges on the idea that one reason we function as readily and as easily as we do, for example, in a doctor's office—signing in, hanging up coats in the closet or on the pegs, sitting quietly in the waiting room expecting to hear our name called, and eventually disrobing for the examination—is that we rely on such stored frames, or scripts. This sort of knowledge representation, or data-structure, hypothesized for human beings, can be exploited in designing computer programs. Instead of just storing individual items, we can store whole scripts that can form the background knowledge lacking in earlier attempts of AI to model facets of human intelligence.

Our own human "script storage" is of course most easily described in terms of language. To outline a given script we employ language, and this is also the way we enter it into a computer. For this reason, it is important not only to focus on the syntax of language, as was done in designing parsers, but to work with meaning as well. If a computer is to understand a script, it must store knowledge of meanings as well as knowledge about what sort of word may follow another in a sentence. Failure to include meaning in the mix might enable a program to "understand" Lewis Carroll's *Jabberwocky,* for instance, but not recognize the difference between this elegant piece of relative nonsense and a portion of a script dealing with going to the doctor or to a restaurant.

One path followed in the late 1960s and early 1970s was the attempt to design a program that could parse English sentences into conceptual representations.

> The basic intent of our work was to provide unique representations for ideas that could be expressed in many ways. Because of this, our programs could understand an event to be the same one as one seen previously, even if the previous expression of that event had been quite different. The conceptual representations that we devised . . . were intended to facilitate the automatic *paraphrasing* of a sentence that the program read, and even the translation of that sentence into other languages. (Schank & Childers, 1984, p. 140)

To paraphrase is to render one formulation of a text into a different formulation of the same conceptual material, that is, to say the same thing in different words. Those who have tried paraphrasing a sophisticated passage—or any but the simplest sort of writing—can attest to the difficulty of the task. Programming a machine to paraphrase is an impressive achievement. Nevertheless, it is limited: Paraphrasing does not go *beyond* the text. When we humans speak or read, on the other hand, our understanding is not limited to the sentences on the page or those that hang in the air. We also make *inferences* based on what we have read or heard. If someone told us, for example, that John paid the butcher and went home to make his dinner, we would most likely infer that John had just purchased meat (not, for instance, applesauce) for this dinner and that he was going home to cook that purchase. We might, of course, be wrong. It is certainly possible that John bought the meat for Sally and dropped it off on the way home to his own vegetarian meal. But our immediate assumption would be that it was for *his* imminent repast.

Inferences are based on a great deal of background knowledge. Had we known John to be a vegetarian, we would not have drawn the particular inference just mentioned. Inferences are also usually based on aspects of background knowledge that make sense to us in a given context. We do not in fact infer a great many of the meanings that are possible, because we know from our experience (i.e., our stored knowledge) that only a limited set will make sense. From John's purchase at the butcher we do not, for instance, infer that he is going to take the bus on the corner, though we know that there is a bus stop there and that it goes past his house. He may be on foot (the store is six blocks from his home), or he may have been traveling home from work by car. If a computer program is to be endowed with a modicum of understanding, it must encompass not only the immediate text but the context as well. The program must deal with the *connections between* sentences as well as with the sentences themselves. This is where scripts come in.

Script Applier Mechanism (SAM)

The 1970s saw interesting developments along these lines in computer programs. One such was the Script Applier Mechanism, or SAM, developed under Roger Schank's direction. SAM was a program that could read stories based on scripts. Scriptlike newspaper stories about specific subjects, such as car accidents, lent themselves particularly well to SAM's capabilities, and SAM was given the task of summarizing such stories. The following snippet of a program illustrates SAM's impressive accomplishments.

Input: Friday evening a car swerved off Route 69. The vehicle struck a tree. The passenger, a New Jersey man, was killed. David Hall, 27, was pronounced dead at the scene by Dr. Dana Blanchard, medical examiner. Frank Miller, 32, of 593 Foxon Rd., the driver, was taken to Milford Hospital by Flanagan Ambulance. He was treated and released. No charges were made. Patrolman Robert Onofrio investigated the accident.

English Summary: [SAM could also produce translations into Russian and Spanish!]
AN AUTOMOBILE HIT A TREE NEAR HIGHWAY 69 FOUR DAYS AGO. DAVID HALL, AGE 27, RESIDENCE IN NEW JERSEY, THE PASSENGER, DIED. FRANK MILLER, AGE 32, RESIDENCE AT 593 FOXON ROAD IN NEW HAVEN, CONNECTICUT, THE DRIVER, WAS SLIGHTLY INJURED. THE POLICE DEPARTMENT DID NOT FILE CHARGES.

Question-Answering Output:
Q1: Was anyone killed?
A1: YES, DAVID HALL DIED.
Q2: Was anyone hurt?
A2: YES, FRANK MILLER WAS SLIGHTLY INJURED.
Q3: Why was Miller hurt?
A3: BECAUSE THE AUTOMOBILE HIT THE TREE.
Q4: Did Miller go to the hospital?
A4: YES, HE WAS IN THE MILFORD HOSPITAL.
Q5: How did Miller get to the hospital?
A5: THE FLANAGAN AMBULANCE COMPANY TOOK HIM TO THE MILFORD HOSPITAL. (Schank & Childers, 1984, p. 145)

The reader will have noticed several instances of "understanding" on SAM's part. That is, SAM has responded with information it has filled in from its background knowledge. SAM's output includes, at the very beginning, a reference to an automobile, though the original passage does not use that word. It only mentions "car" and "vehicle." SAM also *inferred* that the passenger, "a New Jersey man," lived in New Jersey. To readers that fact may seem obvious; but consider a similar construction, such as "the passenger, a *tall* man." We understand that "tall," unlike "New Jersey," is a characteristic of the man. Like us, SAM does not infer that "New Jersey" is a characteristic of the man, as "tall" is; rather, it understands what we understand: that in such a context the modifying phrase indicates that the man *lives* in New Jersey.

Further, the original story states that the passenger was killed. From this term, SAM infers that he *died*. From the original statement that the driver was treated at the hospital and released, SAM infers that he "was slightly injured." And in the question-answering output section, we see that SAM also infers that the driver was hurt because the automobile hit the tree, though the story does not make that connection explicit.

We take for granted that we can understand a story by inferring connections not explicitly stated. When we examine the process carefully, we see that this ability is indeed based on a great deal of implicit knowledge that we have stored. We do not take for granted that a machine can do it. But as impressive an accomplishment as SAM was, its developers were faced with the same "yes, but . . ." difficulty as before. In this case, the "but" resulted from the fact that the stories SAM could deal with were based on highly restricted scripts. In real life, there are no such restrictions. Although it may be that we store certain complex sequences as chunks, or as units, no individual instance of the sequence occurs in a prescribed way. I may function on "automatic pilot," as it were, through the doctor's office scenario, but when a patient who came in half an hour after I did is called before I am, the neat sequence is interrupted. Having rolled up my sleeve and offered my arm to be tightly cuffed, according to the script, I may expect my blood pressure to be judged within the normal range. My reaction to having been made to wait for an unconscionable amount of time while others were taken out of turn may again disturb the smooth flow of the script. When I attempt to pay by credit card before leaving and find that my card is not accepted by the machine, I can no longer expect to rely on my internalized script. Furthermore, if my credit card has never been questioned before, I now have to deal with a truly novel situation.

Suppose, in addition, that I had had a plan when I made my appointment with the doctor: I had arranged to meet a friend afterward for lunch in a nearby restaurant. My goal was to get the visit to the doctor over with as soon as possible and enjoy my afternoon. But now I will be very late; my friend might not wait. I have no credit card with which to pay for lunch. And my stomach, along with my blood pressure, is upset by the unexpected events in what should have been a routine, "scripted" event. If a machine were ever to understand a real-life sort of story, it would have to be able to deal not only with plans and goals but also with possible upsets of these plans and goals. All of this indicates the enormous complexity of what we are asking a machine to do when we ask it to engage in the kind of acquisition, storage, and processing of language and other types of knowledge characteristic of human beings.

Machine Learning: Connectionism and the Neural Network

The preceding discussion gives an idea of the process in which AI researchers engage as they develop programs to carry out some of the cognitive functions of the human brain—which require for this purpose definition at an ever deeper and more precise level. Having endowed SAM with a degree of understanding, Schank and his colleagues addressed the next level. One aspect of what we humans do, but that SAM could not, is to learn something new from what we experience. Reading a story is not, for us, a static experience. Rather, it may cause us to understand something in a new way or to make connections we had not previously thought of. A new story may fill in some blank spaces in our knowledge so that we approach the next one with a richer store against which to interpret it.

> To achieve the level of intelligence we are looking for, we have to provide the computer with more general structures, the same ones that allow people to make connections at a very high level of abstraction. We want the computer to learn something when it reads. We want it to thoroughly integrate a story into its knowledge structures. We want it to be able to distinguish what is important from what is trivial in a story, and remember things it read in the past just when they are most applicable to a situation it is processing currently. We want computers to have flexible, *dynamic* memories that will enable them to be reminded of past experiences and to profit from those experiences. (Schank & Childers, 1984, p. 166)

Making connections is crucial to profiting from those experiences. We humans make simple connections constantly: The color of that house brings to mind Aunt Minnie's house, which is painted the same color; or, at a greater level of abstraction, the story of Richard Nixon's fall from grace may remind us of a Greek tragedy, in which a fatal flaw brings about the destruction of the hero.

Neural Networks

Associative thought of this sort, produced by the connections among stored concepts, is discussed with regard to human cognition in Chapter 2. Recognizing that for machine intelligence to resemble human intelligence it would have to be capable of learning, some AI researchers turned to an approach that, like so much of AI research, had its roots in the 1950s. This was the development of **neural networks**, systems that make use of connections to produce in the machine something of the kind of dynamical memory so essential to human learning.

There is a major difference between this approach to artificial intelligence and the one that produced, for example, the Deep Blue chess program that beat our human champion Gary Kasparov. The latter type relies on symbolic processing, solving problems by applying sequences of formal rules for manipulating symbols. High-level programming languages, such as **LISP** and **Prolog**, facilitate the job. The neural network approach, on the other hand, attempts to solve problems at the level of the structure of the machine. A distinction may be drawn between this approach and that described above

> in terms of the way the two disciplines view knowledge or information. AI attempts to capture intelligent behavior without regard to the underlying mechanisms producing the behavior. This approach involves describing behaviors, usually with rules and symbols. In contrast, neural networks do not describe behaviors; they imitate them. (Caudill & Butler, 1990, p. 26)

Rather than producing intelligent behavior by means of manipulating stored rules and symbols, neural networks actually model the human brain, though in a greatly simplified manner. They are designed to learn in an associative way, as we do.

The symbol/rule approach has been very successful in a number of areas, such as that of the expert system. Neural network researchers note, however, its failure to capture such human cognitive abilities as speech recognition, motor control, object manipulation, and association. They point out that such problems are the ones neural networks are ideally suited for. Indeed, we are learning that even much of the functioning of human experts occurs at a level of

> intuitive understanding of the structure of the task they are performing—from a learned internal model of the process they are involved in—rather than from a set of facts or cognitive rules about the process. This type of model building is more reminiscent of intuition than of symbolic processing and is the natural domain of neural networks. (Caudill & Butler, 1990, p. 26)

What, then, are neural networks, or *neural nets,* as they are often called? Chapter 3 provides a brief introduction to the system of neurons within the human brain, that network of cells and synapses by means of which information is acquired, stored, and recalled. Artificial neural nets are designed on a similar principle. They consist of nodes, or units, connected by input and output links. Of course, human neural networks are realized in the flesh, whereas artificial neural networks, for practical reasons, are generally realized in computer software. They are "virtual" networks, or simulations of physical networks. The neuron is represented in the artificial neural net by the node, and the input and output links are the neural net's version of the brain's synapses.

Before focusing on the artificial neural net, consider for a moment the properties of the human brain-as-learning-system. One important property of this system is that it learns by means of repetition. Indeed, it evolves, changing physically as it learns. Physical changes in the neurons of the brain have been observed in experimental animals as they learn behaviors. As we respond to the environment in a particular way, the response becomes familiar and we tend to repeat it the next time. I remember clearly, for instance, the frustration I experienced in practicing the piano when I was young. I would make a mistake and then repeat the passage to correct it. But instead of playing the correct notes as I expected, I would play the wrong ones again. It seemed that the more I tried to correct the mistake, the more entrenched it became. I was indeed learning by repetition! You may recognize the phenomenon, either in this domain or in some other—perhaps in typing, when, in proofreading, an error is discovered. Try to type the correction, and as likely as not you type it wrong again. It then takes a concerted effort to avoid the mistake and render your manuscript error-free. In the case of music, it takes the same kind of effort to play the correct note so that one is finally able to produce it easily each time the passage is played.

Another property of the learning brain is that a response once made, but not repeated over a period, tends to decay. The system *forgets* through **nonfunctional degeneration.** We may, for instance, remember that we used to be able to do something (in my case, play that Mozart concerto) but, after a long time without actually doing it, find ourselves unable to. We no longer remember how.

Learning by repetition and forgetting from disuse are some of the most important properties of the brain that have been exploited in designing an artificial neural net. Recall from our earlier discussion of memory that in addition to these properties, our system may learn from a single experience, without repetition. Some experiences are so salient, make such an impression on us, that we learn after just one exposure. I do not, for instance, have to put my hand down on a recently turned off electric burner more than once to know from then on not to put my hand down on the burner at all.

In designing a (virtual) learning system, we are of course aware that we cannot yet expect to create anything nearly as complex as the human brain. But incorporating into our learning system the properties just discussed will take us some distance toward our goal. This is accomplished in the following way. We may simulate on the computer a rectangular array of nodes, a very simple instance of which is illustrated in Figure 8.5. We set each **link** in the network at a certain numeric value, or *weight*. We also set the network at a specific level of activation. Each time a link is activated, its weight is increased. At any given time, a node will be either on or off. A node that is on and set to "fire" at a particular time will send a signal to its neighbors, via the links. Some of these links will conduct and some won't. An off node receiving a signal will turn on, and the sending node, having fired, will turn off (unless of course it too receives a signal from a firing node).

As the brain learns by repetition, so can our artificial neural net. If a link conducts, the likelihood of its conducting again increases. The probability that a link will conduct is called its **conductance**, and each time it conducts, its conductance increases. If it fails to conduct, its conductance decreases. The decrease in conductance from non-use is analogous to the brain's property of forgetting knowledge that has not been tapped over time. A way of producing this decrease is to set the links at a particular base conductivity level, which strengthens each time the link conducts, but to which the link reverts if the node it comes from has not fired for a long time. If the conductivity level increases by a little, the tendency to conduct may be compared to our own short-term memory. If it increases a great deal, as more frequent firing of nodes will lead it to do, the tendency to conduct becomes more fixed, a more permanent condition, which is analogous to our long-term memory.

Although neural nets do not now approach the complexity of the human brain, they are a good deal more complex than this brief discussion indicates. Other important properties of the human brain are modeled as well, such as the unpredictable behavior it frequently exhibits. The information coming into it is so diverse, and there is so much interference from the environment and from its very *muchness,* that some degree of chaos is to be expected. The output is never going to be entirely predictable. Although it is at an interior and generally inaccessible level, it is similar to a situation in which, after mulling over a course of action, considering all factors involved and all the possibilities, we finally act—then perhaps turn around and ask ourselves, "Now why did I do *that?*" By including in the design of the neural net a *probability* of firing, a degree of randomness—an element of unpredictability in the brain—is introduced.

Modeling **associative learning** is also possible, because a node that fires causes the firing of another, which connects with the conducting link. Each time this sequence takes place, the likelihood that it will be repeated increases. In this way, the connection between node 1 and node 2 becomes stronger. This process is

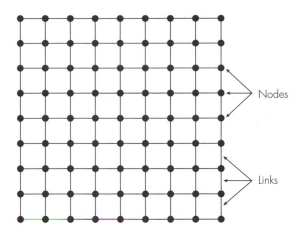

Nodes

Links

FIGURE 8.5 Diagram of a Simulated Array of Nodes

analogous to the associative process within our brains (described in Chapter 2), in which one thought leads to another with which it shares some feature or features.

Early Developments in Neural Net Research

Whereas neural nets are a development of AI research in the 1950s, the work that led up to the concept dates from somewhat earlier. The groundwork for artificial neural networks is generally considered to date from 1943, when McCulloch and Pitts addressed the question of how *biological* neural networks function. Their explanation was framed in terms of logic. The strength of the neurons' impulses being fixed, they assumed that outputs were binary—that is, either active (on) or inactive (off). Further assumptions were, for example, that the excitatory synaptic connections had the same fixed strength, although one neuron could make multiple connections to another. They also assumed that if one input connection directed that there be no output, then there would be none.

The further assumption of a threshold provided an explanation for the firing of neurons: If input reached or exceeded the threshold, there would be activity, or output—that is, the neuron would fire (McCulloch & Pitts, 1943). For artificial neural nets, McCulloch and Pitts posited *threshold logic units*; these could compute logical functions such as OR, AND, and NOT. (The NOT function is illustrated by the following: If input reaches or exceeds a given unit's threshold, it fires; if an inhibitory input reaches it, it will not.) Conventional digital computers are made of components that perform basic logical functions. That is also what the threshold logic units do—so a computer could be built entirely of *them,* and thus they could also, in principle, compute anything a digital computer can compute (Barrow, 1996).

Exemplifying the interdisciplinary nature of the cognitive science initiative, the work in the 1940s of Donald Hebb (discussed in Chapter 3) is important in the conceptualization of neural networks. Hebb's hypotheses concerned biological networks, but his principle of cell assemblies and his concept of connectionism form an important part of the background of the work in artificial neural nets. Readers of Chapter 3 will recall Hebb's explanation, sometimes called Hebb's rule: "When an axon of cell A is near enough to excite a cell B and repeatedly or persistently takes part in firing it, some growth process or metabolic change takes place in one or both cells, such that A's efficiency, as one of the cells firing B, is increased" (Hebb, 1959, p. 62). The similarity of this account to the design of the artificial neural net described earlier is clear. In fact, Hebb's rule, in various mathematical formulations, underlies quite a few self-organizing model neural networks that have since been devised (Barrow, 1996).

Perceptrons

Neural net research really blossomed in the 1950s, when attention to the question of neural net learning focused on what was called the perceptron. Introduced by a psychologist (Rosenblatt, 1958), the notion rested on a biological frame of reference rather than on one of symbolic logic. Involving at once artificial intelligence, biophysics, and psychology, it reminds us once more of the interrelatedness of fields often thought of as quite distinct. The **perceptron** was conceived as a hypothetical nervous system realized as a neural net. This new line of research involved considering how the biological system (of humans, for instance) detects information about the world around it, how this information is stored, and how the stored information influences recognition and behavior.

Stored information represents experience. Our own experience naturally influences our behavior. If we have been bitten by the neighbor's dog, we will not choose to pass close to that nasty animal again. If the supermarket has given out free samples of tasty goods at the end of aisle 6 once or twice, we will make it a point to pass that spot when we do our grocery shopping. If we really liked that tasty tidbit, once or twice is all it takes for us to remember to pass that way on our next shopping expedition to see whether another morsel will be offered. It is also true that a negative experience, such as a mistake, has to happen only once to change our behavior: One fender-bender is enough to keep us from tailgating for a long time, if not forever.

The networks we considered earlier learn from repetition, as we do, but the perceptron is a neural net that learns from "experience." That is, when a stimulus is presented to the network it may produce an erroneous response. When this happens, an error-correction rule is used to change the weights of each response unit. (Recall that values, or weights, have been set for each link in a neural network.) Our own response to the fender-bender is not to drive even closer to the car in front of us in the future. Somehow we know that the correct response is to keep our distance. In working with neural nets, there must be something that decides which responses are correct and which are not. This something is referred to as the *teacher,* though it is not like any teacher you may have had in school. It may even, in fact, be another neural network.

Given such parameters as the number of units in the system, the number that excite and the number that inhibit, and the expected threshold of the excitatory

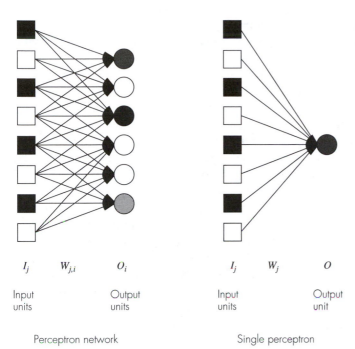

FIGURE 8.6 Perceptron and a Simple Perceptron Network, Showing a Set of Nodes and Their Connecting Links

I_j $W_{j,i}$ O_i I_j W_j O

Input   Output   Input   Output
units   units   units   unit

Perceptron network   Single perceptron

connections, Rosenblatt (1958) theorized that one could predict phenomena such as learning, perceptual discrimination, and generalization. Based in mathematical probability theory (recall the quality of unpredictability in the behavior of the brain), the perceptron was to address the way "an imperfect neural network, containing many random connections," can make predictable the relationships between stimuli and their neurological effects (p. 387). Rosenblatt's original "Mark I" perceptron was an artificial retina and projection area, in this case an actual physical device constructed to respond to stimuli consisting of optical patterns. Figure 8.6 is a diagrammatic rendering of a perceptron and a simple perceptron network. Its responses demonstrated that a machine could be "capable of learning. . . . It could be trained to produce a desired output for each input pattern" (Barrow, 1996, p. 142). Ultimately, this meant that Mark I could learn to perform tasks such as distinguishing between a vertical and a horizontal bar of light, or between letters of the alphabet (Barrow, 1996).

There were, however, limits to what the perceptron could do. A system consisting only of an input layer, or even of an input and an output layer, is not adequate to very complex tasks. The brain, after all, contains *billions* of neurons, each one connected to thousands of others, all of them operating concurrently. These early networks could not interpret their input data or organize them, as the brain does, into an "internal worldview" (Caudill & Butler, 1990, p. 171). That the perceptron was inadequate was demonstrated definitively in an analysis that appeared in 1969 (Minsky & Papert). If, however, one designs a kind of "sandwich" of layers, in which at least one intermediate "hidden layer" is inserted between the input and the output layer of the neural net, and if these hidden layers transmit information in both directions, the power of the net is multiplied. Once such multilayered systems had been developed, they were rendered more powerful by a training procedure known as backward error propagation learning, or **back propagation**. This procedure is implemented in two stages. In the first of these, activation proceeds forward from the input layer to the output layer, as one would expect. But in the second stage, the flow proceeds back from the output layer, as error signals are sent back through the network. The strength of the weights of the connections among all the units is adjusted accordingly, ultimately producing the desired learning. The hidden layers thus contribute to responses in a more complex fashion than is possible without them.

A very interesting project carried out by means of such neural networks addressed an issue that had heretofore been the province primarily of psychologists and linguists: the way in which the past tenses of English verbs are learned. Chapter 5 discusses the kinds of rules linguists have suggested that the child learns when encountering a first language. Children learning English as their first language pass through stages in their acquisition of these past tenses. Briefly described, the first of these is characterized by the production of a limited set of verbs that, whether regular or irregular, are formed with the correct past tense (e.g., *walked, carried, rode, went*). In the next stage, the child produces many more verbs, largely regular ones, but forms the past tense of all of them—including irregular ones—in the regular fashion (i.e., with the suffix usually represented by *-ed: walked* but also *wented*). This observation has led researchers to hypothesize that in the first stage the forms are learned individually, as separate items, and that in the second stage the child has acquired (on his or her own, because it is not specifically taught to small children) the past-tense "rule" and simply generalizes it to all verbs. In the final stage, the child forms the irregular past tenses correctly to known irregular verbs but uses the regular form for newly acquired verbs. The rules are assumed to be stored explicitly in the brain, accessible for instantaneous use but not necessarily available to consciousness.

When the neural nets we have been discussing were developed, a hypothesis was proffered to the effect that the production of correct forms such as the past tense might result from a mechanism that did not in fact contain such a "rule." Rather, it was suggested that the "mechanisms which process language and make judgments of grammaticality are constructed in such a way that their performance is characterizable by rules, but that the rules themselves are not written in explicit form anywhere in the mechanism" (McClelland & Rumelhart, 1986, p. 216). The researchers used a neural net to test this hypothesis. Their goal was to simulate the three-stage learning of the past tense by children, and to see whether the model would be characterized by the same kind of gradual change that marked child-learning and by the same kinds of stages. Could a neural network computer model, in which no explicit rules were represented, learn the past tense of English verbs? And if it could, would it show the same characteristics of the process that children exhibit?

The answer was that it could and did. The model was able to respond correctly to the 460 words it was taught, and, further, it could generalize to unfamiliar words it had not been taught. It learned "not only the dominant, regular form of the past tense [e.g., guard/guarded], but many of the subregularities [e.g., sweep/swept] as well" (McClelland & Rumelhart, 1986, p. 265). The researchers concluded that their "simple learning model shows, to a remarkable degree, the characteristics of young children learning the morphology of the past tense in English" (p. 266).

Developed by means of a three-layer back-propagation neural network, another program was designed within the language domain, though with a very different purpose from the one just described. This was NETtalk (Sejnowski & Rosenberg, 1987), a system that translates English text into the **articulatory features** that describe phonemes (the speech sounds of a language serving to distinguish meaning in that language: /b/ and /d/, for example, which distinguish *bent* from *dent*). NETtalk is designed to produce, by means of these sounds, pronunciations for all the words of English. The sounds it produces can then be passed to an electronic speech generator. The system was trained on a fairly small set of words, then asked to perform on this training set. The results of this part of the experiment were encouraging, but the program performed less well when the task was generalized to other text.

These experiments, in which both artificial intelligence and linguistics were involved, indicate once more the interrelation of fields embraced by cognitive science. We may also note that there is significant practical value in a system that represents text on a page in speech. Readers may have noticed, when listening to their computers or to automated telephone responses, some of the inherent difficulties in such machine "reading" aloud. We humans know we must pronounce the vowel sounds in *nose* and *lose* differently. It is not so easy to get a machine to "know" this.

With machines that can learn, machines that can translate, machines that can make inferences, and machines that can speak, are we not getting closer to the time when our world will more closely resemble those worlds depicted in science fiction? Will there not be real R2D2s and real HALs soon? And is this a frightening prospect? In fact, as you have now seen, each time we create a "piece of the future," the distance between our creation and ourselves is highlighted. Nevertheless, there is interesting—even amazing—work being done in endowing computers with portions of what we have always considered our human birthright: our intelligence. Provided now with some background, you are equipped to judge more realistically how far we have in fact come and how far we have yet to go in the endeavor. So let us now examine some of the accomplishments in the area of robotics.

Robotics

The previous chapter described the Turing test, a notion predicated on the idea that a computer whose cognitive skills are adequate to fool a human being is "intelligent." Recall that the criterion was that the answers provided by the (unseen) computer to questions asked by a human should cause the human to be unable to distinguish the computer from a human being. But in the situation envisioned by Turing, no suggestion was made that the computer and the human should share, for example, perceptual abilities. It was not expected that, confronted simultaneously with human questioner and responding computer, a person would not be able to tell the difference. A person could, for example, see the computer and press the keys of its keyboard. The computer could neither see nor reach out and touch the person. People are capable of image analysis. That is, they distinguish items in their environment, and, further, they make sense of them. Since Turing's time, as we have seen, mechanisms have been developed that perform image analysis. The Mark I perceptron, an early example of a machine that can perform image analysis, can distinguish letters of the alphabet. That was certainly a start in endowing a machine with perception.

What else must a computer do if it is eventually to be able to fool a human being? Certainly it must be able to learn from experience. Well, neural nets learn. It must be able to infer elements of a situation from nonexplicit information it has stored. There are programs like SAM that make inferences. The list goes on, but readers will by now have been convinced of the vast number of capabilities housed in one human brain. Plainly a machine as well endowed has yet to be developed. Nevertheless, it is now time to look at what in fact *has* been accomplished in this direction.

Science fiction has encouraged us to think of robots as systems mimicking, with significant success, the behavior of humans. But the design of "real" robots—that is, those already developed and in operation—is not so ambitious. The real-world robots we read about are not intended to fool anyone; their purpose is, rather, to perform specific functions. The motivation may be practical, such as developing a robot to carry out stereotyped assembly-line chores or a vehicle that can get where it needs to without a human driver (autonomous navigation). The motivation may be, on the other hand, for research purposes: to see whether and how a machine can perform tasks that humans perform.

Research into the functioning of the human brain has provided a good deal of information about how we operate to perceive and interpret our perceptions of the world outside ourselves. Even robots designed for specific purposes will have to deal as well with certain aspects of the world outside themselves. AI research is directing much effort toward those functions that will facilitate interaction between machine and human and between machine and the larger world in which it is designed to accomplish specific tasks.

When we think of robots, often what we envision is, like R2D2, a reasonably efficient entity that moves without bumping into things and that, perhaps, interacts with us by obeying our spoken commands and responding with appropriate (if mechanical-sounding) speech of its own. The discussion of natural language processing some pages back indicates the complexity of such an endeavor. Researchers now understand something of what our robot must be equipped with if it is to navigate our world and perform the tasks we require of it. Let us look at some of what has been accomplished in the design of robots within these two domains.

Automatic Speech Recognition

Keeping in mind the necessity for an adequate knowledge base and for various capacities such as the ability to make inferences if a machine is to be able to "do" human language, we can briefly consider some applications of speech recognition and speech synthesis that have already been implemented. Not long ago I was suddenly startled when my telephone, presumably by recording, informed me I could proceed by simply saying "yes." Tentatively I tried it, saying "yes" far more clearly and distinctly than I do when speaking to a voice I know belongs to a person. It worked! Since then I have also been invited by such a voice to say "one" instead of pressing the button, and that works too. So far I have not been invited to communicate anything more profound or more complex than that. Nor has the voice ever responded to my "hello" with the question "What's the matter?" having judged the state of my mind by cues from my voice, as close friends sometimes do. Nevertheless, this machine "understands" the difference between yes and no, a clear distinction, one might think—but one that my cat can't make. (To be sure, the cat responds to no, but that is probably because of the tone I use when saying it; she has no concept at all of yes.) One might expect the automatic speech recognition (ASR) system to have difficulty because everyone's yes is slightly different from everyone else's—and even from one's own from one time to the next.

Then there are the problems of noise on the line, which (as long as it's not too loud) we humans filter out as we focus on the words. There are also differences in the microphones from one phone to another. Add to that the inclination of human users to talk to the machine voice as though it were human, adding words like "please" and talking while the system is prompting them. So it is no wonder that "the most successful current systems are ones that limit themselves to very small vocabularies, on the order of 10 to 20 words" (Rudnicky, Hauptmann, & Lee, 1994, p. 53), and some to only two words—as you might guess, "yes" and "no." As we require more of such a system, for example, that it permit us to place catalog orders, its vocabulary and ability to interact with us must be increased. Will the day come when I can ask the system to tell me if the sweater pictured on page 17 of the winter catalog runs true to size or whether I should order the next size up or down? Or if it is really the shade of red shown in the picture, and not a bit more orange or blue?

There are, however, systems with much larger vocabularies, on the order of 40,000 words. Some of these systems are designed to take dictation of, for example, business letters, but these are generally intended to work with a single speaker. Furthermore, they perform best in situations where noise can be controlled, such as offices where special microphones eliminate surrounding noise. The error rate has declined in recent years in some of these, to about 3% to 13%, depending on the size of the vocabulary and the number of word alternatives the system must consider at any one point in the decoding process (Rudnicky et al., 1994, p. 54). Again, though progress is evident in what these systems can do, they seem still to be far from achieving what a live stenographer can do: take dictation from just about anybody whose language he or she understands, just about anywhere (from a quiet room to a busy office to a noisy airport), and manage even unfamiliar words.

Speech Synthesis

If our personal robot is to serve all the purposes we might like, it will not only have to recognize and understand our speech well enough under ordinary conditions to respond appropriately; it will also have to be able to respond with speech. Research addressing this aspect of machine use of human natural language has led to the development of systems that synthesize speech, but these are not yet intended for our own personal R2D2. Rather, they convert written text to speech for purposes such as providing blind people with access to the text. In doing so, they face a very difficult task, because unrestricted text can vary widely in complexity.

More mundane uses of text-to-speech synthesis involve, for example, one's personal computer. These days when something goes wrong as I am using mine, the error message on the screen clamors for my attention, if I don't respond quickly enough, by saying, in its distinctive voice, "Alert!" and proceeding to read me the error message. Did I say mundane? How far we *have* come if I can call my computer's addressing me in my very own language (albeit in a mechanical voice) "mundane"!

The lack of these cues, however, indicates one of the complexities of human speech that must be dealt with in text-to-speech synthesis if the result is to sound "right," or natural, to human ears. There are, of course, many facets of what text-to-speech systems involve. They must convert text input into a sequence of sound symbols, usually accomplished by means of mapping rules that derive the pronunciations. (Neural networks have also been used, but not, so far, as successfully as the rule-based approach.) To deal with the problem of unusual (perhaps foreign) words, there may be special rules, or even an "exception dictionary," to handle pronunciations that differ from the expected.

Some systems mathematically model the acoustic qualities of the aimed-for (target) sounds. Some splice prerecorded sound segments of human-produced speech and then smooth the connections among them. But no system yet devised mimics human speech well enough to fool a person into thinking it is the speech of another person. As was earlier noted, babies master the intonation patterns of their language even before they acquire *words*. Improvement in the area of intonation patterns and dynamics will contribute to making synthesized speech sound both more intelligible and more natural ((Rudnicky et al., 1994).

Robot Vision

My computer sits quite still as it "talks" to me. But a robot moves around, whether in a constrained area as it performs specific tasks or, eventually, in the world at large. How can our personal robot get around safely without falling into holes, bumping into walls, or, for that matter, bumping into *us*? To design a system that can navigate the real world, we must consider how *we* do it. And one of the first things we notice is that at virtually every moment of our waking existence we are perceiving and interpreting and acting on the world outside of us by means of our vision. Although individuals deprived of vision compensate in many ways and may succeed very well in navigating this world, the most efficient means of doing so depends on vision. To take a very simple example, suppose you wish to have a sip of juice to help you swallow your daily vitamin tablet. The juice is poured, sitting on the counter, and the tablet is in your hand, on its way to your mouth. You reach out, grasp the glass of juice in your hand, and bring it to your lips. Your mind may have been on other matters as you did so, and you were not, in all probability, paying attention to your actions—so automatic, so simple.

But how did you know just how far to reach for the glass? Reach too far to the side or not quite far enough, and you miss the glass. Reach in the right direction but just a bit too far and your hand collides with it, knocking it off the counter, spilling the juice, and delaying your departure for school or work. Your eyes have provided cues necessary to enable you to reach in exactly the right direction and exactly far enough. Vision combines with the ability we have to make the rapid computations involved in judging distances and in the mechanics of grasping and moving items. This is an important factor in the seamless and effortless actions such as those involved in picking up a glass of juice and in the countless actions, small and large, that we engage in constantly in the process of living. Attempting to create a robot that can do the same both depends on and adds to our understanding of how *we* do it. The potential practical applications of such robots are myriad—and very attractive.

Our immediate aim may be stated at one level as simply to create a robot with vision. The reader should not be misled by my use of the word "simply," for there is nothing easy about the project. Examining the tasks that machine vision involves may lead us to state our aims at a more fundamental level. It will require segmenting the world into objects, classifying the objects into categories, and describing their shapes. To achieve these goals, we might begin with television cameras to simulate eyes, which gather information (input, in computer terminology) from the environment. The positioning of our own two eyes yields stereo vision, which allows us to perceive depth. (Without depth perception, we will be much more likely to knock over our juice glass or, worse, to walk into the path of an oncoming car.) If we design our cameras so that they can swivel, and if we place them on a moving platform, they will not be restricted to "seeing" what is directly in front of them but will be able to alter what they are "looking at" and take in the world around them. We can then send what the cameras "see" to an onboard computer, imitating our own transmission of what we see to those areas of the brain that process it. The computer will be designed to analyze the video stream from both cameras, perhaps using more than one processor, so that it can respond more quickly.

If we stop there in our consideration of this project, we are left with a very general sort of machine that might form the basis of a surveillance system but that is not equipped for any more specialized purpose. Our own extremely complex mechanism deals very well with whatever may be the task of the moment: picking up the juice glass, crossing the street, judging from the distance and configuration of the clouds whether and when rain will arrive, scanning the crowd at a concert for our friends' faces, recognizing as dogs both a beagle and a greyhound. But the simple system I just described must be geared to a particular function if it is to serve a particular purpose. If we want our robot to bring us that glass of juice as we sit comfortably perusing the morning newspaper, it will have to be endowed with a gripper mechanism as well as with vision, and with a means of coordinating the two (Hogg, 1996).

Furthermore, when we humans regard a scene in our environment, such as the clouds or the crowd, we do not fix on a single image for processing; rather, we process and comprehend a sequence of images over time. If an object we are looking at moves, we follow it with our eyes. A machine with vision might need to be able to do that too, which means it will need to know when and how to change the position of its "eye." The processing of all these different capabilities may depend on the integration and implementation of both symbolic reasoning and neural networks (Hogg, 1996).

Now, how can a machine that "sees" in this way be made to make sense of—to understand—what it sees? First of all, the machine, like the infant human (and indeed, humans at every age), needs to be able to identify important individual items in the confusion of images in its environment. So it needs to recognize the salient features of what it sees as it looks around. These are the features that can be interpreted in terms of the shape and the structure of the objects in its view. (An example is "edges," or localized changes in image intensity, which yield depth information.)

Additionally, machine vision, when not dedicated to a restricted and unvarying special purpose, must have the ability (as we do) to deal with unfamiliar objects. One way of providing this is very specific: by means of stored models of objects whose structures are fixed, such as a particular chair or a certain book. Stored in this instance are the particular geometric shapes of the objects. Models of a generic sort may also be stored, such as the model of a generic book or person. Less specifically still, a set of general object properties may be stored. One of these properties might be the way objects' components relate to each other in space: This object holds together in a round sort of way, that one in a long thin sort of way, this other one in an oblong sort of way. Additionally, the round one is at the top of the oblong one, and the others are attached by their ends, two on each side of the oblong one (Lo: a person!). Another general object property has to do with the inertia of a moving body. Is it, for example, moving quickly enough to block my path if I don't move in a hurry? Combining the information based on these two properties, the machine "understands" that a person is bearing down on it and it must move out of the way. By interpreting (understanding) the scene, whether by recourse to stored specific object properties or generic object properties or general object properties—or all three—our general-purpose personal robot will be able to avoid bumping into us. (This discussion benefits greatly from Hogg, 1996.)

One reason machine vision has received so much attention from AI researchers is that human vision has been the object of a great deal of research by cognitive scientists in various disciplines. A lot is known about how it works. It is an enormously complex process, so naturally the implementation of these abilities in a machine is also an enormously complex process. Every aspect of what I have described, which is only a small portion of the process, must be addressed in great detail by designers of machine vision. My purpose here has been to touch on some of the considerations involved in this process, to suggest what is involved and how AI researchers approach the challenge. Let us now look at some recent applications made possible by this research.

Applications of Machine Vision   One area benefiting from machine vision research is the military. Grimson and Mundy (1994) provide a useful discussion to which I am indebted. For example, governments seek information about where missiles are stored. They have been gathering this information largely by photographing areas of countries that are considered to pose a threat. These photographic images must be analyzed. Now that images can be digitized, instead of having humans interpret images on film, machine vision can be employed to interpret digital images. From these, 3D maps of the terrain can be automatically constructed that can be used by the military for simulating fly-throughs. Readers familiar with video games know this virtual reality phenomenon.

If the features of an object mentioned earlier are easily identifiable, machine vision can be used to find instances of the object. This ability has allowed the Space Vision System of the National Research Council of Canada to be used on a space shuttle to find target objects, such as satellites. Learning of this, one almost has the impression that the space vehicles of *Star Trek* have arrived on the scene. Machine vision can now detect and track targets, which an operator can remotely manipulate.

Interesting and important work relying on computer vision is being carried out at the Massachusetts Institute of Technology Artificial Intelligence Laboratory. A collaboration between this lab and the Surgical Planning Laboratory of Brigham and Women's Hospital in Boston has resulted in the development of tools that enable image-guided surgery. Surgeons will be able to "visualize internal structures through an automated overlay of 3D reconstructions of internal anatomy on top of live video views of a patient" (Internet source: http://www.ai.ai.mit.edu/projects/medical vision). This means that planning the surgery can be guided by machine vision, which can also provide guidance, navigation, and instrument tracking during surgery.

A 1995 report from the MIT AI Lab indicates that neurosurgery benefits from "enhanced reality visualization." Via images of a patient's brain, this technology correctly locates brain structures that surgeons cannot see directly, effectively giving the surgeons "X-ray vision" (Mellor, 1995). In providing them with such extensions of their own capabilities, computer vision contributes to the accuracy of the surgery, a great benefit to both surgeons and patients.

Artificial Life: Animats

The list of applications of computer vision is impressive, and computer vision has value in all manner of practical applications. Many other aspects of human intelligence have not yet been conquered, however, for example, the one we call common sense. This is difficult even to define, but it clearly makes use of vast amounts of many kinds of knowledge.

> To exhibit common sense a robot must be able to manipulate models of its world, reason by analogy, carry out useful lines of reasoning automatically, and develop enough of a "Self" to sensibly modify its own behavior. An architecture for the mind of such a robot must be able to reflect the complexity of the world without being overwhelmed by it. Today's computers lack the simple computational power required for such mental architecture. Computer designers have begun to see the limits of traditional methods and are beginning to explore alternatives in which thousands and millions of interconnected computers run at once. In the end, robots will begin to exhibit common sense when we know enough about what is required to build the architecture of a mind [to be able to tailor computer technology] . . . to meet those requirements. (Agre, 1985, p. 95)

Although this may be so, there is another approach being employed in the attempt to endow the machine with intelligence. Human intelligence—or, for that matter, the intelligence of any species—does not start out with some kind of master plan for accomplishing a particular function. Neither the reader nor the reader's pet white mouse is designed, in what is called a "top-down" fashion, to be intelligent in a particular and limited way, for a particular set of purposes, whether analyzing images, running on an exercise wheel and learning where its water bottle is, playing chess, or solving problems in math, logic, or natural language processing. The approach we have seen up to this point exploits this **top-down** method. That is, it begins with a design intended to represent explicitly within the machine the machine's capabilities, the conditions of the world outside the machine, and the goals the machine is to accomplish. Based on these explicit formulations, the machine can search for the data it needs and for the method of applying what it finds to solve a problem. We have seen that introducing probability into the design extends its capabilities, but this addition is still predicated on the explicitness of a description of what the machine does in, say, reasoning or learning. What humans and other animal species do, in contrast, is to produce "adaptive, intelligent behavior in complex, changing environments" (Dean, 1998, p. 60).

Artificial life (AL) is a rather new approach to artificial intelligence. It is based on the following line of reasoning. If the goal is the creation of machines that produce intelligent behavior, it makes sense to use as a model an example of an intelligence already in existence—a living intelligence. Now all living intelligences develop in a physical form—a body. As "embodied" creatures they develop in a physical environment. Using a bottom-up approach, we could model the devel-

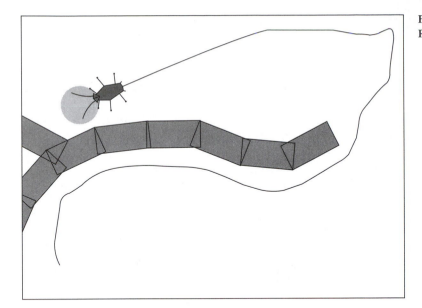

FIGURE 8.7 Simulation of a Roachlike Animat

opment of machine intelligence on that of a living, behaving being. Rather than beginning with a *design*, as in the top-down approach, we might start with some simple *behaviors*. Because human intelligence produces very complex behaviors, we might wish to begin with an animal simpler than a human—an insect, for example. Suppose we give our machine the (mechanical) form of an insect, place it in a real-world environment, and endow it with sensors (visual and others) so it can detect aspects of that environment. Suppose further that we build into it a neural net arrangement so it can learn. Will our machine then demonstrate behaviors, emerging from the interaction of its components, that we would consider intelligent?

Researchers in AL have in fact already produced a number of such animals, called **animats**, either as I have described or simulated on the computer (Figure 8.7). Their designers work under certain assumptions, such as the idea that we can understand adaptive behavior best if we focus on the way a behaving individual and its environment interact. Another assumption is that as systems made up of simple behavioral capabilities become more complex, high-level behaviors will emerge (Dean, 1998). The notion of **emergent properties** is one with which researchers in more than one field of cognitive science are grappling, but it may be new to you. Think for a moment of the elements that go to make up— well, *you*. At a very early level in the scheme are the innumerable molecules of which your cells are constructed. These come to constitute the different tissues that contribute to the construction of your various organs, such as brain, lungs, stomach. These organs participate in subsystems of your body: nervous, respiratory, digestive, muscular, and so on. All of these subsystems work in the service of the larger system that is *you*. But we do not give the label *you* to any of these levels in the hierarchy of elements and systems, until we reach that level at which they all work in concert to produce the behaviors unique to you. This set of behaviors emerges from the interactive functioning of all the elements, organs, and other subsystems of your physical self.

Just so do artificial-life researchers view their effort: "Starting with a collection of entities exhibiting behaviors that are simple and well understood, AL aims to synthesize more complex systems in which entities interact in nonadditive ways and give rise to lifelike emergent properties" (Meyer, 1996, p. 326). The word "nonadditive" suggests that we are not dealing with the usual expectation that the sum of the parts of an entity will equal the whole entity. Rather, the whole is greater than, and thus somehow different from, the sum of its parts. The behaviors of living beings are not the simple sum of the behaviors of all their component parts but are the result of the interaction of those parts. They emerge from this interaction; they constitute an emergent property not just of human life but of all life.

> The emergence of life and intelligence from less-alive and less-intelligent components has happened at least once. Emergent behavior is that which cannot be predicted through analysis at any level simpler than that of the system as a whole. . . . Emergent behavior, by definition, is what's left after everything else has been explained. (Dyson, 1997, p. 9)

When embodied animats are placed in the real world, researchers are taking advantage of the fact that an embodied intelligence, artificial or natural, necessarily works within an entire physical system, comprised of itself and the outside physical world. Interacting with the physical environment is the way living beings develop. In doing so, they work with the properties of the physical world, taking advantage of them to reduce their own effort. When a monkey swings from tree branch to tree branch, for example, it makes use of the physics of its swing, the momentum that carries it up from its gravity-produced dip to the next branch, without the monkey's having actually to plan the whole motion.

Another motivation for placing animats in real situations derives from a consideration of what real animals do:

> First, animals are confronted with a complex environment and multiple tasks to satisfy. Second, animals behave continuously and react to stimuli without significant delays for planning; often a less precise, speedy response is more adaptive than a precise, slow one. Sensory and motor systems in animals are connected by multiple parallel connections that vary in speed and complexity of response. Third, animals typically possess some basic behaviors from birth, and then develop more complex abilities, including many high-level cognitive abilities, but also motor skills . . . in the course of interactions with the environment. (Dean, 1998, p. 62)

Situating animats in real-world environments and having them respond in real time to these environments requires endowing them with the representation of a certain amount of knowledge and the ability to control simple behaviors. Artificial neural networks may be built in to enable learning to occur. Instead of building in explicit goals, one can give animats, by means of parallel distributed processing and more than one behavioral module, the ability to select behaviors each time a response is required. Behavior thus emerges as a result of selection rather than being explicitly dictated by the design.

Project Cog

In the 10 years or so that researchers have been working in the area of artificial life, they have gotten animats to perform some simple tasks, such as purposeful, goal-directed movement. A next and more ambitious step is the design of a mobile **humanoid** (resembling a human) robot known as *Cog*. Researchers working on this project take as a model "the only existing systems which are universally accepted as intelligent: humans" (Brooks et al., 1998, p. 1). The basic assumptions guiding this research include what we have just considered with regard to animats, but they are more complex—just as human intelligence is more complex than that of simpler life forms. It is assumed that human intelligence results from four intertwined attributes. First, as with other species, intelligence in the human individual is achieved over the course of that individual's development. But to an even greater extent than is the case with other species, *our* interactions with the world outside us change over time as we develop from infancy. In the process the activities and functions we are capable of become increasingly complex. Next, all of our development occurs in contact with other people. It relies heavily on social interactions, and we develop our repertoire of behaviors largely from these interactions.

Another important attribute of human intelligence, like the intelligence of other species, is that it is "embodied"—it resides and develops within a body. This body interacts physically with the outside world, its actions motivated in direct response to its perceptions. Further, the control we have over the movements of our bodies is not restricted to complicated programs that explicitly specify all of its functions. Like the monkey swinging in the tree, we exploit the swing as, for example, when we lift objects without having to plan each element of the whole motion. (For a remarkable account of the effects on a person of losing the ability to move through the world without such planning, see Jonathan Cole's *Pride and a Daily Marathon*.)

Another attribute of human intelligence taken into consideration by the researchers involved in Project Cog is that all of our sensory perceptions are processed simultaneously. They are not independent of one another, but are, rather, integrated. Even a newborn, for instance, will turn its eyes in the direction of a sound.

Project Cog is predicated on the notion that these attributes of human intelligence can be exploited in building a robotic system. So the researchers have designed Cog, a humanoid robot, which (or should I say "who") looks a bit more like what we imagine our personal robot will look than does an animat or a computer. It is expected that designing the robot to resemble a human will make it easier for people to interact with it, increasing the learning that occurs through social interaction.

> Humanoid form is important to allow humans to interact with the robot in a natural
> way. In addition, we believe that building a real system is computationally less complex

FIGURE 8.8 One Stage in the Development of Cog, the Humanoid Robot

than simulating such a system. The effects of gravity, friction, and natural human inter-action are obtained for free, without any computation. (Brooks et al., 1998, p. 3)

What has already been accomplished with Cog? As you see in Figure 8.8, the robot approximates the human form from the waist up. It can move its head, torso, neck, arms, and eyes. It is also endowed with sensory systems. Sight is provided by two video cameras. **Proprioception**, which indicates to it where its parts are, comes from the position of its joints and lets it know where its arms, head, and other movable parts are located in space with relation to the rest of itself. In humans, proprioception depends on our largely unconscious perception of the position and movement of our body and our limbs and the force exerted by our muscles. It allows for our sense of balance and our knowledge of where we are physically situated. Without it we could not function; we would simply fall over in a heap (Cole, 1995). Some other senses that Cog possesses or will possess are hearing and touch. It will have sensitive hands, and it will have a system for vocalization. "Cog is a single hardware platform which seeks to bring together each of the many subfields of Artificial Intelligence into one unified, coherent, functional whole" ("Overview of the Cog Project," 1999, p. 1).

Is the humanoid Cog as intelligent as a human being? Clearly not, but this approach is particularly interesting in that Cog is not designed to be "intelligent" in a particular and limited way, for a particular purpose, such as playing chess or solving problems in math, logic, or natural language processing. Human intelligence includes all of these abilities and many more. We will want to tune in next week or next year to learn the progress the humanoid robot known as Cog is making as it is increasingly endowed with systems designed to work together as our own do, yielding the flexible sort of intelligence that, so far, only we possess.

Project Cog relies on knowledge provided by many fields. From psychology's study of human development and perception comes the information that underlies much of the researchers' approach. Physiology and psychology both contribute to an understanding of vision. Knowledge and insights gleaned by linguists are crucial to the development of language capabilities envisioned for Cog. If Cog's intelligence is to resemble ours, the role of emotion must be taken into account. The field of neuroscience has much to contribute in this regard—and the list goes on.

Some Answers; More Questions

We have reached a point in our discussion of the nature of intelligence where we find ourselves once again confronting some knotty questions: If we succeed in endowing a machine with intelligence such that its emergent behaviors closely resemble ours, what sort of being will we be dealing with? If some later-day Cog can, like *2001*'s Hal, react to us, sense and somehow process our own emotional reactions, converse with us, do our spoken bidding—will its emergent behaviors, like Hal's, include doing what we have *not* bargained for? If this robot arrives at a state in which it can function to a large extent on its own, based on experience and learning from exposure to many environmental situations, may it one day act on its own initiative to engage in behaviors we do not expect and are not pleased to encounter?

It should be abundantly clear that we are a long way from having to face any such potential situation. If the results of AI and AL research are impressive, they also serve to impress upon us the complexity of the intelligence we habitually take so much for granted. It is also evident, however, that the questions are valid and important. Would a machine endowed with such intelligence be capable of the kinds of creativity we humans so far consider our own unique capacity? Would it be *conscious,* with a consciousness resembling our own, capable of contemplating and reflecting not only upon its surroundings but upon itself? Would we be forced to face the loss of our own "uniqueness"? Would that matter . . . ?

These questions belong to the domain of philosophy, to whose borders our journey through the terrain of the nature of intelligence has brought us. Part 5 introduces that domain.

Questions to Think About

1. Was humanity somehow diminished by Deep Blue's defeat of Gary Kasparov? Explain your answer.

2. Chapter 8 frequently makes the point that expectations for computer simulation of human intelligence have not yet been met. What do you expect the future to bring along these lines? Have we gone about as far as we can go? Or do you see infinite possibilities? Explain.

3. AI is largely based on a model of thinking that assumes rationality. How like or unlike human thinking do you think such a model is?

4. Which of the following do you regard as the highest hurdle that AI scientists must surmount in approximating human intellectual processes? Why do you think so?
   a. providing the computer with the information it will need to accomplish its tasks
   b. providing the computer with instructions about how to use the information
   c. choosing a productive set of problems to which to apply the computer
   d. another problem (Which?)

5. The preceding question is particularly relevant to the requirements of expert systems. Explain what an inference mechanism contributes to AI.

6. Explain the differences between, and the advantages and disadvantages of, algorithms and heuristics.

7. Why do some workers in AI feel it is necessary to build "embodied robots"? What, exactly, does that mean?

8. List some of the difficulties that inhere in a computer's translating from one natural language to another.

9. Why is it difficult to program a computer to paraphrase text satisfactorily?

10. If we succeed in endowing a machine with intelligence such that its emergent behaviors resemble ours, what sort of being will we be dealing with? What sorts of "human" behaviors will the machine be *un*likely to produce?

11. How might one go about programming a computer to have a sense of humor? Aesthetic appreciation? Religious fervor?

12. Is it at all likely that computers will make human beings obsolete in some occupation or activity? Which? Why?

13. How might a robot be programmed to "compensate" for one of its own inadequacies or deficiencies?

14. How likely is it that a computerized machine will ever develop a mind of its own?

CHAPTER **9**

Philosophical Issues in Cognitive Science

One day in October, the weather being conducive to an outing, we decided to go to the zoo. As my companion and I walked the paths among the fenced-off domains of yaks, polar bears, seals, and wolves, we experienced all the scents and sounds of these exotic animals—and childhood came rushing back. "The primates," I exclaimed. "I want to see the primates." These above all had intrigued me, I remembered, with their hands so much like ours, their faces uncannily reflecting our own, as in a distorting fun-house mirror.

But this time I was not a child, and I was not prepared for the effect the primate house would have on the adult I was now. As my companion and I entered it, coming in out of the bright October sunlight, it took a moment for our eyes to adjust to the relative dark of the interior. As I grew accustomed to it, I made out a very large form facing me from behind a wall of glass. A moment more and I had discerned the features of a huge gorilla, sitting and gazing with red-rimmed eyes at the gaping crowd. For a long moment our eyes met. I read his as plainly as I could have read the eyes of another human being: He was sad to the point of despair, he knew he was trapped, he had given up. But he had not forgotten what he had lost. I saw more: I saw just as plainly that he *knew* I had read his eyes. He knew that I knew what was in his mind. In some unfathomable space, we had connected. It was unbearable. I turned and went out.

As I walked with my companion in a freedom I was suddenly, guiltily aware of, many thoughts swirled in my mind. I contemplated the sorrow and bleakness of the gorilla's life. I reflected on his similarity to me, not in terms of his physical attributes, as I had when a child, but with respect to the nature of his mind and my own. I don't think I'll ever forget the shock of that connection, that recognition. It provoked in me not only the thoughts and feelings I have described but also a persistent sense of wonder: Had I *really* read his eyes, his mind? If I had, how had I done so? And why had I felt so certain that he had read mine? If we were indeed "reading" each other, what was it we were reading, and what were we reading *with*?

These questions express our sense of a mysterious and abstruse extension of ourselves into a realm we conceive of as nonphysical. Although we identify our bodies with ourselves, we have a sense that this mysterious essence is just that, our essence, something more than our physical bodies. Words we use to name it include "soul," "spirit," and "mind." We experience it as distinct from our bodies and conceive of some of our strongest feelings—love, for example—as involving both "body and soul." We admonish ourselves to exert "mind over matter." We yearn for a "spiritual center" in our lives to provide stability and a sense of peace. Above all, we are *aware* of this distinction. The eyes in the primate house seemed to be telling me that at least one other species (to be sure, a species closely related to our own) possesses a spirit, a mind. They seemed to indicate an awareness much like my own. But it is we who, thanks to language, have named the phenomenon and we who have sought to explain it. I suspect that the gorilla, though seeming to recognize that I had understood his feelings, was still sitting as I had left him, lost in his hopeless melancholy, whereas I, walking away, was framing questions and striving to understand. If we had indeed read each other, only I was now asking "what with?" and observing myself, even as I did so, with—what?

When did human beings first notice this aspect of themselves, and when did they begin to ask these questions? We cannot know the origins of our human mind, but still we seek to understand it, and we do have a well-attested history of the search, going back some 2,500 years. It is the history of Western philosophy, and we turn now to this discipline, which has long been the domain of those who consider such questions. As the reader is now in a position to judge, we might have begun our journey across the terrain of human cognition at any of the stops we have made so far. Each has a valid claim to be the starting point. Certainly philosophy has the right to assert its primacy, for the questions asked by philosophers far back in history were the questions that in a real sense sparked the whole endeavor. Our examination of the various approaches taken by cognitive psychologists, neuroscientists, linguists, and researchers in artificial intelligence shows us that these fields confront the same questions, each in its own way. I have chosen to end the journey with philosophy rather than beginning there. The reader, acquainted now with new ways of asking the old questions and with the new methods of approaching them, will perhaps be better equipped to see how the old themes come together, where we now stand with regard to them, and, in the light of what we now know, what areas of ignorance remain.

There are of course countless questions with which researchers and other thinkers have been engaged over the centuries, and I have found it necessary to be selective in order to bring this book to an end in a reasonable number of pages. This selectivity is equally—perhaps especially—characteristic of the unit on philosophy, because philosophy has a far more extensive history than the other disciplines involved in what is now called cognitive science. Given time and space enough, much more could be said about the questions philosophers have addressed and the answers they have attempted—all of which provide the foundation for the current endeavor. Accordingly, I have chosen representative issues in philosophy, focusing on those with us—even, in some cases, matters of hot debate—today.

Philosophy's Role in Cognitive Science

We are accustomed to use the term "philosophy" in everyday life to refer to our approach to some facet of that life. For instance, when we think about the schools our children attend, we may consider the "philosophy of education" that guides them. Or when someone is in the habit of considering large issues—the ethical stance behind a society's treatment of criminals or their victims, perhaps—we may describe him or her as being of a "philosophical bent." We may even object to someone's "philosophizing" when what we are interested in is practical assistance. In our customary framework we don't usually think about the field of philosophy or about what people participating in this field actually do, though we all know the names of such famous philosophers as Plato, Aristotle, Descartes, Locke, and Kant.

But philosophy has long played a very important role in our search for understanding the universe that confronts us and, indeed, for understanding ourselves. The roots of Western philosophy go back to the early Greeks. The term "philosophy" itself derives from the Greek and means love of wisdom (from *phil,* "love," and *soph,* "wise"). Once thought of as the "queen of the sciences," philosophy has taken for its domain questions concerning the nature of reality, the analysis of reasoning, of justice, of beauty, the study of moral values and principles, and the nature and sources of knowledge. Over the course of time the issues addressed by philosophers expanded greatly, and by the 12th century there had developed concern for subjects that today are so large and so diverse that we regard them as separate areas. These include physics, mathematics, logic, ethics, agriculture, medicine, and grammar and rhetoric. Out of philosophy's concern with the nature of reality and the nature of knowledge, and with the means by which we acquire that knowledge, has emerged the modern field of cognitive psychology.

Philosophy and Cognitive Psychology

In Chapter 2 we examined cognitive processes such as the formation and representation of concepts and categories, the representation of propositions, the representation of images, and the functioning of memory. We looked at experimental evidence for hypotheses concerning how the different sorts of knowledge are represented in our brains. We began with two assumptions: that we acquire knowledge and that this knowledge is somehow of "real" things. We did not question the reality of what we know. In fact, except in our philosophical ruminations, when we are alone with our thoughts, we give little consideration to the fundamental essence either of ourselves or of the environment that provides the substance of our knowledge. We operate *as if* we are real, *as if* it is clear that everything we experience as "out there" is really out there. But the questions we seldom ask underlie modern research in cognitive psychology.

Although we rarely dwell on these issues, haven't we all wondered at one time or another whether our conception of what is real is valid? Haven't we all noticed that when we dream we are not usually aware we are dreaming? On the contrary, the dream seems real. We may then wonder whether our current "awake" reality is really a dream. When you remember what you said in an argument, and your opponent in the argument remembers your words very differently (even, perhaps, that you never said anything of the sort!), does the angry certainty of your recollection ever yield to a sense of confusion about what really happened? We read in the news of "recovered memories," supposedly of events that occurred when someone was very young, events buried so deeply (where?) that they were not "recovered" until, with guidance, the individual was ready to face them. Then it may turn out there is proof that the "remembered" events in fact never occurred. When you and three other people witness an auto accident and give four apparently honest but entirely different—even mutually exclusive—accounts of the occurrence, do you wonder what is going on? We recognize today that each of us constructs our world by virtue of a combination of genetic propensity and unique environmental experience. This combination apparently gives each of us a unique reality, such that a scene appears one way to you, another way to your friend, and a third way altogether to me. But if this is so, it speaks against there being an objective reality. And if it is so, whatever can we really (!) count on?

Epistemology: How We Know What We "Know"

Philosophers of the past considered two closely related areas, the nature of reality and the nature of knowledge. How can we tell what exists, what is real? In order for knowledge to be possible—in order to know something—we must have a notion of something out there that is real. How do we determine whether there is? And if we judge that there is something real out there, how do we acquire knowledge of it? And when we appear to have done so, what *is* this knowledge? *Where* is it?

The Rationalist View   The philosophical term **epistemology** refers to the theory of knowledge: its nature and origin. Plato (ca. 427–347 B.C.), in the *Meno,* suggested that certain knowledge, such as mathematical truths (e.g., the properties of a square), is already within us. René Descartes (1596–1650), a renowned proponent of what is known as the **rationalist school**, built on the ideas of Plato. Descartes held that the mind is primary, all knowledge being acquired through reasoning and a certain number of basic innate concepts and elementary logical propositions. (These concepts include God, triangle, mind, and body. The elementary logical propositions are of the nature "it is impossible for the same thing to be and not to be.") In observing the infant's responses to the world, one may say that infants are born with a tendency to cry when they are hungry and a tendency to identify important aspects of their environment, for example, their mothers. They demonstrate other such tendencies as they develop, becoming able to pick out other entities in their environment, such as cookies, kittens, and colors. We considered this subject within psychology's modern framework when we examined concept and category formation. Descartes hypothesized that infants are able to identify crucial entities in their surroundings because the "idea" of these entities is inborn.

> Any man who rightly observes the limitations of the senses, and what precisely it is that can penetrate through this medium to our faculty of thinking must needs admit that no ideas of things, in the shape in which we envisage them by thought, are presented to us by the senses. So much so that in our ideas there is nothing which was not innate in the mind, or faculty of thinking, except only these circumstances which point to experience—the fact, for instance, that we judge that this or that idea, which we now have present to our thought, is to be referred to a certain extraneous thing, not that these extraneous things transmitted the ideas themselves to our minds through the organs of sense, but because they transmitted something which gave the mind occasion to form these ideas, by means of an innate faculty, at this time rather than at another. (Descartes, 1641/1984, pp. 442–443)

This passage tells us that for Descartes nothing in our minds has come to us via the senses; rather, every idea is in there from birth, or is formed by means of an innate mechanism for "forming ideas."

Immanuel Kant (1724–1804) was another philosopher whose ideas provide some of the grounds for present-day considerations in cognitive psychology. Like Descartes, who died nearly 75 years before Kant's birth, Kant presented arguments that the mind is the only source of knowledge. But Kant's framework, unlike Descartes's, did not preclude the existence of a world "out there." According to Kant, the only way we know that world is through our minds and the a priori categories within them (that is, categories that are there prior to experience). These a priori categories shape our impressions of the world we perceive, and what we know of this world depends on the nature of these categories (Kant, 1781/1965). Today we speak not of a priori knowledge, but rather, like Descartes, we use the term "innate." Unlike Descartes, however, we use the term to refer not to ideas but rather to capabilities, such as those that enable us to acquire our first language.

The Empiricist View   Even in its day, the rationalist school represented so notably by Descartes was not unopposed. Any hypothesis that rested on a priori knowledge or innate ideas was rejected by **empiricist** thinking. An important proponent of the empiricist school was John Locke (1632–1704), a younger contemporary of Descartes, who held that, far from being innate, knowledge derives ultimately from experience and sensation. These are encountered by a mind that is at birth essentially a "blank slate." As we develop, this blank slate is written on by the operation of our "natural faculties," such as the faculty of (capacity for) abstraction. Locke proposed that what we do is abstract from qualities that we perceive, such as color and shape. We then reflect on our experience, constructing from these qualities the entities we recognize as mother, cookie, or kitten.

Readers will recall earlier discussions of behaviorism, a theoretical perspective of the early- to mid-20th century that held that mental processes such as thoughts and feelings are not the cause of what we do. Rather, our behavior consists of responses to stimuli in our environment, stimuli that shape our behavior. Therefore, the behaviorists claimed, the appropriate object of study is not mental activity, which, if it exists at all, cannot be seen or measured, but behavior, which *can* be directly observed and measured. These notions, that there is nothing "in there" susceptible to study and that what yields knowledge must first be sensed, bear an obvious relation to Locke's blank slate.

It is not, however, necessary to consider this an either-or issue: either ideas are innate, already "in there," or there is nothing "in there." Consider for a moment the following line of reasoning. Let us take as a starting point the empiricist notion that we abstract from what the world presents to us, to arrive at our eventual knowledge of what there is in that world. And let us focus on the color red, which is a category we may expect that human beings possess. Although it is true that apples and flowers and sunsets and babies' crying faces may be red, each of these entities has many other qualities as well, from round to fragrant to huge to wet. There is no entity that consists of nothing but red. So to arrive at the concept of "red" we must abstract just one feature from each of many entities that have many qualities, one of which is red. Knowing nothing to begin with, how do we get the point? How do we know that redness is something to latch onto, unless there is something innate that responds not simply by perceiving the world in all its colors but also by singling out certain types of characteristics, such as "color" and, more specifically, "red," as concepts? This is an important question, which does seem to lead to the notion that, although we do not come into the world with ideas already implanted, the mind does contain at birth certain elements (in Locke's terminology, natural faculties). We make use of these in the process of sorting out the world. Thus whatever it is, the mind is *not* initially a blank slate. This point of view brings us once more to the present, and readers will recognize in it the underpinnings of modern research in concepts and categories discussed in Chapter 2.

Determinism and Free Will

We are always faced with choices; one might say that everything we do involves a choice. "Should I study or go out? That's an easy one; I'll go out. Okay, now that that's decided, where should I go? I could do some errands or stop for pizza and ice cream. Hmmm . . . If I go out for pizza and ice cream instead of doing home-work or running errands (I need to go to the cleaners and the library), I won't have the suit I need for tomorrow's interview, my books will be overdue, and I may fail the test I should be studying for. I really have no choice. I guess I'd better just run to the cleaners and the library and then come home and study."

Did I make my choices freely, or was it already determined that I would do just as I did? Certainly I felt somewhat compelled to run errands and study, because that's what I decided to do even though what I really wanted to do was go out and enjoy myself. But I *could* have chosen to do that—I've done it before. Despite the sense of "ought" that caused me to choose a particular action over my preferred one, I had a sense all the while that the choice was up to me and I could exercise free will in making it. Was this feeling well founded, or was it deceptive? This is another one of those questions still on the table.

Religion provided the framework for much early thinking on this matter, as on the mind-body problem (a discussion of which follows shortly). Descartes, for example, in his "Meditation IV, Of the True and the False," arrives at a discussion of will from considering his errors and what they are based on. He finds that they depend on a combination of two causes: the understanding that he possesses, and on his power of choice, or free will. If, as he believes, he has received his power of will from God, it cannot be the source of his errors, "for it is very ample and very perfect." No, his errors

> come from the sole fact that since the will is much wider in its range and compass than the understanding, I do not restrain it within the same bounds, but extend it also to things which I do not understand, and as the will is of itself indifferent to these, it easily falls into error and sin, and chooses the evil for the good, or the false for the true. (Descartes, 1641/1984, pp. 175–176)

Thus, Descartes resolves the difficulty of acting according to will in a manner counter to the perfection that must characterize what is God-given. Reconciling the nature of the human will with Western culture's prevalent conceptions of God has been a knotty problem. The question of how—or whether—this can be done is still with us. Also still with us is the issue of the relation of free will, or the lack of it, to responsibility for our actions. If, for example, he is truly at the mercy of "raging hormones," is an act of violence the perpetrator's fault? One's answer to this question affects one's position on the appropriateness of punishment for his transgressions. The question of free will has many ramifications.

An influential development in this arena had to do with the expanding scientific understanding of the laws of physics. The universe, including our corner of it, was seen to obey certain natural laws. This understanding colored trends in the fields of philosophy and psychology: Humans too might function deterministically. This point of view is evident in the behaviorist school of thought, which treats human behavior as obeying the laws relating stimulus and response. There is not much room for free will in such a scheme. More recently, new findings about the complementary roles of genetic and environmental factors in human development and behavior have altered the perspective once again. We may indeed be constrained by our genetic inheritance. But because environmental factors are so important in our development, we can never tease out which factor, if either, has been more influential in shaping any given aspect of ourselves. And we still don't have a handle on the problem. It is difficult to reconcile the notion of free will with what we observe to be the constraining influences of genetic and environmental factors: "Free will is another enigma. . . . How can my actions be a choice for which I am responsible if they are completely caused by my genes, my upbringing, and my brain state? Some events are determined, some are random: How can a choice be neither?" (Pinker, 1997, p. 550).

The American psychologist and philosopher William James discussed the question of free will in terms of effort of attention: If the amount of effort of attention we can bring to bear on an idea is somehow a "fixed function," then we have no freedom of will. If it is not, we have freedom of will. Setting the problem in these terms, however, does not solve it. Part of volition, James points out, is effortless; this part results from "interests and associations whose strength and sequence are mechanically determined by the structure of that physical mass, [the] brain." However, "Even in effortless volition we have the consciousness of the alternative being also possible. . . . *The fact is that the question of free-will is insoluble on strictly psychological grounds*" (James, 1892/1985, p. 323). He suggests handing the free will controversy over to **metaphysics**:

> Psychology will never grow refined enough to discover, in the case of any individual's decision, a discrepancy between her scientific calculations and the fact. Her prevision will never foretell, whether the effort be completely predestinate or not, the way in which each individual emergency is resolved. Psychology will be psychology, and Science science, as much as ever (as much and no more) in this world, whether free-will be true in it or not. (James, 1892/1985, pp. 324–325)

One other point of view will suffice to indicate that the issue is still very much alive, and that is the point of view of the Australian physiologist and 1963 Nobel laureate in medicine, Sir John Eccles (1903–1997):

That we have free will is a fact of experience. Furthermore I state emphatically that to deny free will is neither a rational nor a logical act. This denial either presupposes free will for the deliberately chosen response in making that denial, which is a contradiction, or else it is merely the automatic response of a nervous system built by genetic coding and moulded by conditioning. One does not conduct a rational argument with a being who makes the claim that all its responses are reflexes, no matter how complex and subtle the conditioning. (Eccles, 1985, pp. 159, 161)

The Mind-Body Problem

Some issues that have occupied philosophers through the ages are not easily relegated to one domain or another. One such issue is the so-called mind-body problem. We are all familiar with the advice, when we have a physical ailment such as a headache or a nervous stomach, that we should place "mind over matter." This advice rests on the notion that mind and matter are separate entities. But though we have a clear sense of what the body is (a physical object whose basic structure is well known), we are still puzzled by the mind. Some regard it, as the phrase indicates, as an entity unto itself. Others see it as inseparable from the body, because when the body dies, the mind is also gone. If mental activity occurs in the brain, is *mind* simply another word for *brain*? But the brain is part of the body's physical structure, and we have a strong sense, as the suggestion "mind over matter" again indicates, that something about our mental activity is capable of overcoming the dictates of the body. How then can mind be no more than a manifestation of brain tissue? To the extent that mind involves mental activity, its study is properly the domain of cognitive psychology. To the extent that mind is related to brain, the area of neuroscience is relevant. And in more recent times, a question has arisen as to the relevance of mind to computer. Because the computer can increasingly do what the brain does, is it meaningful to propose that it has a mind? Will we find in the field of artificial intelligence an answer to the age-old question?

Descartes Yet Again   The mind-body problem can be succinctly defined as the problem of explaining the relation between mental processes and bodily processes or states. The philosopher whose reasoned grappling with this problem put it on the map, so to speak, was, again, René Descartes. In a series of *Meditations on First Philosophy* (published in 1642), he set down his thoughts concerning the possibility of proving by means of reason "the fact that the human soul does not perish with the body, and that God exists" (Descartes, 1641/1984, p. 132). The "facts" of which he wrote were, as they are today, generally accepted by believers as matters of faith. Descartes, as a philosopher, approached them from the perspective of reason. In the process, he considered mind, the subject of our present concern. His resolution of the mind-body problem, that mind and body are not one but two entities, is known as **dualism**. In his "Meditation VI" we find a clear statement of this conclusion:

> There is a great difference between mind and body, inasmuch as body is by nature always divisible, and the mind is entirely indivisible. For, as a matter of fact, when

I consider the mind, that is to say, myself inasmuch as I am only a thinking thing,
I cannot distinguish in myself any parts, but apprehend myself to be clearly one and
entire; and although the whole mind seems to be united to the whole body, yet if a
foot, or an arm, or some other part, is separated from my body, I am aware that nothing has been taken away from my mind. And the faculties of willing, feeling, conceiving, etc. cannot be properly speaking said to be its parts, for it is one and the same
mind which employs itself in willing and in feeling and understanding. But it is quite
otherwise with corporeal [bodily] or extended objects, for there is not one of these
imaginable by me which my mind cannot easily divide into parts, and which conse-
quently I do not recognise as being divisible; this would be sufficient to teach me that
the mind or soul of man is entirely different from the body, if I had not already learned
it from other sources. (Descartes, 1641/1984, p. 196)

The Materialist View   Descartes's dualism is one of many approaches to the question of how mind and body are related. Another, known as **materialism**, takes us
once more back to early Greek times—to the philosopher Democritus (ca. 460–
370 B.C.). Democritus conceived of the world of matter as composed of tiny indivisible parts that he called atoms. He hypothesized that the forms material things
take depend on the attributes of these atoms: their size, shape, location, and so
forth, and on their lawful behavior. He proposed that humans, like all other material objects, are also made of atoms. The different aspects of humans, such as their
bodies and their souls, result from the different sorts of atoms of which they are
composed. In part this is a rather modern view: There are currently **reductionist**
philosophers who hold that all objects and events can be reduced to the lawful
behavior of the elements of which they are constructed. The operations of the
mind, in their view, can be understood strictly in terms of the functions of the
brain—leaving us, in fact, with no need of the concept "mind," and thus no more
dualism problem.

Psychophysical Parallelism: The "Monad" Explanation   In the centuries before
the explosion of knowledge led to our age of specialization, philosophical explanations for the "big questions" were expounded by thinkers from a vastly greater
variety of professional backgrounds than is the case today. Gottfried Wilhelm von
Leibniz (1646–1716) was, in fact, a mathematician who "combined physics, biology, introspection, and theology into a worldview that was both strange and complex" (Hergenhahn, 1992, p. 166). The invention of the microscope had recently
allowed people to see living things where living things had not been suspected.
This new view of the world suggested to Leibniz the notion that *everything* was
living. He therefore proposed that, instead of matter being made of tiny nonliving
elements, atoms, everything was made of tiny *living* elements, which he called
"monads." According to Leibniz, these monads do not influence each other. Although everything in the universe was created by God to be in perfect harmony,
nothing in the universe influences anything else. Therefore, "Whenever we perceive in one monad what appears to be the cause of something, other monads are
created in such a way as to display what appears to be the effects of that cause"
(Hergenhahn, 1992, p. 167). Thus perceptions only "mirror" external events; they

are not caused by them. It is like two clocks that agree precisely on the time: They move in parallel but do not affect one another.

Because the monads comprising the mind and those comprising the body also operate in this way, the implication of this worldview for the mind-body problem is that mind and body do not interact. Instead, they function in parallel, corresponding in their perceptions as part of a Divine Plan. This explanation is known as **psychophysical parallelism**.

Ryle's Approach   It is very difficult to find an explanation of mind, especially given today's scientific approach to the physical world and the way it is understood. One well-known discussion was provided by Gilbert Ryle in the middle of the 20th century (Ryle, 1949). Ryle considered the mind-body distinction of Descartes and those who reasoned similarly to have resulted from a mistake in categorizing. Their error was in representing the facts of mental life as if they belonged to one category when actually they belong to another. He described Descartes and others as having fallen into a kind of thinking trap, which he explained by means of an analogy. Imagine a foreign visitor touring Oxford or Cambridge University and being taken to see the various buildings, departments, and offices. This visitor, new to the concept of a university, says, "Well, I've seen all this, but I haven't yet seen the university." We would have to explain to him that the university is not "another collateral institution, some ulterior counterpart to the colleges, laboratories and offices which he has seen. The University is just the way in which all that he has already seen is organized. When they are seen and when their co-ordination is understood, the University has been seen" (Ryle, 1949, p. 16).

The visitor's mistake was in considering the university as belonging to the same category as its components. Ryle (1949) applies this reasoning to what he terms "Descartes's myth," that the mind, like the body, is a complex organized unit, but one "made of a different sort of stuff and with a different sort of structure" from that of the body (p. 18). It is a mistake to treat the mind as though it were the same sort of category as the body. It is not simply one component of two that make up the person. He ridicules the notion, calling it "the dogma of the Ghost in the Machine" (p. 17), and he sets out to prove that, as a category-mistake, it is false not in its details but in principle.

We could go on for volumes, as in fact philosophers have, considering and debating the mind-body problem, but unfortunately (or fortunately, as the case may be) we must move on. We will encounter the issue again, but from a different perspective, in the following section.

Philosophy and Neuroscience

The Mind-Body Problem Revisited

Early philosophers who dealt with the mind-body problem sometimes equated *mind* with *soul*. Whichever term they used, the concept had religious connotations:

a somewhat mystical entity that directs our perceptions and behavior, an entity unique to each one of us in life, yet perhaps part of a larger shared spirit that lives on after death.

For many of us today, the quest to understand ourselves is carried on within a scientific frame of reference. As our foray into the area of neuroscience (Part 2) makes clear, we have new means of studying the brain, which, although still mysterious, is more accessible to us than in the past. Rather than pursuing the relation of mind and body, we have transferred our focus and now seek to discover the relation—if there indeed is a distinction—between mind and that "three-pound universe" that new technologies are making it possible to probe. Some of its mysteries are yielding to our increasingly sophisticated methods of study, and some of the issues explored by philosophers may now be fruitfully examined in the light of contemporary neuroscience. The mind-brain problem is one of them, certainly; the question of free will is another. In this section we will examine some of what neuroscience has enabled us to see in relation to these puzzles.

It would have been very helpful in our quest to understand ourselves if it were possible to peer into the brain of a waking subject with our new tools and spy out exactly where all the "language" function or all the "memory" function is lurking. It would be wonderful if we could do the same with the mind and, spotting the one belonging to our subject, cry "There it is! We've finally found it!" But, as has been made abundantly clear, the brain is far more complex than simply a collection of such elements piled together into a container, each in its own little space. Many conceptualize the mind as the entity that makes our experiences ours alone, enables us to feel like ourselves throughout our lives, makes us conscious of what we perceive *and* of ourselves—*and* of our consciousness. If this is the case, the mind must arise out of many complex processes. It cannot be found in a given location. But that does not mean that studying the brain will be unprofitable. Neuroscientists are now able to contribute a far greater understanding of the effects of brain damage or dysfunction on behavior and on the sense of self and consciousness than was available to those early speculators about mind and body, mind and brain.

Split-Brain Research Revisited

In Chapter 3 we encountered some strange phenomena. A child whose entire left hemisphere—containing areas known to be heavily involved in the language function—had been removed subsequently acquired adequate mastery of language. Limbs that have been amputated—and sometimes limbs congenitally missing—nevertheless are "felt." The two hemispheres of the brain, disconnected by a severing of the corpus callosum, no longer communicate with each other, so that information acquired by one hemisphere remains trapped there. The strange result is that knowledge acquired by the right hemisphere cannot be expressed or even thought, insofar as thought requires language, but it can be expressed in a drawing made with the *left* hand. There are many other odd phenomena manifested by people with various types of brain damage or dysfunction, some of which have been described by the neuropsychologist A. R. Luria (1902–1977) and, more recently, by the neurologist Oliver Sacks (1933–). The accounts they offer are fascinating, not simply because of the behaviors they describe, but because of the effects of the damage or dysfunction on the individuals' senses of themselves and what these effects reveal about mind and consciousness.

The split-brain effects described in Chapter 3 represent one intriguing example. Recall Sperry's summing up of the situation, in which

> each hemisphere seems to have its own separate and private sensations; its own perceptions; its own concepts; and its own impulses to act, with related volitional, cognitive, and learning experiences. Following the surgery, each hemisphere also has thereafter its own separate chain of memories that are rendered inaccessible to the recall processes of the other. (Sperry, 1968, p. 724)

We raised the question there as to whether patients who have undergone this type of surgery have now two "consciousnesses" or, put otherwise, two "minds." We have noted that self-awareness is a crucial aspect of our consciousness. We rely on a continuous stream of awareness for our sense of identity, our very selves: who we *are*. We must now ask whether a person who cannot put the two halves of his or her brain together to form this single stream of self-awareness is truly in the situation of maintaining two separate "streams"—two minds, as it were. Neuroscience has not yet answered these questions, but it has taught us something we didn't know before: that this continuous stream of mind depends on the shuttling back and forth of information from one hemisphere to the other.

Memory Revisited

Luria and Sacks describe other consequences of brain damage or unusual brain function. In two short books, *The Mind of a Mnemonist* (1968) and *The Man with a Shattered World* (1972), Luria presents the cases of, respectively, a man who could remember everything he saw, heard, and experienced, and a man who suffered from the opposite condition: severe amnesia from brain damage incurred in combat during World War II. In the first instance, the man, whom Luria calls S., was characterized by synesthesia, a curious condition in which the senses are "hooked together" so that the individual *hears* colors, *feels* sounds, *tastes* shapes (Cytowic, 1993). Somehow, S. saw colored images when he encountered numbers or heard sounds, whether the sounds were from speech or were simply tones. He might describe a voice as "crumbly yellow" (Luria, 1968/1987, p. 24), or a tone as "a brown strip against a dark background that had red, tongue-like edges" and that, moreover, triggered a taste of "sweet and sour borscht" (p. 23). Somehow, perhaps partly because of all this extra information he associated with everything he encountered, S. was able to remember virtually everything; he simply reviewed his vision of something along with his recollection of the accompanying colors, textures, or flavors it evoked, and even after many years he could call it up in its entirety.

"I wish *I* could remember everything," the reader may be thinking, aware of the advantage such an ability would confer, especially when preparing for an exam. But S. paid a high price for this ability. When he read a passage, for instance, each word in it called up so many associations that he experienced tremendous interference with comprehending or even simply getting through the passage. Images produced by each word in it distracted him, blocking the meaning.

> Inasmuch as S's images were particularly vivid and stable, and recurred thousands of times, they soon became the dominant element in his awareness, uncontrollably coming to the surface whenever he touched upon something that was linked to them even in the most general way. . . . Given such a tendency, cognitive functions can hardly proceed normally. (Luria, 1968/1987, pp. 114–115)

Luria contemplates the mind of such a person. Surely it is composed differently from the minds of more "normal" individuals. Luria (1968) focuses on questions such as

> What effect does a remarkable capacity for memory have on other major aspects of personality, on an individual's habits of thought and imagination, on his behaviour and personality development? What changes occur in a person's inner world, in his relationships with others, in his very life style when one element of his psychic makeup, his memory, develops to such an uncommon degree that it begins to alter every other aspect of his activity? (p. 4)

Most of us with an ordinary sort of memory (the kind that occasionally fails us when we are hoping it will serve us best) don't ordinarily stop to consider what life would be like if we were unable to *forget*. Luria's account makes the point forcefully.

In the second book, *The Man with a Shattered World,* Luria describes the condition of Mr. Zazetsky, whose war wound had destroyed much of his memory. It had also severely damaged the complex and vulnerable region of his brain whose crucial function is to serve to integrate messages to and from the visual (occipital), tactile-motor (parietal), and auditory-vestibular (temporal) sections of the brain (Luria, 1972/1987, p. 30). Because this essential area had been damaged, Mr. Zazetsky's world was devastated: "He no longer had any sense of space, could not judge relationships between things, and perceived the world as broken into thousands of separate parts" (p. 61). One can hardly imagine what such fragmentation must mean for the consciousness, the inner world, the mind of such a person.

The same kinds of issues are addressed in several remarkable works by Sacks, in which are presented accounts of patients suffering various kinds of damage and attendant deficits. Like Luria's account, Sacks's (1995) description of the young man Greg F., discussed in Chapter 2, gives us some additional insight into what happens when memory goes. In this case the damage caused a deficit in the patient's ability to establish *new* memories. Greg F. lacks the "constant dialogue of past and present, of experience and meaning, which constitutes consciousness and inner life for the rest of us" (Sacks, 1995, pp. 49–50). Sacks speculates that therefore Greg may not have such a consciousness and "inner life."

In presenting these case studies, Luria and Sacks are not simply recording facts. They are seeking to understand something fundamental about the human being.

Loss of memory and the capacity to integrate information received by the senses bears on the old mind-body question:

> The patient's essential being is very relevant in the higher reaches of neurology, and in psychology; for here the patient's personhood is essentially involved, and the study of disease and of identity cannot be disjoined. Such disorders, and their depiction and study, indeed entail a new discipline, which we may call the "neurology of identity," for it deals with the neural foundations of the self, the age-old problem of mind and brain. It is possible that there must, of necessity, be a gulf, a gulf of category, between the psychical and the physical; but studies and stories pertaining simultaneously and inseparably to both—and it is these which especially fascinate me—may none the less serve to bring them nearer, to bring us to the very intersection of mechanism and life, to the relation of physiological processes to biography. (Sacks, 1995, p. xiv)

Mindblindness   Certain other conditions observed by neurologists (and psychologists of course) also illustrate the relation the effects of brain malfunction or damage bear to the old questions asked by philosophers. One is the condition known as autism (briefly discussed in Chapter 4). This condition often involves cognitive deficits, as well as other symptoms, such as repetitive movements (perhaps head-banging or hand-flapping) and abnormal sensory responses (intolerance of being touched, for example, and/or insensitivity to pain). But the aspect of this disability that pertains to our present discussion is the characteristic failure of autistic individuals to relate to other people in the usual way. That is, they do not respond to and learn to participate in ordinary social interactions. In our discussion in Chapter 1 of Gardner's theory of multiple intelligences, we noted Gardner's (1983) *interpersonal intelligence:* the ability of people in general "to notice and make distinctions among other individuals and, in particular, among their moods, temperaments, motivations, and intentions" (p. 239, emphasis omitted). The cues people transmit by their facial expressions, body language, and tone of voice are the signals that most of us recognize intuitively, and react to unthinkingly and appropriately. People who do not behave in this regard as others expect are perceived as being "insensitive." In autistic individuals the inability to perceive these cues is much more extreme and not that easily or lightly characterized.

A condition known as Asperger's syndrome is particularly interesting in this regard. Considered by some to be a form of autism, it is in fact not characterized by all the symptoms that usually define that syndrome. Unlike clear cases of autism, it is manifested primarily (though not always solely) in some level of inability to function in the social arena. Thus this aspect of the disability, whether classified as autism or not, is discernible in a relatively "pure" form. Although functioning normally or even at a high level intellectually, individuals with Asperger's syndrome are, in effect, "nearly blind to the feelings and needs of others" (Ratey & Johnson, 1997, p. 256). For this reason their condition is often referred to as "mindblindness" (Baron-Cohen, 1995).

Over the course of their development, people with normally functioning brains acquire the ability to attribute mental states to others. Autistic individuals and those with Asperger's syndrome seem either not to acquire such a "theory of mind" or to acquire it in impaired form. The explanation we seek is at the level of brain function. How does it happen that most people do arrive at an adequate theory of mind, but some do not? What is happening—or failing to happen—in people's brains as they develop in a social context? As one might expect, neuroscientists are at work on this problem. In various experiments involving brain imaging, they are comparing areas of brain activity in autistic and Asperger's patients with those of normal subjects when performing "theory of mind tasks." One such task has been based on the fact that people in general glean information about the mental state of others by "reading" their eyes—much as I inferred the frame of mind of the gorilla at the zoo and felt strongly that he was, at the same time, inferring that I was doing so. Experiments have been carried out in which subjects performed a theory of mind task requiring them to infer the mental state of a person just by looking at photographs of the person's eyes. Positron emission tomography (PET) scans showed that in normal subjects the task was associated with activity in the left medial prefrontal cortex. In patients with Asperger's syndrome, PET scans showed no activity in this region, but the adjoining areas exhibited normal activity. From this result one may infer that a very specific area of the brain is involved in understanding other minds (Baron-Cohen, Jolliffe, Mortimore, & Robertson, 1997).

Dissociative Identity Disorder   Another phenomenon that has fascinated the general public and intrigued researchers is one that used to be called "multiple personality disorder" but is now termed more accurately "dissociative identity disorder." From popular accounts in books and movies, most of us are familiar with the more notorious and shocking symptoms of individuals exhibiting this disorder, in which two or more personality states alternate in controlling behavior. Dissociative identity disorder is thought to derive from a reaction, often traceable to childhood, to intolerable traumatic events. Unable to confront the events, the individual effectively dissociates from them, blanks out, rejects consciousness of the events—"disappears." It is an extreme form of the reaction anyone might have when confronting something unbearable. We may block it out, at least temporarily. But our personalities generally remain intact; we do not "disintegrate." In dissociative identity disorder, aspects of the personality that are required for the person's functioning may surface as distinct entities. It often happens in these cases that at least one of the personalities is aware of the other or others, but that some among them are ignorant of the presence of others. This disorder, in which there seems to be more than one mind occupying a single body, is clearly of interest in any consideration of the relation of mind, brain, and body.

A remarkable fact in cases of dissociative identity disorder is that the different personalities manifested by a given individual may appear to differ in traits that generally characterize different people, but which do not generally coexist in a single body. For example, one personality may have an allergic reaction to a substance that doesn't bother the other personalities, or one may be right-handed and another left-handed. Or the different personalities may exhibit varia-

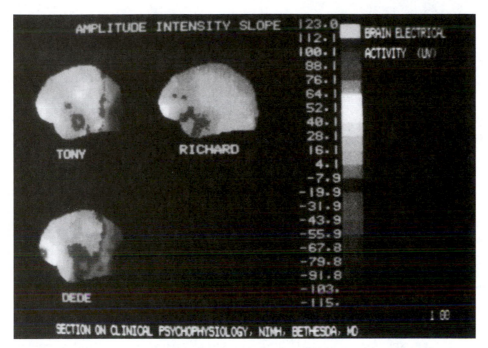

FIGURE 9.1 **Brain Images of a Single Subject in Different Personality Manifestations**

tions in visual function, such as color vision and size of the pupils of their eyes (Birnbaum & Thomann, 1996). No wonder these bizarre cases catch the imagination of the public!

Using its increasingly sophisticated brain mapping techniques, neuroscience may begin to answer the interesting question: Are the different manifestations of personalities in dissociative identity disorder associated with differences in the activity of various brain regions? There are indications that the answer is yes, in at least some cases. For example, in one study (Hughes, Kuhlman, Fichtner, & Gruenfeld, 1990), brain maps were recorded for each of 10 alternate personalities in a single patient. The recordings were taken twice, at an interval of 2 months, and in two different conditions: with eyes open and with eyes closed. The maps of each of the alternate personalities were then compared to those of the personality considered to be the basic one. There were indeed differences noted among four of the personalities. Figure 9.1 illustrates the kinds of differences observed in brain imaging of patients with dissociative identity disorder.

It seems we are learning once again that the relationship of mind and brain will not be easily understood. Information gleaned from studies such as this one takes us a certain distance along the road, but although we are homing in on some answers, we are still left with the fundamental question of what mind *is*. The fact that we can see physiological differences in the brains of dissociated personalities is not yet an answer.

Free Will Revisited

In a 1989 article in *The Sciences,* Benjamin Libet reported an experiment that bears on the question of free will from a perspective quite different from those we examined earlier. His perspective derives from the search for the neural correlates of consciousness. We understand the expression "He didn't lift a finger to help" to involve *will.* But what is involved in willing a finger actually to move? Libet's experiment explored the brain activity associated with what people experience as conscious awareness of the decision to move a finger. Experiments in the 1960s in which subjects were asked to move a finger in a certain prescribed time had indicated that neurological activity occurred four fifths of a second before the subjects "decided" to move their fingers, and this was a mysterious finding. Perhaps it meant that there was a much longer period of "getting ready" to carry out the intended action than is actually required for the command from the motor cortex to reach and activate the muscles of the hand. This idea seems strange, because we don't notice that there is a gap between our decision to move and our movement in response to the decision. Another possibility is that the brain initiates the action on its own, before we decide to carry out its direction. But this notion too is strange, because our general perception is that we decide first and then act on our decision.

Libet's experiment called for the subjects to move a wrist or a hand whenever they wanted to. At the same time, they watched a revolving spot of light on an oscilloscope and reported where the spot was at the exact moment they became aware of the decision to act. Brain wave activity was measured by means of electrodes attached to the scalp of each subject so that the researchers could compare the moment when this activity changed with the moment of decision.

What happened? The result was very much the same as that in the earlier experiments. Even with the freedom to move whenever they wanted to, the subjects' brain activity changed one third of a second *before* they reported the decision to move! Their neurons had fired a surprisingly long time before the subjects were conscious of a decision to act. So our brains seem to prepare even before we are conscious of making a decision.

What does this finding mean? If our brains start the process before we "decide" to move, *have* we decided to move? Has neuroscience proved the answer to the question of free will? Does free will in fact not exist? Libet offers another possibility. Subjects had been aware during the experiment of urges *not* to move. Another experiment was designed to discover when, in the sequence of (a) brain activity, (b) deciding to act, and (c) acting, the "cancellations" occur. The researchers found that most of the subjects could cancel the decision—change their minds—during the last 150 milliseconds before they acted and that at the moment they did so, the electrical activity in their brains diminished.

Libet (1989) suggests two philosophical implications of the experiment. The first is that the human will "seems to have its roots in neurological processes of which we are utterly unaware—processes rooted in some unconscious domain." The second implication is that the brain is "continuously generating possible courses of action and that free will operates . . . by letting us decide which ones to execute" (p. 35). He points out that it is not easy to distinguish the workings of this selection process, but that the process seems to be one of inhibiting action. We may decide *not* to act, or it may be that we need a conscious trigger before we perform any act, and that when there is none the act simply doesn't happen. Whichever it is, says Libet, "The foundation of free will seems to reside not within our unconscious capacity for generating choices but within our conscious ability, in the hundred and fifty milliseconds before taking action, to make up our minds" (p. 35).

Lest the reader conclude, either happily or unwillingly, that the problem of free will has been resolved, let me hasten to add that once again, when something new has been learned more questions arise.

> In fact, we are left with more of a conundrum than might appear at first. We have excluded a conscious freedom of the will. We have relegated any freedom to the nonconscious. Are we left with the conclusion that human acts are predicted by neuronal events, that our consciousness is not necessary for what may appear purposeful? (Spence, 1996, p. 85)

So much for the ordinary situation, the "normal" case. What do these findings imply for pathological cases, such as those in which patients experience a limb as not belonging to their bodies (see Sacks, 1984) or not being under their control? With respect to such limbs, the patients seem to have lost the experience of free will. The limb is perceived as acting "on its own." It has been suggested that in such cases, something about the timing of the sequence of brain activity, deciding to act, and acting has been disturbed. The individual has a different perception, or impression, of the sequence. It should seem as though one's conscious self is generating acts, but it does not. In any event, the case is not closed; there remains much to learn, and neuroscience is a promising source of information.

Philosophy and Linguistics

In Chapter 6 the point was made that the connection between philosophy and the study of language as a human function is complex. Philosophers have addressed themselves to various aspects of it. I have mentioned grammar and rhetoric as part of the subject matter philosophy had early taken as its domain. These areas of study are directed, respectively, toward language as a rule-governed system (see Chapter 5) and speech as a vehicle of expression. But more fundamentally, both grammar and rhetoric involve language as a human capacity. Philosophers such as Thomas Hobbes (1588–1679) and Bishop George Berkeley (1685–1753) have observed and commented on the uses of this capacity. According to Hobbes, "The general use of speech, is to transfer our mental discourse, into verbal; or the train of our thoughts, into a train of words" (*Leviathan,* 1.4, 1651, in Woodbridge, 1930, p. 165). This description relies on the notion that there is something like language that represents our thoughts and exists in our minds before we actually clothe it in language—and that we do this in order to communicate these thoughts. Readers of Chapter 2 will surely be reminded here of contemporary research in the representation of knowledge as concepts and propositions.

Berkeley, writing somewhat later, proposes that "the communicating of ideas marked by words is not the chief and only end of language, as is commonly supposed. There are other ends, as the raising of some passion, the exciting to or deterring from an action, the putting the mind in some particular disposition" (introduction to *The Principles of Human Knowledge,* sec. 20, 1710, in Burtt, 1939, p. 520). With its many uses, language comes to be seen as the vehicle of far more than communication. Today we consider also that the evolution of language may have been the crucial development in enabling us to think in the manner that appears unique to our species.

The Meaning of Words and the Framing of Concepts

Among the aspects of human language that philosophers discuss is the relation between the name of an entity and the entity itself. We do not today generally equate the two. Names are words, and we readily accept that the various words naming the same object are but arbitrary symbols. In English we may call a particular item a *table,* whereas in Spanish it is *mesa,* in Danish it is *bord,* and in German it is *Tisch*. But Plato held to the idea that abstract universals exist, that there is a "tableness" independent of actual tables, and that each of the many types of (actual) table is a manifestation of this abstract universal. Plato introduced the notion of an "ideal name," one that frames a concept in such a way as to enable thought to reflect the nature of its objects (Blackburn, 1995). An ideal language would thus be one in which concepts are formed so accurately that knowledge itself may be correctly framed and communicated.

Fifteen hundred years later, philosophers were actively debating the question of whether there are such abstract universals or whether in fact these are nothing more than verbal labels—names-—that summarize various similar experiences of objects. In a famous disputation, Peter Abelard (1079–1142) argued that words and the things they represent should not be confused. He was asked if the names of nonexisting things such as "chimaera" (a mythological fire-breathing monster with a lion's head, a goat's body, and a serpent's tail) fall into the category of *substantia* (things with substance, real things). He responded, in effect, not unless there is something wrong with a person's mind—in other words, no (Beonio-Brocchieri Fumigalli, 1970). I can freely label entities. Here's one: little green men from Mars. Here's another: perfection. Do these exist because I am able to conceptualize and label them? Perfection is something we may strive for, but we may well question whether anything is ever really perfect. And though we can imagine them, I think we'd be really hard put to argue for the existence of little green men from Mars. It does not seem to be the case, as some have argued, that if you can think of something (as your naming it indicates that you can), there must be something real corresponding to your thought.

The Truth Value of Sentences

With or without implementing Plato's notion of the possibility of framing concepts so accurately that knowledge can be correctly framed and communicated, suppose we succeed in communicating our knowledge. What about the *truth* of what we communicate? Truth is another large issue with which philosophers have been concerned, and our discussion of names for things leads us right to it. Today most of us would say that the object a word names is distinct from its name. We possess it as a *concept,* and although names are arbitrary and conventional, there is nothing arbitrary or conventional about a concept. As long as I understand the languages, it makes no real difference whether I say, pointing to the object, "That is a table" or "Es una mesa" or "Das ist ein Tisch." But to utter any of these sentences while pointing to a tree is a different matter. The sentence is now subject to a judgment regarding its truth. The issue of truth is not entirely distinct, then, from that of meaning, which is, in turn, intimately connected to language.

Jumping across centuries once again, we encounter the concerns of the German-born American philosopher Rudolf Carnap (1891–1970) and the British philosopher Alfred Ayer (1910–1989), representing the **logical positivist school**. This school of thought approached the issue in terms of the "verification principle," which holds that there are two kinds of cognitively meaningful statements. The first are those that are true by virtue of their being empirically verifiable (true because they are true in the world). "My brother is a firefighter" is one such statement. If in fact my brother is a firefighter, this statement is true; if he is not, it is false. The second type of cognitively meaningful statements includes those that are true by virtue of being linguistically verifiable. That is, their truth or falsity depends on the *meanings* of the words. In the example "My brother is a male," *brother* includes as a component of its meaning the feature *male*. It is, therefore, necessarily true, not by reference to the world but entirely because of its meaning.

Semantics   A branch of the study of language known as *semantics* is another area of overlap between philosophy and linguistics. Semantics is concerned with issues of meaning, and the truth value of statements falls within this domain. But we all know that statements are not the only kinds of sentences language contains. They are, however, the only kind whose truth or falsity can in principle be determined. Commands and questions are different from statements, and linguists point out that these kinds of sentences are not subject to judgments regarding their truth. I may ask whether it is true or false that "my brother is a firefighter" and "my brother is a male"; such questions make sense. With regard to the first question, if he is a firefighter I say "true"; if he is not I say "false." To the second question I must answer "true." But if I ask someone "Is your brother a firefighter?" it makes no sense to follow my question with "True or false?" Nor does it make sense to issue the command "Go fly a kite!" and then ask "True or false?"

In the preceding paragraph, I used the expression "in principle" with reference to statements being the only kind of sentences whose truth value may be determined. The reason for the qualification is that there are statements that include a complication that must be dealt with before their truth value can be determined. These are statements containing **presuppositions**, in which some state of affairs is understood to have obtained. "My brother has given up being a firefighter" contains the presupposition that he has at some time been a firefighter. If this presupposition is not correct, then the question "True or false?" cannot be asked. It is like the old joke about the judge who asks the defendant "Have you stopped beating your wife?" The question contains the presupposition that the man has in fact beaten his wife. If he has never done so, he cannot accurately answer the question, because either answer he may give will be based on the same incorrect presupposition and will indicate guilt. Linguists concerned with semantics say that the truth value of a statement cannot be determined unless all of its presuppositions are correct.

The distinction between sense and reference is yet another concern of semantics. **Sense** signifies meaning (*brother* means male sibling), whereas **reference** simply denotes someone or something (*Mary, Connecticut*). Some words have both sense and reference (*chair,* for instance, has meaning and can also refer to a specific chair). Some, such as *Mary* and *Connecticut,* have only reference, and some, such as *Martians*—those little green men I mentioned before—have only sense.

Speech Acts   Another aspect of meaning that concerns both linguists and philosophers is the fact that when one utters a sentence one may be doing something more at the same time: for example, asserting, questioning, giving an order, or promising. The actions embodied in these sentences have been called **speech acts** (Searle, 1969). They are acts as well as statements or questions. We easily recognize that a grouping of words is an assertion ("John is a chocoholic.") or a question ("Is John a chocoholic?") or an order ("Don't give John any more chocolate!"). But some statements are more than they seem. "Don't give John any more chocolate!" is a command, but it does not by itself carry out the action of not giving chocolate to John. Consider the statement "I promise I won't give John any more chocolate." This is subtly different from the other sentences. It is, to be sure, a statement expressing my intention not to give John any more chocolate, but it is also an act—the act of promising. Saying "I promise" is itself an act in addition to the act involved simply in the saying. Such statements are called **performatives**. You can probably think of many performatives: In *saying* "I resign," I in fact resign. The way I indicate at a certain point in a game that I give up is not to get up and walk away (I may intend to finish the game later) but rather to *say* "I give up." In this way, speech acts such as performatives add a dimension to the meaning of utterances beyond that of the sense and reference of the words or word groupings.

Language and Thought Revisited

In matters regarding meaning, such as the truth value of statements, the sense and reference of words, and the additional dimensions provided by speech acts, the overlap between philosophy and linguistics is clear. It is also clear in the matter of the relation of language and thought, which has been considered in some detail in Chapter 6 with regard to the Sapir-Whorf hypothesis. As we saw, the strong version of the hypothesis holds first that our language determines the way we think (linguistic determinism) and, second, that the distinctions found in a given language will not be the same as those in any other language (linguistic relativity).

It is true, however, because thought is encoded in language, that language necessarily reflects thought. We generally take this notion for granted. The way the world is when you first experience it, however, probably does constitute a strong influence on what you perceive as the "natural" way. The weaker version of the Sapir-Whorf hypothesis, that structures of a particular language may render certain thoughts relatively easier to conceptualize, might be invoked to support the notion that the structures of our language may exert some influence on the way we organize our worlds. This notion is illustrated by the different types of kinship terms employed in the languages of the world (see Chapter 6), reflecting the variety of kinship emphases in different cultures. My own experience will serve as an example. In my "real world" (the one I am compelled to recognize over and over again as different from the way things are now), families are composed of mothers and fathers and their children. Each child has as grandparents the parents of his or her parents, and each sibling is the child of those same parents. But the current high rate of divorce and remarriage reformulates families so that terms such as "grandmother" and "brother" are not limited to denoting kin in the way my original experience of culture predisposes me to expect. They are used more broadly by today's generations than "my world" would dictate.

How much does language influence thought? Whatever the answer, it is clear that issues of truth, meaning, reality, and thought are all involved when language is considered. We have not yet resolved these problems. Perhaps we never will. The complexity of the relationship between language and the concerns of philosophy has taken us back many centuries and then forward again, and we have not exhausted (nor can we hope to exhaust) the issues, so let us turn from them to other concerns of philosophers.

The Puzzle of Consciousness

Another aspect of our uniqueness as a species is the sort of consciousness with which we are endowed—a consciousness that may be regarded at the same time as a precious gift and as a curse. Other species, though conscious in the sense of being awake and alert, do not seem to possess consciousness of, for example, *what might be* rather than *what is*. We have no reason to assume a dog thinks anything like "You will take me for a walk next Thursday after dinner"—only that the dog expresses a wish to be taken out right now. Although there is some evidence from studies with apes that they may have a measure of self-consciousness, we do not know that it is as complex or sophisticated as our own.

I called human consciousness a gift because it enables us, for example, to be conscious of what is good and what is bad outside our own immediate environment. We may thus plan to enhance the good and alter the bad. I called consciousness a curse because it allows us to be aware of the inevitable—death—and of the potential for pain and suffering. It creates for us the pleasures of remembering and anticipating—and it produces as well the anguish and anxiety of remembering and anticipating. This suggests a parallel between the kinds of thoughts our sort of consciousness (including our self-consciousness) permits and the kinds of subjects our sort of language permits us to encode, whether simply to think about or also to convey. Both are characterized by being bound neither to the present nor to the actual. Is one (which?) perhaps the handmaiden of the other? Did they arise interdependently? Is each possible only by virtue of the other? Perhaps our unique consciousness is closely allied with our unique language. Consciousness is a hot topic these days, and we return in the next chapter to current work in that area.

Questions to Think About

1. What evidence, if any, have you that your pet (or your friend's pet) has a mind?

2. When do you think little children first become self-conscious? What does that require of them?

3. What makes you think that reality is "real" and that your dreams are not? Or do you have a different view of things?

4. In your opinion, is the rationalist approach incompatible with the empiricist approach? Why or why not?

5. What is your experience with respect to free will? What causes you to make the choices you do? *Are* they up to you? In what sense?

6. Have you ever thought about *where you* are? One writer said that he was located behind his eyes about 2 inches inside the surface of his skin. Where would you locate your*self*? Why? If you think this is not possible, why do you think so?

7. When Dwight Eisenhower was president of Columbia University, he once told members of the faculty that "the university appreciates what you do . . ." and was told in response, "Mr. President, we *are* the university." How would you explain the idea that "a university is not some ulterior counterpart of its colleges, buildings, laboratories and offices"? And how would you evaluate the faculty member's reply to Columbia's president?

8. What are some implications of split-brain research for understanding the nature of the human mind?

9. How do you think researchers might someday account for the finding that alternate personalities of a victim of dissociative identity disorder have different reactions to allergens, the substances that induce allergies?

10. Do you think that neuroscience has clarified or is likely soon to clarify the issue of free will? Why or why not?

CHAPTER 10

Who Are We?

Every spring, when my neighbors are supervising the progress of crocuses and tulips, I am watching the progress of an ant colony I thought I had successfully disposed of the year before. In the flower borders just outside the neighbors' doors are green shoots and early blossoms. Outside *my* front door are little piles of earth, larger and more numerous each day, signaling the presence of active tiny lives that won't take "no" for an answer.

But wait—they are not the same tiny lives I said no to last year. These are new individuals, making up a colony I have without thinking regarded as the same one I encounter every spring. Now, as I watch their traces grow, I do begin to think, and my thoughts turn philosophical. From "Who am *I* to claim this spot and refuse them their home?" I progress to a more simply phrased but equally profound "Who, after all, *am* I?" Am I, like each of them, just an individual member of a larger society, all of us scurrying about, engaged in pursuing our own interests? Are *they* in fact not pursuing individual interests at all, but rather acting as parts of a whole? In this case, is the individual I am (who is, after all, made up of many tiny parts acting as a whole) comparable rather to the larger society the ants comprise? Watching them, I mull over other questions, some of which the reader will recognize as having arisen in Chapter 8 (and been postponed). I think of the individuals as alive. That much is obvious, isn't it? Or is it really the *colony* that is alive? Or both? I am an individual, and I am alive. But what about the cells of which I am composed? Are they alive, or is it just me? What does "alive" mean? Do ants choose their lot? Do I choose mine? Is their behavior goal-directed, or are they simply acting out predestined roles? Can they consciously alter their behavior to meet goals—if in fact they have them? I have goals; there seems to me to be a conscious "director" in me who points me toward them and toward ways of achieving them. Where does this consciousness come from, and what, exactly, is it? Can ants devise new ways of approaching their tasks, or indeed, conceive entirely new ones? Humanly, I can. If I so decide, I can write a book no one has written before. I can be "creative." Well! We will get nowhere if we stand around watching ants and musing. Let us see where our musings take us.

Philosophy and Artificial Intelligence

Chapter 9 purported to treat the relation of philosophy to the other fields of cognitive science, but the reader will have noticed that one of these fields was left out. I have saved the section that treats the relation of philosophy and artificial intelligence for this last chapter. I have done so because AI in recent years, with methods different from those of earlier researchers, brings us back full circle.

Throughout this book we have asked questions about how we humans tick, and we have examined perspectives of some of those seeking answers. Among the accomplishments of researchers into the workings of brain and cognition are those of psychologists. Some have tried to define intelligence and to measure it, and some have discovered a good deal about the locations in the brain involved in such cognitive functions as storing and accessing information and solving problems. Neuroscientists have related many behaviors to functioning or malfunctioning of the brain. They have gleaned much from examining after death the brains of individuals who in life exhibited those behaviors. The development of new imaging techniques has enabled them to examine the functioning of brains of living people engaged in cognitive activities. Linguists' contributions to explaining our unique language behavior have provided another pathway to understanding the human brain and are connected in important ways to all the other fields involved in cognitive science.

The last domain we examined was that of AI. It is time now to consider a few of the many difficult questions at the interface of AI and philosophy. We have reviewed major steps in the attempt to build intelligence into machines. These attempts have approached the subject from the point of view that there is a central "director" in effect driving the machine we are attempting to model—that wonderful brain that seems to us to be the location of the self and of consciousness. We have conjectured that if we can only put into the machine enough elements of the abilities that resemble our own we will have created an intelligent machine. Both earlier and more recent philosophers have, through introspection and analysis of intellectual activities, conceived of intelligence in terms of thought and reason. They have been working within a set of conventions that prescribe the ways of handling the inputs to thought and reasoning, such as the representation of knowledge, and also the outputs—behaviors, such as planning and problem solving, that are expected from thought and reasoning. But it is possible that these conventions are not adequate to explain large chunks of what contributes to intelligence. (In the 1930s the brain was conceived of as analogous to a telephone switchboard, but that analogy has long since ceased to suffice.) Because much of the important research on thought has necessarily been carried out within the technological constraints imposed by the available computers, we have come to think of these constraints as somehow inevitable (Brooks, 1991). That is, we have been building machines out of nonbiological components, and we have been for the most part thinking about developing intelligence within them, giving little consideration to how the intelligence we are endeavoring to model actually develops in biological beings. There is, however, another way of approaching the enterprise: the "bottom up" approach mentioned in Chapter 8, in which elements of *behavior* are the name of the game, and the game is played with very small pieces.

Microrobots

Like me, Rodney Brooks of MIT, whose Project Cog we learned of in Chapter 8, watches ants. But he and his coworkers do more than watch: They *build* them. Their Ants are mobile robots, and the reason for building them involves the following considerations. When we try to model intelligence by traditional means, we fail to take advantage of insights yielded by observation of the way in which intelligence has developed in nature. It was pointed out in Chapter 8 that intelligence that occurs naturally in biological species is *embodied*—it is not placed inside a machine by an outside force (as we instill "intelligence" into a computer).

Rather, it develops within an organism in contact with an environment in which it is *situated*. Biological species move about in the world; they do not simply sit still playing chess or solving mathematical problems. In line with the traditional approach, if we wish to design an intelligent machine to serve a real-world purpose (exploration of other planets or cleanup of nuclear waste, for instance), we will equip the machine with many sensors to enable it to perceive its environment. If it is to move from one point to another, it must be able to perceive its path and the obstacles along it (rocky surface, slippery wet spots) and constantly evaluate its next move. Unlike the living organism, a machine with enough sensors to manage this, and which contains a program massive enough to evaluate its next move, turns out to be very slow. It spends what to a human seems an inordinate amount of time reviewing all the information its sensors transmit, and by the time it decides it must stop for an obstacle in its way, it may already have banged into it. Consider the awesome job our own brains accomplish in just moving us around in space!

The newer approach to modeling intelligence focuses on creating in machines the ability to accomplish specific behaviors. A single behavior, such as avoiding obstacles, will not require a large number of sensors and a massive evaluative capacity. We might aim for a machine—a robot (for now we are really talking about mobile machines functioning within a real-world environment)—that is equipped to accomplish a small number of such behaviors. When a particular behavior suits the needs of the moment, it can take precedence over the others. That is one of the ways *we* function. In playing the piano, for instance, I am not required to consider what scent there is in the air. In deciding to reach for a blanket I am responding to the temperature in the room, and I don't need to be looking at the clock or noticing any other particular aspect of my environment. So instead of equipping our robot with a single massive processor, we can use a number of small processors, each of which takes precedence when called for. Thus the mobile robot Ants.

The Concept of Emergence and the Location of Intelligence

Before I say any more about these microrobot Ants, there is an important aspect of intelligence we must consider. An issue on the table now, a hot topic at the beginning of the 21st century, is the notion of **emergence**. If we seek the "location" of intelligence in an intelligent being—human organism, nonhuman organism, or machine—it is not enough simply to cite the brain or the program. For if we look inside the brain (even with today's methods of imaging a living, functioning brain) or if we examine the steps in the program, we will not "see" intelligence. It is not "in" any of the component parts of the brain, nor is it "in" any of the sequences of operations in the program. The notion many philosophers and AI researchers are proposing is that intelligence emerges as the components of the system, natural or artificial, interact with each other. "Intelligence can only be determined by the total behavior of the system and how that behavior appears in relation to the environment. The key idea from emergence is: *Intelligence is in the eye of the observer*" (Brooks, 1991, p. 16).

FIGURE 10.1 Microrobot Ant

With this in mind, let us pick up the threads of the microrobot Ants. Brooks (1991) points out that intelligence arose over the course of evolution by what he terms a "generate and test strategy" (p. 23). It is not the result of planned incorporation of specific properties, such as representation or problem-solving ability, as in the traditional method of AI. The microrobot Ants in this project are far simpler than Cog, but like Cog they are embodied and they "live" in an environment in the lab. In fact, they constitute a small colony, on the model of the much larger one outside my front door. Though small for robots, they are huge compared to my ants: Each is 1.4" long by 1.4" wide by 1.2" high (not including their whiskers!). Each weighs a little over an ounce. They are battery powered, and each has four infrared receivers, four light sensors, two bump sensors, five food sensors, one tilt sensor, two mandible (jaw) position sensors, and one battery voltage sensor. They can communicate with each other by means of infrared emitters, one on the front and one on the top. They have a quarter-inch wheel radius and are capable of traveling up to 6 inches per second (Figure 10.1).

Subsumption Architecture   The software that enables these Ants to function is designed on a different principle from that of traditional programs used in machines modeling aspects of intelligence. Operating on the principle described earlier, every one of these Ants is equipped with a number of little programs, each of which involves a specific behavior that oversees certain of the robot's sensors. When readings come in from the sensors of a particular behavior program, the program sends a command to the appropriate motors. The distinguishing characteristic of this manner of programming is that the commands are based on a hierarchy in which the commands of those behaviors designated as more important override, or subsume, those designated as less important. This style of programming is thus called **subsumption architecture**. We might consider our own "architecture" to be of this type. Because we cannot function well when there is too much going on, instead of having to be aware of everything at once we are endowed with the capacity for *selective attention*. But though we can decide to focus on a particular aspect of the environment, we can easily be deflected from it by the fact that, in humans, attention focuses automatically on certain high-priority stimuli. Flashy, changing stimuli, for instance, coopt our attention (Farber & Churchland, 1995). (There is an important advantage in this: Although we may find it annoying to be distracted by a siren when we are trying to concentrate, it is to our advantage to shift our attention to an important event such as impending danger.)

With regard to the subsumption architecture of robots, there are, of course, programs of varying complexity. A simple one, Move To Light, has only three behaviors: move-forward, move-to-light, and move-from-bumps. A slightly edited version of the explanation offered on the Internet is as follows:

> Move-forward is always active; it simply makes the robot move forward. Move-to-light is more important than move-forward. When this behavior detects light in one of the robot's light sensors, it heads in that direction, overriding, or subsuming, the output of move-forward. The move-from-bumps behavior is the most important. It checks the bump sensors and backs the robot away from any obstacles it runs into. When this behavior is active, it overrides the lower two. (Brooks, 1999b)

Now, what happens when the tasks are not as simple as that? A hierarchy of several behaviors can be included in the design of the robot, and each such group, or "mood," will be called on as the situation requires. "With all these behaviors behaving and moods mooding, you can get some pretty interesting actions from very simple software. With a little practice, you can even get the robots to do what you want them to!" (Brooks, 1999b). Readers who would like to see some of the activity these microrobots engage in, such as an Ant following light and Ants clustering around food, will find video clips at the Internet site http://www.ai.mit.edu/projects/ants/photo-album.html.

So far all of this sounds like fun. But it has a serious purpose, and there are certain specific goals to be met, beyond that of integrating all the sensors and actuators into a micro-sized robot. Taking their inspiration from natural ant colonies like mine, the researchers involved in this project are initiating social behavior among the robots. Because the individuals can communicate with each other, a structured robotic ant community, one that can engage in social behavior, can form from the interactions among the individual Ants. Such behavior in ants in nature derives, for example, from the need to seek food sources. Anyone who has ever watched them in action has seen long lines of individuals on their way to and from such sources. Somehow a food-finding ant must communicate with the others; somehow even the last one in line must receive a signal that impels it to follow the others to the food source.

So it is with the microrobots. An individual who detects "food" emits an infra-red signal to that effect, and those in the vicinity detect the signal and travel toward the "finder" Ant. As they do so, they emit an infrared "I see an Ant with food" signal. An Ant that receives this signal travels toward the sender, emitting a signal that indicates "I see an Ant that sees an Ant with food," and so on. The sequence continues until all the Ants have clustered around the "food." Other types of social behavior these Ants engage in involve games—or what are considered games when *we* play them, such as Follow the Leader and Tag (http://www.ai.mit.edu/projects/ants/social-behavior.html).

By building in the ability to sense, emit, and respond by appropriate movements to signals, researchers elicit specific behaviors (such as "move to a signal," "move away from bumps") from individual microrobots. From such simple elements social behavior arises that, when observed in the natural world, is considered intelligent. This has been a relatively simple illustration of the bottom-up strategy of implementing machine intelligence—"artificial" intelligence. But even a modest example such as this introduces a profound question: What is the difference, if indeed there is a difference, between this sort of intelligence and "natural" intelligence? Is there a difference, in principle, between this sort of intelligence and *ours*?

The intelligence exhibited by the Ant microrobots is, like ours, situated in a real, not a virtual, environment. The diminutive vehicles must deal with a solid surface underneath them, and there are solid obstacles (walls, each other) that they must avoid bumping into. The intelligence that enables them to do so is, like ours, embodied. They are honest-to-goodness little beings, though not made from living tissue. Expanding their capabilities to a much larger scale is easily imaginable. Indeed, some such expansion has already been accomplished in projects such as Cog, in which a larger, humanoid robot is being developed on similar principles. If their intelligence eventually approaches, or even rivals, ours, how will we characterize the difference between them and us?

This is not an easy question, to be answered merely by reference to the materials of which we are respectively composed. We are accustomed to considering ourselves unique, "masters of all we survey." Yet we have had to give up our self-satisfied view that Earth, our home, is the center of the universe. We have had to confront our close link to other species in the animal kingdom: the emotions, behaviors, and the (in some cases startlingly large) amount of genetic material we share with them. But we have always had recourse to the pride and pleasure of knowing ourselves smarter than anything else we have ever encountered. Now that we are engaged in creating machines that increasingly demonstrate capacities similar to ours, what will serve to distinguish us among the entities of our world? Is the stuff we are made of, which is different from the stuff out of which we create *them,* enough to ensure our position at the top? Or even to ensure that we are distinct in any meaningful way from our intelligent creations?

How much importance we ascribe to the way it all turns out is an individual matter. One person may feel very strongly that it matters a lot to be "special" as a species; another may not care a bit. And some may be most interested simply in straightening it all out—knowing what or how to think about the issue, whichever way it goes. Our intelligence may in fact be unique, or, as an emergent property of the architecture and functioning of our brains, it may be a property that could just as well emerge from another sort of architecture and functioning. Armed with the grounding provided by the earlier chapters of this book, let us consider some of the big questions bearing on the nature of our intelligence—the nature of our*selves*—from a philosophical perspective. Let us first briefly consider the notion that as "reason" has been held to distinguish us from other animals, so it is emotion that distinguishes us from "intelligent" machines.

"Robot Intelligence": Project Kismet

Observing the interactions of parent and infant, we notice that each seems to cue the other. A baby responds emotionally to a stimulus provided by its mother: a facial expression, a song, or the waving of a toy in front of its face. The response may be pleasure or fear or perhaps simply boredom. Whatever it is, it is communicated by an expression on the baby's own face: a smile, a widening of the eyes, perhaps a turned-down mouth followed by a wail. The baby's reaction in turn produces a response on the part of the mother, who modifies her behavior to increase the baby's pleasure or to soothe its distress. Motivated by each other's expressions, mother and baby begin to develop a relationship in which the baby learns to both read and send cues that lead to emotional satisfaction.

To test whether humans really are readily distinguishable from machines by virtue of the emotional capacity of the former, which the latter has thus far lacked, we might begin by trying to design a robot that signals emotions we can recognize. Taking our cue from the way such behavior begins in humans—the model of mother and baby—we might try to develop a relationship between a robot and its "mother" in which the "mother" sends signals and the robot responds to them by facial expressions familiar to us. This project requires that we somehow establish in the robot a motivational system that will lead it to produce expressions appropriate to emotions elicited by the "mother," or the caretaker. An attempt of this sort is currently under way in Rodney Brooks's lab at MIT. Kismet, the robot depicted in Figure 10.2, has been designed specifically to interact socially with humans.

The expressions illustrated here, which have been made possible by the way the robot is constructed and programmed, are neither as varied nor as subtle as those humans produce. They are, however, modeled on human expressions and are easy for humans to read and to understand. When confronted by its caretaker, who waves a small stuffed animal in front of its "face," Kismet reacts first with "interest" and then with "happiness." If the waving is too intense, Kismet becomes overstimulated and indicates its "mood" by progressing from an expression of "disgust" to one of "anger." But Kismet's "behavior engine framework" is yet more complex. The total system consists of

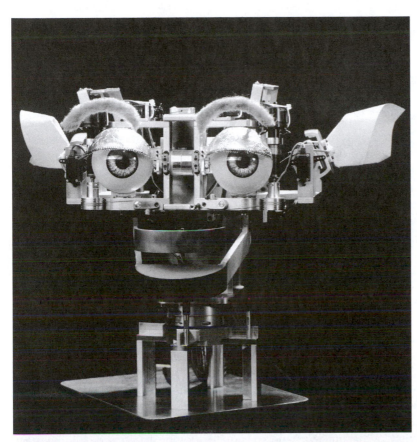

FIGURE 10.2 Photographs Illustrating Kismet's Expressions of "Happiness," "Interest," and "Disgust."

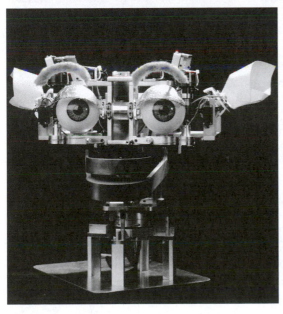

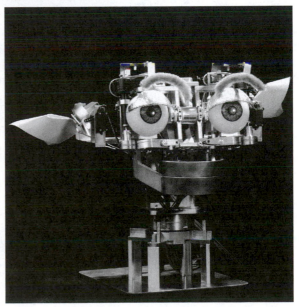

three drives: fatigue, social, stimulation

three consummatory behaviors: sleep, socialize, play

two visually-based percepts: "face," "non-face"

five emotions: anger, disgust, fear, happiness, sadness

two expressive states: tiredness and interest, and their corresponding facial expressions. (Breazeal, 1999)

As the illustrations indicate, Kismet would hardly be mistaken by a person (or by a person's pet dog or cat, for that matter) for a real human being. Its features are more reminiscent of ET than of anything else. And of course it stops at the "neck." But humanoid robot projects such as Cog will ultimately arrive at encompassing the whole of the human form, so it is possible to look toward a robot that models both the physical abilities and the emotional responses of human beings. Researchers involved in these projects already find it easy to react to the robot as to a human, to think of it in human terms, as a "he" rather than an "it." If in the process of expanding the capabilities the design is rendered more humanlike, with a "skin" covering (made of materials already available, by the way), the robot will resemble us enough to make it even easier to fall into a pattern of interacting with it as if it were not just human*oid* but really human.

When machines seem to be responding to stimuli we provide, we do tend to respond to them in this way. In her 1984 book *The Second Self: Computers and the Human Spirit,* Sherry Turkle describes young children interacting in this way with Merlin, an early computer game. Robert and Craig are playing with Merlin, which has a certain amount of unpredictability built in. Because of this unpredictability, which we usually associate with live creatures (that is, in their active behavior; the unpredictability of machine breakdown is quite another story!), the children react to it as if it were alive. "Robert throws Merlin into the sand in anger and frustration. 'Cheater. I hope your brains break'" (Turkle, 1984, p. 29). Along these lines, I myself have felt impelled to give my computer a name, though it looks and acts not at all like my pets and certainly not like my children—nor is it even as "lifelike" as Kismet. When displeased with its "behavior," I speak angrily to it. How easy it would be for me to fall into the habit of regarding and addressing a humanoid machine as if it were human!

Projects such as Cog and Kismet keep us aware of how far we have yet to go to achieve the goal of a humanoid robot that (who?) functions so much like us that we tend to forget it is "only a machine." Nevertheless, these projects indicate that achievement of such a goal is on the horizon. When it is achieved, and when robots include in their interactions with us both a sensing (however achieved) of our moods and appropriate responses to them—what will we have to say about a distinction between them and us? I may assume certain emotions on the part of my fellow humans based on expressions and behavior I have learned to recognize. I have no assurance, however, as Descartes and others have pointed out, that what I think is going on in another's mind is in fact what *is* going on in there. Really, I have no assurance that anything at all is going on in there. When I am interacting with a humanoid robot rather than with a human being, how will that situation differ from this one? Will we still be satisfied to base an "us/them" distinction on the emotions we possess and they lack?

Creativity

Perhaps we can yet save the day by invoking the notion of creativity—a characteristic claimed by humans. We are not limited, the argument goes, to programs that are installed in us by other forces and that constrain our choices and our moves. We are capable of defining a problem and solving it or envisioning a project and carrying it out. We can compose symphonies, or at least songs. We can write sonnets, or at least novel sentences. We can paint masterpieces, or at least pretty pictures. We can reach for and find new explanations for how the world works (the theory of relativity, chaos theory). Can a machine rival these capacities?

I mentioned that we can compose symphonies, or at least songs. In November 1997 an article appeared in *The New York Times* under the headline "Undiscovered Bach? No, a Computer Wrote it" (Johnson, 1997). The article reports on a symposium organized by Douglas Hofstadter and held at Stanford University early in November 1997. The subject of the symposium was an "artificial composer" called Experiments in Musical Intelligence, or EMI, whose programmer is David Cope, Professor of Music at the University of California, Santa Cruz. EMI is capable of composing works in the style of human composers of recognized musical genius: Bach, Beethoven, Mozart, for example. Some of these compositions were performed at the symposium, and "Casual listeners could easily mistake many of the pieces for the real thing" (Johnson, 1997, p. F2). EMI, explained Professor Cope (1996), uses patterns that indicate a particular composer's style and mixes such "signatures" to create new music that people recognize as being in the style of that composer.

> This program thus parallels what I believe takes place at some level in composers' minds, whether consciously or subconsciously. The genius of great composers, I believe, lies not in inventing previously unimagined music but in their ability to effectively reorder and refine what already exists. (p. 1)

Cope (1996) holds that the quality of music depends on its proportions matching those we consider "artistically genuine." How those proportions are created—whether by human or by machine—is irrelevant.

Many definitions of creativity have been offered over the years, within many different conceptual frameworks. A major trend is the position that has been called "combination theory," which involves "coming up with something novel, something different . . . *a novel combination of familiar ideas*" (Boden, 1994, p. 1; italics mine). It will be well to keep in mind the word *involves,* because as we shall see, it has been argued that creativity involves more than just the combining of familiar elements.

This theory is of course not limited to musical compositions. It has application in many realms, one of which is seeing connections—analogies. Analogies are novel combinations of familiar ideas in which "the structural similarity between the two ideas is especially important" (Boden, 1994, p. 1). The reader has surely experienced the sort of analogy included in standardized tests. Baby: human :: puppy : ? is a simple example of the kind used in tests to evaluate a student's capacity for analogical thinking. Naturally, an important instance of creativity will require a more complex exercise of the analogical process. The elements involved in the association may be far more abstract than the relation between newborns and the species to which they belong.

The reader will recall Winograd's SHRDLU, a program examined in Chapter 8, in which the issue being addressed was natural language. Because this is potentially a very big topic, the programmers reduced complexity by limiting the "world" of the program. SHRDLU operates in a very small and constrained "blocks world," in which instructions and responses are limited to a virtual robot endowed only with a hand and an eye and the ability to manipulate toy blocks on a table. In like manner, another restricted domain, or "microdomain," was devised to test the ability of a machine to engage in an analogical process. The program, designed by Douglas Hofstadter and his group, is called Copycat, and its domain is alphabetical letter-strings. Copycat has been asked to discover analogies in a psychologically realistic way, involving the emergence of what in humans would be insightful behavior "as a statistical consequence of myriad small computational actions."

A simple example of the sort of analogy with which Copycat has been challenged is the following, drawn from Hofstadter et al. (1995): "Suppose the letter-string **abc** were changed to **abd**; how would you change the letter-string **ijk** in *'the same way'*?" (p. 206, italics mine). The thought process we might follow here is that because **d** is the next letter in the alphabet after **c** we should take the next letter in the alphabet after **k** to solve the problem, giving us **ijl**. But we might also notice that it is not as simple as that, because we could, after all, interpret "in the same way" a number of different ways:

> change **ijk** to **ijd** (because we changed **c** to **d**);
>
> leave **ijk** as **ijk** (because we have changed only the letter **c** and there is no **c** in this string);
>
> change **ijk** to **abd** (because this is the exact result in the first case).

What seemed like a simple problem at first now looks more slippery, or "fluid." If we complicate the analogy a bit, as follows, the "fluidity factor" becomes much greater. If, for instance, the letter-string **aabc** were changed to **aabd**, how would we change the letter-string **ijkk** in "the same way"?

Noticing that the last element in this string is doubled, we may wonder whether it should be treated as before, yielding **ijkl**, or whether the two **k**s should be treated as a unit, leading us to change both and yielding **ijll**. If we do the latter, we have in a sense allowed the concept of *letter* to slip, "under pressure, into the related concept group of letters" (Hofstadter et al., 1995, pp. 205–206). Here, Copycat is engaging in what some have characterized as an essential component of creativity: ambiguity.

> It is necessary to tolerate *ambiguity* in representations. Thus programs should, under appropriate circumstances, allow the generation of seemingly incorrect associations in order to build connections between concepts. In other words, it should be possible to relax constraints on concepts to enable the activation of more disparate ideas. (Rowe & Partridge, 1993, p. 45)

If novel connections are to be made, a creative person or a creative program must be allowed to range over possibilities that seem at the outset to bear little or no relation to one another.

Without going into detail about how Copycat works, I will mention just a bit about its architecture. This consists of three major components: the Slipnet, the Workspace, and the Coderack. The Slipnet is the site of a network of permanent, interrelated concepts (such as *opposite* and *successor*), rather like a long-term memory. The Workspace is where perceptual activity, and hence the instances of the Slipnet's concepts, are located, combined into temporary perceptual structures such as letters and groups—rather like a short-term memory. The Coderack is a kind of lineup of tasks to be done in a specific order by small, simple agents called *codelets.* The order is random, not predetermined, in order to enable just the sort of ranging over the possibilities predetermined to relate to one another (Hofstadter et al., 1995).

When a task is begun in Copycat, the Workspace consists of unconnected raw data representing the situation the program faces.

> Over time, throughout the actions of many small agents [codelets] "scouting" for features of various sorts . . . items in the Workspace gradually acquire various *descriptions,* and are linked together by various *perceptual structures,* all of which are built entirely from concepts in the Slipnet. (Hofstadter et al., 1995, p. 217)

The Slipnet is used as a guide by means of which useless combinations are avoided and useful ones encouraged. It allows for ambiguity, indicating which concepts may slip into others (Rowe & Partridge, 1993).

The Copycat project is one of several that indicate that at least some aspects of human creativity are already being demonstrated by machines. Another approach to creativity has been taken in which concepts are not recalled whole but rather are reconstructed in appropriate situations—but partial memories continue to exist so that they can continue to be used in other combinations. This process allows for flexibility, because one situation will be similar to, but not the same as, an earlier situation. In this case, the similar portions can be called upon and only the different aspects will need to be filled in. The mechanism that implements this program called GENESIS is termed an "emergent memory mechanism," and it too works with different kinds of agents. Some of these construct representations, and others group the successful agents together to constitute new agents (Rowe & Partridge, 1993).

Like intelligence, creativity is here viewed in terms of emergence, or as an emergent property, and as such has been implemented in machines. Very important among the requirements for a program that is creative is *making its own decisions,* rather than simply carrying out a set of decisions made for it by humans

(Hofstadter et al., 1995). (This, by the way, is a condition clearly related to the question of free will, touched on in Chapter 9.) In a sense, emergentism enables this criterion to be satisfied, because the result of the operations of such a program is not determined by decisions humans have programmed in. But even so, even if we have designed programs that will enable a machine to demonstrate "creativity," we are left still wondering what it is that enables someone or some machine to arrive at newly combined ideas (Boden, 1990). Do EMI's ability to compose a new musical work, and Copycat's ability to produce analogies, mean these programs are "creative"? Many don't think so. The *surprising* quality of new creations is still not explained. "Original ideas are surprising, yes. But what is crucial is the sort of surprise—indeed, the shock—involved . . . genuinely creative ideas are surprising" in that we recognize that "the world has turned out differently not just from the way we thought it *would,* but even from the way we though it *could*" (Boden, 1990, pp. 30–31). An idea, musical, analogical, or otherwise, may well be novel and surprising. But is it novel and surprising simply because it has never occurred before in history, or is it so because there is a sustained (emergent, perhaps) creative capacity characterizing the individual who produced it? Regarded as the latter, the essence of creativity remains a mystery.

Like so many of the knotty problems contemplated by humans, this one, too, depends on where one draws the line. Progress has been made in endowing the machine with what some, at least, consider to be real creative ability. If the machine is capable of this, then one more mark of human uniqueness may have been erased. If this is so, and in light of recent accomplishments in building into machines social behavior, emotional behavior, language behavior (endowing them with at least the rudiments of qualities we thought were unique to animal species, even uniquely human), what is left to us? There is yet, perhaps, a last bastion, a truly real distinction between human and machine: the kind of consciousness that, it seems, distinguishes us from all other entities on earth.

Consciousness Revisited

All right, here at last is the area we can surely delineate as ours, the characteristic we intuitively feel to be a—if not *the*—crucial factor that marks us as different from all else within our purview. Now all we have to do is define it and show that it truly belongs only to us, and we're home free. We will have saved our unique position among the entities of the earth.

Let us begin, then. Consciousness is—consciousness is—well, it's knowing what's going on in and around us, isn't it? It is "the subjective, inner life of the mind" (Chalmers, 1995a, p. 80). When we sleep, we are unconscious. When we have been hit hard on the head, we are unconscious. Otherwise, we are conscious. Right? Well, maybe. But what about when we are asleep and dreaming—yet somehow aware that our dream is in fact a dream? What about when we answer questions under hypnosis? What about those who report after having been under anesthesia or in a comatose state, when everyone around was convinced by every noticeable sign that they were unconscious, that they yet heard—and now remember—what was going on in the room?

What about split-brain patients, whose consciousness seems in some sense divided, each half of the brain knowing only half the picture? What about dissociative identity disorder? What can we say when an individual—someone occupying a body—exhibits behavior when one personality is "out" that can be engaged in only when conscious (carrying on a conversation, driving a car), yet the behavior is unknown to another personality occupying the same body? Or even in an ordinary, nonpathological situation, what about you, the reader, engrossed in a good book (this one, dare I hope?), awake, aware of the actions or ideas being recounted or explored in the book you are reading, nevertheless oblivious to the voice calling you to your chores? What about me, driving the car in the incident I described in the preface, noticing the "Civic" on the car in front of me and nothing else—not the road I traversed, not the traffic, not the lights I must have stopped for—until I arrived home and realized I didn't remember anything about the trip itself?

If it is so difficult to put our finger on what consciousness is, how can we determine first of all whether it is unique to us and, even more puzzling, how it comes about? But being human, we are not about to throw up our hands in despair. I will never know for certain whether that gorilla in the zoo was truly having the thoughts I surmised from the expression in his eyes. I do know, however, that this elusive phenomenon called consciousness is something I will not give up trying to understand. And I am clearly not alone in this. A quick visit to the Internet turns up hundreds of online papers on the subject, 508 on consciousness and related topics at one site alone as of this writing, most by academic philosophers or scientists. The directory has been compiled by David Chalmers, a philosopher at the University of California, Santa Cruz, who indicates as well several other sources of online papers and bibliographies of about 2000 offline papers. (Interested readers will find the directory at http://ling.ucsc.edu/~chalmers/mind.html.) A small sampling of the areas covered includes 18 papers on the *concept* of consciousness, 10 papers on the *function* of consciousness, 20 on consciousness and neuroscience, and 24 on consciousness and physics.

Conferences on issues concerning consciousness abound as well: The third Tucson conference on "Toward a Science of Consciousness" in the spring of 1998 explored, among other areas, the evolution and function of consciousness, the neural correlates of consciousness, and sleep and dreaming. In the spring of 2000, the conference included the relationship between consciousness and volition, neurobiological models of consciousness, and consciousness at the millennium: Where are we now, and where are we going? The third annual conference of the Association for the Scientific Study of Consciousness in June of 1999, at the University of Western Ontario, had as its theme "Consciousness and Self: Neural, Cognitive, and Philosophical Issues." Journals have also sprung up in the 1990s dedicated to the study of consciousness, among them: *Consciousness and Cognition: An International Journal,* and *Journal of Consciousness Studies: Controversies in Science and the Humanities.*

Scholars from diverse disciplines have published their explorations and explanations of the puzzle of consciousness in books that attract readers from a considerably wider public than one might suppose. Some titles the reader may recognize are William Calvin's *The Cerebral Symphony: Seashore Reflections on the Structure of Consciousness* (1990); Gerald Edelman's *Bright Air, Brilliant Fire: On the Matter of the Mind* (1992); Daniel Dennett's *Consciousness Explained* (1991) and his more recent *Kinds of Minds: Toward an Understanding of Consciousness* (1996); Roger Penrose's *Shadows of the Mind* (1994); Francis Crick's *The Astonishing Hypothesis: The Scientific Search for the Soul* (1994); and Lawrence Weiskrantz's *Consciousness Lost and Found* (1997).

The Easy Problem—and the Hard One

If so many are so involved in pursuing solutions to the problem of consciousness, why has it not yet been solved? Can it perhaps not be solved? "What are the specific issues that comprise *the* problem of consciousness? (Is there really a *the* problem of consciousness?) And are we facing a phenomenon the understanding of which lies forever beyond our intellectual capacities?" (Güzeldere, 1997, p. 1). Opinions vary, but a large number of cognitive scientists, neuroscientists, philosophers, and researchers in the other related fields hold to the belief and expectation that although there is a "hard" problem we may yet find a theoretical framework within which to figure it out. But first we must distinguish this "hard" problem from all the other issues involved in thinking about consciousness. Chalmers (1995b) identifies several "easy" problems, which seem in principle to be ultimately explainable scientifically, by the computational or neural mechanisms provided by cognitive science. These include abilities we have examined earlier, such as the ability to categorize, and other phenomena, such as the difference between the sleeping and the waking states and the fact that we can report our mental states. Many of these kinds of abilities may be characterized as aspects of awareness, "the process by which information in the brain is made globally available to motor processes such as speech and bodily action" (Chalmers, 1995a, p. 84). Although it may take us a long time to solve these "easy" problems, at least we have an idea of how to go about doing so.

In a 1974 paper titled "What Is It Like to Be a Bat?" Thomas Nagel pointed out the difficulty of trying to know what it is like to be something we are not. How can we know what a bat experiences as it travels, by means of **echolocation** (using hearing to perceive obstacles in its path, as we use sight)?

According to Nagel (1994), "the fact that an organism has conscious experience *at all* means, basically, that there is something it is like to *be* that organism. . . . Fundamentally an organism has conscious mental states if and only if there is something that it is like to *be* that organism—something it is like *for* the organism. . . . We may call this the subjective character of experience" (p. 436).

This is the really difficult problem with regard to consciousness. We do not know how to relate the awareness we have of both the world outside us and our own inner states, an awareness that is potentially scientifically explainable, to the *felt* experience of, say, purple, or a fog horn, or the scent of lilacs on a mild spring day, or the chill up and down our spines during a horror movie, or the way our toes feel when stepped on. We can discover the mechanisms by which we perform functions such as categorizing or sleeping. But

> even when we have explained the performance of all the cognitive and behavioral functions in the vicinity of experience—perceptual discrimination, categorization, internal access, verbal report—there may still remain a further unanswered question: *Why is the performance of these functions accompanied by experience?* . . . Why doesn't all this information-processing go on "in the dark," free of any inner feel? Why is it that when electromagnetic waveforms impinge on a retina and are discriminated and categorized by a visual system, this discrimination and categorization is experienced as a sensation of vivid red? (Chalmers, 1995b, in Shear, 1995, pp. 12–13)

Over the years there have been a number of different approaches to the problem of consciousness. Although those who ponder and write about it frame questions and thoughts in different ways, one may discern a few major categories into which their approaches fall. Some emphasize, for example, the mysteriousness of it all and propose that as long as we look for answers grounded in the material (the body) consciousness is likely to remain a mystery. For answers we must turn to some immaterial explanation, such as Descartes's thinking entity, which is all we can really know (because we cannot know if anything material is real), or an appeal to the divine (an explanation based in religion). But these leave us still with the old difficulty of relating the immaterial to the material: the soul to the body, or the mind to the brain.

Another tack one might take is to be skeptical about the very concept of consciousness and whether a scientific or philosophical investigation of consciousness is warranted. Maybe, in fact, there *is* no such thing. Maybe it will turn out that the explanation for what we have thought of as consciousness is a notion, like the **phlogiston** explanation of combustion, that will be abandoned once we know more.

The "naturalist" approach is one taken by many today who think that consciousness is not only real but that it is a perfectly natural phenomenon that, given time, increased knowledge, and an appropriate framework, we will ultimately understand.

> The "mystery" of consciousness today is in roughly the same shape that the mystery of life was before the development of molecular biology. . . . It seems mysterious because we do not know how the system of neurophysiology/consciousness works, and an adequate knowledge of how it works would remove the mystery. (Searle, 1992, p. 102)

(The discussion of consciousness is based on Güzeldere, 1997, pp. 3–6.)

Consciousness as an Emergent Property

If we follow this last path, we may avail ourselves of the techniques provided—or potentially provided—by neuroscience and search for the neural correlates of consciousness on the assumption that if we discover what our neurons are doing when we are conscious, we will solve the problem. And so we may. But there is something we must keep in mind. In our quest to understand the nature of intelligence we discovered that intelligence is not something we can see if we look inside the brain, nor have we captured its essence by reporting and studying what we know or feel. We may "explain" emotions in terms of chemicals and cognitive functions in terms of neural development and activity in certain brain areas. But because intelligence is not a "thing" to be found somewhere, it is more fruitfully regarded as an emergent quality arising from the parallel functioning of complex systems. This may be true of creativity as well. And systems need not be constructed like our own for intelligent or creative behavior to emerge. Consciousness can be considered in this light as well: an emergent property arising out of the enormously complex functioning of the human brain.

How Might a Machine Become Conscious?

If a machine can be intelligent, given sufficient complexity, might it not also arrive at being conscious? In an essay titled "The Practical Requirements for Making a Conscious Robot" (1998), Daniel Dennett considers the issue. He presents several arguments on the subject of whether a robot could, in principle, ever be conscious. Among them he discusses the position some would take that because robots are strictly material and consciousness requires "immaterial mind-stuff" (p. 154) robot consciousness is in principle impossible. This is the dualism we examined earlier, largely abandoned by modern science. Dennett points out that, over the course of scientific investigation, all the phenomena at first invested with a supernatural or mysterious aura, from magnetism to reproduction, have been shown by science to be perfectly natural. Why should consciousness turn out to be different?

Another argument against the possibility of robot consciousness is that consciousness can exist only in an organic brain—and robots are by definition not organic. Dennett's response to this is twofold. One aspect of it is his recognition that we may indeed never arrive at a conscious inorganic machine, but not because it is impossible in principle. Rather, there may be engineering factors that would cause an inorganic robot brain to be too clumsy or poorly coordinated to perform tasks necessary for consciousness. The other aspect of his response is addressed to the feasibility, in principle, of creating consciousness in a robot: "As biochemistry has shown in matchless detail, the powers of organic compounds are themselves all mechanistically reducible and hence mechanistically reproducible at one scale or another in alternative physical media" (Dennett, 1998, p. 155). We have already accomplished by inorganic means much that had been strictly the domain of the organic. Why, then, not consciousness?

A further claim that robots can never be conscious rests on their simplicity. We humans are enormously complex, composed as we are

> of trillions of parts (if we descend to the level of the macromolecules). . . . We consist of billions of cells, and a single human cell contains within itself complex "machinery" that is still well beyond the artifactual powers of engineers. (Dennett, 1998, p. 158)

To create a robot—a machine—as complex as this is certainly out of the question, now and for the foreseeable future. But, Dennett points out, perhaps that degree of complexity isn't necessary. We already construct artificial heart valves that work very well despite the fact that they are much simpler than the original organic ones. Artificial ears and eyes are in the offing. Because of their relative simplicity, their efficacy will not be nearly as impressive as that of the real thing. But such prosthetic devices will serve to replace at least some of the lost functions. Following these developments, why could there not *in principle* be a brain whose parts are artificial, a brain much simpler than organic ones, whose functioning would be relatively crude, yet which develops consciousness?

That I have used the word "develop" is not an accident. It is precisely what *humans* do during their earliest months and years. Humans are characterized by a very extended period of infancy and childhood. It takes time for them to amass the knowledge relevant to "just living," knowledge that includes not only the physical facts of the world but also the social factors involved in growing up human. Cog, the embodied and situated humanoid robot discussed earlier, has not been planned as an "adult" who arrives on the scene fully developed, cognitively or any other way. On the contrary, Cog is "being designed to pass through an extended period of artificial infancy, during which it will have to learn from experience, experience it will gain in the rough-and-tumble environment of the real world" (Dennett, 1998, p. 161). The motivation for this is that

> by confronting and solving *actual, real time* problems of self-protection, hand-eye coordination, and interaction with other animate beings, Cog's artificers will discover the *sufficient* conditions for higher cognitive functions in general—and maybe even for a variety of consciousnesses that would satisfy the skeptics. (Dennett, 1998, pp. 165–166)

If a robot such as Cog can learn to manage its environment and react in an appropriate manner to other beings in its environment, and if, in the process, it develops higher cognitive functions, there is yet a question we may wish to ask: Does such a machine *understand* its environment and the actions it produces in response to that environment? We will need to define "understand," of course, and for that let's turn to a well-known discussion presented in 1980 by the philosopher John Searle. This is usually referred to as the "Chinese room argument."

The argument was constructed to refute the claim of so-called strong AI that "the appropriately programmed computer really *is* a mind, in the sense that computers given the right programs can be literally said to *understand* and have cognitive states and that the programs thereby explain human cognition" (Searle, 1980, p. 509). Programs such as Weizenbaum's ELIZA, Winograd's SHRDLU, and the inference-making programs of Schank and his group (see Chapter 8) seemed able to pass the Turing test, because, based on their results, human observers could not necessarily distinguish them from humans. Searle argued that these results in no way indicate that the computers producing them understand, in the sense that a person understands, what they are doing. To clarify what it means to understand, Searle suggested a little thought experiment. We are to imagine a man locked in a room full of boxes of Chinese symbols and a set of instructions for manipulating these symbols. The boxes of symbols are in effect a database, and the instructions are analogous to a program. People outside the room send the man additional Chinese symbols, which are actually questions in Chinese. These represent the input. The man then follows the instructions for manipulating the symbols and gives the results (the output) to the people outside. These results are the correct answers to the questions.

Here's the catch: the man speaks only English. *He knows no Chinese!* As far as the people outside are concerned, he has answered correctly the questions they have posed, so in effect he passes the Turing test—but he doesn't understand a word of what he's done. He has answered the questions based only on a set of instructions, which really correspond to the syntax of a language, the rules for arranging words into sentences of that language. He has no grasp of the semantics—the meaning, the mental content.

Searle draws an analogy between this man and a computer, and points out that what the computer is doing to "fool" people is *simulating* mental capacities. But simulating the original is not duplicating it, and the fact that the Turing test can't tell the difference does not mean there isn't one. The machine that performs as the man in the room does is not thinking (Searle, 1980).

Will it be possible to conclude eventually that a robot such as Cog, on the other hand, *is* thinking? Will Cog's cogitations remain only simulations? Or will it be possible to say that Cog truly *understands*? Cog will not, after all, be merely manipulating symbols that are not "grounded" in the world, because anything in him that "might be a candidate for symbolhood will automatically be grounded in Cog's real predicament, as surely as its counterpart in any child" (Dennett, 1998, pp. 168–169).

One further point can be made bearing on the possibility of Cog's becoming conscious. We have looked at the so-called hard problem and easy problems involved in the attempt to explain consciousness. The latter include our ability to categorize and the fact that we can report our mental states. These may be characterized as aspects of awareness, "the process by which information in the brain is made globally available to motor processes such as speech and bodily action" (Chalmers, 1995a, p. 84). If, as may happen, Cog and his ilk arrive at this capacity for awareness, even reporting their own states, what then will we say, with regard to them, about consciousness? Will their perceptions and awareness be characterized by *experience,* the explanation of which is the hard problem? Our attempts to create machine intelligence stem largely from our wish to learn about our own intelligence. Perhaps, if it should happen that from the interaction of very complex systems in robots consciousness emerges, we will also come to understand our own. Or perhaps this is truly a problem we shall never solve.

Questions to Think About

1. If in some distant time robots were capable of learning and self-direction much as humans are, would you wish to room with one in college? What sorts of issues would you likely consider in deciding?

2. Do you think that any of the age-old questions about consciousness will ever be satisfactorily answered? Why or why not?

3. What would be necessary to design a robot that can laugh—but only at funny things?

4. Choose any hour of any day you wish and record all the decisions you make about which actions you gave priority over others. Could your actions have been anticipated by a subsumption architecture model of *human* behavior? Why or why not?

5. With respect to question 4, did particular senses or behaviors dictate your decisions? How much of your behavior do you think is governed in this way?

6. Could you fall in love with a robot that expresses affection for you? Would it matter if the robot *felt* affection? Why or why not?

7. As far as you're concerned, does it make a difference whether a piece of music is written by a computer rather than by a person? Why or why not?

8. If you were required to take an analogies test as a prerequisite for graduate school, would you have some wish to hand the job over to Copycat? Why or why not?

Glossary

Agent An entity that perceives and acts.

Agnosia A deficit in the ability to recognize a specific category, such as animals or tools.

Agrammatic aphasia An inability to produce grammatical sentences, characterized by the loss of grammatical elements such as those indicating person or tense.

Algorithm A set of precise instructions for solving a problem or attaining a goal (e.g., a formula or a recipe).

Alzheimer's disease A progressive degenerative disease in which brain cells are destroyed, leading to loss of memory, loss of other functions, and ultimately death.

Ambiguous sentence A sentence whose words or structure offer more than one possible interpretation.

American Sign Language (ASL) A linguistic system of hand signals and gestures, used by much of the deaf population of North America.

Amnesia Loss of memory.

Analytical Engine An early computer, invented by Charles Babbage, that was to be a general-purpose programmable computing machine able to add, subtract, multiply, and divide.

Anatomy The branch of biology dealing with the structure of the body.

Angiography A method of imaging the human brain by injecting a dye that is detectable by X ray.

Animat An artificial simulated or embodied animal.

Aphasia Partial or total loss of language caused by injury to certain areas of the brain.

A priori knowledge See *innate knowledge*.

Arbitrariness of the sign An expression referring to the fact that the sounds of which words are constructed bear no logical or necessary relation to the meaning of the words.

Argument One of the concepts in a proposition that stands in relation to the other concepts in the proposition.

Article A word indicating the specificity or non-specificity of a noun (expressed in English by *the* and *a*, which are placed before the noun).

Articulation The way in which the vocal organs produce a sound (e.g., by closing the lips and pushing air out of the nose while vibrating the vocal cords, as in the sound *m*).

Articulatory features The characteristics of speech sounds (e.g., voiced vs. unvoiced, aspirated vs. unaspirated).

Aspiration The puff of air accompanying certain speech sounds (e.g., the first *p* in *paper*).

Associative learning The strengthening of connections, whether in the brain or in a computer model, through the repeated linking of concepts or nodes, as when one experience or event repeatedly occurs simultaneously with or immediately after another.

Autism A syndrome characterized by, among other behaviors, repetitive movements (e.g., head banging), abnormal sensory responses (e.g., intolerance of being touched), and an inability to understand and relate to others.

Axial tomography A method of imaging the body using a rotating X-ray beam, which exposes the body to much less radiation than do traditional X rays.

Axon A portion of a neuron consisting of a single long fiber terminating in the branching structures (end feet) that form the "sending part" of synapses.

Back propagation A two-stage process in the functioning of a neural network. During the first stage, activation goes forward from the input layer to the output layer. In the second stage, error signals are sent back through the network.

Basal ganglia Masses of gray matter embedded in the white matter of the brain, associated with the control of movement.

Behaviorism A school of thought operating on the principle that the only appropriate subject matter of psychology is behavior, because that is all that can be objectively measured. Mental activity not directly observable or measurable is therefore not an appropriate or useful subject of research.

Bilingual A person who speaks two languages with native fluency.

Bipolar disorder A condition in which a manic state, characterized by, for example, excessive excitability and activity, alternates with depression.

Bottom-up approach The approach (to modeling intelligence) in which the starting point of processing is sensory stimuli rather than a master design, or higher level knowledge (see *top-down approach*).

Brain mapping The endeavor to achieve, by means of a variety of techniques, a representation of the components of the surface of the human brain and the structures beneath it, as well as an understanding of the functions performed by these components.

Brain plasticity The ability of areas of the brain to perform functions for which they would

not ordinarily have been used, as, for example, when the areas usually employed for those functions have been damaged.

Broca's aphasia A type of language deficit, caused by damage to Broca's area, in which patients omit grammatical elements of sentences and demonstrate difficulty in expressing themselves in speech.

Broca's area A portion of the left frontal hemisphere of the brain that is crucially involved in the ability to produce spoken language.

Carotid artery A major artery located in the neck that carries blood to the brain. There is one on each side of the neck.

Categorization The organization of concepts into classes. It is this capacity that enables us to make sense of a world that would otherwise consist for us of a mass of unrelated perceptions.

Caudate A portion of the basal ganglia of the brain.

Cell assembly A set of neurons that, having frequently been involved in a given action, are activated as a unit.

Cerebrospinal fluid A clear liquid that surrounds the brain and the spinal cord and fills the cavities in the brain (see *ventricles*).

Cerebrum The upper part of the brain, consisting of the left and right hemispheres.

Chronograph An instrument for recording short durations and rapid changes.

Chunks (chunking) Grouping discrete items so that they are learned and recalled as a unit (e.g., the prefix *1-800,* which precedes toll-free telephone numbers).

Cognition The mental processes engaged in by the human brain, including perception, learning, memory, problem solving, thinking, and imagining.

Computer axial tomography (CAT) A procedure in which computer technology is used to reconstruct and sharpen a complete image from multiple views provided by a rotating X-ray beam.

Concept One's notion or idea of what an entity, concrete or abstract, *is.*

Concordance A frequency count of all the words and, in some cases, phrases and sentence constructions in a given text along with their exact locations within the text.

Conductance The probability that a link in a neural network will conduct a signal.

Contralateral Pertaining to the "opposite side" and referring to the fact that activity of each side of the body is largely governed by the cerebral hemisphere on the other side of the brain (as in the situation of paralysis on the left side of the body accompanying damage to the right cerebral hemisphere).

Corpus callosum A thick bundle of fibers connecting the two hemispheres of the human brain, by means of which information is transferred from one hemisphere to the other.

Cortex The outer layer of gray matter of the brain, within which most of the higher functions of cognition are carried out.

Cortical functions Activities of the outer layer of the brain's gray matter.

Counterfactual A statement presenting a situation that is not so and (in English) indicating recognition of that fact by means of an if-then construction employing the subjunctive form of the verb (e.g., *If* I *were* you, [then] I would go to Paris).

Craniometry An early approach to understanding the nature of intelligence, involving the measurement of cranial capacity on the (mistaken) assumption that the larger the brain, the more intelligent the individual.

Craniotomy A procedure in which the scalp and skull are opened surgically in order to reach the brain.

Critical period The period during which a cognitive behavior is normally acquired. If the environmental stimulus (e.g., birdsong for birds, language for humans) is missing during this period, the behavior may never be acquired.

Cyclotron An accelerator for protons or other positively charged ions.

Declarative (factual) knowledge The kind of knowledge embodied in concepts and propositions. For example, "George Washington was the first president of the United States."

Declarative memory Memory to which one has direct access and of which one can be consciously aware.

Dendrite A portion of a neuron that extends like a thin ribbon from the cell body. Its ends form the "receiving parts" of synapses.

Descriptive linguistics The study of language involving description of actually occurring patterns and processes.

Descriptive rules Those rules occurring naturally and spontaneously in language and described by linguists, as opposed to *prescriptive rules,* which are formulated and taught by grammarians and teachers.

Developmental psycholinguistics The branch of linguistics concerned with the development of and changes in mental processes and actions as people use language.

DNA Deoxyribonucleic acid, the component of chromosomes that contains the genetic instructions.

Dualism The philosophical idea that the mind and body are two distinct entities.

Dyslexia A condition in which language development is impaired to some degree, most noticeably in the ability to read.

Echoic memory Transient auditory memory in which perceived sounds remain in memory briefly.

Echolocation A process of perceiving obstacles in one's path by means of hearing (employed, for example, by bats).

Elaboration The process by which new information is linked to associations already in the long-term memory store.

Electrode A device for applying electric current to, for example, specific sites on the surface of the scalp or within the brain.

Electroencephalogram (EEG) A recording of electrical activity in the brain. (See *electroencephalography.*)

Electroencephalography The process of recording as line tracings on paper patterns of electrical activity in the brain, by means of electrodes attached to the scalp.

Electrophysiology The study of the electrical aspects of a bodily function.

Emergent property, or **emergence** A property of a system that is realized (emerges) through the interaction of the component parts of the system.

Empirical Based on experiment and observation rather than on theory or deduction.

Empiricism The school of thought that holds that we derive all knowledge from our senses and our reflection on the sensations they yield.

Episodic memory A non-word-based aspect of declarative memory that stores occurrences of events or experiences (as opposed to facts).

Epistemology The study of the nature, origin, and limits of knowledge.

Event-related potential (ERP) The voltage changes, recorded during an EEG during a specified period of time, that are specifically related to the brain's response to a stimulus presented during that period.

Exemplars Within a particular model of categorization, the instances of an experience, such as "dog," that, taken together, constitute an individual's category *dog*.

Explicit memory Memory one is aware of as one retrieves it (see *implicit memory*).

Feature detectors Neurons that respond to specific features of the environment.

Features Characteristics of a category that are both necessary and sufficient for membership in that category.

Feral Wild, untamed.

Finite-state machine A computing machine that, by means of a finite number of symbols, instructions, and states of memory, performs a sequence of steps to achieve its results. It is at any moment during its functioning in one of a finite set of states in which part of the computation has been performed and the results stored.

First-language acquisition The learning of one's first language(s), beginning in infancy.

First-language attrition The loss of an individual's native language.

Fluent aphasia See *Wernicke's aphasia*.

Fluoroscope A machine making use of X rays to register on a fluorescent screen the image of a portion of the body.

Frame An invariant background situation stored as a complex whole, leaving only the details of a specific instance to be filled in.

Frontal lobe The largest of the four lobes of the cerebrum, situated under the frontal bone, or forehead. It plays an important role in planning and decision making.

Frontal sulcus A groove between the frontal lobes of the brain resulting from the folding of the cortex.

Functional magnetic resonance imaging (fMRI) A technique used to image the brain, in which MRI scanners detect the changes occurring in the magnetic state of the blood, which depend on the amount of oxygen in the blood flowing to activated tissues of the brain.

g The label for *general intelligence;* the idea that intelligence has a single major component.

Game tree A branching structure depicting all the possible moves in a game and their consequences.

Generative transformational grammar A grammar developed by Noam Chomsky, based on the notion that language is generative, or creative, allowing speakers to understand and produce sentences they have never heard. In this account, phrase structure rules generate the deep structures of sentences; transformational rules convert these to the surface structures that are actually uttered.

Grammar The set of rules pertaining to every component of a language that are internalized by the speaker of the language; also the linguist's account of those rules.

Grammatical relations The relations among the grammatical elements in a sentence, such as the constant relation between the subject and the object regardless of whether the sentence is expressed in an active or passive form.

Grimm's law The sound shifts, noted by Jacob Grimm, that explain the historical relationship between certain Latin and Germanic consonants, for example, Latin *p* (as in *pater*) and English *f* (as in *father*).

Gyrus The convex portion of a convolution of the cerebral cortex.

Hallucinations The perceptions of, for example, sounds, images, and scents that are not in fact present.

Hemorrhage Heavy bleeding, as from a ruptured blood vessel.

Heuristic A "rule of thumb" used in reaching a goal, as opposed to the more definitive *algorithm*.

Hippocampus A region in the temporal lobe that has been associated with memory.

Humanoid Resembling a human; in the form of a human.

Iconic memory The brief persistence of a visual impression.

Idiots savants Individuals who demonstrate less than normal intelligence but are nevertheless endowed with far more than is usual of a *particular* ability.

Implicit memory Memory retrieved without conscious awareness (see *explicit memory*).

Indo-European A language or group of languages spoken some thousands of years ago, from which many of the languages extant today derive (e.g., English, French, and Russian).

Inflectional suffix A suffix that adds information to a word without changing its meaning or its grammatical category (e.g., the plural -*s* and the past tense -*ed*).

Innate knowledge Knowledge one is (assumed to have been) born with.

Insight The grasping of the inner nature of a phenomenon, or the solution to a problem, by an intuitive process rather than, for example, by application of rules.

Introspection The practice of looking inside of one's own experience, of attending to and becoming conscious of one's own mental states.

IQ Intelligence quotient, determined by dividing mental age (as determined by a set of tests of mental function) by chronological age and multiplying by 100.

Language acquisition device A hypothetical cognitive faculty by means of which one acquires one's first language(s).

Langue The linguistic system internalized by speakers of a language (as suggested by Ferdinand de Saussure), as opposed to *parole,* the act of speaking.

Least noticeable difference The smallest amount of change in sensory perception that an individual is capable of noticing.

Lesion An injury or damage to an organ or a tissue of the body.

Lexical retrieval The finding of words from one's lexicon; the vocabulary stored in one's memory.

Linguistic competence The ability to use one's language; what one knows about the rules and the usage of one's language even without being aware of knowing it.

Linguistic determinism See *Sapir-Whorf hypothesis.*

Linguistic performance What one actually says, as opposed to one's linguistic competence.

Linguistic relativity See *Sapir-Whorf hypothesis.*

Link In the human brain, a synapse between neurons that readily transmits nerve impulses as a result of repeated experience; in a propositional or semantic network (whether relevant to human cognition or to artificial intelligence), a line relating concepts or nodes.

LISP A high-level computer programming language.

Localization of function The notion that different cognitive functions of the human brain reside in particular locations in the brain.

Logical positivist school The school of thought concerned with the issue of the nature of truth that holds to the verification principle that there are two kinds of cognitively meaningful statements. The first are those that are true by virtue of their being empirically verifiable (true in the world), and the second kind includes those that are true by virtue of being linguistically verifiable (true because of the meanings of the words).

Longitudinal studies Studies carried out over an extended period of time on a particular subject or group of subjects.

Long-term memory The component of our memory system that retains material for a long time.

Magnetic resonance imaging (MRI) An imaging technique that applies radio-wave pulses to protons in the body that have been aligned by means of a magnetic field and that emit detectable radio signals.

Materialism A school of thought holding that the world of matter, including human beings, is composed of tiny indivisible parts, and that the form of each material object depends on the attributes of these parts—their size, shape, location, and so forth—and on their lawful behavior.

Mental imagery Images not currently visible to the eye but present to the mind's eye.

Mental rotation A process of imagining the rotation of imagined objects (objects in the mind's eye) as if one were physically rotating actual objects.

Metacomponents The executive processes used to plan, monitor, and evaluate problem solving.

Metaphysics Originally a branch of philosophy seeking to explain the nature of reality, of knowledge, of the universe; more recently, speculative philosophy in general.

Mnemonic device A device to aid in remembering facts, such as the word "HOMES" to remind one of the names of the Great Lakes.

Modal memory model A model of the memory system in which the permanent, structural features of the system are distinguished from the modifiable control processes, and in which a number of different structural components are hypothesized (see *multistore model*).

Monolingual A person who speaks only one language.

Morphology The study of the rules governing word structure.

Multistore model A model of the memory system in which several components are hypothesized, for example, the sensory store, the short-term store, and the long-term store.

Narcosis A condition of deep unconsciousness, often caused by narcotics.

Natural categories Those cognitive categories arising from real-life experience.

Nature–nurture question The question involving the relative importance of heredity and environment in the development of the individual and his or her behavior.

Neural network (neural net) A system designed to make use of connections to produce in a machine something of the kind of dynamical memory involved in human learning (parallel distributed processing).

Neuroendocrine Having to do with the relation between the endocrine system and the brain.

Neuroimaging The constructing of images of the brain by various techniques (see, e.g., *computer axial tomography, magnetic resonance imaging*).

Neuron A cell that makes up part of the nervous system; a component of a nerve.

Neurosurgeon A physician whose field of expertise is the brain.

Node In a propositional or semantic network, the representation of a concept.

Nonfluent aphasia See *Broca's aphasia.*

Nonfunctional degeneration A system's process of forgetting of learned material through disuse.

NP Noun phrase: the portion(s) of a sentence containing a noun.

Occipital lobe The posterior area of the brain in which the visual capacity is located.

Onomatopoeia The creation of a word such that it sounds like what it means (e.g., *clang, meow*).

Parallel processing See *neural network.*

Parole The act of speaking, as opposed to the linguistic system internalized by speakers of a language (see *langue*).

Parser A computer program that assigns grammatical categories (parts of speech) to the words in a sentence and groups them into phrases.

Perception Interpretation or understanding of sensory experiences.

Perceptron A hypothetical nervous system realized as a neural net.

Perceptual Having to do with perception.

Performatives Statements that perform what they state (e.g., "I resign.").

Phlogiston An imagined substance invoked to explain combustion, which was thought to occur as a result of the loss of the substance to the atmosphere.

Phoneme A sound of a language that makes a difference in the meaning of words in that language (e.g., the *s* and the *b* of *sand* and *band*).

Phonology The study of the sound systems of language.

Phrenology A 19th-century system of attributing character traits to an individual based on the relative prominence of regions on the surface of his or her skull.

Physiology The branch of biology dealing with essential life processes and functions.

Plural marker The indication on a noun that it refers to more than one (in English, generally the suffix *-s*).

Polyglot One who speaks many languages.

Positron emission tomography (PET) An imaging technique that uses radioactive isotopes (positrons) to measure cerebral blood flow while a subject is carrying out certain cognitive tasks.

Preposition A word occurring in a sentence before a noun, ordinarily locating the action of the sentence in space or time (e.g., *under* the house, *before* noon).

Prescriptive rules Rules imposed on a language and on its speakers by grammarians, teachers, and so on, as opposed to descriptive rules.

Presuppositions Statements in which a state of affairs is presumed to obtain. In the sentence "Evan didn't want any more potatoes," there is a presupposition that Evan had already had some potatoes.

Priming An effect of the activation of nodes and links associated with a particular concept or proposition. The priming effect is produced when a proposition relatively unrelated to the initial one is activated through the association of nodes and links. Thus access to a more distant concept will be faster if an associated concept has already been activated—and the closer the relation between the two, the faster the access.

Principles and parameters The approach taken by Chomsky and others to factor out general principles that hold for all languages and that govern application of the rules of languages. The finite set of ways in which the principles apply, triggered by the language to which the learner is exposed, are called parameters.

Procedural knowledge The kind of knowledge required for tasks performed so often that they become automatic.

Procedural memory The various forms of unconscious memory expressed in performance rather than by recollection (e.g., memory for how to ride a bicycle).

Prolog A high-level computer programming language.

Proposition A thought that is in some sense complete (e.g., "That is a fire hydrant.").

Propositional representations Thoughts stored, largely unconsciously, as propositions in some language-like form, translatable into actual language when required.

Propositional (semantic) network A network of associated propositional representations.

Proprioception The (partly unconscious) perceived sensations of one's balance, one's movements and position in space, the force exerted by one's muscles, and the position and location of one's limbs.

Prosopagnosia The loss of ability to categorize or recognize faces.

Prototype A version of an entity that one might think of as the "average" of the type, that is, a representation formed of average values for the features characterizing the entity (e.g., the "typical" bird, the "typical" house).

Psychometrician A researcher who devises and studies methods for measuring intelligence.

Psychometrics The theory and practice of measurement of psychological variables such as intelligence.

Psychophysical parallelism The position, espoused by Leibniz, that the mind and the body do not interact but, rather, function in parallel.

Radioactive isotopes Atoms emitting radiation.

Rationalist school A school of thought, a major proponent of which was René Descartes, taking the position that all knowledge is acquired through reasoning and certain basic innate concepts and elementary logical propositions.

Receptive field A region comprising the receptor cells that function together via a single neuron in transmitting sensation to the central nervous system.

Recursion The property of a system that permits the embedding of an element of the system within itself (e.g., in computer programs, a loop).

Reductionism The position that all objects and events can be reduced to the lawful behavior of the elements of which they are constructed.

Reference What a word refers to, or denotes, as opposed to the meaning of the word. For example, the word *Joe* has no particular meaning; it merely refers to a person of that name (see *sense*).

Rehearsing The repetition, either aloud or to oneself, of an item one wishes to remember temporarily; rehearsing keeps the item in short-term memory as long as it is continued.

RNA Ribonucleic acid, an essential component of all cells, which functions in combination with DNA (see *DNA*).

Rube Goldberg contraption An extremely complex machine consisting of commonplace items organized in a very imaginative and surprising fashion in order to accomplish an absurdly simple task. Rube Goldberg was a cartoonist who drew such devices in the 1940s and 1950s.

Sapir-Whorf hypothesis The hypothesis that our language determines the way we think (linguistic determinism) and that the distinctions found in a given language will not be the same as those in any other language (linguistic relativity).

Schizophrenia A very severe mental disorder characterized by such symptoms as thought disorders, hallucinations, delusions, and difficulty in relating to others.

Schoty A Russian version of the abacus.

Scripts Sequences of frames stored as a unit (see *frame*).

Second-language acquisition The learning of another language after a first language has already been acquired.

Second-language attrition The loss of a language acquired subsequent to one's native language.

Semantic memory The complex structure, or network, in long-term memory that includes such components as concepts and words, enabling us to understand ideas, solve problems, and use language.

Semantics The area of language and language study that pertains to the meaning of words and sentences.

Sense In the context of words, the meaning of a particular word, as opposed to the entity it denotes (see *reference*).

Sense receptors Specialized nerve cells that respond to sensory stimuli leading to the propagation of nerve impulses.

Sensory discrimination The ability to distinguish between differing intensities or other qualities of similar stimuli.

Sensory store, or **register** Within the multistore model of memory, the structural component of the system where incoming sensory information remains only very briefly before "decaying" and being completely lost.

Short-term (working) memory store The structural component of the memory system where the work of the current moment is carried out.

SHRDLU An early program in artificial intelligence intended to model natural language processing.

Single photon emission computed tomography (SPECT) A technique for imaging body structures that relies on radioactive entities (photons) introduced into the bloodstream, whose emissions are sensed by detectors and whose patterns are then reconstructed by computers.

Soma The main body of a nerve cell.

Spatial relations The manner in which entities in space are perceived to relate to one another and to the perceiver, the sense of which enables an individual to maneuver in the world and to adjust and readjust perceptions in order to do so efficiently.

Speech acts See *performatives*.

Stream of consciousness A process in which one thought or perception leads to another, which in turn stimulates a third, and so on.

Subordinate semantic category A category that falls within another (e.g., *chair,* a category containing high chair, desk chair, easy chair, etc., falls within—is subordinate to—the category *furniture*).

Subsumption architecture The type of programming in artificial intelligence (and, in a sense, in human intelligence) in which commands to act are carried out based on a hierarchy according to which those behaviors designated as more important override, or subsume, those designated as less important.

Sulcus The "valley," or concave region, between one gyrus and another in a convolution of the cerebral cortex.

Superordinate semantic category A category that subsumes another (e.g., *animal* is superordinate to cat, dog, lemming).

Synapse A link from one neuron to another.

Syntax The rules for the arrangement of words into sentences.

Temporal lobe One of the major lobes in each cerebral hemisphere, located along the temples and containing the auditory projection area (the area involved in the receiving of information provided by the sense of hearing).

Thalamus A structure in the forebrain, under the cortex, that is the principal gateway for most sensory input, serving an integrative function.

Theory of spreading activation The theory advanced to explain the rapid associations we make between and among the nodes that represent concepts. It holds that during the thought process, activation from a given node spreads out in every direction in the network, lessening at weaker links and strengthening at stronger ones. This activation continues as long as the node is in use, with many associated nodes becoming activated and continuing their simultaneous activation in parallel fashion.

Threshold The point at which we become aware of a thought or a sensation.

Top-down approach The approach to modeling intelligence in which the starting point of processing is a master design, or higher level knowledge, rather than sensory stimuli (see *bottom-up approach*).

Truth value The truth or falsity of a proposition.

Turing machine Alan Turing's hypothetical machine with an infinite tape from which it reads or to which it writes. The machine is at any given time in a particular state and is able, on reading a symbol on the tape, to determine successive changes in its state. Such a machine would, by means of algorithms, be able to perform any computational process that can be performed.

Turing test Devised by Alan Turing, the Turing test is a game in which an interrogator asks questions of both a human being and a programmed computer simulating a human being, to determine whether the computer is adequately simulating the human mind. If the interrogator cannot tell from their answers the difference between them, the simulation is deemed successful.

Unipolar disorder A condition characterized by either a persistent manic state or a persistent state of depression (see *bipolar disorder*).

Universal grammar A hypothesized fundamental structure shared by all human natural languages that specifies the forms that are possible for the grammar of any human natural language, thereby accounting for the range of linguistic variation they exhibit.

Universal machine A machine that carries out any program it is equipped to read. The main principles and future applications of the universal machine were formulated by Alan Turing. In effect, the combination of a modern-day computer and the programs it can read constitutes a universal machine.

Ventricles Four relatively large spaces in the brain, generally filled with cerebrospinal fluid, serving to protect the brain and the spinal cord.

Visual field The area visible to an individual while his or her eyes are not moving.

VP Verb phrase: the portion of a sentence that contains the verb.

Waveform A wavelike image yielded by changes in energy and viewable by means of tech-nologically sophisticated equipment such as the EEG.

Wernicke's aphasia A language deficit, caused by damage to Wernicke's area, in which flu-ency of speech is retained but comprehension is disturbed.

Wernicke's area A portion of the brain, typically in the left temporal lobe, that is crucially involved in the ability to comprehend spoken language.

X ray Electromagnetic radiation that penetrates the body and is absorbed to different degrees by different anatomical structures within it. The unabsorbed radiation passes through the body and registers on a photographic plate, providing an image of the internal structures.

References

Agre, P. E. (1985). Robotics and common sense. In M. Minsky (Ed.), *Robotics* (pp. 71–97). Garden City, NY: Anchor Press/Doubleday.

Ahn, W-K., & Medin, D. L. (1992). A two-stage model of category construction. *Cognitive Science, 16,* 81–121.

Atkinson, R. C., & Shiffrin, R. M. (1968). Human memory: A proposed system. In K. W. Spence & J. T. Spence (Eds.), *The psychology of learning and motivation: Advances in research and theory,* (Vol. 2, pp. 89–195). New York: Academic Press.

Babbage, C. (1864). *Passages from the life of a philosopher.* London: Longman, Green. (Reprinted 1968 by Dawsons of Pall Mall, London)

Baddeley, A. (1986). *Working memory.* Oxford, England: Clarendon Press.

Baddeley, A. (1992). Working memory. *Science, 255,* 556–559.

Banks, C. A., & Turner, J. R. (1991). *Mozart: Prodigy of nature.* New York: Pierpont Morgan Library.

Baron-Cohen, S. (1995). *Mindblindness: An essay on autism and theory of mind.* Cambridge: MIT Press.

Baron-Cohen, S., Jolliffe, T., Mortimore, C., & Robertson, M. (1997). Another advanced test of theory of mind: Evidence from very high functioning adults with autism or Asperger Syndrome. *Journal of Child Psychology and Psychiatry and Allied Disciplines, 38*(7), 813–822.

Barrow, H. (1996). Connectionism and neural networks. In M. A. Boden (Ed.), *Artificial intelligence* (pp. 135–155). San Diego, CA: Academic Press.

Barsalou, L. W. (1992). *Cognitive psychology: An overview for cognitive scientists.* Hillsdale, NJ: Erlbaum.

Bartholow, R. (1874). Experimental investigation into the functions of the human brain. *American Journal of Medical Sciences, 67,* 305–313.

Bavelier, D., Corina, D., Jezzard, P., Clark, V., Karni, A., Lalwani, A., Rauschecker, J. P., Braun, A., Turner, R., & Neville, H. J. (1998). Hemispheric specialization for English and ASL: Left invariance–right variability. *Neuroreport, 9*(7), 1537–1542.

Bechtel, W., Abrahamsen, A., & Graham, G. (1998). The life of cognitive science. In W. Bechtel & G. Graham (Eds.), *A companion to cognitive science* (pp. 1–104). Malden, MA: Blackwell.

Beonio-Brocchieri Fumigalli, M. T. (1970). *The logic of Abelard.* Dordrecht, Holland: D. Reidel.

Berkeley, G. (1939). Introduction to *The Principles of Human Knowledge.* In E. A. Burtt (Ed.), *The English philosophers from Bacon to Mill* (pp. 507–579). New York: Random House, the Modern Library. (Original work published 1710)

Berko, J. (1958). The child's learning of English morphology. *Word, 14,* 150–177.

Berlin, B., & Kay, P. (1991). *Basic color terms: Their universality and evolution.* Berkeley: University of California Press.

Berton, L. (1997, August 15). The front lines: A young, blind whiz on computers makes a name in industry. *The Wall Street Journal,* p. B1.

Bever, T. G. (1970). The cognitive basis for linguistic structures. In J. R. Hayes (Ed.), *Cognition and the development of language* (pp. 279–362). New York: Wiley.

Binet, A., & Henri, V. (1895). La psychologie individuelle. *L'Année psychologique, 2,* 411–465.

Birnbaum, M. H., & Thomann, K. (1996). Visual function in multiple personality disorder. *Journal of the American Optometry Association, 67*(6), 327–334.

Blackburn. S. W. (1995). History of the philosophy of language. In T. Honderich (Ed.), *The Oxford companion to philosophy* (pp. 454–458). Oxford, England: Oxford University Press.

Bloom, A. (1981). *The linguistic shaping of thought: A study in the impact of language on thinking in China and the West.* Hillsdale, NJ: Erlbaum.

Boden, M. (1990). *The creative mind: Myths and mechanisms.* New York: Basic Books.

Boden, M. (1994). Agents and creativity. In D. Riecken (Ed.), *Communications of the association for computing machinery,* Special Issue on Agents [On-line]. Available: http://www.ozemail.com/~caveman/Creative/Authors/mbagents.htm

Bower, G. H., Black, J. B., & Turner, T. J. (1979). Scripts in memory for text. *Cognitive Psychology, 11,* 177–220.

Breazeal, C. (1999). *Kismet: A robot for social interactions with humans* [On-line]. Accessed 5/1/99. Available: http://www.ai.mit.edu/projects/kismet/kismet.html

Britton, J. L. (Ed.). (1992). *Collected works of A. M. Turing: Pure mathematics.* Amsterdam: North Holland.

Brooks, R. A. (1991). *Intelligence without reason* [On-line]. Massachusetts Institute of Technology Artificial Intelligence Laboratory, AI Memo No. 1293. (Prepared for *Computers and Thought,* IJCAQI-91.) Accessed 4/24/99. Available: http://www.ai.mit.edu/projects/ants/tech-specs.html

Brooks, R. A. (1999a). *The Ants: A community of microrobots* [On-line]. Accessed 4/25/99. Available: http://www.ai.mit.edu/projects/ants/

Brooks, R. A. (1999b). *The Ants: A community of microrobots* [On-line]. Accessed 4/25/99. Available: http://www.ai.mit.edu/projects/ants/antware.html

Brooks, R. A., Breazeal (Ferrell), C., Irie, R., Kemp, C. C., Marjanovi, M., Scassellati, B., & Williamson, M. M. (1998). Alternative essences of intelligence. *American Association for Artificial Intelligence* [On-line]. Accessed 2/9/99. Available: www.aaai.org

Buchanan, B. G., & Shortliffe, E. H. (Eds.). (1985). *Rule-based expert systems: The MYCIN experiments of the Stanford heuristic programming project.* Reading, MA: Addison-Wesley.

Buchanan, B. G., Sutherland, G. L., & Feigenbaum, E. A. (1969). Heuristic DENDRAL: A program for generating explanatory hypotheses in organic chemistry. In B. Meltzer, D. Michie, & M. Swann (Eds.), *Machine intelligence* (pp. 209–254). Edinburgh, Scotland: Edinburgh University Press.

Calvin, W. (1990). *The cerebral symphony: Seashore reflections on the structure of consciousness.* New York: Bantam Books.

Carnegie, D. (1936). *How to win friends and influence people.* New York: Simon and Schuster.

Carroll, J. B. (1956). *Language, thought, and reality: Selected writings of Benjamin Lee Whorf.* Cambridge: MIT Press.

Cattell, J. McK. (1890). Mental tests and measurements. *Mind, 15,* 373–380.

Caudill, M., & Butler, C. (1990). *Naturally intelligent systems.* Cambridge: MIT Press.

Chalmers, D. J. (1995a, December). The puzzle of conscious experience. *Scientific American, 273*(5), 80–86.

Chalmers, D. J. (1995b). Facing up to the problem of consciousness. In J. Shear, (Ed.), *Explaining consciousness: The hard problem* (pp. 9–30). Cambridge, MA: MIT Press.

Cheney, P. D. (1996). Electrophysiological methods for mapping brain motor and sensory circuits. In A. W. Toga & J. C. Mazziotta (Eds.), *Brain mapping: The methods* (pp. 277–309). San Diego, CA: Academic Press.

Chomsky, N. (1957). *Syntactic structures.* The Hague, The Netherlands: Mouton.

Chomsky, N. (1964). A review of B. F. Skinner's *Verbal Behavior.* In J. A. Fodor & J. J. Katz (Eds.), *The structure of language: Readings in the philosophy of language* (pp. 547–578). Englewood Cliffs, NJ: Prentice-Hall.

Chomsky N. (1965). *Aspects of the theory of syntax.* Cambridge: MIT Press.

Chomsky, N. (1995). *The minimalist program.* Cambridge: MIT Press.

Chute, D. L. *MacLaboratory for psychology: Research.* (1994). CD-ROM Version 3.0. Pacific Grove, CA: Brooks/Cole.

Clarke, A. C. (1968). *2001: A space odyssey.* London: Hutchinson/Star.

Cohen, J. D., Perlstein, W. M., Braver, T. S., Nystrom, L. E., Noll, D. C., Jonides, J., & Smith, E. E. (1997, April 10). Temporal dynamics of brain activation during a working memory task. *Nature, 386,* 604–608.

Cole, J. (1995). *Pride and a daily marathon.* Cambridge: MIT Press.

Coles, M. G. H., & Rugg, M. D. (1995). *Electrophysiology of mind: Event-related potentials and cognition.*

Oxford Psychology Series No. 25. Oxford, England: Oxford University Press.

Colley, A., Banton, L., Down, J., & Pither, A. (1992). An expert-novice comparison in musical composition. *Psychology of Music, 20,* 124–137.

Collins, A. M., & Loftus, E. F. (1975). A spreading activation theory of semantic processing. *Psychological Review, 82*(6), 407–428.

Cope, D. (1996). *Experiments in musical intelligence.* Madison, WI: A-R Editions.

Copeland, J. (1993). *Artificial intelligence: A philosophical introduction.* Oxford, England, & Malden, MA: Blackwell.

Courtney, S. M., Petit, L., Maison, J. M., Ungerleider, L. G., & Haxby, J. V. (1998, February 27). An area specialized for spatial working memory in human frontal cortex. *Science, 279,* 1347–1351.

Crevier, D. (1993). *AI: The tumultuous history of the search for artificial intelligence.* New York: Basic Books.

Crick, F. (1994). *The astonishing hypothesis: The scientific search for the soul.* New York: Charles Scribner's Sons.

Cushing, H. (1909). A note upon the faradic stimulation of the postcentral gyrus in conscious patients. *Brain: A Journal of Neurology, 32,* 44–53.

Custers, E. J. F. M., Boshuizen, H. P. A., & Schmidt, H. G. (1996). The influence of medical expertise, case typicality, and illness script component on case processing and disease probability estimates. *Memory and Cognition, 24*(3), 384–399.

Cytowic, R. E. (1993). *The man who tasted shapes.* New York: G. P. Putnam's Sons.

Damasio, A. R. (1994). *Descartes' error: Emotion, reason, and the human brain.* New York: Avon Books.

Damasio, A. R., & Tranel, D. (1993, June). Nouns and verbs are retrieved with differently distributed neural systems. *Proceedings of the National Academy of Sciences, 90,* 4957–4960.

Damasio, H., Grabowski, T. J., Tranel, D., Hichwa, R. D., & Damasio, A. R. (1996, April 11). A neural basis for lexical retrieval. *Nature, 380,* 499–505.

Davis, K. (1947). A final note on a case of extreme isolation. *American Journal of Sociology, 52,* 432–437.

Dean, J. (1998). Animats and what they can tell us. *Trends in Cognitive Science, 2*(2), 60–67.

Deep, S., & Sussman, L. (1996). *Yes, you can: 1200 inspiring ideas for work, home, and happiness.* Reading, MA: Addison-Wesley.

Dehaene, S., van de Moortele, P.-F., Dupoux, E., Lehérici, S., Cohen, L., Perani, D., Mehler, J., & Le

Bihan, D. (1997). Cerebral substrates of bilingualism: A 3-T fMRI study. In A. W. Toga, R. S. J. Frackowiak, & J. C. Mazziotta (Eds.), *NeuroImage: Third international conference on functional mapping of the human brain* (Vol. 5, No. 4, Part 2 of 4 parts, p. 57). San Diego, CA: Academic Press.

Dennett, D. C. (1991). *Consciousness explained.* Boston: Little, Brown.

Dennett, D. C. (1996). *Kinds of minds: Toward an understanding of consciousness.* New York: Basic Books.

Dennett, D. C. (1998). The practical requirements for making a conscious robot. In D. C. Dennett, *Brainchildren: Essays on designing minds* (pp. 154–170). Cambridge: MIT Press.

Descartes, R. (1984). Meditations. In E. S. Haldane & G. R. T. Ross (Trans.), *The philosophical works of Descartes* (Vol. 1, pp. 144–199). Cambridge: Cambridge University Press. (Original work published 1641)

Drevets, W. C., Price, J. L., Simpson, J. R., Jr., Todd, R. D., Reich, T., Vannier, M., & Raichle, M. E. (1997, April 24). Subgenual prefrontal cortex abnormalities in mood disorders. *Nature, 386,* 824–827.

Dreyfus, H. L. (1992). *What computers still can't do: A critique of artificial reason.* Cambridge: MIT Press.

Dubois, P., Graham, S., & Sippola, L. (1995). Early lexical development: The contribution of parental labeling and infants' categorization abilities. *Journal of Child Language, 22*(2), 325–343.

Duda, R. O., & Shortliffe, E. H. (1983). Expert systems research. *Science, 220*(4594), 261–267.

Duncker, K. (1976). On problem solving (L. S. Lees, Trans.). In J. E. Dashiell (Ed.), *Psychological monographs.* Westport, CT: Greenwood Press. (Reprint of the 1945 edition, issued as Vol. 58, No. 5, Whole No. 270 of *Psychological Monographs Series,* Washington, DC: American Psychological Association)

Dyson, G. B. (1997). *Darwin among the machines: The evolution of global intelligence.* Reading, MA: Addison-Wesley.

Eccles, Sir John. (1985). Cerebral activity and the freedom of the will. In Sir John Eccles (Ed.), *Mind and brain: The many-faceted problem* (pp. 159–174). New York: Paragon House.

Edelman, G. (1992). *Bright air, brilliant fire: On the matter of the mind.* New York: Basic Books.

Eichenbaum, H. (1997). Declarative memory: Insights from cognitive neurobiology. *Annual Review of Psychology, 48,* 547–572.

Eimas, P. D. (1975). Speech perception in early infancy. In L. B. Cohen & P. Salapatek (Eds.), *Infant percep-*

tion: From sensation to cognition: Vol. 2. Perception of space, speech, and sound (pp. 193–231). New York: Academic Press.

Eimas, P. D., Quinn, P. C., & Cowan, P. (1994). Development of exclusivity in perceptually based categories of young infants. *Journal of Experimental Child Psychology, 58*(3), 418–431.

Estes, W. K. (1994). *Classification and cognition.* New York: Oxford University Press.

Farah, M. (1990). *Visual agnosia.* Cambridge: MIT Press.

Farber, I. B., & Churchland, P. S. (1995). Consciousness and the neurosciences: Philosophical and theoretical issues. In M. S. Gazzaniga (Editor-in-Chief), *The cognitive neurosciences* (pp. 1295–1306). Cambridge: MIT Press.

Ferrier, D. (1886). *The functions of the brain.* New York: G. P. Putnam's Sons. (Cited in D. Krech, 1963, Cortical localization of function, in L. J. Postman (Ed.), 1962, *Psychology in the making: Histories of selected research problems,* p. 50, New York: Alfred A. Knopf)

Franz, S. I. (1902). On the functions of the cerebrum: The frontal lobes in relation to the production and retention of simple sensory habits. *American Journal of Physiology, 8,* 1–22.

Franz, S. I. (1912). New phrenology. *Science 35,* 321–328.

Franz, S. I. (1923). Conceptions of cerebral functions. *Psychological Review, 30,* 438–446.

Frazier, J. A., Giedd, J. N., Kaysen, D., Albus, K., Hamburger, S., Alaghband-Rad, J., Lenane, M. C., McKenna, K., Greier, A., & Rapoport, J. L. (1996). Childhood-onset schizophrenia: Brain MRI rescan after 2 years of clozapine maintenance treatment. *American Journal of Psychiatry, 153*(4), 564–566.

Fritsch, G., & Hitzig, E. (1968). Über die elektrische Erregbarkeit des Gosshirns. *Archiv für Anatomie, Physiologie, und Wissenschaftliche Medecin,* 308–314. In R. J. Herrnstein & E. G. Boring (Eds.), *A source book in the history of psychology* (D. Cantor, Trans.). Cambridge: Harvard University Press. (Original work published 1870)

Fromkin, V., & Rodman, R. (1993). *An introduction to language* (5th ed.). Austin, TX: Harcourt Brace Jovanovich.

Gabrieli, J. D. E., Brewer, J. B., Desmond, J. E., & Glover, G. H. (1997, April 11). Separate neural bases of two fundamental memory processes in the human medial temporal lobe. *Science, 276,* 264–266.

Galton, F. (1928). *Inquiries into human faculty and its development* (2nd ed.). New York: E. P. Dutton. (Original work published 1883)

Gardner, H. (1983). *Frames of mind: The theory of multiple intelligences.* New York: Basic Books.

Gardner, H. (1998). An interview with Howard Gardner. In R. Durie (Ed.), *Mindshift connection* (p. 2). Tucson, AZ: Zephyr Press.

Gazzaniga, M. S., Ivry, R. B., & Mangun, G. R. (1998). *Cognitive neuroscience: The biology of the mind.* New York: W. W. Norton.

Gevins, A. (1996). Electrophysiological imaging of brain function. In A. W. Toga & J. C. Mazziotta (Eds.), *Brain mapping: The methods* (pp. 259–276). San Diego, CA: Academic Press.

Goldstine, H. H. (1972). *The computer from Pascal to von Neumann.* Princeton, NJ: Princeton University Press.

Goodglass, H. (1993). *Understanding aphasia.* San Diego, CA: Academic Press.

Gould, S. J. (1981). *The mismeasure of man.* New York: W. W. Norton.

Greeno, J. G. (1978). The nature of problem-solving abilities. In W. K. Estes (Ed.), *Handbook of learning and cognitive processes: Vol. 5. Human information processing* (pp. 239–270). New York: Wiley.

Grimson, W. E. L., & Mundy, J. L. (1994). Computer vision applications. *Communications of the ACM, 37*(3), 45–51.

Güzeldere, G. (1997). The many faces of consciousness: A field guide. In N. Block, O. Flanagan, & G. Güzeldere (Eds.), *The nature of consciousness: Philosophical debates* (pp. 1–67). Cambridge: MIT Press.

Haldane, E. S., & Ross, G. R. T. (Trans.). (1984). *The philosophical works of Descartes* (Vol. 1, pp. 144–199). Cambridge: Cambridge University Press.

Hamilton, S., & Garber, L. (1997). Deep Blue's hardware-software synergy. *IEEE, 30*(10), 29–35.

Hebb, D. O. (1949). *Organization of behavior: A neuropsychological theory.* New York: Wiley.

Hebb, D. O. (1959). A neuropsychological theory. In S. Koch (Ed.), *Psychology: A study of a science: Study I. Conceptual and systematic, Vol. 1. Sensory, perceptual, and physiological formulations* (pp. 622–643). New York: McGraw-Hill.

Helm-Estabrooks, N., & Albert, M. L. (1991). *Manual of aphasia therapy.* Austin, TX: ProEd.

Helmholtz, H. von. (1910). *Handbook of physiological optics* (3rd German ed.) J. P. C. Southall (Ed.). (J. P. C. Southall, Trans.). *Optical Society of America,* vol. 3, 1925. (Cited in J. E. Hochberg, 1962, Nativism and empiricism in perception, in L. Postman (Ed.), *Psychology in the making: Histories of selected research problems,* pp. 255–330, New York: Alfred A. Knopf)

Hergenhahn, B. R. (1992). *An introduction to the history of psychology* (2nd ed.). Belmont, CA: Wadsworth.

Herrnstein, R. J., & Boring, E. G. (Eds.). (1968). *A source book in the history of psychology.* Cambridge: Harvard University Press.

Herrnstein, R. J., & Murray, C. (1994). *The bell curve: Intelligence and class structure in American life.* New York: The Free Press.

Hickok, G., Bellugi, U., & Klima, E. (1998). The neural organization of language: Evidence from sign language aphasia. *Trends in cognitive sciences, 2*(4), 129–136.

Hobbes, T. (1656). *Elements of philosophy: The first section, concerning body.* London: Andrew Crooke.

Hofstadter, D., & the Fluid Analogies Research Group. (1995). *Fluid concepts and creative analogies: Computer models of the fundamental mechanisms of thought.* New York: Basic Books.

Hogg, D. C. (1996). Machine vision. In M. A. Boden (Ed.), *Artificial intelligence* (pp. 183–227). San Diego, CA: Academic Press.

Hubel, D. H. (1981). *Autobiography of David H. Hubel* [On-line]. Accessed 3/29/98. Available: http://www.nobel.se/laureates/medicine-981-2-autobio.html

Hughes, J. R., Kuhlman, D. T., Fichtner, C. G., & Gruenfeld, M. J. (1990, October 21). Brain mapping in a case of multiple personality. *Clinical Electroencephalography, 4,* 200–209.

Hyman, R. A. (1982). *Charles Babbage: Pioneer of the computer.* Princeton, NJ: Princeton University Press.

James, W. (1890). *The principles of psychology* (2 vols.). Henry Holt & Company. (Dover reprint, New York, 1980)

James, W. (1985). *Psychology: The briefer course.* Notre Dame, IN: University of Notre Dame Press. (Original work published 1892)

Jensen, A. R. (1999). *Precis of: The g factor: The science of mental ability* [On-line]. Accessed 5/2/00. Available: http://www.cogsci.soton.ac.uk/psyc-bin/newpsy?article=10.023&submit=View+Article

Johnson, G. (1997, November 11). Undiscovered Bach? No, a computer wrote it. *The New York Times,* p. F1.

Johnson, J., & Newport, E. (1989). Critical period effects in second language learning: The influence of maturational state on the acquisition of English as a second language. *Cognitive Psychology, 21,* 60–99.

Johnson-Laird, P. (1988). *The computer and the mind: An introduction to cognitive science.* Cambridge: Harvard University Press.

Jung, R., & Berger, W. (1979). Fiftieth anniversary of Hans Berger's publication of the electroencephalogram. His first records in 1924–1931 (Authors' Trans.). *Archiv für psychiatrie und nervenkrankheiten, 227*(4), 279–300.

Kant, I. (1965). *Critique of pure reason.* (N. K. Smith, Trans.). New York: St. Martin's Press. (Original work published 1781)

Karbowski, K. (1990). Sixty years of clinical electroencephalography. *European Neurology 30*(3), 170–175.

Kosslyn, S. M. (1980). *Image and mind.* Cambridge: Harvard University Press.

Kosslyn, S. M. (1994). *Image and brain.* Cambridge: MIT Press.

Kosslyn, S. M. (1995). Mental imagery. In S. M. Kosslyn & D. Osherson, *An invitation to cognitive science: Vol. 2. Visual cognition* (2nd ed., pp. 267–296). Cambridge: MIT Press.

Kosslyn, S. M., Ball, T. M., & Reiser, B. J. (1978). Visual images preserve metric spatial information: Evidence from studies of image scanning. *Journal of Experimental Psychology: Human Perception and Performance, 4*(1), 47–60.

Krasuski, J., Horwitz, B., & Rumsey, J. M. (1996). A survey of functional and anatomical neuroimaging techniques. In G. R. Lyon & J. M. Rumsey (Eds.), *Neuroimaging: A window to the neurological foundations of learning and behavior in children* (pp. 25–52). Baltimore: Paul H. Brookes.

Krech, D. (1962). Cortical localization of function. In L. Postman (Ed.), *Psychology in the making: Histories of selected research problems.* New York: Alfred A. Knopf.

Kuhl, P. K., Williams, K. A., Lacerda, F., Stevens, K. N., & Lindblom, B. (1992). Linguistic experience alters phonetic perception in infants by 6 months of age. *Science, 255,* 606–608.

Lashley, K. S. (1929). *Brain mechanisms and intelligence.* Chicago: University of Chicago Press.

Lashley, K. S. (1937). Functional determinants of cerebral localization. *Archives of Neurology and Psychiatry, 38,* 371–387.

Leary, W. E. (1998, October 6). Ion propulsion of science fiction comes to life on new spacecraft. *The New York Times,* p. F1.

Lettvin, J. Y., Maturana, H. R., McCulloch, W. S., & Pitts, W. H. (1959). What the frog's eye tells the frog's brain. *Proceedings of the Institute of Radio Engineers, 47,* 1940–1951.

Levinthal, C. F. (1983). *Introduction to physiological psychology* (2nd ed.). New Jersey: Prentice-Hall.

Libet, B. (1989, March/April). Neural destiny: Does the brain have a will of its own? *The Sciences, 29*(2), 32–35.

Lojek-Osiejuk, E. (1996). Knowledge of scripts reflected in discourse of aphasics and right-brain-damaged patients. *Brain and language, 53*(1), 58–80.

Luria, A. R. (1987). *The mind of a mnemonist.* Cambridge: Harvard University Press. (Original work published 1968)

Luria, A. R. (1987). *The man with a shattered world.* Cambridge: Harvard University Press. (Original work published 1972)

Martin, A., Wiggs, C. L., Ungerleider, L. G., & Haxby, J. V. (1996). Neural correlates of category-specific knowledge. *Nature, 379,* 649–652.

Matlin, M. W. (1994). *Cognition* (3rd ed.). Fort Worth, TX: Harcourt Brace.

Mazziotta, J. C. (1996). Time and space. In A. W. Toga & J. C. Mazziotta (Eds.), *Brain mapping: The methods* (pp. 389–406). San Diego, CA: Academic Press.

McClelland, J. L., & Rumelhart, D. E. (1986). On learning the past tenses of English verbs. In D. E. Rumelhart, J. L. McClelland, & the PDP Research Group (Eds.), *Parallel distributed processing: Explorations in the microstructure of cognition: Vol. 2. Psychological and biological models.* Cambridge: MIT Press.

McCulloch, W., & Pitts, W. (1943). A logical calculus of the ideas immanent in nervous activity. *Bulletin of Mathematical Biophysics, 5,* 115–133.

McKeon, R. (Ed.). (1941). *The basic works of Aristotle.* New York: Random House.

McKoon, G., & Ratcliff, R. (1980, August). Priming in item recognition: The organization of propositions in memory for text. *Journal of Verbal Learning and Verbal Behavior, 19*(4), 369–386.

Mellor, J. P. (1995, January 13). Enhanced reality: Visualization in a surgical environment. *AI Technical Report, 1544.*

Melzack, R. (1990). Phantom limbs and the concept of a neuromatrix. *Trends in Neurosciences, 13*(3), 88–92.

Meyer, J.-A. (1996). Artificial life and the animat approach to artificial intelligence. In M. A. Boden (Ed.), *Artificial intelligence* (pp. 325–354). San Diego, CA: Academic Press.

Miller, G. A. (1956). The magic number seven plus or minus two: Some limits on our capacity for processing information. *Psychological Review, 63,* 81–97.

Minsky, M. A. (1975). A framework for representing knowledge. In P. H. Winston (Ed.), *The psychology of computer vision* (pp. 211–280). New York: McGraw-Hill.

Minsky, M., & Papert, S. (1969). *Perceptrons.* Cambridge: MIT Press.

Moray, N. P. (1996). Flying high on AI. *Contemporary psychology, 41*(2), 164–165.

Moyne, J. A. (1985). *Understanding language: Man or machine.* New York: Plenum Press.

Murphy, G. L., & Medin, D. L. (1985). The role of theories in conceptual coherence. *Psychological Review, 92,* 284–316.

Murray, D. J. (1999). Wundt, Wilhelm. In R. A. Wilson & F. C. Keil (Eds.), *The MIT encyclopedia of the cognitive sciences* (pp. 896–897). Cambridge: MIT Press.

Musso, M., Weiller, C., Kiebel, S., Rijntjes, M., Jüptner, M., & Bülau, P. (1997). Brain plasticity induced by language training after stroke. In A. W. Toga, R. S. J. Frackowiak, & J. C. Mazziotta (Eds.), *NeuroImage: Third international conference on functional mapping of the human brain* (Vol. 5, No. 4, Part 2 of 4 parts, p. 60). San Diego, CA: Academic Press.

Nagel, T. (1974). What is it like to be a bat? *The Philosophical Review, 83*(4), 435–450.

Nairne, J. S. (1996). Short-term/working memory. In E. L. Bjork & R. K. Bjork (Eds.), *Memory* (pp. 101–126). San Diego, CA: Academic Press.

Neisser, U. (1967). *Cognitive psychology.* Englewood Cliffs, NJ: Prentice-Hall.

Newell, A., & Simon, H. A. (1972). *Human problem solving.* Englewood Cliffs, NJ: Prentice-Hall.

Newell, A., & Rosenbloom, P. S. (1981). Mechanisms of skill acquisition and the law of practice. In J. R. Anderson (Ed.), *Cognitive skills and their acquisition* (pp. 1–55). Hillsdale, NJ: Erlbaum.

Newport, E. L. (1990). Maturational constraints on language learning. *Cognitive Science, 14,* 11–28.

Niznikiewicz, M. A., O'Donnell, B. F., Nestor, P. G., Smith, L., Law, S., Karapelou, M., Shenton, M. E., & McCarley, R. W. (1997). ERP assessment of visual and auditory language processing in schizophrenia. *Journal of Abnormal Psychology, 106*(1), 85–94.

Nobre, A. C., Price, C. J., Turner, R., & Friston, K. (1997). Selective processing of nouns and function words in the human brain. In A. W. Toga, R. S. J. Frackowiak, & J. C. Mazziotta (Eds.), *NeuroImage: Third international conference on functional map-*

ping of the human brain (Vol. 5, No. 4, Part 2 of 4 parts, p. 53). San Diego, CA: Academic Press.

Overview of the Cog Project. (1999). Accessed 2/10/99. Available: http://www.ai.mit.edu/projects/cog/OverviewOfCog/cog_overview.html

Paradis, M. (Ed.). (1995). *Aspects of bilingual aphasia.* Oxford, England: Pergamon Press.

Penfield, W. (1958). *The excitable cortex in conscious man.* Liverpool, England: Liverpool University Press.

Penfield, W. (1959). The interpretive cortex. *Science, 129,* 1719–1725.

Penfield, W., & Rasmussen, T. (1950). *The cerebral cortex of man: A clinical study of localization of function.* New York: Macmillan.

Penfield, W., & Roberts, L. (1959). *Speech and brain-mechanisms.* Princeton, NJ: Princeton University Press.

Penrose, R. (1994). *Shadows of the mind.* Oxford, England: Oxford University Press.

Phantom limbs. (1998, February). *Discover, 19*(2), 20.

Pinker, S. (1997). *How the mind works.* New York: W. W. Norton.

Piven, J., Arndt, S., Bailey, J., Havercamp, S., Andreason, N. C., & Palmer, P. (1995). An MRI study of brain size in autism. *American Journal of Psychiatry, 152*(8), 1145–1149.

Posner, M. I., & Raichle, M. E. (1994). *Images of mind.* New York: Scientific American Library.

Posner, M. I., & Rothbart, M. K. (1994). Constructing neuronal theories of mind. In C. Koch & J. L. Davis (Eds.), *Large-scale neuronal theories of the brain* (pp. 183–199). Cambridge.: MIT Press.

Postman L. J. (Ed.). (1962). *Psychology in the making: Histories of selected research problems.* New York: Alfred A. Knopf.

Proust, M. (1954). *À la recherche du temps perdu.* Paris: Librairie Gallimard. (Original work published 1913–1927)

Pullan, J. M. (1969). *The history of the abacus.* New York: F. A. Praeger.

Purves, D., Augustine, G. J., Fitzpatrick, D., Katz, L. C., LaMantia, A.-S., & McNamara, J. O. (Eds.). (1997). *Neuroscience.* Sunderland, MA: Sinauer Associates.

Quillian, M. R. (1968). Semantic memory. In M. L. Minsky (Ed.), *Semantic information processing* (pp. 216–270). Cambridge: MIT Press.

Quinn, P. C., & Eimas, P. D. (1996). Perceptual cues that permit categorical differentiation of animal species by infants. *Journal of Experimental Child Psychology, 63*(1), 189–211.

Ramachandran, V. S., & Blakeslee, S. (1998). *Phantoms in the brain: Probing the mysteries of the human mind.* New York: William Morrow.

Ratey, J. J., & Johnson, C. (1997). *Shadow syndromes.* New York: Bantam Books.

Roediger, H. L. (1999). Ebbinghaus, Hermann. In R. A. Wilson & F. C. Keil (Eds.), *The MIT encyclopedia of the cognitive sciences* (pp. 251–253). Cambridge: MIT Press.

Rosch, E., & Mervis, C. B. (1975). Family resemblances: Studies in the internal structure of categories. *Cognitive Psychology, 7,* 573–605.

Rosenblatt, F. (1958). The perceptron: A probabilistic model for information storage and organization in the brain. *Psychological Review, 65,* 386–408.

Rosenbloom, P. S. (1991). Climbing the hill of cognitive-science theory. *Psychological Science, 2*(5), 308–311.

Rosenbloom, P. S., Laird, J. E., & Newell, A. (Eds.). (1993). *The Soar papers: Research on integrated intelligence* (Vols. 1 and 2). Cambridge: MIT Press.

Rosier, A., Cornette, L., Dupont, P., Bormans, G., Michiels, J., Mortelmans, L., & Orban, G. A. (1997). Positron-emission tomography imaging of long-term shape recognition challenges. *Proceedings of the National Academy of Sciences, 94,* 7627–7632.

Rowe, J., & Partridge, D. (1993). Creativity: A survey of AI approaches. *The Artificial Intelligence Review, 7*(1), 43–70.

Rudnicky, A. I., Hauptmann, A. G., & Lee, K.-F. (1994). Survey of current speech technology. *Communications of the ACM, 37*(3), 52–57.

Russell, S., & Norvig, P. (1995). *Artificial intelligence: A modern approach.* Upper Saddle River, NJ: Prentice-Hall.

Ryle, G. (1949). *The concept of mind.* New York: Barnes & Noble.

Sachs, J. S. (1967). Recognition memory for syntactic and semantic aspects of connected discourse. *Perception and Psychophysics, 2*(9), 437–442.

Sacks, O. (1984). *A leg to stand on.* New York: Summit Books.

Sacks, O. (1995). *An anthropologist on Mars.* New York: Vintage Books.

Sandell, J. H., Gross, C. G., & Bornstein, M. H. (1979). Color categories in macaques. *Journal of comparative and physiological psychology, 93,* 626–635.

Sankaran, N. (1995). *Looking back at ENIAC: Computers hit half-century mark* [On-line]. Available: http://www.the-scientist.library.upenn.edu/yr1995/August/birth_950821.html

Schacter, D. L., Alpert, N. M., Savage, C. R., Rauch, S. L., & Albert, M. S. (1996). Conscious recollection and the human hippocampal formation: Evidence from positron emission tomography. *Proceedings of the National Academy of Sciences, 93,* 321–325.

Schacter, D. L., Norman, K. A., & Koutsaal, W. (1998). The cognitive neuroscience of constructive memory. *Annual Review of Psychology, 49,* 289–318.

Schank, R. C., & Abelson, R. P. (1977). *Scripts, plans, goals, and understanding: An inquiry into human knowledge structures.* Hillsdale, NJ: Erlbaum.

Schank, R. C., with Childers, P. G. (1984). *The cognitive computer: On language, learning, and artificial intelligence.* Reading, MA: Addison-Wesley.

Searle, J. R. (1969). *Speech acts: An essay in the philosophy of language.* London: Cambridge University Press.

Searle, J. R. (1980). Minds, brains and programs. *Behavioral and Brain Sciences, 3,* 509–526.

Searle, J. R. (1992). *The rediscovery of the mind.* Cambridge: MIT Press.

Searle, J. R. (1999). The Chinese room argument. In R. A. Wilson & F. C. Keil (Eds.), *The MIT encyclopedia of the cognitive sciences.* Cambridge: MIT Press.

Sejnowski, T., & Rosenberg, C. (1987). Parallel networks that learn to pronounce English text. *Complex Systems, 1,* 145–168.

Shallice, T., & Warrington, E. K. (1970). Independent functioning of verbal memory stores: A neuropsychological study. *Quarterly Journal of Experimental Psychology, 22,* 261–273.

Shaywitz, B. A., Shaywitz, S. E., Pugh, K. R., Constable, R. T., Skudlarski, P., Fulbright, R. K., Bronen, R. A., Fletcher, J. M., Shankweiler, D. P., Katz, L., & Gore, J. C. (1995). Sex differences in the functional organization of the brain for language. *Nature, 373,* 607–609.

Shaywitz, S. E., Shaywitz, B. A., Pugh, K. R., Fulbright, R. K., Constable, R. T., Mencl, W. E., Shankweiler, D. P., Liberman, A. M., Skudlarski, P., Fletcher, J. M., Katz, L., Marchione, K. E., Lacadie, C., Gatenby, C., & Gore, J. C. (1998). Functional disruption in the organization of the brain for reading in dyslexia. *Proceedings of the National Academy of Sciences, 95,* 2636–2641.

Shepard, R. N., & Metzler, J. (1971). Mental rotation of three-dimensional objects. *Science, 171,* 701–703.

Sheridan, J., & Humphreys, G. W. (1993). A verbal-semantic category-specific recognition impairment. *Cognitive neuropsychology, 10*(2), 143–184.

Skinner, B. F. (1957). *Verbal behavior.* New York: Appleton-Century-Crofts.

Smith, E. E. (1995). Concepts and categorization. In E. E. Smith & D. N. Osherson (Eds.), *An invitation to cognitive science: Vol. 3, Thinking* (2nd ed., pp. 3–33). Cambridge: MIT Press.

Spence, S. A. (1996). Free will in the light of neuropsychiatry. *Philosophy, psychiatry, and psychology, 3*(2), 75–90.

Sperling, G. (1960). The information available in brief visual presentations. *Psychological Monographs, 74,* 1–29.

Sperry, R. W. (1968). Hemisphere deconnection and unity in conscious awareness. *American Psychologist, 23,* 723–733.

Springer, S. P., & Deutsch, G. (1997). *Left brain/right brain: Perspectives from cognitive neuroscience* (5th ed.). New York: W. H. Freeman.

Squire, L. R. (1997). *Memory and brain.* Oxford, England: Oxford University Press.

Squire, L. R., Knowlton, B., & Musen, G. (1993). The structure and organization of memory. *Annual Review of Psychology, 44,* 453–495.

Sternberg, R. J. (1985). *Beyond IQ.* Cambridge: Cambridge University Press.

Sternberg, R. J. (1988). *The triarchic mind: A new theory of human intelligence.* New York: Penguin Books.

Stork, D. G. (Ed.). (1997). *Hal's legacy: 2001's computer as dream and reality.* Cambridge: MIT Press.

Swade, D. D. (1993). Redeeming Charles Babbage's mechanical computer. *Scientific American, 268*(2), 86–91.

Swick, D., & Knight, R. T. (1999). Contributions of prefrontal cortex to recognition memory: Electrophysiological and behavioral evidence. *Neuropsychology, 13*(2), 155–170.

Tuddenham, R. D. (1963). The nature and measurement of intelligence. In L. Postman (Ed.), *Psychology in the making: Histories of selected research problems* (pp. 469–525). New York: Alfred A. Knopf.

Tulving, E. (1972). Episodic and semantic memory. In E. Tulving & W. Donaldson (Eds.), *Organization of memory* (pp. 381–403). New York: Academic Press.

Tulving, E. (1997). *What has PET taught us about human memory?* Keynote address, Third International Conference on Functional Mapping of the Human Brain, May 23.

Turing, A. M. (1986). Proposal for development in the mathematics division of an automatic computing engine (ACE). In B. E. Carpenter & R. W. Doran (Eds.),

The Charles Babbage Institute reprint series for the history of computing: Vol. 10. A. M. Turing's ACE report of 1946 and other papers (pp. 20–105). Cambridge: MIT Press, and Los Angeles: Tomash Publishers. (Original work published 1946)

Turing, A. M. (1950). Computing machinery and intelligence. *Mind LIX, 2236,* 33–60.

Turkle, S. (1984). *The second self: Computers and the human spirit.* New York: Simon & Schuster.

Von Frisch, K. (1971). *Bees: Their vision, chemical senses, and language* (Rev. ed.). Ithaca, NY: Cornell University Press.

Waitley, D. (1993). *The new dynamics of winning.* New York: William Morrow.

Waldrop, M. M. (1988). Toward a unified theory of cognition. *Science, 241,* 27–29.

Wechsler, D. (1958). *The measurement and appraisal of adult intelligence* (4th ed.). Baltimore: Williams & Wilkins.

Weiskrantz, L. (1997). *Consciousness lost and found.* Oxford, England: Oxford University Press.

Weizenbaum, J. (1965). ELIZA. *Communications of the Association for Computing Machinery, 9*(1), 36–45.

Weizenbaum, J. (1976). *Computer power and human reason: From judgment to calculation.* San Francisco: W. H. Freeman.

Werker, J. F., & Desjardins, R. (1995). Listening to speech in the 1st year of life: Experiential influences on phoneme perception. *Current directions in psychological science, 4*(3), 76–81.

Wertheimer, M. (1987). *A brief history of psychology* (3rd ed.). New York: Harcourt Brace Jovanovich.

Whitehead, A. N., & Russell, B. (1910). *Principia mathematica.* Cambridge: Cambridge University Press.

Wiesel, T. N., & Hubel, D. H. (1963). Effects of visual deprivation on morphology and physiology of cells in the cat's lateral geniculate body. *Journal of Neurophysiology, 26*(6), 978–993.

Winograd, T. A. (1972). Understanding natural language. *Cognitive Psychology, 3,* 1–91.

Winograd, T. A. (1984). Computer software for working with language. *Scientific American, 251*(3), 131–145.

Woodbridge, F. J. E. (Ed.). (1930). *Hobbes: Selections.* New York: Charles Scribner's Sons.

Wright, A. A. (1972). Psychometric and psychophysical hue discrimination functions for the pigeon. *Vision Research, 12*(9), 1447–1464.

Wright, A. A., & Cumming, W. W. (1971). Color-naming functions for the pigeon. *Journal of the Experimental Analysis of Behavior, 15,* 7–17.

Zuger, Abigail. (1997, August 19). Removing half of brain improves young epileptics' lives. *The New York Times,* p. C4.

Credits

Text and Illustrations

Chapter 1— Fig. 1.2 From J. Sternberg, *The Triarchic Mind: A New Theory of Human Intelligence,* 1988, p. 60, Brockman, Inc. Reprinted with permission from the publisher.

Chapter 2— P. 31, definition of "concept" copyright © 1996 by Houghton Mifflin Company. Adapted and reproduced by permission from *The American Heritage Dictionary of the English Language,* Third Edition. Table 2.2 From E. E. Smith, *Concepts and Categorization* in E. E. Smith and D. N. Osherson, editors, *An Invitation to Cognitive Science,* Second Edition, Vol. 3: *Thinking,* 1995, p. 23. Fig. 2.5 From A. M. Collins and E. F. Loftus, "A Spreading Activation Theory of Semantic Processing," *Psychological Review,* 82, No. 6, 1975, p. 412. Copyright © 1975 by the American Psychological Association. Reprinted with permission. Figs. 2.6, 2.7 Reprinted with permission from R. N. Shepard and J. Metzler, "Mental Rotation of Three-Dimensional Objects," *Science,* 171, 19 February, 1971, p. 702. Copyright © 1971 American Association for the Advancement of Science. Fig. 2.8 From S. M. Kosslyn, T. M. Ball, and B. J. Reiser, "Visual Images Preserve Metric Spatial Information: Evidence From Studies of Image Scanning," *Journal of Experimental Psychology: Human Perception and Performance,* 4 (1), 1978, p. 51. Copyright © 1978 by the American Psychological Association. Reprinted with permission. Fig. 2.9 From R. C. Atkinson and R. M. Shiffrin, "Human Memory: A Proposed System" in K. W. Spence and J. T. Spence, editors, *The Psychology of Learning and Motivation: Advances in Research and Theory,* Volume 2, p. 93, Academic Press, 1968. Copyright © 1968 by Academic Press. Reproduced by permission of the publisher.

Chapter 3— Fig. 3.3 From Purves et al., *Neuroscience,* Sinauer Associates, 1997, p. 3. Reprinted with permission from the publisher.

Chapter 4— Fig. 4.1 From *Journal of Comparative Neurology,* R. J. Nelson, 1980, Vol. 192, pp. 611–643. Reprinted by permission of Wiley-Liss, Inc., a subsidiary of John Wiley & Sons, Inc. Fig. 4.5 From Penfield and Jasper, "Epilepsy and the Functional Anatomy of the Human Brain," in B. Kolb and I. Q. Whishaw, *Fundamentals of Human Neuropsychology,* Fourth Edition, W. H. Freeman, 1980. Reprinted with permission from Lippincott Williams & Wilkins. Fig. 4.14 Reprinted with permission from A. Rosier et al., "Positron-Emission Tomography Imaging of Long-Term Shape Recognition Challenges," Proceedings of the National Academy of Sciences 94, p. 7628, 1997. Copyright © 1997 National Academy of Sciences, U.S.A. Fig. 4.15 From D. Swick and R. T. Knight, "Contributions of Prefrontal Cortex to Recognition Memory: Electrophysiological and Behavioral Evidence," *Neuropsychology,* 13, (2), 1999, p. 162. Copyright © 1999 by the American Psychological Association. Reprinted with permission.

Chapter 5— Pp. 156, 157 Excerpts from J. B. Carroll, *Language, Thought, and Reality: Selected Writings of Benjamin Lee Whorf,* The MIT Press, 1956, pp. 213–214, 216. Reprinted with permission from the publisher.

Chapter 6— Fig. 6.1 From Jean Berko Gleason, *The Development of Language,* Fourth Edition, Allyn & Bacon, 1997. Copyright © 1997 Allyn & Bacon. Reprinted by permission of the publisher. Fig. 6.3 From E. L. Newport, "Maturational Constraints on Language Learning," *Cognitive Science,* 14, 1990, p. 19. Copyright © 1990 Cognitive Science Society, Inc. Used by permission.

Chapter 7— Fig. 7.5 From M. R. W. Dawson, *Understanding Cognitive Science,* Blackwell Publishers, Inc. 1998, p. 16. Reprinted with permission from the publisher.

Chapter 8— Pp. 226–229 Excerpts from T. A. Winograd, "Understanding Natural Language," *Cognitive Psychology,* 3, 1972, pp. 1–2, 8–10. Reprinted with permission from Academic Press. Pp. 231, 232, 234 Excerpts from R. C. Schank with P. G. Childers, *The Cognitive Computer: On Language, Learning, and Artificial Intelligence,* Addison-Wesley Publishing Company, 1984, pp. 140, 145, 166. Reprinted with permission from the authors. Fig. 8.2 From B. G. Buchanan and E. M. Shortliffe, editors, *Rule-Based Expert Systems: The MYCIN Experiments of the Stanford Heuristic Programming Project,* Addison-Wesley Publishing Company, 1985, p. 4. Used with permission of the authors. Fig. 8.4 From T. A. Winograd, "Understanding Natural Language," *Cognitive Psychology,* 3, 1972, p. 8. Copyright © 1972 by Academic Press. Reproduced by permission of the publisher. Fig. 8.6 From S. Russell and P. Norvig, *Artificial Intelligence: A Modern Approach,* Prentice-Hall, 1995, p. 574. Copyright © 1995 Prentice-Hall, Inc. Reprinted by permission of Prentice-Hall, Inc., Upper Saddle River, NJ. Fig. 8.7 From Randall D. Beer, *Intelligence as Adaptive Behavior: An Experiment in Computational Neuroethology,* 1990, p. 158. Copyright © 1990 by Academic Press. Reproduced by permission of the publisher.

Chapter 9— Pp. 259, 261, 263, 264 Excerpts from René Descartes, *The Philosophical Works of Descartes,* Vol. I, Elizabeth S. Haldane and G. R. T. Ross, translators. Reprinted with the permission of Cambridge University Press.

Photos

1.4, Damasio, H., Grabowski, T. J., Frank, R., Galaburda, A. M., Damasio, A. R. "The return of Phineas Gage: Clues about the brain from the skull of a famous patient." *Science* 264:1102–1105, 1994. Department of Neurology and Image Analysis Facility, University of Iowa. Reprinted with permission from *Science.* © 1994 American Association for the Advancement of Science.; **2.1**, © Alan G. Nelson/Animals Animals; **2.2**, © Fritz Prenzel/Animals Animals; **3.1**, © A. Glauberman/Photo Researchers, Inc.; **3.3**, From Purves, et al.: *Neuroscience,* 1997. Fig. 1.2. © Sinauer Associates, Inc.; **3.5**, From *The Cerebral Cortex of Man,* by Penfield & Rasmussen, Macmillan Company. Reprinted by per-

mission of The Gale Group; **4.2**, © Scott Camazine/Photo Researchers, Inc.; **4.3**, © Scott Camazine/Photo Researchers, Inc.; **4.4**, © Mehau Kulyk/Science Photo Library/Photo Researchers, Inc.; **4.7**, © Wellcome Department of Cognitive Neurology/Science Photo Library/Photo Researchers, Inc.; **4.8**, Courtesy Georg Deutsch, University of Alabama, Birmingham; **4.9**, Bavelier, D., Corina, D., Jezzard, P., Clark, V., Karni, A., Lalwani, A., Rauschecker, J. P., Braun, A., Turner, R., & Neville, H. J. (1998). "Hemispheric specialization for English and ASL: Left invariance-right variability." *Neuroreport,* Vol. 9 (7), (pp. 1537–1542), page 1540.; **4.10**, Gabrieli, et al. (1997). "Separate neural bases of two fundamental memory processes in the human medial temporal lobe." *Science,* 276, 11 April, p. 264. Reprinted with permission from *Science.* © 1994 American Association for the Advancement of Science.; **4.11**, Courtney, et al. (1998). "An area specialized for spatial and face working memory in human frontal cortex." Reprinted from *Science.* 279, 27 February, p. 1349.; **4.12**, Schacter, D. L., et al. (1996) "Conscious recollection and the hippocampal formation: Evidence from positron emission tomography." Proceedings of the National Academy of Sciences, 93, p. 323; **4.13**, Cohen, et al. (1997). "Temporal dynamics of brain activation during a working memory task." Reprinted by permission from *Nature* 386 (10), p. 606 © 1997, Macmillan Magazines, Ltd.; **4.16**, Martin, A., Wiggs, C. L., Ungerleider, L. G., & Haxby, J. V. (1996). "Neural correlates of category-specific knowledge." Reprinted by permission from *Nature* 379, p. 650, © 1996, Macmillan Magazines, Ltd.; **4.17**, Damasio, H., Grabowski, T. J., Tranel, D., Hichwa, R., Damasio, A. R.: "A neural basis for lexical retrieval." *Nature,* 380:499–505, 1996. Department of Neurology and Image Analysis Facility, University of Iowa. Reprinted by permission from *Nature* 380:499–505, © 1996, Macmillan Magazines, Ltd.; **4.18**, Damasio, H., Grabowski, T. J., Tranel, D., Hichwa, R., Damasio, A. R.: "A neural basis for lexical retrieval." *Nature,* 380:499–505, 1996. Department of Neurology and Image Analysis Facility, University of Iowa. Reprinted by permission from *Nature* 380:499–505, © 1996, Macmillan Magazines, Ltd.; **7.1**, From J. M. Pullan. *The History of the Abacus.* 1969. New York: F. A. Praeger, p. 100; **7.2**, © Bettmann/Corbis; **7.3**, © Science Museum/Science & Society Picture Library; **7.4**, © Science Museum/Science & Society Picture Library; **7.6**, © Bettmann/Corbis; **8.8**, © Sam Ogden; **10.1**, Courtesy MIT Artificial Intelligence Laboratory; **10.2**, © Sam Ogden

Index